CW01022553

THE ROYAL NAVY IN THE COD WARS

Britain and Iceland in Conflict

1958-61

1972-73

1975-76

by

Captain Andrew Welch FNI Royal Navy

"Naval operations in high altitudes provide unique challenges to planning, seamanship, ingenuity, endurance and foresight. The elements, always dangerous, become hostile. Mountainous seas, storm-force winds and near-zero visibility for days on end put tremendous strain on men and material."

From the Preface to NATO's Naval Arctic Manual, ATP-17 (B)

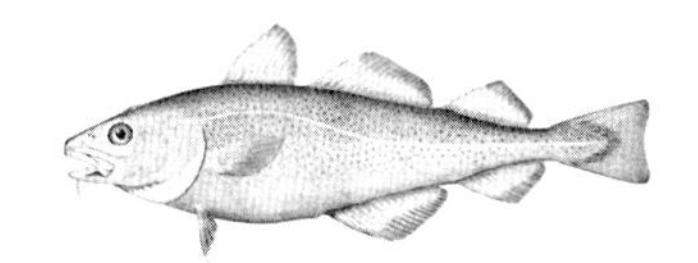

First published in the United Kingdom in 2006 by Maritime Books, Lodge Hill, Liskeard, Cornwall, PL14 4EL

FOREWORDS

Commander Gudmundur Kjærnested[1] Of the Icelandic Coastguard Service

It was an honour and privilege to be able to devote my career to rescue operations and law enforcement on the seas around Iceland. All those who are acquainted with the history of Iceland know that our economic existence has been based on the riches of the seas. Indeed, this line from a famous poem, "the ocean is one half of our fatherland", is the maxim of the Icelandic Coast Guard Service. Our fishermen sailed the rough seas and sometimes they did not return. Sometimes, however, we managed to rescue those in dire trouble. Those were the proudest moments of my career. This also applied to foreign sailors who worked the fishing grounds off Iceland. Fortunately, we were sometimes able to come to their rescue. We always respected their courage and bravery, for a common bond unites fishermen across the world.

Sometimes, however, conflicts arose as this book describes. We Icelanders gained independence in 1944. Yet, we realised all too well that a full victory in our struggle for independence would not be achieved until we had gained complete sovereignty over the Icelandic fishing grounds, the basis of our existence. Unfortunately, this fact led to conflicts with our friends in Britain. We were convinced that right was on our side, and that justice won in the end. But I must emphasise that we never regarded these conflicts as "a war". We respected the Royal Navy and the British trawlermen. We did our duty; they did theirs.

Iceland now has full control over its fishing grounds while the same cannot be said about Britain. One might wonder if the British should not have sided with us in the struggle for increased national jurisdiction on the oceans! As I said, it was an honour to perform one's duty with the Icelandic Coast Guard Service. It is also an honour to write a foreword for this book about the fishing conflicts between Britain and Iceland.

[1] Sadly Gudmundur Kjærnested died on 2nd September 2005, shortly after writing this foreword, which was used in his obituary in Iceland.

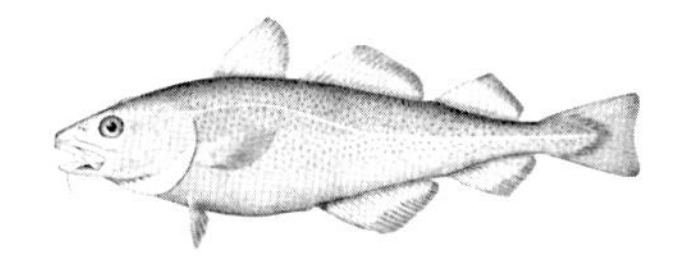

Vice Admiral Sir James Weatherall KCVO KBE DL

The story of the cod wars was really about a small country exerting political and physical pressure to make what it firmly believed to be necessary changes to international law concerning fishing limits. There was in the international community, some acceptance of the need for change, Iceland proceeded in graduated steps to force this acceptance and the political history in this book throws a fresh light on this process.

As a 22-year-old lieutenant navigating the Battle-class destroyer *HMS Lagos*, I gained huge experience of freezing cold, severe icing, gales and fog from the discomfort of an open bridge over Christmas 1958. Having taught ship handling to specialist navigating officers in my second command I was well equipped for the challenges of the last Cod War in command of *HMS Tartar*. I found using my ship as an aggressive defensive physical barrier a rather strange task for a warfare-trained naval officer. A large number of our captains were in command for the first time and ship-handling skills were mostly acquired on the job.

The up side was that the Royal Navy relearned a great deal about coping with appalling conditions at least two days away from any base support. Our opponents, but they were also our friends, were home based, could choose the conditions in which to operate and were all old hands at the game of fishery protection. They could select time and place and take shelter when prudent. We remained at sea.

The upshot was a monumental change to Britain's deep-water fisheries and a sad and continuing decline in the British fishing industry within the European Union which caused and is still causing hardship within the fishing communities at home.

This book makes fascinating reading because it links the political manoeuvring with the demands placed upon a warfare trained navy to perform a very different set of tasks. The author has drawn the threads together to present an excellent analysis of all participating parties in a well-balanced and informative manner.

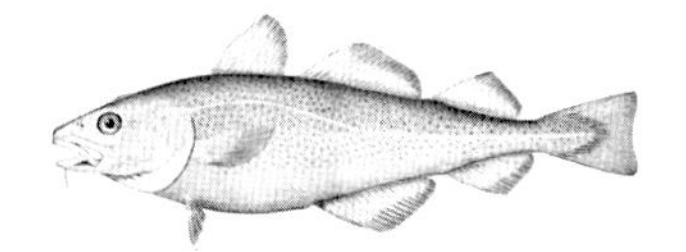

INTRODUCTION

Between 1958 and 1976, Britain and Iceland fought three wars over fishing rights in the waters around Iceland. By most reckonings, International Law, as it was at the time, was on Great Britain's side, but Iceland had the propaganda advantage of being the David vs. Britain's Goliath. Her unilateral action in claiming and enforcing 12, 50 and then 200 mile fishing limits triggered the world-wide change from the 3 or 4 mile limits of antiquity to the near-universal 200 miles limits of today.

There were many factors that caused this dispute to spill over from the diplomatic into the military sphere - from domestic politics (both in the UK and Iceland) to the Cold War, via Britain's failure to understand the International changes brought about by the Second World War, the end of Empire and the aftermath of Suez and the intransigent refusal ('though 'inability' might be kinder and possibly nearer the truth) of Iceland to negotiate. In this book I hope to explain why the so-called Cod Wars (a catch phrase apparently coined by the Daily Express on 3 September 1958) between two NATO allies happened, as well as recount what happened and to give a feel for what life was like in the ships on patrol.

I have tried to read between the lines of the sources I have utilised and to offer an impartial view of who did what when. Some of the collisions were, to me, clearly rammings - usually, but definitely not always, in the heat of the moment, rather than premeditated. The Icelandic view, at the time, was that every collision was a deliberate ramming by the British. In the 2000 TV documentary The Last Waltz there is an admission from one of the Coastguard Captains that he did ram one of HM Ships deliberately. He wasn't the only one in my view. However, to balance this, there are occasions that I have identified when Royal Navy ships deliberately rammed Icelandic Coastguard vessels. The risk in trying to be, at least partially, impartial is that I will have managed to offend both sides! Unless clearly indicated as such, all the opinions expressed are my own.

Note: Timings throughout are in GMT, the 'Navy' is always the Royal Navy, the 'Coastguard' is always the Icelandic Coastguard and, for simplicity, I have referred to the Coastguard vessels as 'gunboats' throughout, although in quoted later passages, they are referred to as ICGV - Icelandic Coastguard Vessels. .

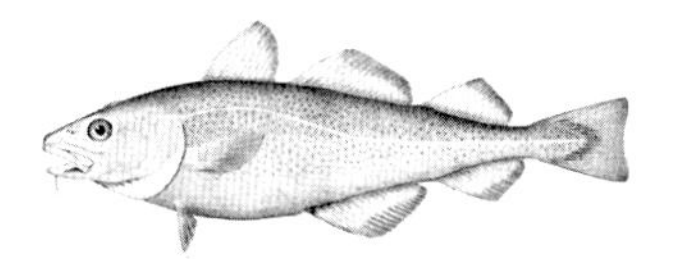

ACKNOWLEDGEMENTS

Thanks are due to Captain Chris Page, Head of the Royal Naval Historical Branch, for allowing me to make full use of BR 1736(57), the official Naval Staff History - "*The Cod War. Naval Operations off Iceland in Support of the British Fishing Industry (1958-76)*" and to Captain David O'Sullivan, the author of the Naval Staff History.

I am also most grateful to Dr. Gudni Thorlacius Jóhannesson for allowing me to read and quote liberally from his unpublished University of London PhD thesis "*Troubled Waters. Cod War, Fishing Disputes, and Britain's Fight for the Freedom of the High Seas, 1948-1964.*" His research in the British, Icelandic and several other governments' archives was extensive and his balanced insights into the varying views from Iceland have been invaluable. He has also offered me extensive support throughout &, without his assistance, it would have been impossible to achieve any degree of balance in this book. Any lack of balance is certainly my fault and not Gudni's.

I must also give thanks to Margrét Jónasdóttir, from whose TV documentary, *The Last Waltz,* I have quoted extensively.

I am most grateful to the following for their help, advice, memories and/or photos: Tom Adams, John (Jack) Armstrong, John Armstrong, Jon Pall Asgeirsson, Alan Barnett, David Barron, Nick Bates, Russ Bates, Les Beck, Carl Beeson, David Berry, Alfie Blackburn, Ken Bonning, Alan Boxall, Tim Boulton, Michael Boydon, Peter Brady, Sir John Brigstocke, Tony Britten, Chris Brown, John Brown, Clare Bunkham, Bruce Burniston, Keith Caldwell, Paul Canter, Owen Carlile, Bill Carr, Tim Charlesworth, John Cheney, Roy Clare, Bill Clarke, Stephen Clement, Ken Clynes, Michael Codner, Rex Cooper, David Crabb, Mike Critchley, John Crosby, Alan Croskill, John Curt, Ian Daniels, Fred Deeks, Charles (Neal) Dempsey, Elisabeth Dempsey, Chris Downie, Andy Du Port, Taff Edwards, Leslie Edworthy, Michael Ellis, Melanie Etches, Mick Evans, Trevor Filtness, Jim Findlay, Mike Franklin, Joe Fraser, David Frost, Matthew Fyfe, Henry Gale, Jock Gardner, Sir Bob Gerken, John Gerring, Alec Gill, Chas Gillespie, Denis Glassett, Roger Godfrey, Ted Grafton, Jan Graham, Jonathan Grobler, Bragi Gudmundsson, Thórarinn Gudnason, Allan Gunniss, Nigel Hadley, Geoff Hammond, Chris Handley, Lez Hardy, Toby Harnden, Harry (Donald) Harrison, Larry Harris, Peter Harrison, Christine Hawk, Geoff Hegarty, Bryan 'Tiny' Height, Gísli Helgason, John Hession, Tony Hewitt, John Hills, Matthew Hodkinson, John Hollidge, Alan Hopper, Alex Hopper, David Howard, Graham Howard, Charles Howeson, Sir Nicholas Hunt, Kelvyn Inch, Roddy Jardine, Dave Jefferson, Alan Jennings, Robin Johns, Colin Johnson, Eric Johnson, Stuart M Johnson, Margrét Jonasdottir, David Jones, Peter Jones, Ray 'Taff' Jones, Shaun Jones, Taff Jones, Eric Johnson, Gary Kearns, Bim Kerr, Jim King, John Knapp, Ken Knox, Peter Lankester, Peter Lannin, David Larmour, John Lawson, Doug (George) Laybourne, Mike Lewis, Guy Liardet, Betty Lillie, Richard Ling, T (Lofty) Loftus, Nigel Lowther, Charles R Lucas, Dougie MacDonald, Tony MacManus, Anton Maguire, Robert Marshall, Barkley Stuart (Perry) Mason, David Mathias, Mike McAllister, Peter Miles, Chris Miller, Jim Miller, Debbie Molyneaux, Robert Moore, Peter Musslewhite, David Nealon, Peter Neate, Sir Roy Newman, Isaac Newton, Christopher Notley, M O'Connell, Agusta Oskarsdottir, Chris Page, Christopher Parker, Alan Paterson, Mike Payne, Chris Petherbridge, Chris Pink, Jim Porter, Ragnar Rangarsson, Sid Reeves, Willie John Reid, Vic Richards, Linda Roberts, David Robinson, Norman Robinson, Robb Robinson, Dave Rogers, Keith Rouse, Roger Sear, Sir Jock Slater, Geoff Sloan, Roger Smith, David Snelson, David Squire, Julian Stockwin, Michael Stubbs, Baldur Sveinsson, Óttar Sveinsson, Myles Swales, Joe Sweeney, Sir Hilary Synnott, Ann Tait, Alfred Taylor, Mick Tolhurst, Doug Thomas, Dick Thorn, Barbara Tomlinson, Bob Trayhurn, Bob Turner, Jane Ward (and Davis Johnson & Co Marine Solicitors), Richard Walker, Ben Warlow, Sir James Weatherall, Mary Welch, Brian Westmore, Paul Willerton, Jimmy Williams, David M Willis, John Wills, Dave Winning, Dave Wood, Ken Voller and a couple of 'Anons'.

Please accept my humble apologies if I've left you out. I also had assistance from the *Grimsby Telegraph*, the *Hull Daily Mail*, the National Maritime Museum, the *Navy News*, the Office of National Statistics, the Royal Fleet Auxiliary Association, the Royal Maritime Auxiliary Service Association Devonport, the Royal Naval Communicators' Association, the Royal National Mission to Deep Sea Fishermen, the Sainsbury Archive in the Museum in Docklands, *Saga Magazine*, the SW Maritime History Society & United Salvage Limited.

And finally, I must thank my wife, Carole, who supported me throughout the lengthy, much longer than either of us had expected, process of writing this book, who read my drafts, tried to de-jargonise my text, coped when I was grumpy and made many cups of tea and coffee.

CONTENTS

Chapter 1	The First Thousand Years	1
Chapter 2	Politics, British Indecision and the Law of the Sea	7
Chapter 3	Fishery Protection before the First Cod War	21
Chapter 4	The First Law of the Sea Conference and the Icelandic Declaration of a 12-mile limit	27
Chapter 5	The First Cod War *The Opening Shots: 1st September - 31st December 1958*	35
Chapter 6	The First Cod War *Routine: 1st January 1959 - 14th March 1960*	49
Chapter 7	The First Cod War *Outside 12 miles, the Second UN Conference on the Law of the Sea (UNCLOS2) and, finally, negotiations: 15th March 1960 - 11th March 1961*	73
Chapter 8	Ten Years of Peace and The Common Fisheries Policy: 1961 - 1971	83
Chapter 9	The 50-Mile Limit	93
Chapter 10	The Second Cod War *Under Civilian Protection: 1st September 1972 - 19th May 1973*	101
Chapter 11	The Second Cod War *Under Naval Protection: 19th May - 20th June 1973*	117
Chapter 12	The Second Cod War *Continued Naval Protection: 21st June - 14th August 1973*	127
Chapter 13	The Second Cod War *A Short Lull before the Storm and the Withdrawal to outside 50 miles: 14th August - 3rd October 1973*	141
Chapter 14	Peace Negotiations *The Third UN Conference on the Law of the Sea (UNCLOS3) and the Icelandic Declaration of a 200-mile Limit -3rd October 1973 to 15th July 1975*	157
Chapter 15	The Run up to the Third Cod War *200-mile Limit and the Start of the Third Cod War: 15th July - 14th November 1975*	163
Chapter 16	The Third Cod War *Phase One: November 1975 - January 1976*	167

Chapter 17 The Third Cod War 187
The Lull: January - February 1976

Chapter 18 The Third Cod War 193
A Break in Diplomatic Relations: February 1976

Chapter 19 The Third Cod War 201
A Policy of Ramming?: February - March 1976

Chapter 20 The Third Cod War 215
A Policy of Avoiding Damage to Frigates: March - April 1976

Chapter 21 The Third Cod War 231
Creeping Towards a Settlement: April - May 1976

Chapter 22 The Third Cod War 241
A Bruising Finale: May - June 1976

Chapter 23 Aftermath and Assessment 263

Chapter 24 A Tailpiece 275

Appendix 1 Chronology of the First Cod War 279

Appendix 2 Chronology of the Second Cod War 287

Appendix 3 Chronology of the Third Cod War 293

Appendix 4 Icelandic Coastguard Vessels 299

Appendix 5 Royal Navy Patrol Dates 305

Appendix 6 RFA, RMAS and Defence Tug Patrol Dates 315

Appendix 7 Cast List 319

Appendix 8 Acronyms and Abbreviations 321

Bibliography 323

CHAPTER 1

THE FIRST THOUSAND YEARS

Cod has been fished commercially for over a thousand years and was a major factor in international trade well up until the nineteenth century. As such, it is not surprising that cod has been the cause of wars, not just the three Cod Wars between Iceland and the United Kingdom between 1958 and 1976, but also a brief conflict off Iceland in 1532 and was even one of the major factors leading up to the American Declaration of Independence and the subsequent war. Closer to home, the extraordinary expansion of the fishing industry in Victorian times - with new technologies being brought into widespread use in amazingly short times - helped to feed the hungry masses who poured into the new industrial cities to provide the workforce for the Industrial Revolution.

But before looking at the first thousand years of cod as a business, a bit of background on the cod itself. There are nearly sixty species in the cod family, of which the best known, and most valuable commercially, is the Atlantic Cod. It usually lives in cool or cold water between depths of 600 to 1200ft (180-360m), often close to the bottom and can migrate long distances. Cod, these days, are generally of moderate size, but can weigh up to 200lb(98kg) and grow to 6ft (1.8m) in length. As I'm sure many others who served in the Cod Wars remember, that the fish that the trawlers used to give the Royal Navy (when they weren't grumpy with us) were often four or five feet long.

The flesh of a cod is almost fat-free and is about 18% protein. When dried, this figure reaches nearly 80% concentrated protein. This was one of the factors that made exploration and long sea journeys possible over a thousand years ago. The Norsemen had established plants for drying cod in Norway and Iceland in the ninth century and traded the products into northern Europe. The Icelandic sagas record that the Vikings made five journeys as far as the North American coast between 985 and 1011AD. Dried cod was almost definitely the food that enabled them to survive the trip from Iceland to Greenland and on to what is now the Canadian east coast.

The Basques were the other pioneers in the Cod business. However, they had ample salt supplies and cod that has been salted before it is dried lasts much longer than just plain dried cod. By 1000AD, the Basques had established an international market for dried, salted cod and were trading well into the Mediterranean. The mystery was - where did their cod come from and where did they salt and dry it? Like all fishermen, the Basques kept the location of their fishing grounds to themselves, but it seems most likely that they were fishing off what is now Newfoundland and salting/drying the cod ashore before bringing it back to Europe. When John Cabot, the Genoese adventurer/explorer in the pay of King Henry VII, claimed Newfoundland for England in 1497, he commented on the vast quantities of cod in the sea and the suitability of the coast for salting and drying it. Similarly, when Jacques Cartier 'discovered' the St Lawrence in 1534, he reported seeing about 1000 Basque fishing vessels. For a fleet that size to have been established, the Basques must have been working the area for many years, but now their secret was out. By the middle of the sixteenth century, 60% of all the fish eaten in Europe was salt cod and this would remain so for the next couple of hundred years.

British fishermen were, initially, slow to follow up Cabot's claim of Newfoundland for the British Crown, as they were already well established on the Icelandic fishing grounds, where they had been active since the mid 1400s. The other group involved in fishing off Iceland was the Hanseatic League. The Hanseatic League was a company founded by a group of merchants in Lübeck in 1159. Their original aim was to protect the commercial interests of North German traders. Over the years it expanded, until there were branches across Europe, from Iceland to the Ukraine and Riga to Venice. The League developed a reputation as a force for good -

standing up against abusive rulers and developing marine infrastructure, such as lighthouses. However, in due course, it started to be increasingly aggressive in defence of its monopoly position. In 1381, there was a violent campaign against Hanseatics in England and in 1475, the League stopped Bristol merchants from buying Icelandic cod. This hostility continued and in 1532 an Englishman, John the Broad, was murdered in Grindavík, in Iceland. This led to the first 'Cod War', a minor conflict between the British and the Hanseatic League. Unusually for a race not noted for retreating until they had no choice, the British withdrew completely from Iceland after the first skirmish and concentrated their efforts on the Grand Banks off Newfoundland.

In due course, the Newfoundland Fishery became a vital part of Britain's mastery of the seas, partly because the Admiralty became the biggest customer by far, as salted cod was part of every warship's stores and gave the Royal Navy the ability to operate worldwide. However, this reliance on one major customer had its downside. The home market was small as, before the age of frozen food, or even widely available ice, fish was very difficult to keep fresh and inland transport was rudimentary and slow, to say the least. If the British ate fish at all, it was probably fresh. Additionally, salt was not available in volume or at a price that made its use for preserving economical. For all these reasons, Britain never became one of the major players in the international salted dried cod trade.

The Newfoundland fishery was only open in the summer months and, in due course, it lost out to the Cape Cod area, where there was year-round fishing - inshore in the winter and offshore in the summer. By the seventeenth century, the British colony of New England was flourishing - Boston was founded on the cod trade and the businesses that supported it. Initially, much of the New England trade was with the West Indies, where salt cod was used to feed the slaves on the sugar plantations. A series of triangular trade routes developed - for example, best cod was shipped to Bilbao, and then the ships went on to the West Indies with wine, fruit, iron and coal. Poor quality cod (to feed the slaves) and some of the Spanish goods were sold in the West Indies and then the ships returned to Boston with sugar, molasses (for rum), tobacco, cotton and the, all-important, salt. Much of this Indies trade was with the French colonies - a source of great concern to Britain. The American colonies were also trading directly with Mediterranean countries. This economic independence of the American colonies (founded, as it was initially, on cod) eventually triggered the enforcement of the British Navigation Acts, which had been passed in 1660 and 1663 to force all trade to and from the Colonies to travel in British ships. The original reason for passing these Acts had been to keep the Dutch from trading with British colonies, but they were not repealed until 1849. It is possible that the Americans could have been satisfied with economic liberalisation - which was certainly their initial aim, but the British Government was steadfast in its defence of British trade and shipping. Eventually the

The trade continues - Icelandic salted cod on sale in the market in Kalamata, Greece in 2005 (Andrew Welch)

series of Acts passed to limit international trading by the American colonists forced the issue and the Americans declared independence.

One of the consequences of the war and the subsequent independence of the American colonies was the destruction of much of the New England fishing business. The newly-independent states could no longer export to the British West Indian colonies, import cod from Newfoundland or Nova Scotia or, eventually, even fish on the Grand Banks. It was some years before Newfoundland and Nova Scotia were able to fulfil the need for low-grade salt cod to feed slaves and between 1780 and 1787, 15,000 slaves died from starvation in Jamaica alone. The end of the Caribbean salt cod trade was triggered by the abolition of slavery by the British in 1834, the French in 1848 and the Dutch in 1849.

On this side of the Atlantic, there was already a commercially significant market for fish in Britain by the mid 18th century. The limiting factor was transport - the problem of getting fish to the inland markets, using horsepower as the only available transport, before the fish went off. The Industrial Revolution, with its expansion of the railway system and the mass migration into the new industrial cities, provided both a much-enlarged market and the means to service that market. Another significant factor was the potato famine in Ireland, which led to mass immigration to Britain - the Irish population in Britain doubled between 1841 and 1861. As most of these Irish were catholic, they expected to eat fish on Fridays. That great institution, the British fish and chip shop, started in this period. At the peak of the business, there were over 30,000 fish and chip shops trading and they took over 25% of the total fish landed in Britain[2] and used nearly 500,000 tons of potatoes.

Hull and Grimsby expanded enormously in this period and by 1860, they were the two largest fishing ports in the world - with several hundred sailing smacks working the North Sea. The smacks (sailing trawlers) in this period dragged a wooden beam across the seabed. Cod are demersal fish - which means that they live at the bottom of the sea. The beam held the mouth of the net open, but was only effective when the seabed was flat. As we have seen in recent years, there were disputes between the different sectors of the fishing community over who should work which fishing area and how. The liners blamed the trawlers for destroying their gear, the Scots complained if the English fished north of the Border etc etc - not much has changed in the last 150 years, except that the disputes are now international, rather than local.

These disputes led to the formation of a Royal Commission in 1863, chaired by Professor Thomas Huxley, one of the most highly respected scientists of the time. The Royal Commission had three remits. To establish:

a. Whether the supply of fish was increasing, stationary or diminishing.

b. Whether any of the methods of catching fish involved wasteful destruction of fish or spawn; and, if so, whether legislative restrictions would increase the supply of fish.

c. Whether any existing legislative restrictions operated injuriously upon any of the fisheries.

Sadly the Royal Commission had very little scientific, either biological or statistical, evidence upon which to base its conclusions. They travelled widely and listened to many 'experts' and their opinions. Unfortunately, they came to the conclusion, as they recommended to Parliament in 1866, that:

'All Acts of Parliament which profess to regulate, or restrict, the modes of fishing pursued in the open sea be repealed; and that unrestricted freedom of fishing be permitted hereafter.'

Three factors were to revolutionise trawling in a comparatively short period - ice, steam and the 'Otter' trawl. Ice was first taken to sea in smacks in about 1847 and soon proved its worth in extending the shelf life of the catch. Ice companies were established to cut the ice during the winter and store it in

[2] Comparisons are very difficult as the humble fish & chip shop now has much greater competition in the take-away food business and many fish & chip shops serve much more than just fish & chips. However, the best comparison I can manage is that in 2006 there were between 10-11,000 fish & chip shops, they used between 20-25% of the demersal fish landed in the UK & still use 500,000 tons of potatoes per annum

insulated icehouses until it was needed. This became a big business, and not just in Britain - for example, by 1865, 45,000 tons of ice were being imported from Norway - mainly for the fishing business. Artificial ice was first used in the fishing industry in 1874, but did not really catch on until the turn of the century.

The first steam-fishing vessel was built in Scotland in 1853 and several vessels were built for the Grimsby trade in the years thereafter, but none was a commercial success - mainly because the primitive steam engines were too low-powered and used too much coal - and their engines were removed. Steam was successfully tried by those involved in 'fleeting', where a fleet of smacks would remain on the fishing ground and the steam cutters would run their catches into shore - sometimes, even directly down to Billingsgate, London's fish market. Steam vessels could also be used to tow smacks from one fishing ground to another if the wind was foul. The steam capstan also reduced the effort needed to recover the trawl. So whilst steam began to have an impact on the fishing business in the 1860s, it was not that significant. The steam revolution really started in 1877, when a severe depression found paddle-tug owners in the Tyne with no work for their ships. One North Shields owner decided to try using his paddle-tug as a trawler. There is anecdotal evidence that some smacks had already attempted trawling whilst under tow. Within a month, there were fifteen paddle-tugs trawling and over forty by the end of that winter. Many continued through the next summer and the idea spread to other fishing ports. Paddle-tugs, however, were not efficient fishing vessels - they had limited storage for coal or fish and so had to operate quite close inshore. Nevertheless, they continued in service for many years and the last working paddle-wheel vessel was wrecked off Scarborough in 1910.

The first real steam trawler, the *Pioneer*, was built in Scarborough in October 1881. Hull followed with two vessels in December of the same year and by 1890, sixty-one steam-screw trawlers were operating out of Hull and forty-two out of Grimsby. Whilst the Victorians did have the advantage that they were not hampered by the likes of the Health and Safety Executive, you do have to admire their entrepreneurial drive and industry. They were prepared to put their own money into untried technologies - albeit, they were not usually risking their own lives.

The next major and, arguably, final significant development in trawling for about 100 years was the use of 'kites', instead of a beam, to keep the mouth of the trawl open. These first appeared on the trawler Otter in Scotland in 1892 and the 'kites' are still called Otter Boards. The beam was replaced by a chain along the bottom edge of the net, with rollers (called bobbins) to help it run along the bottom. Within three years, the Otter Trawl was standard equipment.

Powered trawlers, an effective bottom trawl and ice were the three crucial developments in the battle between the fisherman and fish stocks. In 1883, Professor Huxley spoke at the International Fisheries Exhibition. He repeated his views from twenty years before:

> *'the cod fishery, the herring fishery, the pilchard fishery, and probably all the great sea fisheries are inexhaustible; that is to say that nothing we do seriously affects the number of fish. And any attempt to regulate these fisheries seems consequently, from the nature of the case to be useless.'*

This view from such a well-respected figure was wrong, but was widely accepted - both because there was very little evidence to support conservation (the British government only started to collect data in 1868) and because unbridled Victorian capitalism and conservation were like oil and water. A lecturer from Plymouth University described the owners of fishing vessels to me as 'the last unbridled capitalists' and he was referring to the second half of the twentieth century!

Despite Professor Huxley's confident assertions, evidence was beginning to accumulate, as early as the mid 1870s, that catches were beginning to diminish. The immediate reaction of the industry was to move to new and unexploited fishing grounds, to build bigger smacks and to adopt fleeting - the use of vessels to transfer catches to market, whilst the trawlers remained longer at sea. The increased efficiency of the steam trawler defeated these short term palliatives and so fishermen from the English North Sea coast moved north into Scottish waters - with predictable consequences. As this was strongly Presbyterian country, the fact that the English fished on the Sabbath just poured oil on the fire. There were mass protest meetings up and down the coast during the winter of 1884/5 and violence finally broke out in Wick in the spring of 1885. That same year, both James Sellars, an owner in Scarborough, and Alfred Ansell, a Hull owner, admitted that catches were falling and that trawlers were being forced further afield. The Royal Commission on Trawling, in 1885, agreed that inshore trawling and trawling on narrow grounds could affect stocks, but not that fishing could affect overall levels. However, as a result of this second Royal Commission on fishing, a nationwide body was established to collect statistics and the establishment of a central body to oversee fishing was recommended. Eventually, the Board of Agriculture and Fisheries became responsible for regulating English and Welsh fishing. The Scots, needless to say, had their own body.

Concern continued to be voiced about stocks and over fishing, with conferences held by the National Sea-Fisheries Protection Association in 1888 and 1890, followed by an international conference, attended by Belgium, Denmark, France, Germany, the Netherlands and Spain in London in 1891. This conference passed a resolution calling for an international convention on the landing and sale of immature fish. Gradually fishing restrictions were imposed, led by the Scottish Fishery Board who closed most of the territorial waters under its jurisdiction to trawlers. By 1892, nearly 1500 square miles of the Moray Firth (well outside the three-mile limit) had been closed to British vessels. So a number of Grimsby trawlers were re-registered abroad - so being exempt from the legislation and in 1897, a Danish company began to work the 'prohibited' area off the Moray Firth. All this was happening exactly a hundred years before the row between Britain and the rest of the EU over quota hopping. There is not much new in the efforts that fishermen will make to get round restrictions.

The difficulties of introducing any kind of international agreement on regulating fishing should not be underestimated. Such statistical information as there was, was patchy and comparatively short-term; added to this was the thorny principle of the freedom of the high seas. This was a principle that the British government took very, very seriously and this was the age of Pax Britannica, when the Royal Navy was the world's policeman and so needed to be able to operate as and where it wished.

There is no doubt that Britain could have used its strength to pressurise the other North Sea nations into agreeing to international fishing restrictions - both geographical and quota. Some sections of the British fishing industry were even calling for the extension of territorial waters. However, the steady development of the steam trawler was to kill off these proposals for the next 75 years. The Iceland fishing grounds were now within reach - albeit only during the summer season. The first British vessel since 1532 to be recorded fishing off Iceland was the Grimsby trawler *Aquarius* in 1891. The following summer, there were nine British trawlers fishing off southeast Iceland. They were at the limit of their range, but it was not long before bigger trawlers were working the area. They were still not up to working off Iceland in the winter and would work the Faeroes areas then. By 1903, there were a couple of hundred British fishing vessels, mostly trawlers, working the rich fishing grounds off Iceland all the year round.

Iceland had been a Danish colony since 1397 and had had little contact with the rest of the world since the British had been driven out in 1532. There was some exporting of salted fish, but only about 12,000 tons per annum by the end of the nineteenth century, when the British were already taking over 100,000 tons of fish from Icelandic waters per annum. The arrival of the British fishing fleet caused great concern in Iceland. The Icelandic economy was essentially a subsistence one based on farming and fishing. There were great fears that trawlers would destroy both their fishing gear and the stocks on the grounds on which they fished. After all, had the British not arrived off Iceland because they had destroyed their own fish stocks in the North Sea? Demands were made to ban trawling off Iceland, but before long the success (or depredations - depending on from where and when the judgement is made) of the British trawler fleet led to the purchase of the first British-built steam trawler by an Icelandic owner in 1905.

Over the following years, any call from the British industry for restrictions was silenced. One of the Hull owners put it very clearly to yet another government commission in 1909:

> *'Seeing that the number of British fishermen is at least six to one of any other nation, it is of paramount importance that the three mile limit be maintained and that Great Britain do*

nothing whatsoever in making representations to any other nation whereby their fishing vessels might be influenced not to fish in waters which are international and so give a viable pretext for other nations to close, or prohibit British fishermen from fishing in similar waters off their coasts. I do not think that I can put it much clearer than that.. trying to make terms or to enter into negotiations on any matter affecting the three mile limit will be disastrous to the fishing and mercantile interests of this country.. We say further that any such tampering with the three-mile limit is in our opinion pregnant with international difficulties'

This trenchant statement well expressed what was to remain the industry's position until the end of the First Cod War, fifty-two years later.

By 1915 (when most British trawlers had been requisitioned for the First World War and were either minesweeping or on patrol), there were twenty British trawlers working off Iceland. At the time, the British Ministry of Agriculture estimated that a fishing boat working Icelandic waters could catch three times as much fish as one boat working the North Sea. By the 1920s the British catch was exceeding 200,000 tons per annum and it peaked at nearly 350,000 tons in the early 1930s. This was about 60% of the cod caught in Icelandic waters. There was a dramatic drop in the British catch during the Second World War - to 6,000 tons/per annum and, as dramatic, an increase to nearly 400,000 tons per annum by the early 50s.

There were many protests from Icelandic inshore fishermen from the 1920s onward, both about the damage that trawlers did to fishing gear and to the fishing grounds. However, Iceland was a colony of Denmark and the Danish were not prepared to support the Icelandic case against their powerful trading partner (and buyer of much Danish bacon and dairy products), the United Kingdom.

The main consequence of the absence of the British from Icelandic waters between 1939-1945 was that the Icelandic fishing fleet grew and Iceland became, for six years, the only major fishing nation in Europe. When the war was over, Iceland became independent; but exports of cod to Britain had made this a much richer Iceland than in 1939.

Whilst cod had become a less important part of international trade over the centuries, for Iceland it had become the key to national prosperity. The Icelanders had no intention of returning to their prewar place in the society of nations and the stage was set for the First Cod War.

CHAPTER 2

POLITICS, BRITISH INDECISION & THE LAW OF THE SEA

From the perspective of many today (2006), at least as portrayed on the world wide web (www), there was no agreed International Law of the Sea until UNCLOS[3] came into force on 16th October 1994. This is a contentious statement, as the perceived strength of the UK's legal case, based on international law, against Iceland was one of the main factors underpinning the British justification for fighting the Cod Wars. However, whilst simplistic, International Law is only what Nations agree to be, or are forced to be, bound by. If they don't agree, as Britain and Iceland didn't, then there is either a stalemate or military action. As the history of the immediate post-war period shows, Britain limped from one poor decision to another, losing ground all the way until it stumbled into the First Cod War in September 1958.

From well before they obtained independence from Denmark in 1944, the Icelanders had wished to take complete control of 'their' fishing grounds. It took them just over twenty years to achieve this, mainly by remaining doggedly focussed on the aim. For a country, like Iceland, with only one significant export commodity, this was much easier than for Britain, where Foreign Policy is always about balancing many, often mutually contradictory, objectives. In retrospect, it is obvious that Britain was never going to defeat Iceland over fishing limits. The Icelanders were pushing (indeed shoving) at a door that was opening quite rapidly in the post-World War II and post-Colonialist eras; in this they had international sympathy and support, especially from the less developed world. The British were trying, almost single-handedly, to keep the same door shut.

Conservation was an idea to which only lip service had been paid before the Second World War. There had been many who had suggested that over-fishing was affecting stocks, but the response had always been to move elsewhere or to develop more efficient equipment with which to catch fish. In the second half of the Twentieth Century, it became obvious that the world's fish stocks were being over-exploited. The, now almost barren, Newfoundland Grand Banks are the clearest proof of this. Even the most blinkered fisherman can no longer deny that conservation measures are necessary - as long as they affect someone else's livelihood!

The first 'Law of the Sea' is shrouded in the mists of time, but may well have originated in Rhodes, in the eastern Mediterranean. The first documented Sea Law seems to be the Law of Oleron, dating from 1152AD. This was adopted by Eleanor of Aquitaine, Queen of England, in 1190AD and became one of the foundation stones of international maritime law. In due course, most maritime States claimed sovereignty over as much of the sea as they thought they could. For example, Venice claimed the Adriatic, England the North Sea, the Channel and a large part of the Atlantic and Sweden claimed the Baltic. Sometimes these States would justify their claim by providing some kind of service, such as policing their area against piracy, but there was no real international acceptance of their sovereignty.

In 1493, Pope Alexander VI issued a Papal Bull giving Spain and Portugal sovereignty over the Pacific, the Indian Ocean and most of the Atlantic. Queen Elizabeth I of England's reply is one of the first public statements of the principle of the 'Freedom of the Seas':

'The use of the sea and air is common to all. Neither can title to the ocean belong to any

[3] UNCLOS has two meanings - either the UN Convention on the Law of the Sea, which came into force on 16th November 1994 - or the UN Conference on the Law of the Sea, of which there were three. I will use UNCLOS2 or UNCLOS3 if I am referring to the conferences and plain UNCLOS if I mean the Convention. For reasons best understood by those who are deep into 'UN-speak', UNCLOS1 is always referred to as the First Law of the Sea Conference.

Three miles off. (Ken Knox)

people or private persons for as much as neither nature nor public use and custom permitteth any possession thereof....'

The famous Dutch lawyer, Hugo Grotius, in 1609 made the same case when he published *Mare Liberum*, in which he claimed that the sea was *res communes*; that is that it belonged to all and could not be made the property of any State. John Seldon, an Englishman, made the opposite case in *Mare Clausum*; that a State had the right to sovereignty over waters adjacent to its coast. In 1625, Grotius agreed with the principle of State sovereignty over adjacent waters and from then onwards the principle of territorial seas[4] and the open seas was generally accepted throughout Europe. As the European maritime nations began to trade throughout the world and establish their colonies, these concepts became international and, by the eighteenth century, the nominal 3-mile range of a cannon had come to be the normal limit of territorial waters. At a conference of North Sea states in 1882, Britain persuaded all but one to agree to a 3-mile limit. Only the Kingdom of Norway and Sweden continued to hold to the traditional Scandinavian 4-mile limit.

This conference was followed, in 1901, by a treaty between Denmark and the UK, which extended the agreed 3-mile limit to the Danish dependencies of Greenland and Iceland. This treaty was most unpopular in Iceland, where it was believed that Denmark had, in effect, traded Icelandic fish for Danish pork and butter imports into the UK market. The British felt that maintaining territorial waters as narrow as possible was a vital national interest so that the Royal Navy could operate as and where it wished to. As the British Foreign Secretary, Sir Edward Grey, said in 1911, this was '*a principle on which we might be prepared to go to war with the strongest power in the world.*' Danish attempts to extend the territorial waters of Iceland and the Faeroes in the 1920s were resisted by Britain, as were the Soviets intentions to maintain the Tsarist declared 12-mile limit in the Barents Sea. This latter disagreement was solved with a 1930 treaty allowing the British to fish up to 3 miles from the Kola Peninsula, whilst agreeing to disagree on the actual limits of territorial waters. The Norwegians kept to their 4-mile limit, but did not really enforce it. So whilst the British managed to hold a de facto territorial waters limit of 3-miles, cracks were appearing in the international consensus that were only to be put on hold because of the Second World War.

On the High Seas, whilst there might be generally agreed legal norms, there were no binding multinational agreements, as there are now, and, it was up to Nation States to enforce the law (such as against pira-

[4] Territorial seas is the correct legal terminology, but territorial waters is also widely used. I have used both interchangeably.

cy and slavery) as they saw fit. One of the effects of the long period of Pax Britannica after Trafalgar in 1805, was that the Royal Navy became the world's maritime policeman and so led the British to the view that their interpretation of maritime law was not only right, but also that the freedom of the high seas was a vital national interest. As Hannes Jónsson says in his dogmatic book about the Cod Wars, *"Friends in Conflict"*, 'It was primarily the might of the British Navy, that made the British views on the law of the sea right.' These British beliefs were to be sorely tested in the post-World War II de-colonialisation period and were to founder on the rocks of Icelandic intransigence.

The Truman Declarations

The first blow to the principle of the freedom of the high seas was dealt by the Americans, although they had long been ardent supporters of the *Mare Liberum* principle, with the Truman Proclamations of 28th September 1945. In one the USA declared:

> *'The Government of the United States regards the natural resources of the subsoil and sea bed of the continental shelf beneath the high seas but continuous to the coasts of the United States as appertaining to the United States, subject to its jurisdiction and control..... The character as high seas of the waters above the continental shelf and the right to their free and unimpeded navigation are in no way thus affected....'*

This proclamation was aimed at facilitating the exploration for, and production of, oil and specifically maintained the principle of free navigation on the high seas; however, the second proclamation claimed the right to establish fisheries conservation zones in areas of the high seas contiguous to the coast of the United States. Together, they opened the door to other nations to claim new offshore rights and Peru, Ecuador and Chile quickly used the same logic to claim a 200-mile fishing limit off their coasts. As a Foreign Office mandarin minuted in 1953, the Truman Declaration caused 'enormous damage' to the principle of the freedom of the high seas.

In the immediate aftermath of the Second World War, it was not obvious to the British that their status in the world had changed significantly. Much has been written about the 'decline' of Britain's power, influence and status in the period after the Second World War and some of it has been wishful exaggeration. However, it is clear that Britain no longer had the unfettered ability to use force to impose its will on other countries - the American 'veto' that forced the withdrawal from Suez was to make this very clear. International politics had become much more complicated. The UN was founded in 1945, the Cold War started a couple of years later and NATO was founded in 1949. Britain was being bound more closely into international organisations.

Iceland, having declared independence in 1944, from a Denmark that was still occupied by the Nazis, was less enthusiastic about getting involved in an anti-Soviet alliance (about 20% of Iceland's population voted communist in the 1944 Independence plebiscite). However, the Americans were keen to have a base in Iceland for geo-strategic reasons and, once it became clear that Norway and Denmark were also joining, the Icelandic government accepted the invitation to join NATO.

The first post-war dispute about territorial waters was between the UK and Norway. British trawlers were back on the North Norwegian fishing grounds in the winter of 1947-8. Local fisherman complained vociferously and on 26th June 1948, the Norwegian Parliament, the Storting, decided, in closed session, that the 4-mile limit would be strictly enforced. Not only was this limit greater than the 3-mile accepted by Britain, but it was measured from baselines across fjords and between islands, the longest of which was 44 miles long. Other countries accepted the British definition that territorial limits were measured from the low-water mark. On being informed that the 4-mile limit (initially declared in 1935, but never strictly enforced) would now be strictly policed, the British Ambassador in Oslo was instructed to express 'our surprise and dismay at the Norwegian decision to apply without warning a measure which is known to be utterly unacceptable to His Majesty's Government'. He was also instructed to say that the Royal Navy would have to protect British trawlers. Britain suggested a reversion to the old limits whilst there were negotiations or a referral to the International Court of Justice at The Hague.

The Norwegian Fishery Minister, Jens Bull, reminded the Storting of Sir Edward Grey's assertion of 1911, but the Norwegian Ambassador in London was more realistic when he reported that 'in this day and age, the British response was outrageous.' As so often, there was a personal thread here - the British Ambassador had dealt with the Norwegian fishing problem as a young man in the Foreign Office in 1935, when the original 4-mile Royal Decree had been published. Then, active consideration had been given to sending the Navy in to protect British trawlers, but, at the time, the Norwegians decided on just enough enforcement to satisfy their fishermen, but not so much as to trigger a British reaction.

The Five Ps

The British over-reaction was driven by five factors[5] - Pressure, Prestige, Principle, Precedent and Power. These five Ps were to continue to drive policy throughout the Cod Wars with Iceland and so it is worth explaining their significance.

Pressure - although fishing only accounted for 1% of Britain's GDP in 1948, Hull and Grimsby were still the two largest fishing ports in the world and many thousands were employed, both directly and indirectly, in the industry. The trawler owners were united in the view that there should be no concessions. As the Norwegian Ambassador was told, half-apologetically, by the Foreign Office, they were 'very tough people'. This tactic of looking for sympathy by claiming to be trying to keep the more extreme elements in the dispute under control was to be used later by the Icelandic Government, over worries that the communists would pull Iceland out of NATO if Britain did not withdraw.

Prestige - how could a great maritime power (at this time, it was only about 5 years since the Royal Navy had been overtaken by the USN as the largest navy in the world) allow its publicly expressed 'vital national interests' at sea to be so clearly ignored?

Principle - the principle of the Freedom of the High Seas was, rightly, one that was, and still is, very important to Britain. As the Admiralty pointed out, wider territorial seas could impede or exclude access to vital outposts of the British Empire and neutral states might be unwilling or unable to prevent the abuse of their territorial waters. Internally, the British government would have been prepared to accept a Norwegian 4-mile limit, but not one based on the principle of baselines.

Precedent - London was well aware that Reykjavik was watching the dispute with Norway very carefully and that there were strengthening calls in Iceland for an extension of their territorial waters. The Icelandic fishing grounds were much more important to Britain's fishermen than those off Norway.

Power - if you have power, why not use it? To quote Frederick the Great, 'diplomacy without arms is like music without instruments'. However, the reality was that Britain was no longer completely free to use her power - even in support of perceived vital national interests. To have used the Royal Navy to protect British trawlers might well have prejudiced any British case at the International Court of Justice in The Hague and, internationally, many countries would have agreed with the Norwegian Ambassador's assessment of Britain's reaction, quoted earlier. The, possibly, decisive factor was that Britain and America were still trying to coax the Scandinavian nations into joining NATO. The use of armed force by one of their putative allies just off their coast would have made it impossible for the Norwegian government to join the Atlantic Pact and, if the Norwegians hadn't joined, Iceland wouldn't have done so either.

The Norwegians called Britain's bluff and the first British trawler was arrested for poaching in November 1948. Serious consideration was never given to deploying the Royal Navy to Norwegian waters and the Cabinet decided that an application to the International Court of Justice was the best solution. Both governments judged that the ICJ would find in favour of Norway over the extension to 4 miles and in favour of Britain over the baseline method. The Norwegian Foreign Minister was irritated that foreign policy had been hijacked by the fishermen from northern Norway and their supporters in the Storting - he told the British Ambassador that he was 'most anxious to avoid Anglo-Norwegian friction over such matters in view of the present European situation'.

Ernest Bevin, the British Foreign Secretary, several times expressed his concern that the dispute would

[5] I am deeply indebted to Gudni Jóhannesson for allowing me to quote from his unpublished thesis (see bibliography), which is the source of many of my quotations in this chapter and for my understanding, such as it is, of the politics behind Britain and Iceland's decisions.

hinder the efforts to get Norway to join NATO. No doubt the Norwegian Ambassador in London was well aware of these concerns, for he also played the Pressure card and emphasised how hard it would be to make concessions against the wishes of the fishermen. Talks were held in London, a compromise fishing limit was agreed, but subsequently rejected by the Storting and eventually Britain applied to the ICJ in The Hague for a ruling on the baseline method. Whilst awaiting the court's verdict, British trawlers continued to break the 4-mile limit, to be arrested and to be fined heavily. Britain made diplomatic protests, there were calls for naval protection and an embargo on Norwegian imports, but nothing was actually done.

The pragmatic reality was that encouraging Norway to join NATO and maintaining Western unity in the face of the Soviet threat was, rightly, more important than maintaining the 'vital national interest' on territorial waters. Interestingly, a request to the US - who, despite the Truman Declaration, still supported 3-mile limits and rejected the baseline method - to join Britain's case at The Hague was received with sympathy, but politely rejected. Britain's ability to use force in support of national interests was now reduced by its membership of the NATO alliance.

The situation over Iceland was more acute for Britain. Not only were the fishing grounds of more importance to her fishermen, but the potential willingness of Iceland to have a NATO (in reality, American) base on their soil, something that Norway has never permitted, gave the Icelanders more power in the Atlantic Charter negotiations. In his review of the Norwegian attitudes[6] to all the Anglo-Icelandic fishing disputes, Gudni Jóhannesson asserts that Norway's regular willingness to mediate was based upon self-interest. If NATO was not allowed to have bases in Iceland, there would be intense pressure to permit NATO bases in Norway.

Allied to their realisation of Iceland's strategic importance to NATO, was the fact that fish accounted for 90% of Iceland's exports and therefore its foreign income. This was a live and constant domestic political factor and as soon as Iceland gained independence from Denmark on 17 June 1944, there were moves to extend the fishing limits. The 1901 Anglo-Danish Treaty establishing a 3-mile limit was viewed as a colonial relic.

A Bosun gutting a large cod (Ken Knox)

In 1946, the International Council for the Exploration of the Sea (ICES), established in Copenhagen in 1902, had issued a report recommending that Faxa-Bay, the rich breeding grounds in Iceland's west coast should be closed to all trawling for 10 years. This was intended as an experiment to judge the effect of conservation measures and Iceland invited interested nations to a conference in 1949 to discuss the implementation of the ICES recommendations. Britain refused to participate, which was, in retrospect, an unfortunate decision and probably triggered the first of Iceland's moves towards unilateral extensions of her fishing limits. An international agreement in support of establishing some agreed facts on conservation would have shown that Britain was prepared to take Iceland's concerns over conservation seriously and would not have damaged

[6] *'Sympathy and Self-Interest. Norway and the Anglo-Icelandic Cod Wars.'*

the case in support of the 3-mile limit. Between the ICES recommendation and the aborted conference, the Althing, Iceland's Parliament, promulgated the 'Conservation Law', giving Iceland the right to regulate fisheries above all of their continental shelf, which extended to a maximum of 55 miles from the coast.

Despite the mood in the Althing, which accurately reflected that of the whole country, the government moved slowly. Partially because they hoped to reach an agreement with all the parties concerned and partly because they assumed that a unilateral extension to the full extent of their desires would be widely resisted. However, having failed to draw Britain into negotiations, in October 1949, the Icelandic government withdrew from the 1901 3-mile treaty, giving two year's notice to the British, as required by its terms. In April 1950, a 4-mile limit, using the baseline principle, was established off Iceland's north coast and everyone, Icelanders included, was banned from trawling inside it. The only exception was that the British, as per the 1901 treaty, could continue to fish between 3 and 4 miles until the two-year notice period had expired. As about 25% of Britain's distant-water catches came from this area, a strong reaction could have been expected.

The Mate releases a rich haul (roughly 1 tonne) of cod from the cod ends. (Ken Knox)

British fishermen did, indeed, claim that this extension would lead to the virtual extinction of fishing off Iceland and threatened boycotts on the landing of fish by Icelandic trawlers. The British government's reaction to the extension to 4 miles was to do nothing; as nothing had actually changed (yet!), the Foreign Office's view seemed to be that nothing needed to be done - and, it could be said that, the ruling of the ICJ on the Norwegian 4-mile limit using the baseline method would apply equally to the Icelandic claim. However, there should have been no doubt in London that the Icelandic government, of whatever political hue, was intent on more than just an extension to 4 miles - the 1948 Conservation Law made that very clear, with its reference to the whole of the Continental Shelf. Iceland had a long-term plan to get full control of 'her' fish. Without a plan of her own, Britain was going to be constantly wrong-footed - having to react as and when the next stage of Reykjavik's plan was unveiled.

The government was taking the 4-mile extension calmly and the use of the Royal Navy was quickly dismissed, however the fishing industry was pushing for a ban on Icelandic landings. The Ministry of Agriculture and Fish was willing to support this proposal on the basis that '...it may be necessary - in spite of all the arguments against it - to stop Icelandic imports for a time, until Iceland agrees to act more reasonably.' The Foreign Office, whilst agreeing that a boycott would be a powerful weapon against Iceland, observed that it would go against the free-trade rules that Britain had recently signed up to in the Organisation for European Economic Co-operation (part of the Marshall Plan). The Ministry of Food was against any interference with imports and the Board of Trade noted that any ban would be in conflict with the trade treaty with Iceland. Once again, the interdependence of the post-war world was reducing Britain's scope for action.

A landing ban would have hurt Iceland severely. From a near subsistence economy, the country had become wealthy during the war years - both by selling fish to the Allies and by providing services to the occupying forces (British and then American). The first post-Independence government decided to build freezer plants, fish-processing factories and to order 30 new trawlers from Britain. This planned expansion was very over-ambitious. Assisted by rampant inflation, a thirst for consumer goods and mistakes in setting the exchange rate, the new-found wealth of the Icelanders was gone within three years of Independence - 'Iceland is just about bankrupt', a Board of Trade official noted in 1947. Whilst this may have underestimated the underlying strength of the Icelandic economy, there were clearly very major problems and a British boycott might have brought Iceland to its knees - but then, who would have had to pick up the pieces? As it was, the start of the Cold War and the strong desire to include Iceland in the Western world saved the Icelanders. Once Iceland was within NATO, Marshall aid started to flow strongly from America and Iceland received, proportionately, a bigger share of aid than any other nation.

The American position on the 3-mile limit had not changed and low-key warnings were given to the Icelandic government not to make unilateral extensions of their fishing limits. Maybe these warnings were too low-key, because the government ignored them and promulgated the 4-mile limit along the north coast. This caused the State Department to instruct the American Minister in Reykjavik to register the US government's formal objections to the move. On receiving the diplomatic note, the Icelandic Foreign Minister expressed his dismay over the lack of US understanding of Icelandic politics – American intimidation over this vital national interest would cause uproar and play into the hands of the Left. The American envoy followed his instructions, but then 'suspended' the protest note, as he agreed with the Minister's assessment. After a further appeal by the Icelandic Minister, the Americans withdrew their diplomatic note.

This American 'appeasement' encouraged the Icelandic government and it is interesting to speculate as to what would have happened had the two great maritime powers stood firm on the principles of 3-mile territorial waters based on the low-water mark. British officials tried to persuade the Americans that this was in their mutual interest, but the fear of driving Iceland into the Soviet camp was too strong. Iceland's strategic position on the North Atlantic sea-lanes gave their government a powerful weapon. The Americans were not yet grumbling that Iceland was 'blackmailing' them, but this would come (in 1957).

Whilst this dispute was developing, the (Socialist) British government was actually lending money to Iceland to develop its own fishing fleet. This move was not without critics - on being asked by an opposition MP why the British government was lending money to Iceland to build trawlers that would then land their fish on Humberside where there were already enough British trawlers to satisfy the market, the Minister, Douglas Jay, replied 'I should have thought that the modernisation of the fishing fleet of a country which is a member both of the Stirling area and of the OEEC was a very desirable object'. The Conservative MP, William Shepherd, retorted with 'Would not the Honourable Gentleman also think that the preservation of the livelihood of our own people was equally important?' This was not the only exchange in Parliament on this topic and there were those in government who felt that Iceland had not really been on the Allied side in the war, but had merely been profiteers - this despite the facts that Iceland had lost, proportionally as many men as the United States to enemy action, as well as 20% of its fishing fleet and 50% of its merchant ships. Despite these doubts, the British government's position was that Icelandic development should be assisted.

The principled British support was not reciprocated. As an example, in February 1949, there was an Icelandic delegation in London negotiating a contract for frozen fish and fish products with the Ministry of Food. The Icelanders wanted a price well above world market-rates and when the British officials refused to accept this, the Icelandic delegation leader hinted at a deal with the Soviet Union, at whipping up left-wing anti-British sentiment in Iceland and even at offering his resignation to the Icelandic Prime Minister, who was in Washington at the time negotiating over NATO membership. In the end, the Foreign Secretary had to intervene himself, saying that he could 'not sanction endangering the Atlantic Pact for the sake of a few hundred thousand pounds.' This was hardly the action of friends and allies, but as will become clearer later in this saga, Icelanders do not negotiate in any meaningful sense - they state their position and then stick to it.

Meanwhile off the Kola Peninsula, the British had decided, de facto, to accept the Russian claim to a 12-mile limit. The 1930 Treaty, allowing British fishing activity into 3-miles, despite the declaration of a 12-

mile limit was not actually abrogated until 1953, but four British trawlers were arrested for poaching in 1950 and the Admiralty and the Foreign Office were entirely in accord that a military confrontation with the Soviet Union over fishing was not sensible. Trawlers were encouraged to keep outside 12 miles. The government in Reykjavik cannot have been unaware of this precedent.

The departmental disagreements in British policy over fishing limits and territorial waters caused the Foreign Office's Legal Adviser, Sir Eric Beckett, to open a debate between Departments. This produced a 'first class row' between the Admiralty, who Beckett accused of being too rigidly wedded to the 3-mile limit, and the Foreign Office. He also said there was '...practically a belief that international law can be made for the whole world by a series of British protests of which, in fact, other countries took remarkably little notice..'. He went on to describe the policy as being in a 'cloud cuckoo land'. However, the Admiralty still believed that there could be a need for 'gunboat diplomacy' - or more formally 'Naval Assistance in Support of Foreign and Colonial Policy'. In this belief in the need to preserve the maximum freedom of the seas, the Ministry of Transport and Agriculture and Fishery were on the Admiralty's side.

The Lawyers get involved...

The core question, however, was the attitude of the Americans. Together, the two major maritime nations could slow down, if probably not defeat, the burgeoning moves towards wider territorial waters, fishery limits and generally less freedom of the seas. Indecisive talks were held between Britain and the US and time was running out for the *Mare Liberum* camp. Scottish fishermen wanted the Moray Firth and the Minches closed to foreigners, the Norwegians pointed out to the ICJ in the Hague that the British colonies of Honduras and Fiji used the baseline method, Bermuda, the Bahamas, Canada and Australia all insisted on fishery controls outside 3 miles and, finally, the UN General Assembly accepted Iceland's proposal that the International Law Commission should debate the issue of the width of territorial waters. The International Law Commission's task was 'to promote the progressive development of international law and its codification'. Britain had resisted the move to allow the ILC to look at the territorial waters issue, but the UN General Assembly had decided otherwise.

The International Court of Justice's ruling, when it came on 18th December 1951, was a shock to the British - the court found for the Norwegians over both the Baseline issue, but also unexpectedly over the 4-mile limit. Having unilaterally put the issues into the hands of the ICJ, the British could no nothing but accept the ruling. In the subsequent post-mortems, in which scholars of the decline in Britain's status post-WWII are still actively engaged, questions were raised about the wisdom of approaching the court in the first place - with 4 judges from South America, where the 200-mile fishing limit was already being proposed. The reality was probably that Britain, after the experiences of the 1930s and the Second World War felt morally bound to make maximum use of the available international institutions and was very wary of using armed forces except in genuine self-defence. Whatever the reasons, Palmerston would have been amazed at the failure of the government to use its military force early and unequivocally in defence of a 'vital national interest'. The reality was that the world (and especially Britain's place in it) had changed and worse was to come.

Once the dust had settled, a territorial waters committee was established in London. The battle lines were soon drawn - the Scottish Office (supporting Scottish fishermen) were for baselines, as were the Colonial Office (on behalf of archipelagic colonies) and the Ministry of Fuel and Power (oil interests). The Foreign Office was in favour of measured retreat - the Assistant Legal Advisor said that narrow territorial waters depended 'on the existence of naval powers with (a) the will[7] and (b) the power to enforce them.' More and more small and medium powers were bound to decided to extend their territorial waters and Britain could not stop them. The Fisheries Department were in support of the deep-

[7] Many will be aware of Professor Dixon's excellent book on the psychology of Military Incompetence. The Professor used to lecture to the Royal Navy's Staff Courses at Greenwich in the 1970s and one of his lectures was on the psychology of deterrence. In this he used to propose that deterrence (either nuclear or conventional) depended upon the 3 factors of a weapon, an organisation or person capable of using that weapon & thirdly, the political will to use the weapon. The repeated failure of the British Government's will to use the Royal Navy's full capability against the Icelandic Coastguard meant that the result of all three Cod Wars was inevitable.

water fishermen and against any increase, as were the Admiralty, who stated:

'It is true that no Foreign Secretary could say today, as Sir Edward Grey did, that we should go to war for the sake of the three-mile limit. But even the Foreign Office, in their most dejected frame of mind, would admit that the narrowing of territorial waters limits is still a major object of foreign policy.'

With this level of disagreement between departments, it was obvious that the Cabinet was going to have to discuss the issue. After a vigorous discussion, with Winston Churchill in the chair as Prime Minister, it was agreed that 'it was to the advantage of a great maritime power to keep free of territorial control as large an area as possible of the sea and of the air above it.' Before making a final decision, however, the Ministry of Defence were invited to staff all the naval implications and the Foreign Office were to consult with the United States and the Commonwealth. Churchill will, no doubt, have remembered his outrage when Chamberlain had refused to sanction the laying of mines to stop the Germans using Norwegian territorial waters in 1939-40.

The MoD stuck firm on its opposition to any extension, the Foreign Office received ambivalence from the Americans and active support for wider limits from Canada and Australia. Finally, on December 14th, 1953, the Foreign Secretary, Selwyn Lloyd, made a statement to Parliament. He declared that, whilst baselines would be of some advantage to local inshore fishermen, especially in Scotland, he felt that wider considerations, arising out of the naval, mercantile and deep-sea fishery position of Britain must take precedence. Britain would neither implement baselines, nor accept them anywhere, except off northern Norway. It had taken nearly two years from the ICJ's decision for the British government to produce a policy (in reality, a non-policy) statement on this issue.

It may have taken the British two years, but it only took Iceland two hours. On the same day as the ICJ announced their verdict, the Foreign Minister, Bjarni Benediktsson, suggested to the British Ambassador, John Dee Greenway, that they should have a discussion to resolve their differences. The talks were held in London in January 1952 and the Icelandic delegation was led by Ólafur Thors, Fishery Minister, chairman of the Conservative Party (part of the governing coalition) and already three times Icelandic Prime Minister. The British side was led by an Under-Secretary in the Foreign Office and this disparity caused much offence. When no Minister was 'available' to even see the Icelandic delegation, this was perceived as a deliberate slight. In Britain's defence, the issue of Iceland's fishing limits was of far more importance to Iceland than to Britain, but had Eden, the Foreign Minister, been prepared to see Thors and to discuss their relative concerns face to face, the outcome could have been very different. As it was, the British felt that the Icelanders were looking for unconditional surrender[8] and the Icelanders were angry that the British refused even to discuss baselines, despite precedent created by the ICJ's decision.

There is some evidence that the Icelandic team had come prepared to be flexible over the basis for drawing the baselines, which were in reality a much bigger problem for British fishermen than the extension to 4-miles, but the attitude of the British had caused so much offence that Ólafur Thors had decided to stick to his original position. No real discussions took place and no agreement of any kind was reached. Iceland extended her limit to 4 miles on 15th May, drawn from the most ambitious baselines, one of which was 78 miles long and drawn from a small offshore rock. The Grimsby Evening Herald called this 'Black Thursday' and flags flew at half-mast in the distant-water fishing ports. An Icelandic historian was later to say that this day marked both the start of the implementation of the 1948 Icelandic Continental Shelf Act and the start of the end of the British distant-water fishing industry.

The British government protested, but decided to take no further action, even instructing the Royal Navy's Fishery Protection vessel off Iceland not to interfere if an Icelandic gunboat tried to arrest a British trawler inside the 4-mile limit. The first British trawler was arrested in July. Hull and Grimsby were enraged. Sir Pierson Dixon, in the

[8] I am indebted to Gudni Jóhannesson for the observation that there is no proper word for 'diplomacy' in Icelandic and neither does the noun 'loser' exist. On the other hand, there are over thirty synonyms for 'battle' and roughly the same number of expressions to denote the act of conquering. No wonder the British found Icelanders impossible to negotiate with.

In Cod we Trusted (1990 - 2005. David N. Barron & Post This! Inc. www.PostThisInc.com)

Foreign Office, admitted that the British government's freedom of action was constrained:

> *'This is part of the price we have to pay for our fidelity to the principles on international co-operation under the UN Charter and our partnership with Iceland in NATO.... On the other hand, I do not think that we need be restrained by tenderness for Icelandic feelings from allowing the natural indignation of British trawling interests to vent itself through ordinary channels. After all, in the spirit of NATO partnership, the Icelanders ought to have proceeded less brusquely, and consulted us more fully about their regulations, before they were introduced.'*

On 2nd October 1952, the British Trawler Federation (BTF), the trawler owners' group declared that Icelandic trawlers would not be given any landing facilities until the Reykjavik government gave a satisfactory answer to the British objections over the new fishing limits. The British Government stood back and said that Icelandic owners must negotiate with their British opposite numbers. This abrogation of responsibility was not sustainable and Antony Nutting, Under Secretary at the Foreign Office, negotiated, with the Icelandic government, a reference of the dispute to the Overfishing Commission, the international committee on fishery conservation. He had no sooner told the House of Commons that an agreement had been reached with Reykjavik, when the British owners said that they would not back down. The government was no longer in control of this area of foreign policy. One Icelandic trawler did try to break the embargo in November and landed her catch in Grimsby. The Trawler Officers Guilds in Hull and Grimsby immediately went out on strike and the fish merchants agreed to accept no more Icelandic landings.

As 80% of Iceland's catch was usually exported to Britain as fresh fish, this embargo was effective - however, it was almost certainly illegal and it could play into the hands of the Communists in Iceland. In December, Ólafur Thors was in London again - this time he saw Foreign Secretary Eden with no difficulty. Having paraded the 'Communist spook' in front of Eden, he went to Paris and delivered a fiery speech in the Organisation of European Economic Co-operation about the landing embargo. He then raised the matter in the North Atlantic Council, NATO's ministerial level committee. General Alfred Gruenther, Supreme Allied Commander in Europe, told Eden privately that something had to be done. Meanwhile, a backlash was developing against the owners' actions - other people's livelihoods were being affected by the lack of visiting Icelandic fishermen and British exporters to Iceland were worrying about reciprocal action. On top of all this, there were plenty of fish in Icelandic waters and the 4-mile limit had made no difference to the British fleet's catch.

The British government wished to find a path to negotiations, but the owners would not back down. And for the same reason that the Icelandic government was unwilling to cage the Communist bogey, because of the extra pressure they could apply on the British, the British government were unwilling to overrule the trawler owners.

By the summer of 1953, when the landing ban had been in place for nearly a year, George Dawson, known as the 'Cockney Millionaire', came to Iceland's aid. Dawson was an entrepreneur who had made his fortune trading in army surplus after the war. He offered to buy Icelandic fish and then sell it in Britain. Because of his reputation, the Icelandic owners were initially unwilling to enter into a contract with Dawson, but eventually they did and he landed a total of seven catches in Grimsby. As many had predicted this was a short-lived effort - fish merchants who bought from him were blacklisted, he had no proper distribution network and he defaulted on payments to his Icelandic partners.

As George Dawson disappeared from the scene, another 'saviour' appeared. This time it was that NATO bogey - the Soviet Union. In August, Iceland and the Soviet Union signed an extensive barter agreement - frozen fish and herrings for, primarily, oil with some industrial and agricultural goods. For Iceland, this was very good news as, even when the UK landing embargo finished, they would no longer be dependant on one market. The West's initial reaction was that this was mainly a political move by the USSR and, despite Icelandic assertions, right up until recently, that the trade agreement was primarily commercial, recent research in the Soviet archives supports the Western assessment. The Soviet envoy, Igor Sysoev reported to Moscow, on 16th December 1953, that the trade agreement

> *'should increase both the popularity of the Soviet Union and negative feelings over the American occupation.'*

The typical Western reaction was well reported by the "*Yorkshire Post*"[9]:

> *'Iceland, vital link in the NATO chain of defence, with the largest United States air base in the North Atlantic.... has entered into closer economic relations with Russia than any country this side of the Iron Curtain. In Reykjavik I saw more Hammers and Sickles than Stars and Stripes, more Russian diplomats than British.'*

This kind of view increased US pressure on the UK to settle the dispute, but as the US was still committed to a 3-mile limit, this pressure remained low-level. The US helped Iceland find alternate markets and refused demands by New England fishermen to restrict the import of Icelandic fish into the USA.

And Trouble with the Faeroes too...

The next twist in the UK's fishing problems was the 1952 declaration by the Faeroes (a Danish dependency) of a 4-mile limit, with news that a similar declaration around the Greenland coast was imminent. After some quite tough negotiations over three years, a compromise agreement was reached between the British and Danish governments that suited neither the fishermen in the Faeroes, nor those on Humberside. The British had hoped that this deal would be seen as a sensible compromise, but in Iceland it was dismissed, as had the 1901 Anglo-Danish Treaty been, as Faeroese fishermen's interests being sacrificed for Danish bacon imports. Negotiations with the Soviets over fishing off the Kola Peninsula from 1952-6 were less successful and, whilst allowing some limited British rights for 5 years up to 3 miles off the coast, effectively acknowledged Soviet jurisdiction out to 12 miles, including a baseline that was longer than the Icelandic Faxa-Bay one. When Iceland declared her 12-mile limit in 1958, the Anglo-Soviet agreement was to be one of the precedents.

The stalemate between Britain and Iceland dragged on. Iceland was managing without the British market ('though British prices were better), but the political chill between NATO allies needed to be lifted. In 1954, an attempt was made, under a Swiss chairman, to find an agreement through the OEEC; this coincided with the Humberside fishmongers complaining that they wanted more competition

[9] 23 July 1954

in prices and supplies. Even in Iceland, there was a slight thaw, when Ólafur Thors, now Prime Minister again, asked for research to be done to see if some concessions could be offered on baselines, without damaging Iceland's right to follow the ICJ's ruling on Norwegian limits. Simultaneously, there were concerns being expressed within the Icelandic government that they were becoming too dependent on the USSR - suppose the USSR said 'pull out of NATO or we'll buy no more of your fish?' In February 1955, Winston Churchill even wrote personally to Ólafur Thors looking for a way out.

This olive branch was well received, but the sad fact was that both sides were too dug in, even then politicians had a fear of perceived 'u-turns'. It was easier not to embark on a course of action that was going to involve loss of face and there was, as yet, no crisis to force the issue up the agenda. The new British Minister responsible, Derick Heathcote Amory, noted that 'the fish problem was the least of his troubles' and one of his civil servants observed that 'if we withdraw our only bargaining weapon ... (the Icelanders) ... may feel that they have gained complete victory'. To balance the picture, the Danish Minister, Bodil Begtrup, observed 'It is typical for Icelandic politics that the authorities tend to excite the population so much through their own propaganda that sensible negotiations become impossible'. For both sides, there was too much to lose domestically and no clear gains for either side to be willing to risk real negotiations. The Swiss chairman of the OEEC committee complained that he 'was in the presence of two parties who would not meet each other'.

Neither side was willing to risk an application to the ICJ - the British because they were certain that they would lose as they had over the Norwegian case, and the Icelanders because they were afraid that the ICJ might say - so far and no further. When Ólafur Thors actually told the British Ambassador in Reykjavik (that) 'that whatever result he got by negotiation would preclude him from doing what he intended to do - to move the fishery limit gradually outwards as occasion offered', alarm bells started ringing loudly in London. The Permanent Under Secretary (PUS) in the Foreign Office quickly recommended that, if any further extensions were announced, the Royal Navy should give protection to British trawlers. Between May 1952, when the 4-mile limit came into force, and the end of 1956, 15 British trawlers had been arrested for illegal fishing within Iceland's claimed limits. Others had escaped, sometimes whilst under fire from the Icelandic gunboats. The crisis was approaching.

The Permanent Under Secretary's forthright view was not shared at lower levels in the Foreign Office, nor was it shared in the Admiralty, who were concerned about both NATO and the force levels necessary to protect the trawlers - estimated to be at least three fishery protection vessels and two frigates or destroyers on station. These figures need to be multiplied by three to estimate the total force levels required because of the transit time to the patrol areas and the need for leave for the ships' companies and maintenance/repair to the ships. It must be remembered that ships in this era needed regular boiler cleans to remain effective. And then there was also the question of tanker support. The Admiralty's cautious approach caused the Foreign Office's PUS to note that it was 'sadly lacking in the Nelson touch'.

In December 1955 a Cabinet Paper was prepared stating that in the case of further extensions by Iceland, warships would protect trawlers and 'take all necessary steps to prevent arrest and to rescue any arrested vessel'. Had this come about, there is little doubt that Iceland would not have been brought to the negotiating table, but would probably have withdrawn from NATO - the Left was very strong and, only just over 10 years after throwing off the Danish 'colonial yoke', the population were very sensitive to anything that smacked of colonialism. Lieutenant Bob Gerken, who was the Navigating Officer in HMS *Bramble*, remembers arriving in Reykjavik on the day after British paratroopers landed at Suez - the men on the jetty refused to catch the ship's heaving lines, shouting 'get off to Egypt, you murdering British pigs'. However, once *Bramble's* crew had secured the ship alongside, the rest of the visit passed peaceably.

Fortunately, the OEEC negotiations in Paris were, albeit slowly, giving some cause for optimism and so Iceland held off from declaring their intended extension to 12 miles. At the end of 1955, a draft agreement had been reached with the British giving de facto recognition to Iceland's 4-mile limit in return for a quota on Icelandic landings in the UK, permission for British trawlers to shelter in Icelandic waters without stowing their gear and an assurance that there would be no further extension of Icelandic territorial waters until the UN had conferred on the subject. The politicians in Iceland were just about prepared to accept this - the delay on further extensions was their difficulty, but the trawler owners wanted an agreement on no further extension for at least ten, and preferably fifty, years. There was also an outbreak of inter-departmental warfare in Whitehall that delayed things further.

Finally in January 1956, all parties convened in Paris to hammer out the details of the Icelandic quotas - issues about territorial waters were specifically not on the agenda. The trawler owners were obdurate[10] and no agreement was reached. To compound the problem, an election was now looming in Iceland and so the Progressive (left wing) party decided to oppose any agreement. The British government had also, perhaps belatedly, come to the conclusion that the strategic consequences of the Humberside embargo were no longer acceptable. The Foreign Secretary, Selwyn Lloyd, told the Cabinet on 21st February:

> *'A prolongation of the dispute would increase the economic dependence of Iceland on the Soviet bloc; it would also strengthen the hands of the Communists in Iceland, whose aim is to deny the United States the use of the vital air base at Keflavík and to bring about the withdrawal of Iceland from NATO.'*

In Iceland the left wing parties (government in Iceland is always by coalition, quite often unstable) tabled a resolution in the Althing proposing a revision of the 1951 defence agreement with the USA so, although Iceland would remain in NATO, the Keflavík base would be exclusively manned by Icelandic nationals. The Americans immediately stopped all construction work on the air base; this had a significant effect on the local economy. The US Joint Chiefs of Staff stated that a withdrawal from Iceland was 'unacceptable'. There was also concern that other smaller nations in NATO, which was suffering from a Soviet 'charm offensive', might be attracted to the concept of 'neutrality' under NATO's protection. Action was needed and the US leant heavily on the UK to lift the embargo. NATO and the fishing limits dispute were now firmly entangled. The British resisted forcing the trawler owners to lift the ban, pointing out that to do so just before the Icelandic General Election would only add to the controversy.

The left wing coalition won the election and, for the first time, there were Communists in government in a NATO country. The US position changed overnight. It became impossible for the new government to raise any loans in the West and London was asked to do nothing about the landings embargo until 'a more viable government was in power in Iceland'. At the end of July (1956), the US Ambassador in Oslo actually suggested that '*in Washington the possibility of forcing through a change of regime in Iceland was being considered.*' In September, all NATO classified documents in Iceland were destroyed.

However, as so often, the pre-election rhetoric was not matched by post-election action and there was no real push for the Americans to be ejected from Keflavík. In October, negotiations were opened about the air base, with simultaneous talks on economic assistance and loans. Any doubts about the outcome were quashed when the Soviets invaded Hungary on 4th November 1956.

With Iceland firmly back into the NATO fold, the subject of the landing embargo came back to the top of the hoist.[11] The Icelanders had asked for loans to purchase new fishing vessels, but needed access to the 'Free World's markets' to make this loan viable. Meanwhile, in Paris, quiet diplomacy had established that the only remaining obstacle was a commitment from the new left-wing government over any future expansions of territorial waters. The stated policy was:

> *'The government places great emphasis on the Icelandic Coastal Jurisdiction and is of the opinion that an increase of the conservation areas around the country is now a pressing necessity for the security of employment of the Nation and will therefore do its utmost to implement this policy.'*

In November, the British government finally decided to recover control of foreign policy between Britain and Iceland from Humberside and the owners

[10] Causing one Foreign Office official to say 'I now feel about these negotiations rather as Napoleon (I think) said about some of his business when he remarked, "Heaven preserve me from my friends; I can deal with my enemies"'.
[11] A gunnery expression – the next round to be fired is that at the 'top of the hoist'.

were told firmly that the ban must be lifted as it was ineffective, causing international problems and probably illegal. On 14th November, the British and Icelandic owners signed an agreement over the resumption of Icelandic landings and quotas in Paris. The government in Reykjavik stated that British trawlers could enter Icelandic waters with their gear unstowed and that there would be no further extension of territorial waters until the UN General Assembly had considered the issue. Apart from this agreement to delay the next extension, the Icelanders had won everything they set out to achieve.

Elsewhere, the battle to preserve the freedom of the seas had not been going much better. In 1954 only about twenty states, mainly Western or old Commonwealth, were still adhering to a 3-mile limit. Peru, having declared a 200-mile limit in November 1954, seized five of Aristotle Onassis's whaling ships. They were released after payment of a fine of $3,000,000 (about US$20,000,000 in today's terms). As the Marine and War Risk insurance was held in Lloyds, the British insurance market had to pay this fine and naval protection of the British whaling fleet was called for. In similar circumstances, the Ecuadorian Navy fired on and seized Californian Tuna fishermen within their claimed 200-mile limit. The US was unwilling to act because, as one of the Ecuadorian Ministers told the US Ambassador in Quito 'you know the Russians are breathing down our necks'. It was not only the Icelanders who were using the tensions of the Cold War to pursue their own agenda.

'Conservation' had also become another weapon in the campaign to enclose more of the seas. The South American states, at a conference held by the Food and Agriculture Organisation of the UN used conservation as a reason for justifying their 200-mile limits, not that they pretended to impose any limits on catches; they just wished to keep foreigners out. Iceland was not guilty of this hypocrisy – as already noted, the initial 4-mile limit on Iceland's north coast, came with a complete ban on trawling for conservation reasons. Initially, this ban applied to everyone (including Icelanders) except the British, who had a two-year period of grace under the old 1901 territorial waters treaty.

The International Law Commission, established by the UN, did, after several years' debate, manage to agree that 'International Law does not permit an extension of the territorial sea beyond twelve miles', however it also recommended that 'the breadth of territorial seas should be fixed by an international conference.

The International Law Commission organised the First Conference on the Law of the Sea in Geneva between February and April 1958. This conference resulted in the adoption of four conventions - on the high seas, on the territorial sea and the contiguous zone, on the continental shelf and on fishing and the conservation of the living resources of the high seas. This Conference was unable to muster the two-thirds majority necessary to adopt the 12-mile limit on territorial seas and Iceland decided on unilateral action. The First Cod War was to start on 1st September 1958.

CHAPTER 3

FISHERY PROTECTION BEFORE THE FIRST COD WAR

Before moving on to the First UN Law of the Sea Conference and the final diplomatic moves before the outbreak of the First Cod War in late 1958, I would like to look at the activities of the Fishery Protection Squadron in 'peacetime'. Deep sea fishermen are tough, independent men[12], the last 'hunters' of food left in the modern world, so not surprisingly, they don't like being told what to do, even (especially?) by the Royal Navy, although it should be remembered that many of the fishermen active in the distant-water trade had been members of the Royal Navy Patrol Service ('Harry Tate's Navy') in the Second World War and so knew about the Royal Navy and its way of doing things. Equally, the Royal Navy has been involved in fishery protection in one form or another for many hundreds of years - there is record of the Admiralty stationing a 'Wafting Ship' in the North Sea during the herring season in 1586 and Nelson did his time as Captain Fishery Protection Squadron in HMS *Albemarle* in 1781 - so the fishermen were used to having the Navy around. Fishery protection duties cover much more than enforcing regulations, although that is the area that inevitably gets most publicity. Warships on patrol would have provided medical and technical assistance, as well as search and rescue cover when necessary. They would also have provided a liaison link with foreign authorities, for example, the Icelandic Coastguard in case of any disputes or arrests of British fishermen.

In the late 1950s, the First Division[13] (also called the Arctic Division) of the Royal Navy's Fishery Protection Squadron (FPS) consisted of two Algerine class Ocean Minesweepers, HMS *Wave* (Captain Fishery Protection Squadron's flagship) and HMS *Hound*, and two Type 14 frigates, HM Ships *Russell* and *Palliser*. The two Algerines were due to be replaced by two new Type 14s (HM Ships *Duncan* and *Malcolm*) in 1959. These four ships were responsible for covering all of the distant-water fishing grounds used by British fishermen, including Icelandic waters.

Life onboard these ships was never dull or routine - the weather saw to that, and off Iceland they were operating pretty close to their physical limits. In fact HMS *Hound*, who did the initial patrol of the First

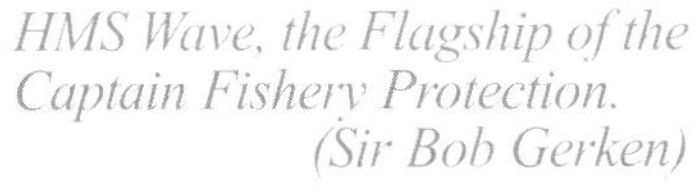

HMS Wave, the Flagship of the Captain Fishery Protection. (Sir Bob Gerken)

[12] I hope I shall be forgiven the use of men, rather than people. At this period, there were no women deep-sea fishermen. The Russians were probably the first nation to employ women in the deep-sea fishery trade in the 1960s.

[13] The Second (or Home) Division of 4 Coastal Minesweepers covered UK waters except for the Channel & the Third (or Channel) Division which consisted of one or two Inshore Minesweepers.

Cod War, was never employed off Iceland again as, mainly because of her limited speed, she was not capable of fulfilling the task. The mainstay of the FPS throughout the First Cod War was to be the Type 14 frigates. These were small (1100 ton standard displacement, 310' LOA) single-screw ships built as anti-submarine convoy escorts for the Cold War.

Life in the FPS was very busy and fairly hard, even by the usual standards of the day. As a consequence, the FPS Type 14s were manned to a 'war complement' of 120, rather than the nominal 90. Charles Dempsey, who was the Leading Sick Berth Attendant (LSBA) in HMS *Palliser*, was the 'Doc' or 'Sick Bay Tiffy' onboard for two years from March 1958. The memories that he has written down for his grandchildren provide a good idea of what life was like onboard and I am very grateful for his permission to quote a few extracts below.

> *'I was messed right aft in a small room that ran the width of the ship; we slept in hammocks and there were 15 other men in the mess. One entered the mess through a vertical hatch and down a ladder. There was another smaller mess branching off it, with 8 men in. Once we got to sea, the main deck bulkhead door was closed and we had to walk aft over the deck housing and drop through two vertical ladders to get to the mess, because the main deck would be awash in heavy weather. In harbour, there was just 8 feet of freeboard between the sea and the main deck; often at sea there was nothing, which I was soon to find out for myself. This created obvious difficulties because all meals were eaten on the mess deck, which meant it had to be carried up one deck, taken out through the weather door and along the upper deck around all the funnels and ventilator shafts for the engine room etc, then down two vertical ladders to the mess deck. If it was cold or raining, it was a perilous journey.'*

The LSBA had a fairly busy life looking after the ship's company; a Medical Officer was only carried when the ship was actually on distant-water fishery patrol. HMS *Palliser* sailed from Rosyth for northern waters three days after Charles Dempsey joined. To continue his story:

> *'The Thursday morning we set sail; it was a cold bleak day. There was a damp mist saturating everything and we seemed to be the only boat moving. We left the dockyard (Rosyth) and turned east to pass under the Forth Bridge (this is before the road bridge was built) and on out to the open sea; the side was manned until we passed the Flag Officer's Residence, then the stand down was piped. The weather continued grey and the sea was completely flat until we came out of*

HMS Palliser in a Norwegian Fjord. *(Norman Robinson)*

the Forth and turned north into the North Sea; now it began to get choppy. As we progressed, the weather deteriorated and towards the evening we were heading into a force 8 gale. The weather continued to be unpleasant for the next three days.
It is not at all unusual for some of the crew members to be seasick for the first couple of days, then they settle down and don't notice what it's like after that. The long-term problem I learnt with constant heavy weather was not seasickness, but back pain. This is caused because a person is constantly moving against the motion of the ship, mostly completely unconsciously and even in one's sleep. Most men had applied to stop shaving, but foolishly, I didn't and I was to regret this later.'

Liferaft transfer. (Charles Dempsey)

His first patrol was in an area off the northwest coast of Iceland. Over Easter weekend, the weather was actually good enough for sunbathing, but on Monday it deteriorated again and reports of injuries started to come in from trawlers. Charles Dempsey was about to learn about liferaft transfers:

'The liferaft was a normal 10-man rubber raft, which was constructed of two inflated circular tubes with a double skin bottom, again inflated.
Inflated tubular arches crossed the raft with a skin between two opposing arches and openings between the other two for access and egress.
There was a large hoop of steel, the circumference of the raft, with canvas stretched across it on which the raft sat. This was held in place by four canvas straps, which met over the top centre of the raft in a metal ring. The raft was lowered over the side by a crane hooked onto this ring and, similarly, when the raft returned, it was hooked on and lifted out of the water, hopefully complete with passenger. Little did I know that this was going to be my busiest form of transport for the next two years.'
'In fine weather, and the seas as you see it in the pictures would be considered fine weather, there is a nylon line shot over the trawler; this is then attached to a thick line and the raft would be pulled across. It can only be done in fine weather, because it means both ships remaining on station with the frigate on the weather side. In inclement weather, they couldn't do this because it would mean that the frigate would be blown onto the trawler. Looking back, I suppose this could be thought of as highly dangerous, but I thoroughly enjoyed it.
We wore what was referred to as an immersion suit to do the transfers in the raft. An immersion suit comprised a rubberised blouse with a hood. It had a tight rubber seal around the wrists of the sleeves and a rubber seal around the neck. It also had a long rubber skirt, which came down to my knees. The trousers were of similar material with rubber boots like Wellingtons sealed to the bottom. They were worn with strong braces. The trousers also had a rubber skirt attached at the waist, which again came down to the knees. With both articles on, the rubber skirts were rolled up together to give a watertight seal at the waist. It was a very comfortable piece of clothing to wear and very warm. It didn't keep ones face and hands warm

Charles Dempsey alongside the Hull trawler Faraday. (Charles Dempsey)

though and that is why I should have grown a beard. Having to do a life raft transfer early in the day after having a shave, it felt as if a thousand knives were cutting into my face and my hands froze into claw shapes as I tried to manipulate the freezing wet ropes. Many, many times I had to get my hands thawed once I got onto trawlers before I could even think of doing anything for the patient.

Getting onboard a trawler was never an easy task and one had to be a bit of an athlete and chancy with it on occasion. In this picture I am alongside a Hull trawler and, as you can see, the liferaft is on the crest of a swell; now is the time to get on the trawler. The large board hanging from the side of the trawler is one of the doors that keep the net open whilst it is being pulled along the seabed. I can just be seen on the far side of the raft. The most common injury we had to deal with was when trawler men caught a particular fish, which had poisonous spines. If the spines pierced their hands, their arms would swell up and they suffered fearful agonies with the pain, but they were a stoic bunch and the masters of understatement. To them, a slight cut finger-would probably mean their arm was hanging off.

Returning back to the frigate could be a difficulty as well, particularly if there was more than one in the liferaft. The raft was lifted out of the water on a hoist, which was raised by manpower, not by machinery. Therefore one of us (the Medical Officer was often in the liferaft with Charles Dempsey) had to get out and climb up the scrambling net. In these pictures, the weather has deteriorated a little since we started on this particular little jaunt. The ship has to remain stationary while this manoeuvre is carried out, otherwise the raft would dip under and fill with water, so everyone gets involved very quickly.'

Norman Robinson, who was Charles Dempsey's predecessor as LSBA in *Palliser*, has one abiding memory of these transfers - the cry of 'Don't whatever you do fall overboard, as you've only got three minutes in these waters.' Charles Dempsey has a couple of particular memories of his time, which well illustrate the way of life and the humour that was always around:

'One trawler was complaining that they had lost a man overboard while they were gutting their catch. They actually said he had jumped ship. They were going to try to search for him. Our skipper was on the bridge in seconds to organise a search. The next thing we heard was that another trawler half a mile away from the first started to complain that they had a stowaway onboard and hadn't they got too many mouths to feed as it was? The subject of all this sardonic humour was the deckhand of the first trawler, a man in his fifties who was wearing a fisherman's frock apron, thigh boots and a neckerchief around his neck to stop

water getting inside his oilskin.
Waves 10 or 15 feet high were sweeping across the decks; he had been lifted by a wave. A pocket of air had been trapped under his oilskin. He was carried over the top of the lifeline rigged three feet above the gunwhale and carried on the crest of the wave until he was thrown onto the lifeboat of the second trawler and impaled by his buttock on the lifeboat's anchor blade. There was no possibility that we could do a transfer in that sea, so we had to wait until it calmed. The doctor intended that I should get him from the second trawler, bring him back to Palliser, then we would clean his wound and stitch him up if necessary, to finally return him to his own ship afterwards. The ribald humour was fast and furious at the poor chap's expense. The first mate wanted to know where he put his gutting knife before he swam off, among many others not so kind.'

Once the injured man was onboard *Palliser*, it became clear that the wound in his buttock was going to require minor surgery and the Doctor decided that he'd exercise the emergency operating theatre - otherwise known as the wardroom. The patient was told to have a good bath (he hadn't had a chance to wash himself fully since he'd left home a couple of weeks before), and was issued with a complete set of new clothing. In the absence of any anaesthetic machine onboard, the trawlerman was given a bottle of whisky, whilst the dead flesh was cut away, the rust and debris cleaned out and the resulting hole stitched up. The Supply Officer was detailed off to assist the LSBA and the Petty Officer Steward was in charge of the autoclave for sterilising instruments. The Captain, Lieutenant-Commander Geoff Hammond came down to the wardroom to observe and to see how the ship's motion was affecting the operation. Several times the Navigating Officer, who had the watch on the bridge, was told to 'stop rocking the boat' - not so easy in 10-12 foot waves. Once the operation was successfully completed, Charles Dempsey said that he realised that the Petty Officer Steward, who had been watching through the pantry hatch ready to supply whatever might be needed, had also been giving a running commentary to the off-watch members of the ship's company who were packed into the wardroom flat.

Geoff Hammond remembers another medical incident where a warp parted and struck a young trawlerman across the mouth. Once onboard *Palliser*, his lips were both sewn up and the remains of his smashed front teeth were removed. On asking the trawler's skipper, next day, how the deckhand was, he got the reply 'Oh he's OK. Out on deck now. The only problem is that he has to dunk his biscuits before he can eat them.'

On the return passage from his first fish patrol, the ship hit severe weather north of the Faeroes. Both boats were stove in, in fact nothing was left of the whaler except for a few bits hanging off the falls at each end, the derricks were twisted as if made of plastic and the quarterdeck had been cleared of everything - including the (aft) 40mm Bofors gun. A period in dockyard hands was to follow. This sort of damage was not unusual - later in his time onboard, during another liferaft transfer (of which Charles Dempsey did 179 during his time onboard), he was able to see that both the ship's bilge keels had gone - which indicates how much the ship was rolling during this particular transfer. Invariably he returned onboard with a couple of basket's worth of fish in the raft - 'though on one occasion, from a 'long-liner', he came back with just one fish - a flounder. Charles explains that this photo is so worn because he has won many pints on the strength of a fish bigger than him and he keeps having to show it to people to prove his yarn!

Charles Dempsey's flounder.
(Charles Dempsey)

And another story from Charles Dempsey's memoirs:

'I was transferred to a Belgian trawler; the sea

was too heavy for a line transfer, so I had gone over on a free drift[14]*. When I climbed onto the trawler, the crew had the deck alive with their catch, which they were gutting. I noticed that all the crew were in oilskins and seaboots, except one man who was in a shirt and jeans and wearing wooden clogs. With water surging onto the deck and out again through the scuppers, I asked the skipper why that man wasn't dressed for the weather. He told me that the man was from a prison in Belgium. He had created trouble in the prison and the magistrate had sentenced him to four weeks on a fishing trawler. He had been brought to the trawler the day the ship sailed and his escort left him when they were about a mile at sea. He had to work like all the other deckhands until they returned, but he only had the clothes he stood up in. When they returned, he would be met and taken back to prison to finish his sentence. The skipper said it was unknown for a prisoner to go to sea twice!'*

Before the start of the First Cod War in September 1958, the Iceland patrol was filled for about 15 weeks a year and, during these patrols, regular visits were made to Icelandic ports - HMS *Hound* had visited in May and HMS *Wave* in June of 1958. Although there was some tension over fishing limits, these port visits were very friendly and the FPS had a good professional relationship with the Icelandic Coastguard (ICG). In fact, during a visit in 1957, when Captain Eric Bailey was Captain Fishery Protection Squadron (CFPS), the British Ambassador, Andrew Gilchrist, had invited the Icelandic President, Ásgeir Ásgeirsson, to spend a day onboard HMS *Wave*. The guard was paraded and the Chief Yeoman had managed to make up a President's Standard, which flew from *Wave's* masthead throughout the visit. The ship went up the Hvalfjordur, past the remains of the old British naval base and then on past the American-run fuelling jetty. Noting the lack of visible activity ashore, the President asked where all the Americans were. Captain Bailey responded that they were probably having their afternoon kip, which led the President to suggest that they be woken up - perhaps by firing a gun. This 'invitation' was much too good to turn down and a clip of 40mm 'break-up' (the shell was made of bakelite and filled with shot) rounds was swiftly provided. The President was asked if he'd care to do the deed himself, and after a brief lesson on the Bofors 40/60, he personally fired 5 rounds over the fuelling jetty, upon which there was much visible activity ashore.... The Americans weren't the only ones to be shaken up - as Andrew Gilchrist recounts in '*Cod Wars and how to lose them*', this section of Hvalfjordur was covered in eider and long-tailed ducks preparing for the imminent breeding season. As the first round was fired, the chatter of their courting was replaced by the sound of 50,000 ducks getting airborne simultaneously. On return to harbour, the President was presented with a suitably inscribed 40mm cartridge and, hopefully, he departed with warm feelings towards Britain and the Royal Navy in particular.

Whilst HMS *Wave* and the British Ambassador were attempting to foster good relations with the Icelandic President, the two countries were moving inexorably, as it seems in retrospect, towards conflict. The Icelanders were intent on expanding their fishing limits and on imposing conservation measures around their coasts. The British - far from as single-minded as the Icelanders, even within government, let alone between government and the fishermen, were intent on keeping territorial waters, and particularly Icelandic waters, as narrow as possible.

[14] A 'free drift' was when the liferaft was not attached to either frigate or trawler during the transfer from one ship to the other.

CHAPTER 4

DECLARATION OF A 12 MILE LIMIT - SPRING 1958

As so often in the real world, the first Law of the Sea Conference wasn't really the first. That had been held in The Hague in 1930 as part of the Codification Conference under the auspices of the League of Nations. The subject of the width of territorial waters was on the agenda in 1930 and, of the 48 States participating, 35 declared a preference. Nineteen declared for 3 miles, four for 4 miles and twelve for 6 miles. As the Icelanders would claim - the Icelandic representative at this conference, Sveinn Björnsson, became the first President of the Icelandic Republic in 1944 - this was hardly wholehearted international acceptance of the 3-mile limit. As it was, there was never a sufficient majority in either the territorial seas committee or the plenary session to codify the law on territorial waters. Thereafter, the world situation deteriorated, the League of Nations - to quote Gudni Jóhannesson 'the epitome of the futility of principle without power' - became even less influential and this early effort to agree on the width of territorial waters petered out. That, in 1958, the UN's International Law Commission convened the Law of the Sea Conference in their headquarters in Geneva, which had also been the premises of the old League of Nations, was, perhaps, not a good omen.

The British government was well aware that the tide was moving strongly against 3-mile territorial waters and had considered supporting 6-miles. The arguments were well rehearsed - more than 3-miles might deny access to Gibraltar, Hong Kong and Singapore (all still colonies in the 1950s), but 6-miles would allow Scottish fishermen exclusive use of the Moray Firth and the Firth of Clyde; however, British deep-water fishermen gained more from 3-miles. So the circular discussion continued between government departments and a Whitehall position paper in March 1956 noted that Britain might have to accept 6 miles, but noted 'this is not a step we wish to take before we have to'. As before, 'wait until there is a crisis' - by the time Britain was ready to accede to 6-miles, the bandwagon had moved on and most countries wanted 12.

The International Law Commission was finely balanced on the issue of territorial waters and, after much diplomatic pressure by the British, on 20th June 1955, pronounced by 7 votes to 6, that the 3-mile limit was legal and that anything over 12 miles was not. The British hailed this as a success - their member on the ILC stating that it 'comes as near an affirmation of the three-mile rule as is ever likely to emerge.' The Icelandic delegate described it as 'hardly comprehensible' and in the eyes of many in Iceland, over 12 miles being illegal, meant that up to 12 miles was legal. The ILC also stated that it 'considered that the breadth of the territorial seas, about which international practice was not uniform, should be fixed by an international conference'. The ILC also acknowledged that exclusive fishing rights might be able to be claimed on the basis of 'special economic circumstances' - a ruling that harked back to the International Court in The Hague's Norwegian decision. This last point gave Iceland great comfort. It should be noted that the ILC was a legal (and legalistic[15]) body - and the question of territorial waters now moved to the political arena. The British dele-

---

[15] For those confused, or at least wondering, about the different kinds of law that affect the mariner, I am indebted to Paul Willerton and Sidney Harley of and ex Plymouth University respectively for simplified definitions:
Law of the Sea - or to give it its full name The International Public Law of the Sea is that branch of international law dealing with the relationships between States in the conduct of their maritime affairs.
Maritime Law - the generic name for International Private law of the Sea, i.e. commercial law involving Bills of Lading, Charter Parties, etc.
Admiralty Law - a subset of Maritime Law concerned with collisions and other losses especially the commercial outcomes thereof.
Marine Law is not a legal term, but Hydrographers use it in the context of that law appertaining to boundaries, zonation, etc.

gate to the ILC noted that in the UN General Assembly 'no amount of legal argument, however cogently put and however much supported by authority, will make the slightest impression.' It would be a political battle and concessions would have to be made - even the Admiralty was prepared to concede that 6-mile limits might have to be supported - but this was caveated with 'we shall have to wait and see'!! (my exclamation marks) Further advice from the British team in the UN was 'For your information, the point that is worrying is the possibility that *strategic and other factors* requiring a narrow breadth of territorial seas may eventually be made to prevail, but only by admitting a wider breadth for the specific purpose of fisheries' (the italicised words are underlined in the Admiralty copy of this memo). In other words - fish for security.

On receipt of the ILC's report, in late 1956, the UN General Assembly voted almost unanimously (only Iceland voted against) to hold a Conference on the Law of the Sea. Iceland voted against, almost in pique it seems, because the intention had been to announce an extension of territorial waters to 12 miles in 1956 or early 1957. At the time, a left-wing coalition had just been elected to power in Reykjavik and their manifesto had, specifically, promised an extension of the fishery limits. The UN's decision (or really non-decision) caused a crisis in the governing coalition, with the Communist Fishery Minister demanding that a 12-mile limit be in place by the autumn and the Prime Minister threatening to resign if the limits were changed before the Law of the Sea Conference. Under the 1948 Fundamental Conservation Law, the Fishery Minister was entitled to, unilaterally, declare new fishery limits and, as the British Ambassador, Andrew Gilchrist, noted 'I should not expect to find any Icelander anxious to take the responsibility for withdrawing it.' Fortunately for the UK, in the end the more left-wing members of the Icelandic coalition government were persuaded to await the outcome of the Conference, but only with the condition that a 12-mile limit would be declared as soon as the Conference was completed - regardless of the Conference's decision.

There was also a degree of realpolitik in the coalition's position. Once the threat to Keflavík had subsided, Washington had provided much-needed loans and Reykjavik wished to remain on-side with the US, from where the message was 'no base - no money' - however, the opposite was also potentially true - 'no money - no base'. In the spring of 1957, the Soviet Union had provided a huge loan in exchange for fish and the Icelanders were very happy to play NATO and the Soviets off against each other. This was the period when a National Security Council in Washington asked 'Is Iceland blackmailing us?' Whilst the answer to this question obviously depended on one's viewpoint (the British Ambassador thought that blackmail was undoubtedly the right word), it was clear that Washington would put its and NATO's strategic interests well above Britain's concerns over fishery limits.

The US Department of Defense, in its preparations for the Law of the Sea Conference stated that 'the security interests of the US must outweigh all other considerations', that the 3-mile limit of territorial waters must be guarded and that a 12-mile fishing limit should be accepted as the quid pro quo. The US did not commit itself to this position in advance, but was prepared to compromise as necessary. Canada's starting position was 3-miles territorial waters with an additional 9-mile fishing zone. Both Norway and Denmark had similar views, albeit there was some ambivalence in the Norwegian position because the fishermen off Northern Norway would benefit from 12 miles, but the herring fishermen, who worked close up to other coasts, would lose out. Norway, as part of an extension of fishing limits to 12 miles, was prepared to reduce her territorial waters from 4 to 3 miles. Britain was increasingly isolated.

The Foreign Office's Legal Adviser, Sir Gerald Fitzmaurice, who had been the British Delegate on the International Law Commission when the decision on territorial waters that led to the Law of the Sea Conference, opened the debate within Whitehall by stating that the 3-mile limit would never be ratified at Geneva and that compromises would have to be made to avoid a 12-mile limit. He suggested either the Canadian position of 3 miles territorial waters + 9 miles of exclusive fishing zone or 6 miles of each. Whilst there was agreement in Whitehall that something had to be done, the departments could not agree as to what that something should be. The British Trawler Federation (BTF) claimed that a 12-mile limit would 'ruin' the industry. This claim by the BTF was accepted unquestioningly in Whitehall; the similar, apocryphal claim over the consequences of the earlier Icelandic increase from 3-4 miles was unfortunately forgotten. The Admiralty opted for the 3 + 9 position, claiming that 6 + 6 would only be acceptable if naval and air rights of free passage would still be guaranteed into 3 miles.

After much debate, the Cabinet did not discuss the problem until one week before the Conference opened. Prime Minister, Sir Harold Macmillan, summed up by saying 'our aim must be to promote a majority decision by the Conference which would inflict the least damage to our own interests, both strategic and economic'. This anodyne statement indicates how little real thought had gone into the problem - it really amounted to more 'wait and see'. A proper examination of the looming international threat to one of Britain's 'vital national interests' would, surely, have produced a plan, with a series of agreed options to fall back on as the UK delegation was forced, as it was bound to be, to retreat. A proper plan would have included discussions with other members of the Commonwealth and with the United States, but none of this happened.

The British position was, no doubt, framed as much with the objective of appeasing opinion on Humberside, as of achieving a favourable outcome. However, by starting from a position that had almost no support and then having to be dragged towards the middle ground, the British lost any goodwill that they might have had. Andrew Gilchrist, the British Ambassador in Reykjavik, believed that, although the Icelandic Government was intent on an extension of their fishing limits, they still hoped to be able to build some kind of bridge with Britain - they did not want a complete falling out. Just before the Conference started, he said 'if we don't build a bridge, we shall be confronted with unilateral extensions, as sure as eggs is eggs'. He was right, as events were to show.

The First UN Law of the Sea Conference opened in Geneva[16] on 24th February 1958. This was the largest conference that the UN had ever organised and 87 nations were represented. The main item on the agenda was the breadth of territorial waters, but fishing, navigation on the high seas, the continental shelf and the rights of landlocked states were also to be considered. Initial discussions took place in committees, with the final decisions requiring a two-thirds majority in the plenary session.

This being the era of decolonialisation, many delegates were mainly interested in grandstanding for the benefit of their publics back home. The first four weeks were spent in procedural wrangling and in demonstrating that everyone was going to stand their ground. Four blocs were established; The Soviets, who were disciplined and focused and were for 12 miles; The Afro-Asians who were against colonialism and western exploitation, did not accept the established international law (clearly of 'colonial' origin) and wanted extended limits; the Latin Americans, who wanted more, but were split between the 200 mile camp and those who would be happy with less and the West - who were not united, but accepted established international law as the baseline.

It was clear that the historic 3-mile limit, on its own, was not going to get any significant support and behind the scenes, the British were trying to get the US to support 6 miles, whilst the US were trying to get the British to accept the Canadian proposal of '3+9'. The US resorted to the 'Dear Harold' ploy and President Eisenhower wrote personally to Sir Harold Macmillan, the British Prime Minister, asking for a unified Western front in support of 3+9. The British delegates in Geneva supported this proposal, but back in Whitehall, the British Trawler Owners continued to exercise influence over the Fisheries Ministry and the Chiefs of Staff, having previously conceded that it might be necessary to support 3+9, now expressed concern that a 12-mile fishing limit, could easily become 12 miles of territorial waters. Britain should stick to the principle of 3 miles.

Macmillan wrote back to Eisenhower:

> *'You ask that commercial considerations should not be permitted to control. It is not merely a matter of commerce, but of the livelihood of a large number of people of this country.*
> *Arrangements which denied to our nationals our traditional fishing grounds on the high seas, as a general extension of limits to 12 miles would do, would put in jeopardy the very existence of the most modern part of our*

[16] Just before the Conference, the *Manchester Guardian*, ominously, described Geneva as 'the last resting place of so many lost causes'.

fishing fleet...which is of great strategic importance to us in terms of both men and ships.'

Macmillan followed this four days later with another letter expressing his belief that there 'may be quite a measure of support for a 3-mile limit for all purposes'. This was wishful thinking and, as the US delegation in Geneva commented '...longer UK postpones facing up to hard decision, the more difficult it will be to keep those who want to help us in line'. Despite further personal requests from President Eisenhower and advice from the British delegation that 'the UK's position at the Conference was one of the most intransigent', Macmillan and his Cabinet decided to tough it out. The domestic concerns over Humberside's reaction to a retreat from the 3-mile limit were more important that the US (and NATO's) fears about a Communist takeover in Reykjavik.

On 29th March, the Canadians formally tabled their 3+9 proposal, which was quickly followed by another 20 proposals with variants of 6 and 12 miles plus certain fishing limits. Manningham-Buller, the senior British Delegate tabled a proposal for 6 miles, with caveats allowing innocent passage within 3 miles. He put this forward as a great sacrifice by Britain in search of an agreed solution. No one else saw this as a concession and the net result was to diminish support for the Canadian's 3+9 proposal. As 3+9 now looked to be doomed, the United States came forward with a 6+6 proposal, with historic fishing rights preserved in the outer 6-mile zone. A number of the supporters of 3+9, including Norway and Denmark, declared their support for 6+6 and this proposal would certainly have been better for the British trawler industry than the Icelandic proposal of 12 miles. After Cabinet had overruled a flurry of disagreement from the Ministry of Defence, the British also declared support for 6+6.

The Canadians were indignant that Britain had broken the developing consensus around 3+9 - 'he attacked me personally and was most abusive' Manningham-Buller complained after one exchange with George Drew, the leader of Canada's delegation. The Canadians counter-proposed a variant of 6+6 with greater fishing rights. A united Western position remained elusive. In Iceland, where a variant of 3+9 had been generally supported, there was also fury at Britain's actions, as the 6+6 proposal's preservation of historic rights would allow British trawlers to continue fishing into 6 miles. In Reykjavik the Communist bogey was dusted down and presented to the Americans once again. As expected, they took fright and tried to engineer a compromise that would keep both Iceland and Britain on side.

But time had run out. Agreement was reached on the use of baselines, a 12-mile contiguous zone for fiscal and sanitary purposes and the right of innocent passage through international straits, as well as on the exclusive rights of coastal states to mineral resources on their continental shelf – but not on the main agenda point of the width of territorial waters. In the final vote, no proposal received the required 2/3rds majority - the American 6+6 came closest, with 45 in favour, 33 against and 7 abstentions. The British view was that the Conference had been a success as the, Soviet supported, 12-mile limit had been defeated and the 3-mile limit was still, just about, in place. Sir Gerald Fitzmaurice summed up more realistically when he said that the Conference was 'a prolonged holding operation ..... But time is not on our side'. Hans G Andersen, the legal adviser to the Icelandic Ministry of Foreign Affairs, warned that 'Iceland could not wait much longer'.

The last real hope for an agreement between Britain and Iceland was lost at Geneva on 27th April 1958. There now followed three weeks of intense international politicking - the Communist bogey was given much airtime in Reykjavik, Washington and NATO. The US tried to pressurise the British into protesting, but not using force - the US Secretary of State, John Foster Dulles, hoped that 'war would be waged on paper rather than with bullets'. Reykjavik secretly offered a compromise of 12 miles, with 3 years of historic fishing rights in the outer 6 miles, but the British rejected this compromise. Britain suggested a limitation on trawler numbers, a reduction of the total catch, closed areas, joint scientific investigations of fish stocks and even recourse to the International Court in The Hague. The Icelandic government nearly fell and the five Ps[17] reappeared in Britain. Pressure from Humberside: Prestige - could a great maritime power be defeated by a tiny island in the North Atlantic? Principle - Britain believed the law

[17] See Chapter 2

was on her side: Precedent - Denmark would not accept a Faeroes limit smaller than Iceland's and Power - despite the 1957 White Paper's severe naval cuts, the Royal Navy still had the power. On 15th May, the British Cabinet decided that the Royal Navy would protect trawlers if Iceland unilaterally declared a 12-mile limit.

NATO appealed to the Icelandic government for more time to negotiate and the NATO Secretary General, Paul Henri Spaak, proposed a compromise of 6 miles, with an outer 6 mile zone with permanent historic rights, subject to certain conservation restrictions. The British rejected this and Spaak complained that Britain was being both 'unnecessarily legalistic' and was completely isolated within NATO. This caused a rethink in London, where the Fisheries Secretary and the Foreign Office's Assistant Legal Adviser concluded that the compromise could be accepted if the conservation restrictions were caveated 'under conditions to be negotiated with the Icelandic Government'. Macmillan was furious that this agreement 'seems to concede everything (the Icelanders) want under the weak phase 'conditions to be negotiated'. I was not asked; I would like to know which Minister authorised the Foreign Office to make this decision'. The Foreign Secretary, Selwyn Lloyd, did not support his department and conceded that there had been an error. So Macmillan completely overrode the advice of his experts - his telling phrase was 'I am not an expert ... but'.

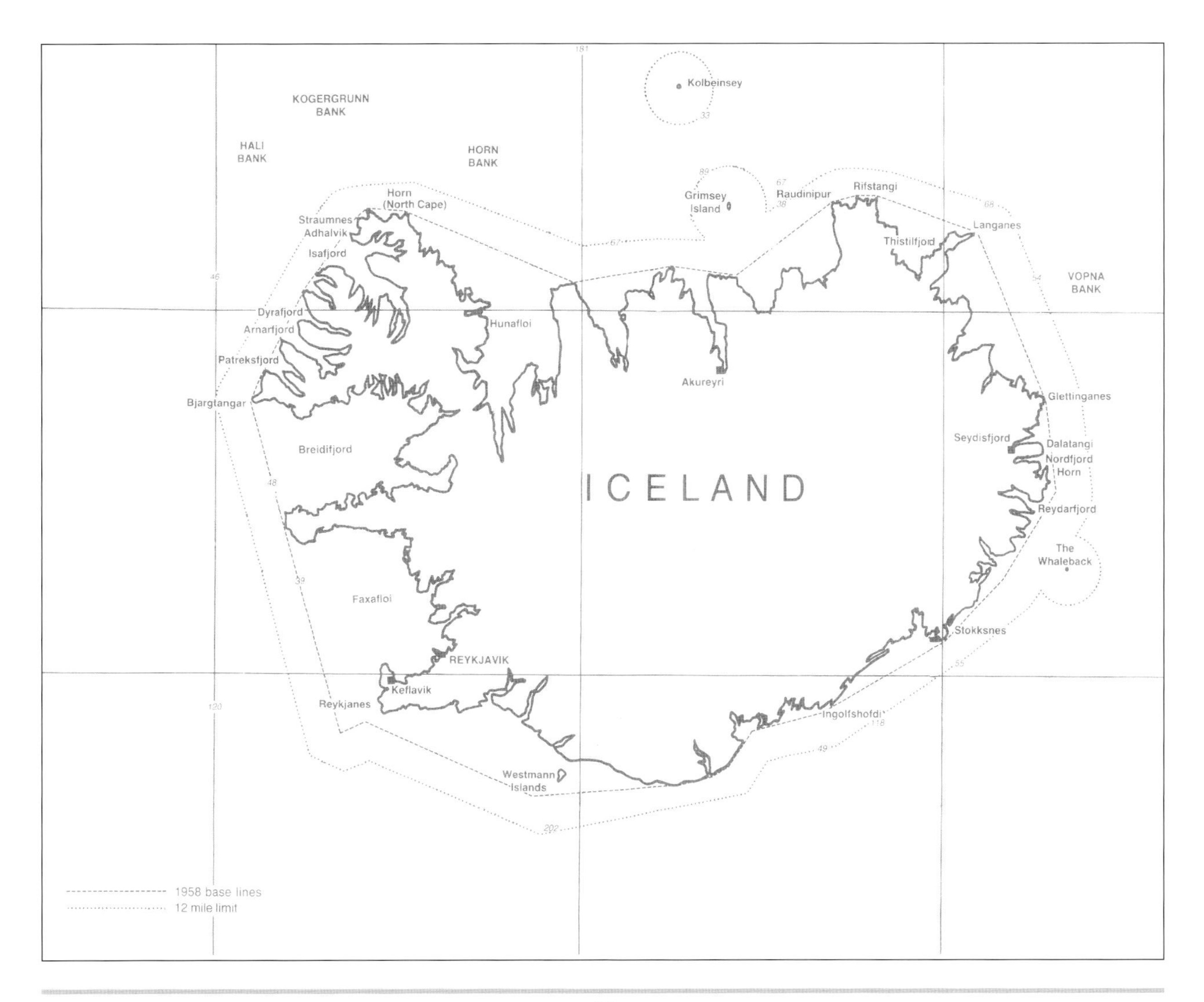

However, the Icelandic coalition government could not survive any further negotiations and whilst Macmillan was laying down the law in London, on 24th May, the Icelandic government announced that new regulations on a 12-mile fishing zone would be issued on 30th June. They would take effect on 1st September. The immediate crisis had been averted, but only three months were left to find a political solution before two NATO allies were publicly committed to using force against each other.

On 4th June, Britain formally expressed 'surprise and regret' at the Icelandic declaration and declared that they would prevent all attempts to interfere with trawlers 'on the high seas'. In Iceland this produced the following from Visir, the most pro-Western newspaper:

> *'It is as though the British government thought that we were living in the 17th or 18th century when it was thought wonderful to use cannons unhesitatingly. ... It is ... in the nature of the Icelanders that one can get him to do various things by kindness, but by nastiness he will not be induced to do anything at all, not even that which might benefit him most. The British note is, therefore, having completely the opposite effect to what was intended.'*

Britain was not alone in her opposition to the new fishing limits and in The Hague on 14th July, Belgium, Britain, France, the Netherlands, Sweden, Spain and West Germany issued a joint statement condemning the Icelandic action as illegal and declaring that they would all continue to fish up to the 4-mile limit. This solidarity did not last.

There were deep reservations in the Foreign Office about the course of action on which Britain was now embarked, but as Lord Vansittart, the former Permanent Secretary on the Foreign Office, wrote in the same year 'the soul of our service is the loyalty with which we execute ordained error'. The Cabinet had decided and, quite rightly in a democracy, the organs of government must do what they are told. As will be seen later, this concept of obedience to the will of the elected government was not always shared in Iceland.

There was a flurry of diplomatic action in late August. Hans G. Anderson, the Icelandic Ambassador to NATO, floated the idea of a 6-mile limit with limited short-term historic rights out to 12 for three years, or until the next Law of the Sea Conference. The British Cabinet concluded that this was a possible way ahead, but Anderson had completely exceeded his brief and the Ambassador in Reykjavik was told, very clearly, by the Minister for Foreign Affairs, that the proposed (Icelandic) text was 'unacceptable'. Maybe Ambassador Anderson was hoping to force the issue - on Aug 29th the British offered, if there was an initial 6-mile limit for 3 years or less, to 'note' the Icelandic intention to extend to 12 miles. Iceland would have got nearly everything they wanted, but Anderson, maybe knowing that he was far out on a limb, said that this concession was insufficient. In reality, it was too late - both sides had allowed themselves to become the captives of domestic politics. Even without the concerns that reaching an agreement would be a surrender to the Communists in Iceland, selling an agreement acknowledging a 12-mile limit to the British trawlermen would have been difficult enough, but no Icelandic government would have survived a retreat from the 'principle' of 12 miles.

Albert Jónsson, an Icelandic Political Scientist, believes that the British Government sent the Royal Navy in for three main reasons[18]:

> *'It was a matter of principle for the British and they tend to place great emphasis on principles.*
> *They claimed that Iceland was in breach of the law and that we threatened interests that they had and had had for a long time, on the oceans.*
> *Secondly there were sentimental reasons. Their origins were that the trawlermen of Hull and Grimsby had earned credit because of their performance during the Second World War and this was not forgotten. This was more a factor in the First Cod War than later on.*
> *Finally, there were strong local interests in Hull and Grimsby and, in the beginning, in Fleetwood.'*

[18] Quotes from *The Last Waltz*

Clauswitz is much over, and often incorrectly, quoted, but it is hard to resist his best-known quotation, which so neatly defines what was about to happen:

'War is not an independent phenomenon, but the continuation of politics by different means.'

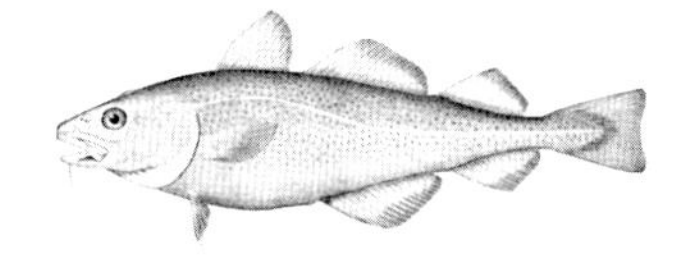

CHAPTER 5

THE FIRST COD WAR
SEPTEMBER - DECEMBER 1958

Whilst the politicians and diplomats were continuing to agree to disagree, the Royal Navy was preparing detailed plans for the protection of British Trawlers. Captain Barry Anderson, the Captain, Fishery Protection Squadron (FPS) issued the operation order for Operation WHIPPET in June 1958 and detailed Instructions to Skippers were agreed with the British Trawler Federation (BTF) and issued through the owners. The missions stated in Operation WHIPPET were:

- *To prevent interference with British fishing vessels on the high seas outside 4 miles and in particular between 4 miles and 12 miles from the Icelandic coast.*

- *To prevent the arrest of any British fishing vessel on the high seas outside the 4-mile line.*

- *To secure the release of any British fishing vessel so arrested.*

Three havens were to be established - Butterscotch, Spearmint and Toffeeapple (perhaps Captain Anderson's children chose the names?) between the 4 and 12 miles limits. Each haven would be 30 miles long and would be guarded by one warship. A fourth ship would be on station as a back up and a Royal Fleet Auxiliary replenishment tanker would also be in support. The havens would move in accordance with the seasonal movement of the fish and the advice of the Liaison Skippers (experienced trawlermen) embarked in the naval ships. The Operation Order emphasised the importance of remaining inside a haven. As Captain Barry Anderson said:

'Remember how stragglers in the last war were easily snapped up!'

One thing that this warning emphasizes is how close the First Cod War was to the Second World War - many of the people, fishermen as well as naval personnel, had fought in WWII and many of the ships had too. Interestingly, I served in HMS *Charybdis* in the Second Cod War and the TAS[19] Officer had joined up in 1944 and had been on a Russian Convoy.

Ashore, the British Ambassador was wondering if the British community needed to be evacuated before 1st September. He agreed with the Foreign Office that the Icelanders were unlikely to take reprisals and the community wasn't that large, so could be evacuated if it really had to be.

The Instructions to Skippers instructed the trawlers to report their arrival to the warship guarding their haven and told them not to fish outside a designated haven for their first 3 days. They were also instructed not to fish within 4 miles and not to fish between 4 and 12 except when in a haven. The Royal Navy was, justifiably, concerned that the trawler skippers would sometimes, if not often, ignore these instructions.

The prime threat was seen to be of arrest by a boarding party, but this was thought to be unlikely in the presence of a warship - hence the instruction to trawlers to remain in an established haven or outside 12 miles from the coast. The British Trawler Federation's Instructions to Skippers advised on methods of avoiding boarding, short of the use of real weapons or of inflicting actual bodily harm. Trawlers were also asked to report every sighting of an Icelandic Coastguard vessel to their haven warship. As trawlers that had been observed within the 12-mile limit were likely to be arrested if they tried to enter an Icelandic port for stores, repairs or medical reasons, the Royal Navy had to be ready to offer a greater degree of technical and medical support than before.

[19] Torpedo and Anti-Submarine

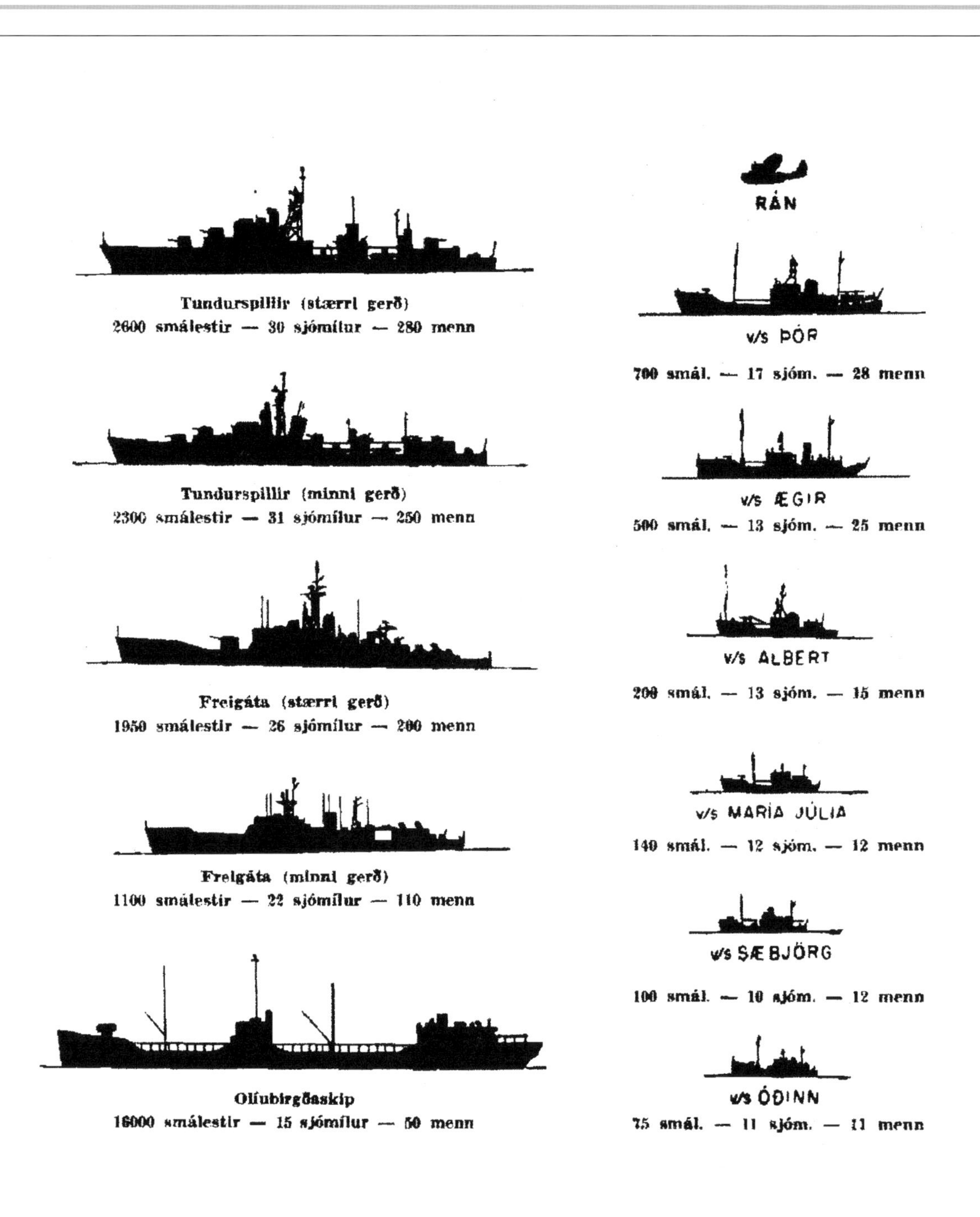

Royal Navy vessels vs. the Icelandic Coastguard fleet' as seen in Iceland at the start of the First Cod War (Gunnar M Magnúss)

The Commanding Officers of all warships on patrol were issued with detailed instructions as to when, what and how much force they could use either to prevent the arrest of a trawler or to rescue a trawler once arrested. This included, ultimately, the use of live gunfire, but only in response to Icelandic gunfire, after warnings and only to disable the Icelandic Coastguard vessel's gun, not to sink her. Although they were not yet called this, these instructions were the beginning of the process that led to today's codified and voluminous Rules of Engagement - an aspect of warfare that is now fundamental to the way that the use of armed force is controlled, especially in non-hot war situations, such as UN embargo operations. Then, as now, it was important for the British to maintain as much of the moral high ground as possible and not to be seen as the aggressors.

Control of operations was to be by the senior naval offer embarked at sea off Iceland, who was fully briefed before assuming this duty and who received regular instructions from the Admiralty covering the political dimensions of the dispute. This was also the first time that single side band radios, capable of direct voice contact with Whitehall, and routed through to the Cabinet Office, was embarked. In other words, the era of Ministerial control of Naval Operations, in real time, had begun.

In fact, Commodore Anderson's briefings (he had been promoted to Commodore so that his authority over other senior captains at sea off Iceland would be clear) included meetings with Harold Macmillan, the Prime Minister, Selwyn Lloyd, the Foreign Secretary and Admiral Lord Mountbatten of Burma, the First Sea Lord. Commodore Anderson's summary of his briefing with the Prime Minister was:

'Stand no nonsense from anybody, neither the trawlermen nor the Icelanders, and do your best to avoid incidents.'

Interestingly, an Icelandic interpretation[20] by Captain Helgi Hallvardsson, a junior officer at the time, was:

'When the warships arrived, they were commanded by Commodore Anderson and he seemed to be rather keen to issue threats. If the Coastguard vessels were disturbing the trawlers, he immediately threatened to sink the Coastguard vessel and only one shot would be needed to sink it.

I have been inclined to call the first fishing dispute a war of nerves of sorts. We tried to make the British nervous and the warships tried the same against us.'

An inter-departmental Whitehall Icelandic Fisheries Group was set up to coordinate the UK government's response to events at sea and to provide advice to Ministers when required. HM Ambassador in Reykjavik, Andrew Gilchrist, was asked to provide intelligence and advice and was copied on all the relevant signals. This was to be a solely British operation - despite their governments' protests, German, Belgian and French trawler owners had decided not to breach the 12-mile limit. Nevertheless, from time to time, the Royal Navy did provide medical and technical support to foreign fishing vessels.

When the First Cod War started, the Icelandic Coastguard had seven ships and two aircraft. The largest of the ships, *Thor*, was of 920 tons and the smallest two were converted fishing vessels. The *Thor* was the only vessel really capable of boarding a trawler and then towing her into port if necessary. The head of the Icelandic Coastguard, Pétur Sigurdsson, quietly admitted that his tiny fleet was 'utterly incapable' of fending off up to 100 British trawlers under Royal Navy protection. Much was to be made in the Icelandic press and in their propaganda campaign of the disproportionate force being ranged against them.

Like much propaganda, this was disingenuous in that the Icelandic Coastguard Vessels were operating very close to their bases and so had no need to stay at sea in all weathers, nor the requirement to be large enough to be self sufficient for a two week patrol 700 miles from the nearest naval base. Also to the Icelandic advantage, was that the costs of the British operation were many, many times greater than the Icelandic costs and, almost certainly, greater than the value of any fish that might be caught. Icelandic Prime Minister Jónasson presciently said to Ambassador Gilchrist on the evening of 31st August 'You will make cheap cod as expensive as salmon'

[20] From the TV documentary *The Last Waltz*

HMS Russell (MoD/Crown Copyright)

and, of course, he was right. The concept of asymmetric operations (e.g. Al-Qaeda vs. the West) and the disproportionate force levels needed by the defence had yet to be recognised.

Icelandic intentions had been accurately assessed by the British. Their aim was to police their newly declared fishing limit, arrest any offending trawlers and bring their skippers to trial. They also hoped to minimise the use of force and recognised that they would not be able to arrest a trawler in the presence of a British warship. Nevertheless, they believed that they would catch a lone trawler sooner or later and that time and the weather were on their side - in this they were correct. There was however, an assessment within the Admiralty that the Icelandic government believed that the British Government would withdraw naval support after a few weeks - but here the Admiralty were only partly correct and may well have been the victim of wishful thinking, as Admiralty minutes express the hope that the RN would only be needed for about three months 'until the situation is cleared up by approach to the United Nations or other authority'. At the same meeting where he commented on the future price of cod, the Icelandic Prime Minister said that he foresaw a 'long-term operation' with time on his side. 'Would the British have the stomach for that?' The British Ambassador reported this conversation to the Foreign Office next day, but this view clearly did not get across Whitehall into the Ministry of Defence. In fact, the First Cod War was to last for two and a half years and to involve 63 RN warships and 11 Royal Fleet Auxiliaries over 192 individual patrols.

By the end of August 1958, both sides had made their preparations and the diplomats and politicians had failed to resolve the dispute. The baton now passed to those at sea, in particular to Commodore Barry Anderson.

31st August 1958 - Final Preparations

On 31st August 1958, HMS *Eastbourne* (commanded by Lieutenant-Commander Dickie Mayne with Commodore Barry Anderson and his staff embarked), HMS *Russell*, HMS *Palliser* and HMS *Hound* were on patrol off Iceland. Sub-Lieutenant Christopher Notley was serving in HMS *Eastbourne*. He remembers that they had embarked the press (3 plus a TV cameraman) in Chatham and then had proceeded up the North Sea at 25 knots, embarking Commodore Anderson by light jackstay when they joined *Russell* & *Palliser*. The Commodore was ceremonially piped as he came onboard & then rather unceremoniously dumped on his bottom. RFA *Black Ranger*, commanded by Captain Basil Dobbie, arrived on station on the 2nd September. There were about 75 trawlers on the fishing grounds - about two-thirds in Toffeeapple and Butterscotch to the NW and the remainder in Spearmint to the east. HMS *Hound* (Commander Arthur Clark) was 'Haven Chief' in Spearmint, HMS *Russell* (Lieutenant-Commander Peter Corson) had Butterscotch and HMS *Palliser* (Lieutenant-Commander Geoff Hammond) had been allocated Toffeeapple. The names of the three havens were to become well known throughout the Navy and amongst the population of Hull, Grimsby and Fleetwood over the next few months. Fishermen's wives would be heard to say 'my husband's in Toffeeapple' or whatever. The protection system swung easily into effect; trawlers reported their positions and remained in the havens and the Icelandic Coastguard vessels *Thor*, *Albert* and *Ægir* were reported to be at sea. That evening, Commodore Anderson was able to report:

> *'Trawlers are approaching havens and getting organised. So far teamwork between RN and trawlermen is excellent. Weather much better (the day had started rough, with a Force 7 wind). The 'long ships' are lurking tonight.'*

In Iceland, Pétur Sigurdsson gathered all his gunboat captains in Reykjavik and instructed them 'to show the utmost caution at the onset when everyone is tense and the situation is a powder keg'. Based on the messages he was getting from his many Icelandic contacts, the British Ambassador was able to tell London that if a trawler refused to obey ICG orders and immediately appealed for naval assistance 'no boarding attempt will be made.' In London, Harold Macmillan wrote 'We shall protect our trawlers as best we can, but there is no future in it'.

1st September - the 12-mile limit comes into force

Next morning the gunboats appeared. The wind had dropped and there was some fog in Spearmint to the east. In Butterscotch, where there were six trawlers, *Albert* and *Ódinn* warned them by loudhailer and radio that they were fishing illegally. In Toffeeapple (nine trawlers working), *Aegir* passed close by the trawler *Lord Askaig*, but was warned off by HMS *Palliser* (Lieutenant-Commander Geoff Hammond) and withdrew. Later *Ægir* returned and, observed by HMS *Palliser*, made a very close pass on the trawler *Vascana*, but did not attempt to board. HMS *Eastbourne* was backing up HMS *Hound* (whose radar was defective) in the foggy Spearmint, where there were ten trawlers working. Both *Thor* and *Maria Júlia* had been observed inshore of the haven and the Commodore had exchanged greetings with them. That evening's Sitrep noted:

> *'During the day ships of the task group have been in contact with the three major Icelandic gunboats and two of the smaller ones. First impressions indicate that the majority of these are anxious to avoid incidents. With the exception of Ódinn and Ægir, friendly and*

ICGV Thor (Norman Robinson)

HMS Eastbourne, ICGV Maria Julia & the trawler Stella Canopus - 2nd September 1958.

(Icelandic Prime Minister's Office Papers, National Archive, Reykjavik)

> *chatty signals have been exchanged after which the gunboats have gracefully withdrawn. In my opinion, a gunboat will undoubtedly attempt to arrest an unprotected trawler inside 12 miles.'*

At 0200 next morning, *Ódinn* approached a trawler within Butterscotch and illuminated her with a signal lantern. Lieutenant-Commander Peter Corson in *Russell* warned *Ódinn* off and then followed *Ódinn* out of the haven. *Ægir* was also observed to be in the area. The 2nd September dawned calm and foggy. At 0800 Commodore Barry Anderson in *Eastbourne* received a report that the trawler *Northern Foam* had been arrested by a boarding party from two gunboats - later established as being *Thor* and *Maria Júlia*. This had happened right in the middle of Spearmint, off the eastern point of Iceland and about 6.5 miles from the coast when HMS *Eastbourne* was about 20 miles away. *Thor* and *Maria Júlia* had looked for and found a lone trawler fishing in the fog. *Maria Júlia* had cut close ahead of the trawler, forcing her to stop, whereupon *Thor* had come alongside and transferred an unarmed 5-man boarding party to the *Northern Foam*, with 4 more men following from *Maria Júlia*.

Onboard *Northern Foam*, the wireless operator had locked himself in the wireless office and was calling for help on 2182khz - the coastal MF distress frequency and one that could also be heard by all the other trawlers. Denis Glassett, who was one of the radio operators onboard HMS *Hound*, remembers taking the original distress call. *Northern Foam's* radio officer sounded agitated and excited said that 'he had been boarded by some Icelanders and had locked the wheelhouse door; he had an axe' and went on to say that 'the first bastard that tried to get through the door would have his f...ing hands chopped off'. *Hound's* CO, Commander Arthur Clark, was informed that there was a problem with one of the trawlers and came down to the radio office to speak to the *Northern Foam*. The skipper of *Northern Foam* was encouraged not to do anything rash, but to resist arrest and to immobilise his engines (the Royal Navy's Rules of Engagement would not have allowed 'hot pursuit' inside the 4 mile limit if the ICG had managed to get *Northern Foam* underway), whilst *Hound* took a bearing of the distress call (her radar was still defective) and headed for the incident at her best speed.

Initially, the boarding party were friendly, asking to see the secret Instructions to Skippers and trying to persuade the skipper to go over to the *Thor*. When he refused to comply, they tried to get the trawler underway, but the skipper had managed to get his engines both stopped and immobilised. Meanwhile, HMS *Eastbourne* had heard the distress call and had taken control of the incident. She had gone to action stations and was proceeding to the scene at full speed. The boarding party had just managed to get *Northern*

Foam underway when HMS *Eastbourne* arrived and put her own 12 man boarding party into *Northern Foam*.

The British boarding officer, Sub-Lieutenant Christopher Notley, was armed with a pistol, but otherwise, the boarding party were unarmed. The press were embarked in HMS *Eastbourne* and, it was important that the UK was not seen to be using any more than minimum force - hence *Eastbourne's* armament remained trained fore and aft and the boarding officer carried the boarding party's token armament.

To try to resolve the situation, Commodore Barry Anderson used the loudhailer to call Captain Eiríkur Kristófferson saying, 'Kris, Kris, this is bloody daft! I'm coming over to talk to you.' Commodore Anderson went onboard the *Thor* where he discussed the situation (in Norwegian) calmly, but forcefully, with Captain Kristófferson. Captain Kristófferson insisted that he was entitled to arrest the *Northern Foam* under Icelandic Law for fishing inside the 12-mile limit and Commodore Anderson insisted that Britain did not recognise the new Icelandic law and so the *Northern Foam* must be released, as she was legally fishing on the high seas. The captain of *Thor* refused to withdraw his boarding party and it was eventually agreed that they would be transferred to HMS *Eastbourne*.

Christopher Notley remembers that one of the problems faced by Barry Anderson was that there was a complete radio blackout with Whitehall during this incident due to a severe electical storm. This blackout persisted for several hours and so Barry Anderson had to act without being able to consult the MoD. This blackout also frustrated the efforts of the Press embarked in HMS *Eastbourne* to report events and the most 'vivid' accounts of events came from reporters, who were far from the scene. Christopher Notlwey remembers that the *Daily Mail*, in particular, carried some wonderfully colourful reports.

Meanwhile, the *Maria Júlia* tried to arrest the Grimsby trawler *Lifeguard*, but her crew resisted strongly, wielding boathooks, rope-ends and an axe. After a running scuffle, fortunately without any injuries, *Maria Júlia*, having sustained slight damage, withdrew. By 1115, the boarding incident was over, the *Northern Foam* was fishing again, both boarding parties were onboard HMS *Eastbourne* and *Thor* and *Maria Júlia* had left the scene. The first skirmish was over and it seems likely that the subsequent report in the *Daily Express* on 3rd September 1958 coined the name by which the British and Icelandic fishing disputes would become known - the Cod War.

The British may have won the first engagement of the Cod War and the ICG would never again keep a boarding party in a trawler once the Royal Navy was involved, but the British now had the difficult problem of returning their Icelandic 'guests' or 'prisoners' as they were called in Iceland. And what had happened to the Head of the Icelandic Coastguard's instructions to his captains about 'utmost caution'? These instructions still stood, but Captain Kristófferson, who was the senior captain, did not see eye to eye with his boss, Pétur Sigurdsson, and was 'determined to act as he saw most fit when the nation's honour was at stake.' As an official in the Icelandic Prime Minister's office later recalled 'I remember that we were rather worried about Eiríkur, because he was considered rather too pugnacious'. Any hopes for an incident-free initial period after the imposition of the 12-mile limit, allowing for a gradual reduction of tension and possible talks had been shattered by one man's pride and unwillingness to obey orders - but a man who had now made himself a hero in the eyes of most, if not all, Icelanders.[21]

In Reykjavik, the British Ambassador, who admits in "*Cod Wars and how to Lose them*" that he was in a 'rather anti-Icelandic mood' at the time, had anticipated trouble in the wake of the *Northern Foam* incident and suspected that his Residence (separate from the Embassy, which was, at the time, in a commercial building in the down-town area) would be the scene of any popular demonstration. He had been warned that truckloads of stones, suitable for throwing, had been dropped off near the Residence and so as to avoid any of his staff being isolated, he had invited them all to join him for dinner that evening. In the Residence, they would, at least, be under the protection of the single policeman who was usually on guard there. In order to ensure fair reporting of any trouble, Andrew Gilchrist also decided to invite three of the dozen foreign journalists who had gathered in Iceland to join this dinner.

[21] Arguably, Captain Kristófferson's action actually helped the British. Having been presented with an early opportunity to demonstrate their resolve, this resolve was never seriously tested again.

In fact the crowd outside were fairly quiet until Eddie Gilmore, the Associated Press correspondent, complained that he was there under false pretences as AP wouldn't get a headline out of the 'serenade' from outside, where there was a bit of shouting and the singing of the Icelandic national anthem, but really, a comparatively well-behaved crowd. Unfortunately one of the Embassy staff suggested that the crowd might like some music - it might soothe them! The Ambassador's 7-year-old son was dispatched to put a record on the new radiogram and he chose his favourite - the Edinburgh City Police Band playing The Barren Rocks of Aden - at full volume. Although the record was fairly quickly switched off, it was too late and a volley of stones flew up at the house. This did, at least, prove that ammunition had been provided and, whilst the Pipers may have provided the signal, there would probably have been an attack at some stage anyway. As the stone-throwers got their eye in, more police arrived and were able to keep the crowd out of the Residence gardens and at a comparatively safe distance. Ground floor windows were being broken by now and so the Ambassador had the heavy curtains drawn and got the children out of range. The reporters headed down to the cellar, where a special phone line to London had been established and proceeded to file their reports from 'the embattled British Embassy'.

Meanwhile, some people in the crowd had started firing steel ball bearings from powerful catapults. These penetrated both the glass and the heavy curtains, forcing an evacuation to the back of the house. The final act was an attack with firecrackers and smoke bombs, which gave the impression that the Residence was on fire (and dramatic photos for the world's press), but in fact there was no significant damage apart from the windows. As things were dying down, Andrew Gilchrist went out to survey the scene with his dog Kitz (dogs are illegal in Iceland so Kitz, having 'diplomatic immunity' was the only dog on the island). More stones were thrown, one of which hit Kitz. This provoked a robust outburst from the Ambassador, which was witnessed by some of the journalists who had not been invited to dinner. Their reports accused him of deliberately trying to provoke the mob. Geoff Hammond, who was the Commanding Officer of HMS *Palliser* in the Fishery Protection Squadron described him as a 'fool' and compared his 'blunt' manner to that of today's Deputy Prime Minister, John Prescott. Geoff Hammond was in command both before and at the start of the First Cod War and so had met the Ambassador several times and dined formally in the Residence with Icelandic VIPs.

One of the other unfortunate effects of having press outside the residence, who could only see part of what was going on, was that the story of a burst of recorded bagpipe music was 'improved' to one in which Andrew Gilchrist had donned his kilt and personally played the bagpipes to show defiance to the crowd. Anthony Sampson in his *Anatomy of Britain* quotes this story as fact; Gudni Jóhannesson in his well-researched 2002 thesis dismisses it as journalistic licence.

In the 1950's, attacks on Embassies, Ambassadors and their dogs were very rare events and most of the world's press were critical of the reported attempt to 'burn down the British Embassy' in Reykjavik. Associated Press's reporting (from within the 'embattled' Residence) in America, where there was great concern over Iceland's possible withdrawal from NATO and therefore the future of the US airbase in Keflavík, did, for a time, help to reduce US pressure on the UK to go easy on Iceland. However, the way the evening's 'riot' was reported, added to Captain Kristófferson's 'principled' stand against his boss's instructions, ensured that compromise was now almost impossible for both sides.

3rd September and onwards - into the routine

Several unsuccessful attempts were made to arrest trawlers in the next few days, including one in Butterscotch (to the west) where *Ægir* collided with the trawler *Burfell*. As the winter drew on, it became clear to the Icelanders that the Royal Navy would remain on patrol and could provide the medical and technical support that the trawlers needed to continue fishing. In his daily summary, Commodore Anderson signalled 'I appreciate the political problems, but urge a face saving interim solution be found quickly for both countries if only to save needless loss of life.'

On the 4th September 1958, to the west, in Butterscotch, *Ægir* made to collide with HMS *Russell*, forcing her to sheer away. It is unlikely that this was a real attempt to inflict damage - more a game of cat and mouse, but Lieutenant Commander

Peter Corson, the Commanding Officer of HMS *Russell*, was not going to be pushed around by a gunboat 1/5th of his size and responded over the loud-hailer ' *Ægir*, if you try to ram me, I will blow you out of the water.' This was probably bluff, as his Rules of Engagement (RoE) only allowed him to open fire when he or a trawler under his protection has first been fired at and then only to disable the gunboat's gun - specifically not to sink her. However, whilst London and Reykjavik may have promulgated 'keep it cool' RoE to their respective representatives at sea, in the harsh seas off Iceland toughness and determination were going to be necessary and the experienced seamen on both sides were inclined to trust to their own judgement.

That evening one of the largest gatherings ever held in Iceland's history took place in Reykjavik, where speakers from all of Iceland's ever-quarrelling political parties were united in their calls for unity against the common enemy - the British - the battle cry became 'We don't deal with the Brits, we beat them'. Any call for caution or compromise by an Icelandic politician or diplomat would now be seen as treason - both sides were dug in for the long haul.

Whilst Iceland benefited in the propaganda battle from being the 'little boy' subjected to bullying by the 'colonialist' British, her position was not universally supported. The Secretary General of NATO noted

> *'Whatever Iceland's strategic value to the Alliance, it would be a grave mistake to give way before such blatant blackmail on the part of small countries.'*

The American Secretary of State, Dulles, similarly said to the British Ambassador

> *'it would be quite wrong that (Britain) should yield on what was an important question of principle affecting other parts of the world.'*

To balance this, however, the American Ambassador in Reykjavik said to one of the British Embassy staff

> *'You damn British, you can't do this to the Icelanders. You know, you're sending those damn warships up there. They're just off the .... coast, people in their houses can see them off their doorstep. You must stop this whole thing.'*

No doubt some of those supporting the British position were irritated with Iceland's refusal to consider any compromise, despite the standing British offer to start with a 6-mile limit and work outwards.

The problem of the Icelandic 'guests' in HMS *Eastbourne* remained unresolved. Once it became clear that the Coastguard were not going to accept their boarding party back, the first thought was that they would have to be sent to Britain in the first ship returning home, but the UK government law officers assessed that this course of action was full of legal pitfalls - for example, once in the UK, the Icelanders might apply for a writ of habeas corpus against the Commanding Officer, or perhaps the First Sea Lord or maybe even the Prime Minister. After several days of legal and diplomatic discussions, during which *Eastbourne*'s 'guests' refused to eat any fish, in case it had been caught within their 12-mile limit, the Icelanders were dropped off at 0300 on 13th September near Keflavík and rowed themselves ashore in HMS *Eastbourne's* whaler, which was therefore lost to the ship.[22]

Christopher Notley remembers that they were actually quite sorry to lose their visitors as the two officers were always willing to make up a bridge four. They were all given some spending money whilst onboard and, as the 'office boy', Sub-Lieutenant Notley charged these payments against NATO Forces. This, somewhat unusual, procedure was, fortunately, accepted by the Base Supply Officer when the ship returned to her base port of Chatham. The visitors were kept out of the operational compartments, but otherwise had a free run of the ship and were frequent customers of the ship's NAAFI.

HMS *Hound* was relieved by the Battle-class Destroyer HMS *Lagos* (Commander Denis Jermain) on 5th September. *Hound's* radar problems had continued from 31st August until the moment when *Eastbourne* closed on her, so that Commodore Anderson could address the ship's company and tell then that they were going back to Portsmouth for repairs. This good news caused the radar to begin rotating again and the Commodore to remark 'It

[22] This must have given rise to an interesting Form C.126 – Report into Loss of Stores!

HMS Diana (MoD/Crown Copyright)

looks like there's life in the old dog yet!'

Denis Glassett remembers that they had a *Manchester Guardian* reporter onboard and his reports, which all began 'Aboard HMS *Hound* off Iceland...' were transmitted in morse by the ship's radio office. For security reasons, the ship's name was not allowed to be reported and as there is no blank in morse, the ship's name had to be sent out as HMS *Blank*. Algerine Class minesweepers would not be employed off Iceland again as, with a 16 knots maximum speed, they were too slow to be able to protect a whole haven.

Over the next couple of weeks, all of the ships on the initial patrol were relieved, with Commodore Barry Anderson (Commodore Fishery Protection Squadron (CFPS) and his very small staff transferring to HMS *Hogue* on 13th September. From 8th November onwards, the patrol was reduced to three destroyers or frigates, with one RFA tanker in support. The average patrol length on station was 18 days. As the patrol settled into a routine, consideration had to be given to how fishing was going to be conducted during the winter months, when gales are frequent. The 'Arctic Pilot' states that for the six months from November to April there are, on average, just over 10 days of gales per month at the Westmann Islands off Iceland's south coast and that the mean daily windspeed, throughout the year, is 21 knots or Force 5-6. Icing can also be a significant problem - several trawlers had been lost with all hands after they capsized due to the weight of ice on their superstructure. By midwinter, the sea ice edge approaches the north and northwest coasts of Iceland, in bad years, can close the Denmark Strait. The other important factor, well remembered by almost everyone who was involved in any of the Cod Wars, is the sheer speed at which the weather can change. Before the Cod War, trawlers working Iceland's north coast in winter had been able to shelter inshore from the worst of the gales and ice, but now they risked being arrested if they did so.

September was a foggy month and on the 25th a sailor in the trawler *Paynter* was diagnosed with appendicitis. HMS *Diana* cleared all the trawlers out of the 12-mile limit and with *Maria Julia's* permission, entered Patreksfjord at 1100 to land the casualty. *Diana's* motor cutter was obstructed in her efforts to land the sick man and was nearly trapped in the harbour by a floating crane that was moved, surely deliberately, across the harbour entrance. Meanwhile, *Ódinn* and *Maria Júlia* had arrested the *Paynter*, at the time 2 miles outside the claimed 12-mile limit, and had sent a boarding party onboard. *Diana* recovered her motor cutter and headed for the scene of action at 25 knots. *Paynter's* crew forcibly resisted and minor injuries were sustained on both

The Paynter with HMS Diana's whaler alongside. *(Alan Boxall)*

sides, giving the skipper time to both anchor and immobilise his engines.

As *Diana,* commanded by Captain Bill Graham, arrived, the Icelandic boarding party retired. They subsequently claimed that they could have taken *Paynter* into port if their Prime Minister had not personally intervened and ordered that no arrest was to take place whilst a British warship was away on an 'errand of mercy'. There was an uproar after this incident, as the Icelanders felt that they were being deprived of their legitimate prey. The press had a field day over the Prime Minister's 'boy scout attitude' - as the communist newspaper said, 'If this man wants to give an imitation of Jesus Christ, it is time he left Iceland!' The consequence was that the Prime Minister had to state that, in future, sick fishermen could only be landed from their own trawlers, and that British warships could only land sick crew members if they could prove that they were not trawlermen in disguise.

Sid Reeves, who was serving in HMS *Diana* at the time, recounts that they arrived on patrol on 20th September directly from the Mediterranean Station. Food, including fresh local bread, was embarked in Bilbao on the way north, but there was no cold weather clothing onboard. Ratlines were rigged along the upper deck and going on watch involved trying to estimate the gap between waves so as to avoid getting "goffered"[23]. Usually he started his watch with cold water down his neck. Relations between the fishermen and the Royal Navy were already beginning to fray a bit - on arriving at speed to see off an Icelandic gunboat, the cry would go up 'Here goes that big grey bastard frightening all the fish away'. Another source of friction was the relative pay rates - an engineer from one of the trawlers, who was victualled onboard *Diana* for a week to recover from burns to his hands, told the After Stokers Mess that he was paid £100 per week, which may have been a bit of an exaggeration (and, anyway, was very much dependant on the size of the catch the market price when the catch was landed), but didn't go down well with those protecting him, who were on only £7 10s 6d (£7.52) a week.

Alan Boxall, who was also onboard *Diana* during this patrol, remembers that the ship's mail used to come up in trawlers, who would transfer it to the warships. These transfers were usually effected by using a liferaft. On one occasion, the First Lieutenant, Lieutenant-Commander Beatty, who was newly engaged, 'volunteered' to do the transfer himself. He appeared on deck dressed in his dinner jacket, with trousers rolled up to the knees and bare feet. It was rough and the trawler was regularly being lost from sight in the waves. Not surprisingly, the majority of *Diana's* ship's company came up on deck to watch the fun. There was much cheering as the rope holding the liferaft was paid out towards the trawler and even more as, once alongside, the expected cascade of fresh cod covered the First Lieutenant.

With both arms clasped firmly around the mail sack, the liferaft was hauled back alongside and recovered. The Coxswain (who was responsible for mail onboard) tried to take the bag from him, but Lieutenant-Commander Beatty would not give it up and they went into the Coxswain's office together to sort the mail. There were further cheers, when Lieutenant-Commander Beatty emerged waving the

[23] A Royal Naval expression for being overwhelmed by a huge sea.

precious letter from his fiancée.

By the time *Diana* was relieved, Sid Reeves remembers that the Spanish bread was hard and dry, the Canteen had sold out of any foodstuff and they were down to hard tack and jam, albeit supplemented by wonderfully fresh fish. The situation was such that HMS *Adamant*, the submarine depot ship that, according to naval legend, only went to sea when required to do so in order to retain her full duty-free privileges, was sailed north from Scotland to meet them and replenish their food stocks.

The *Paynter* incident highlighted the ambivalent attitude that the trawlermen were to show towards the Royal Navy throughout all three Cod Wars. On 28th September, the Grimsby Trawler Officer's Guild expressed satisfaction at the way the Royal Navy was carrying out its protection duties, but then called for stronger measures and more warships. The presence of Liaison Skippers in warships did much to ease things and to foster a greater understanding of each side's problems. Communication between trawlers and between trawlers and the Royal Navy was on HF and VHF voice circuits. The trawlers usually had more powerful commercial radios, but they had no facility for encrypting their messages. Paul Willerton, who was a cadet on two of the RFAs, remembers that they sometimes had to relay traffic for the Royal Navy using their more-powerful MF transmitters. As always, anything transmitted can be received by anyone else with a suitable receiver and it was nigh on impossible to keep the trawlermen fully informed about what was going on without equally informing the Icelandic Coastguard. 'Edited' tapes of conversations between the Royal Navy and trawler skippers would be regularly transmitted on Icelandic radio. As Sir Andrew Gilchrist reported, 'the bloodthirsty threats of the trawler skippers and the increasingly unenthusiastic and pacific tendencies of the British naval captains' made it clear that there were very firm limits on how far the Royal Navy would be allowed to go in protecting the trawlers.

Used out of context, bits of these radio conversations could be, and were, used to demonstrate British aggression and as time went on, the Coastguard realised that they could record this traffic and replay it on air later to cause confusion. For example, trawlers were asked to report all sightings of gunboats and did so. These messages were recorded and then retransmitted when the gunboats were elsewhere. Once the Royal Navy realised that they were receiving false reports, they would tell the trawlers to ignore them. This message was itself recorded and then re-transmitted later to counter a real sighting report from a trawler. The trawlers also joined in this war on the airwaves, by broadcasting 'Rule Britannia' on VHF channel 16 (the International circuit on which initial radio contact was to be made) when they were called by a gunboat. Captain Gudmundur Kjærnested of the *Ægir* is said to have responded with "*The Last Waltz*", hence the title chosen for the Icelandic TV documentary of the Cod Wars.

At the time, the technology did not exist which would have allowed the British to get their version of an incident to the world's press as quickly as the Icelanders could and so Iceland could always get their version published first, leaving the British on the back foot. Initially, there were British press embarked in HM Ships and in some of the trawlers, but as the First Cod War settled into a routine and there were very few incidents to report, the press lost interest.

For the first seven weeks, Commodore Anderson and his staff transferred from ship to ship, so maintaining continuity of command; the very real difficulties of maintaining long-haul communications off Iceland in this era were probably a significant factor in the decision to keep CFPS on station for nearly two months. On 24th October, the Captain 3rd Training Squadron, Captain Adrian Northey, took over in HMS *Zest*. CFPS was back on station from 16th November to 19th December. Thereafter, as the patrol settled into a routine, Commodore Anderson shared the CTG (Commander of the Task Group) role with several senior Captains, although he remained the Admiralty's principal adviser and the overall operational planner.

The Royal Fleet Auxiliaries were an essential part of the CTG's assets. The destroyers and frigates would normally be refuelled every three days. This may seem surprisingly often, but there were several factors driving this frequency; amongst them the need to keep the warships ready to react to any eventuality and the fact that they were more stable with full fuel tanks. On 12th November, HMS *Orwell*, commanded by Captain Peter Compston, had to return to Lyness for fuel, because the tanker was on the other side of Iceland, the weather had been too rough to refuel for three days and the risk of *Orwell* running low was too great. This was one of only three times during the two and a half years of the First Cod War that a ship had to leave Icelandic waters to refuel. Lieutenant-Commander Geoff Hammond, the Commanding Officer of HMS *Palliser*, remembers that the single-screw Type 14 frigates rapidly abandoned stern refuellings and always used to refuel abeam down sea at, at least, 15 knots to avoid the risk of being pooped. One problem was that this replenishment course needed lots of searoom.

Paul Willerton, who was a cadet in *RFAs Wave Ruler* and *Wave Chief* at the time, recalls that the ships operated a 1 month on/1 month off pattern, usually running out of Glasgow or Rosyth. Whilst on station, they would loiter at slow speed, except when required to transit to another area to R/V with a warship for Replenishment at Sea (RAS). RASs, which were almost always conducted abeam, apart from those conducted for training purposes, would normally take 45-60 minutes for the FFO[24] ships, but 3-4 hours for the Cathedral class diesel[25] frigates. The tankers carried 90% FFO and only about 10% dieso; over a one month patrol, they would only distribute about 30% of their cargo, so their stability was never a problem. Another of the RFAs' tasks was to act as the film library - inevitably films would be transferred to and from the warships during replenishments.

Jim Findlay was a stoker in HMS *Decoy*. He remembers the 19th September 1958 very well:

> *'We had been chasing the gunboat Thor around half of Iceland. I had the afternoon watch down the boiler room on the turbo alternator. It was in the Denmark Strait and it was blowing a hooligan Force 9 to 12. Bodies lying seasick everywhere.*
> *I had half my rum ration (I'm not admitting where the other half went). Just to crown it all, it was my 21st birthday. Who can forget their 21st? We had come straight from the Med to do fishery protection and didn't get a run ashore for almost three months. I don't think I've eaten cod ever since.'*

[24] Furnace Fuel Oil - 'heavy' fuel.
[25] Marine diesel fuel.

On 12th November 1958, there was another incident involving *Thor*. The trawler *Hackness*, who was off Breidifjord on Iceland's west coast and was not fishing at the time, was intercepted by *Thor*, who fired a warning shot. HMS *Russell* prevented an arrest and when *Thor* threatened to fire at *Hackness* again, Lieutenant-Commander Peter Corson in *Russell* told *Thor* that he would sink her if she did. Fortunately, the incident ended there. Lieutenant-Commander Geoff Hammond, of HMS *Palliser*, recalls that Captain Eiríkur Kristófersson of *Thor* once asked him if he would really open fire on his ship. To which Geoff Hammond replied that, if he tried to capture a British trawler, yes, but that his 40mm gun would hardly do much damage. He'd rather use the Anti-submarine mortar - which fired a pattern of 3 550lb mortar bombs and would surely blow *Thor*'s bottom in, sending them all to the bottom.

As the winter weather set in, affecting every activity from refuelling to fishing, the decision was made to shift the north and north-westerly havens, Butterscotch and Toffeeapple, round to the south coast from 2nd December. By then the number of trawlers on the fishing grounds had begun to decrease, in accordance with the usual pattern, and by Christmas there were only about 20 still working - most of whom were fishing outside the 12 mile limit, because there seemed to be more fish there.

As the year closed, 22 Royal Navy ships and 5 RFA tankers had shared the patrol. There had been 30 serious, but unsuccessful, attempts to arrest trawlers. The ships had conducted 125 RASs, 42 jackstay transfers and 300 liferaft transfers. On December 2nd the UN General Assembly decided to call the second Law of the Sea conference (UNCLOS2) for spring 1960. The NATO Council had debated the dispute without any result and the Icelandic Government had resigned (for reasons unconnected with the fishery dispute). The interim government (elections were to be held in May or June 1960) may have been further to the right, but there was no doubt at all that every Icelander, whatever their political persuasion, was united in their determination to win the dispute with Britain. As the new Prime Minister, Emil Jonsson, said to the British Ambassador

> *'As you can see, we are a weak government,*

therefore we cannot make concessions. You know what public feeling[26] *is like. Any party in Iceland that gives up on the 12-mile limit is committing suicide. Don't pay any attention to us if we tell you anything different.'*

With no political solution in sight before UNCLOS2 in the Spring, the Royal Navy was now committed to a long-term holding operation.

[26] It is arguable that the British never really understood how strongly the Icelanders felt about this issue. In the TV documentary *The Last Waltz* the historian Dr Valur Ingimundarson compared it to the struggle leading to the founding of the Icelandic Republic.

CHAPTER 6

THE FIRST COD WAR
JANUARY 1959 - MARCH 1960

Over the next 15 months, 37 warships and six RFAs shared the patrol. The four Type 14 frigates of the Fishery Protection Squadron (FPS) were the backbone of the patrol cycle - they were invariably either on patrol, between patrols or under maintenance and taking leave. Unusually, in late March 1960, Commodore Anderson had all four of his squadron on patrol simultaneously and was moved to quote Psalm 133 Verse 1 in one of his reports - "*Behold how good and how pleasant it is for brethren to dwell together in unity.*" The Icelandic Coastguard continued with their policy of attempting to arrest trawlers when there was no British warship around. This meant that the CTG and his Liaison Skipper had to balance several conflicting priorities, including tracking both the gunboats and all the trawlers whilst allowing the skippers to fish with as little interference as possible. There were some skippers who preferred to fish on their own and would even give false position reports if they had found good fishing, so as to avoid others taking 'their fish'. The Liaison Skippers were invaluable in advising the CTG on fishing problems, on shifting the havens to follow the fish and on reigning-in recalcitrant skippers. One of their other tasks was translating the communication between skippers (of which over 50% could easily be expletives). The skippers just 'knew where they were' and had their own names for the geography of Iceland and for the different areas where fish could be found. Charles Dempsey of HMS *Palliser*, one of the patrol stalwarts, tells a story of boarding a Dutch trawler to deal with an infected wound. The doctor wanted to see the injured man a week later and the CO of *Palliser* set a rendezvous off an island known as 'Ingolfshöfdi' (which means 'horse's hoof' and is what the island looked like). The Dutch skipper had no charts and didn't need them. Charles drew a diagram of where they wanted him a week later and the Dutchman headed north to fish off Greenland. Slightly to everyone's surprise, at

Extract from the kind of charts used by fishermen before the days of modern electronic navigational aids.
(Ken Knox)

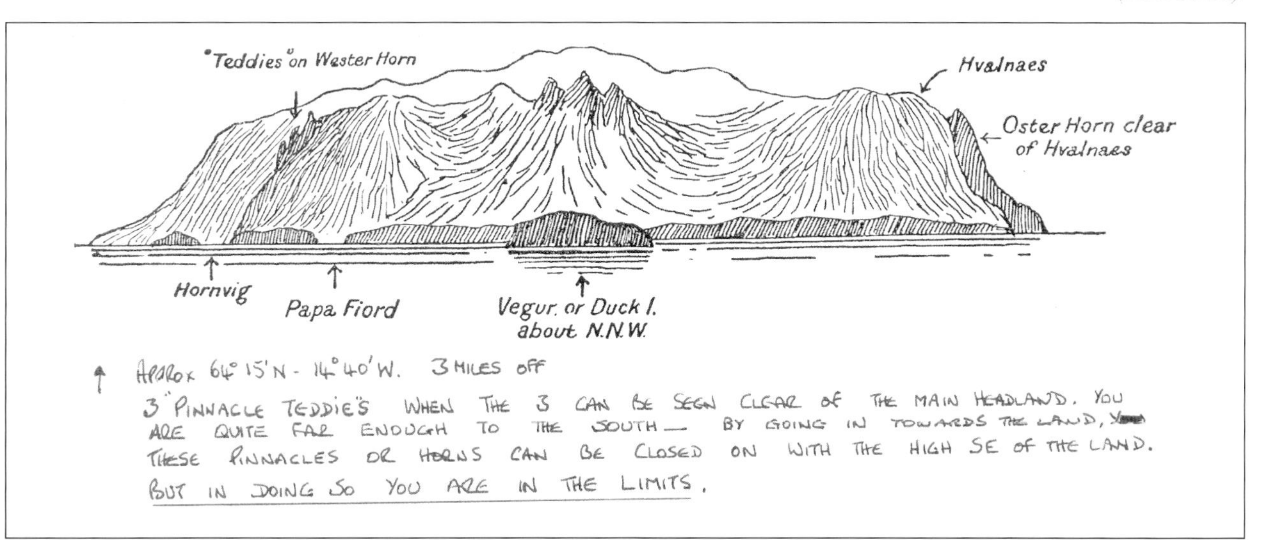

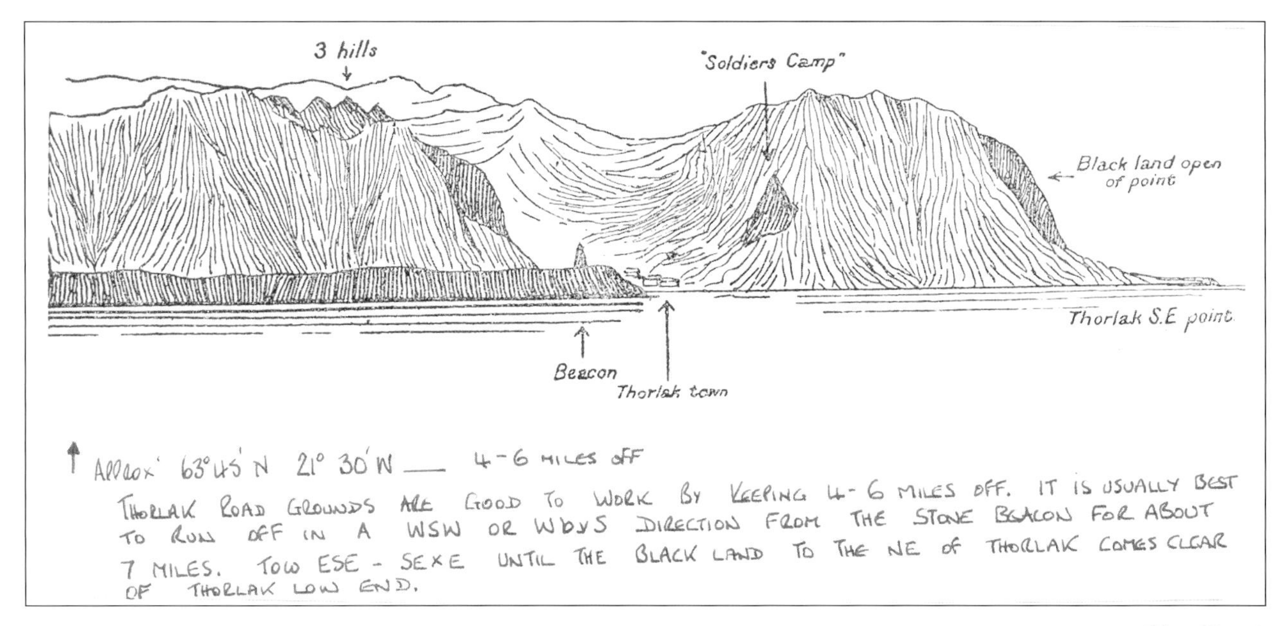

(Ken Knox)

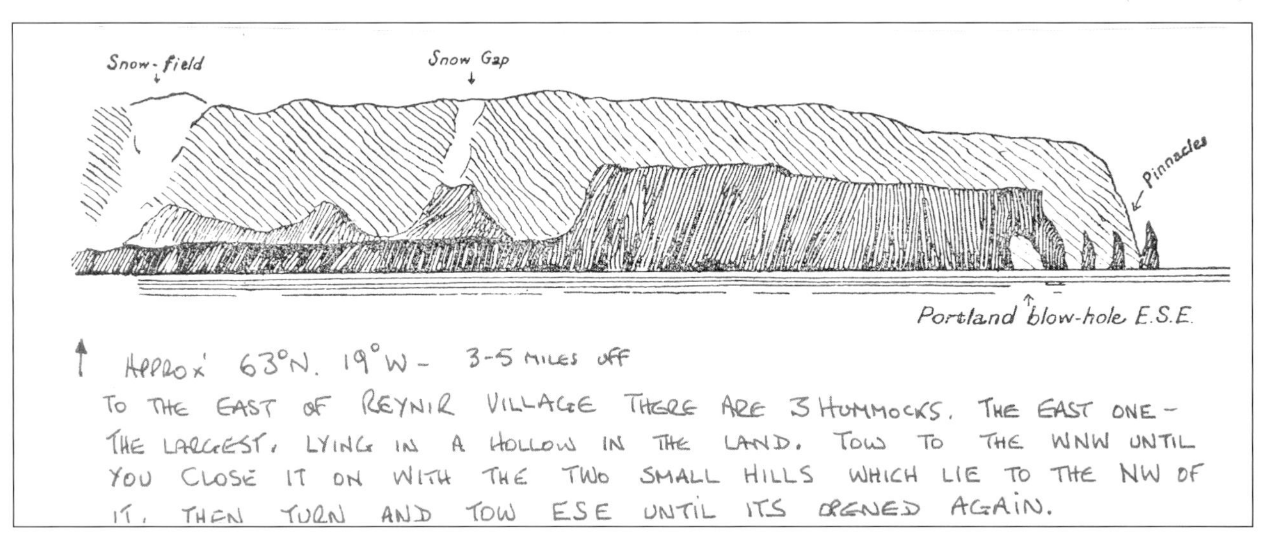

the appointed time, there he was at the rendezvous.

Trawler Navigation

As the limits off Iceland were extended, the methods of navigation had to change. Accuracy was important, especially when fishing as close as possible to the limit. From the late 60s, Decca[27] could be used off southern Iceland, but it wasn't always that accurate.

Within 6 miles, visual navigation, both bearings and views of the coast, combined with soundings were accurate enough. The fishermen's charts are liberally supplied with views of the coast, as can be seen from Skipper Ken Knox's diagrams - note the warning about the 3-mile limit.

The skippers would often annotate their charts with vessels names and 'The Lot' or 'Pt'd both warps' - this would indicate places where the skipper had come foul and lost his full set of trawling gear.

[27] Decca was a radio fixing aid, initially developed for the D-day landings.

Outside 6 miles, in good visibility, visual navigation was often still possible, using the more mountainous bits of Iceland. Once radar became available, this became a prime fixing aid out to 30 miles, because the Icelandic coast is often sheer and gives very good echoes. Decca Scottish Chain 6 was useable when the signal was strong enough, but the signal was often too weak to be of use.

Another navaid that skippers would often use was a marker buoy - to mark good fishing, bad ground or a wreck. This buoy was mainly used when out of sight of land in the absence of any other means of fixing. The buoy would be stowed in the portside rigging and was kept at the ready for dropping. The anchor and ground cable, with several lengths of wire attached, usually kept it in position with little drifting.

It was in the spring of 1959, on 18th February, that the Icelandic Coastguard lost one of their ships, with all hands, in a storm off the SW coast. The *Hermodur*, a 200-ton vessel, was primarily employed as a lighthouse tender, but had been used on fishery protection work. The 100-ton converted fishing vessel *Manatindur* replaced her.

The gunboats' main effort was directed at catching trawlers fishing alone and without Royal Navy protection close-by, in the area between 4 and 12 miles from the shore. They considered that they had an undisputed right to arrest 'poachers' inside 4 miles and so were much less worried about the proximity of a British warship. Whilst Britain had never legally recognised the Icelandic government's unilateral 1952 extension from 3 to 4 miles, the British government's advice and the trawler owners' instructions were clear - that there should be no fishing inside 4 miles.

Problems with the 4-mile limit

This inconsistency was first put to the test on 1st February 1959. At 1110, *Thor* approached the trawler *Valafell* in the Spearmint haven off Glettinganes on the eastern coast. *Thor* accused her of fishing inside 4 miles and whilst ordering her to stop, fired a shot across *Valafell's* bow. The Captain of *Thor* then told *Valafell* that unless she stopped, he would fire directly at her.

HMS *Corunna* was in company and her CO, Commander Cecil Gordon DSC, told *Thor* that if he did so, *Corunna* would retaliate in kind. The Captain of *Thor* invited Commander Gordon onboard to discuss the problem. He declined, saying that the CTG, Captain Erroll Sinclair in HMS *Agincourt*, was on his way and that they should wait for his arrival. Both *Thor* and *Agincourt* fixed the trawler's exact position and it was clear that *Valafell* had been fishing 5

ICGV Hermodur - lost with all hands on 18 February 1959. (Landhelgisgæslan)

cables inside the 4-mile limit. Captain Sinclair did not admit this to *Thor* and he was not prepared to allow a trawler to be arrested in the presence of British warships. Nor could he instruct the *Valafell's* skipper to follow the *Thor* into an Icelandic port; this was a decision for the owners. The CTG recommended to London that *Valafell* should be protected and allowed to continue fishing, whilst the matter was resolved. After four days of discussions between the different government departments involved, the owners and the Ambassador in Reykjavik, the owners decided to take a conciliatory line and HMS *Agincourt* escorted the *Valafell* into Seydisfjord, where the skipper was tried on one charge of illegal fishing and fined £1700, with the expected confiscation of gear. Many in Iceland considered this fine to be unduly lenient.

Whitehall attempted to clarify the legal position with respect to fishing between 3 and 4 miles, but the end result was a *de facto* acceptance of 4 miles, even if the Icelanders were not to be allowed to police it themselves. The owners instructed skippers to keep well outside 4 miles and announced that skippers caught inside 4 miles, or inside 12 miles but outside a haven, would be suspended for 3 months on the first offence and 6 months on the second. This statement did not solve the problem and confrontations with the ICG continued.

Whilst all this was going on off Iceland, the British and Danish governments had reached an agreement on new fishing limits off the Faeroes. This was based on the 6+6 formula with some historic rights to fish in the outer 6 miles. The Danes did, however, insist that any agreement finally reached with Iceland should be reflected in the Faeroes agreement. Any hope that this compromise with Denmark would put pressure on Iceland to negotiate was stillborn. To the Icelanders, the Danes had sold out the Faeroese interests because of their own bacon trade with Britain.

Back off Iceland, the confrontations over the 4-mile limit continued. On 26th March, *Thor* tried to board *Carella*, who was accused of fishing just inside the 4-mile limit[28]. Lieutenant-Commander Geoff Hammond in HMS *Palliser* refused to allow the arrest, refused to even discuss *Carella*'s navigational position and told *Carella*, who had just hauled and was full of fish, to return home immediately. *Thor* set off in 'hot pursuit' with *Palliser* in company. After about 24 hours, *Thor* broke down & the skipper of *Carella* asked Geoff Hammond if he should offer assistance! Geoff Hammond told him to 'not be so stupid & to bxxxxx off home', offered assistance himself (it was declined) and then stood by *Thor* until she managed to get underway and return to Iceland.

This hard line on poachers by the British did sour the professional working relations with the Coastguard, but saved a lot of time and effort in often fruitless negotiations. There was another, similar, incident between HMS *Scarborough*, commanded by Captain Edward Usherwood, and *Ódinn* over the Hull trawler *Swanella* on 14th April.

On 23rd April, there was yet another incident inside 4 miles - this time with one of the trawlers on the Coastguard's blacklist of frequent 'poachers' - the *Lord Montgomery*. HMS *Tenby*, commanded by Commander William Gerard-Pearse, prevented arrest by *Ægir*, but the owners agreed that the skipper should stand trial. However, once in court, he was not only charged with fishing inside 4 miles, but also with several charges of fishing within 12 miles. He was fined £3000, had his gear confiscated and was sentenced to three months in prison. Although, the skipper was released after 2 days on payment of a bond, this upping of the ante by the Icelandic authorities persuaded the owners that there should be no more surrenders to Icelandic justice.

Charles Lucas was in the RNR at this time and joined HMS *Exmouth* just as she sailed for patrol on 19th April 1959, but to let him tell his own story:

> *'My bags thrown onto the deck of this frigate where all hands were at sailing stations. By the time I reached the bridge, the vessel was well under way ..... I'm not sure to this day whether I was there as a navigator or because I had spent 3 months on* HMS *Orestes in the Fishery Protection Squadron. We arrived at the NW corner of Iceland coming up from the south on 22 April. There were three supernumeraries onboard, myself a Lieutenant RNR, a Lieutenant Doctor on National Service right out of medical school and a retired trawler skipper as liaison.*
> *The weather was pretty bad and for the first few days the crew was used to clear ice from the vessel. Our protection area was 30 miles*

[28] Geoff Hammond remembers that Carella was certainly inside the limit.

Icelandic Coastguard Catalina. Note the Fishery Protection flag painted on the fuselage.

(Icelandic Coast Guard via Baldur Sveinsson)

north to south and 10 miles east to west starting at 66 North 24 West. I kept the bridge watch from 9pm to 6am and the Captain (Lieutenant-Commander Mike Wilson) took the daylight hours.

Probably the hardest worked man onboard was the Doctor who was dropped alongside trawlers in a rubber dinghy on a towline and was retrieved the same way, only this time with a full load of live fish. We ate fish three times a day for the rest of the month after our arrival. On top of that their Lordships in their wisdom gave us a can of sardines every day since we were above the Arctic Circle. It was many years after before I could look at a piece of fish. The first incident was the boarding of a trawler by an Icelandic Gunboat.[29]

Exmouth's boarding party boarded on the opposite side as the Icelanders left on the other side. The Icelanders usually beat up on the old men and the boys.[30] *Our boarding party was armed with pickaxe handles with the exception of the Officer in Charge who carried a loaded pistol.*

The second incident involved the Icelandic Air Force.[31] *The weather had moderated and it was decided that a little R&R was needed so a shooting match was arranged. Teams competed with .22 bore rifles at targets on the fore deck.*

During the competition, a Catalina flying boat flew over and within a couple of hours, the Admiralty was asking us why we were shooting at the plane.

We kept a radar plot of all trawlers in our area and it was interesting that most of the trawler skippers were not familiar with this. At night they would trawl up towards the coast and turn their lights out and steam out of the protected area. We would then call them on R/T and bring them back into the fold.

Most nights the liaison trawler skipper would come up and sit with me for a couple of hours and listen to the skippers on the R/T. A lot of them had code whistles and my liaison skipper could identify them and what they were trying to do. Most of it was to do with where the fish were running.'

---

[29] This would have been *Albert* attempting to arrest *Ashanti* on 29th April 1959.

[30] I have discussed this statement with Charles Lucas, as it is the only record I have of this kind of behaviour by the Coastguard. He says that 'bullying' might be a better word - the Coastguard boarding party would sometimes pick-on the old men and the boys (some only 15) amongst the trawler's crew.

[31] In fact the Coastguard. Iceland has no armed forces.

The increase in gunboat activity in April was no surprise. Two havens were shifted to the southwest corner of Iceland - to an area where Icelandic trawlers were forbidden because of the damage they could do to local line and net fishermen. This haven move was regarded as unnecessarily provocative by many observers and the Americans protested strongly. These protests were not taken seriously in London; indeed a Foreign Office minute about the American protests is marked 'The Foreign Secretary did not have time to see this.'

With excellent fishing available, trawler numbers were back up to 80, there was plenty of fish and the weather was better. From the Icelandic side, the election was due and no politician could be seen to be soft on the dispute with the British. The trawler owners, once again, reminded their skippers to keep to the rules and to be ready for trouble. The CTG (Captain Patrick Bayly in HMS *Cavendish*) signalled the following reminder to the ships on patrol on 29th April 1959:

"1. The gunboats seem to be concentrating on nabbing trespassers inside the 4-mile limit rather than on the forcible capture of trawlers between 4 and 12 miles. Nevertheless, persistent buzzing of trawlers continues and with the advent of good weather in the southern havens, boardings will be possible more often than not. Haven Chiefs must, therefore, be ready to deal with both nuisances.

2. In spite of Valafell and Lord Montgomery, a few trawlers are still singularly carefree near the 4-mile line, even when a gunboat is in the vicinity.

Also, I suspect that familiarity has bred contempt, since most trawlers do not show any sign of anti-boarding measure when being buzzed. They would probably be an easy prey to a surprise attack.

3. Unless there are good reasons to the contrary, the Haven Chief should be breathing down a gunboat's neck whenever she is near

HMS Cavendish *(MoD/Crown Copyright)*

any of our trawlers. This is particularly important when the trawlers are near the 4-mile limit.
4. If there are two gunboats amongst our trawlers, the one nearest the 4-mile limit will usually be the one to watch.
5. If you are dogging the gunboat, it should be possible to warn any trawler which is dangerously near the 4-mile limit well before she can be accosted, and the surprise boarding of trawlers outside the 4-mile limit will be improbable."

Commodore Anderson summarised about a week later:

"1. In my opinion, recent aggressive and provocative action by Icelanders is largely due to:
(a) Last autumn, Icelandic gunboats continually warned trawlers that when winter storms came, trawlers would be forced to get shelter from weather for medical and defect assistance in Iceland, when they would be captured. Also that Royal Navy would be unable to fuel in all weathers and would not always be present to protect and assist trawlers. These warnings have proved wrong in all respects.
(b) Excellent spring fishing being enjoyed by all trawlers and Navy still on the job.
2. Our orders are quite clear and the Task Group policy remains the same, namely to be firm, just and polite. We stand for no nonsense from anyone.
3. Trawlers will again be reminded to look to their anti-boarding devices and warned to keep clear of 4-mile capers.
Co-operation between HM ships, trawlers and tankers has been magnificent. 'Well done, all hands.'"

Ken Knox was on trawlers at the time. He remembers the anti-boarding preparations:

"The Skipper's and Mate's requisition list handed into the owners at the end of each fishing trip often got reduced by the operations manager or ship's husband. Deck brush handles were always a very rare commodity onboard; several seamen sharing one deck brush for cleaning the decks. During the Cod War, we could receive a bundle of a dozen broom handles to fight off the boarders. Heaven help us if they ever decided to fire their forward gun.
How many times had fishermen shaken empty pepperpots at meal times, the cook shouting "that's yer lot"? Sailing into the Cod War zone some trawlers could release their secret weapon. A large bag of pepper was put onboard to make small pepper bombs. Look out you boarders!
One skipper I sailed with came up with an idea for anti-boarding, lower the portside derrick on the foremast at right angles, have a large round 21-inch iron bobbin (drilled to fill up with water). Swung out on a rope, the idea was to cut the rope if an Icelandic gunboat or boarding craft got underneath. I think our own crew were more in danger.
When the gunboats or boarding craft came close, it was all hands to the port side to repel. The one-deck hosepipe (donkey) was manned and the chief or 2nd engineer ordered 'give full force on the donkey'. If we were on a port tack, this resulted in all hands being soaked, the Icelandic crew getting some good laughs and pictures.
One sound idea, and used by most trawler skippers, was to stretch a sheet of netting, something we had in abundance, the full length of the port side area between the fore and aft gallows - approx 80'x 8'. Rigged with rope and blocks, this anti-boarding net could very quickly be raised, closing up the port side, usually the main point of attack."

HMS *Contest,* commanded by Commander Richard Reynolds, was another of the destroyers on task at this time. Tony Britten was onboard at the time; *Contest* was patrolling the southwest haven and he remembers how cold it was:

It's true to say that special winter clothing had not been issued. The Icelandic gunboats would harass the fishing boats by going very close and playing exceptionally loud music from loudspeakers along the upper deck. .... We would 'race' to a scene and were greeted with jeers and derisory comments from the Thor, which seemed to be the main protagonist. ... This sort of incident happened almost daily, day or night, and I remember one night (I could be wrong![32]) we fired a live warning round from the 4.7 in addition to the starshells which lit up the area. ... We ran out of fresh food and the trawlers began to send fish daily to us. ... On our return to UK, ... into Portsmouth, which was not our home port. We spent the next month taking school children out daily for a trip around the Isle of Wight. This to us was more harrowing than the so-called Cod War.'

Every attempt had been made by the Royal Navy to maintain good professional relations with the Icelandic Coastguard. Inevitably, incidents where trawlers had been protected inside the 4-mile limit had soured relationships a bit, as the Coastguard thought that this was unfair, especially when Royal Navy Commanding Officers would not even discuss whether the trawler was inside 4 miles or not. The attitudes of the gunboat captains varied considerably. The Admiralty assessment was that Eiríkur Kristófersson of *Thor*, the senior and most experienced captain, was straightforward and dour, but understanding; Thórarinn Björnsson of *Ægir* was usually reasonably mild and friendly; Lárus Thorsteinsson in *María Júlía* was irritable, but on the whole amenable; Pétur Jónsson in *Ódinn* was thoroughly aggressive and Jón Jónsson in *Albert* was believed to be violently anti-British.

On 22nd May 1959, HMS *Chaplet,* commanded by Captain Bob White, had a minor collision with *Ódinn*. *Ódinn* had been very aggressive for several days and was being very closely marked by *Chaplet*. She appeared to act rashly by turning across the destroyer's bow at close quarters. *Ódinn* claimed that *Chaplet* had turned towards her. Fortunately very little damage was done and no one was injured. The Icelandic version of this incident reached the British press before the Admiralty were even aware that there had been an incident and much was made of the 'big brother is bullying us' line. However, as this type of incident was very unusual at the time, the press soon lost interest in what was going on off Iceland. In general, the First Cod War was conducted in a chivalrous way, with both sides trying to ensure that their actions would not be misunderstood and aiming to avoid direct confrontation. There were regular exchanges of polite signals, sometimes even Biblical quotations[33] between Captain Eiríkur Kristófersson of *Thor* and Commodore Barry Anderson and, on several occasions, joint search and rescue operations were undertaken. Both sides tried hard to keep the situation under control.

In May, the Admiralty assessment was that the Coastguard had been instructed to act only in the following circumstances:

- *When trawlers were inside the 12-mile limit, but outside a haven*
- *When trawlers were inside the 12-mile limit in a haven, but any protecting warships were either a long way away or otherwise occupied*
- *When trawlers were inside 4 miles.*

The ships on patrol were able to confirm this assessment from their contacts with the Coastguard. Nevertheless tension was high and there was considerable aggression on both sides. After one incident where *Maria Júlia* had fired shots towards a British trawler, Commodore Anderson trained his guns on the Icelandic Coastguard vessel. He later broadcast to all the trawlers (and any listening gunboat):

'I want you boys to fully understand that I was not bluffing. I will not have this nonsense from these people.'

As the Icelandic elections approached, the Norwegian and Danish governments warned Britain that the political situation in Iceland was very delicate. They believed that a serious incident on the fishing grounds could help a left wing government

[32] I don't think that he is wrong as Peter Musslewhite, a Leading Seaman onboard at the time, also remembers a warning shot being fired towards *Thor*.

[33] Sadly, as one senior serving officer put it to me, "Alas Biblical quotes very seldom used now because (a) Non PC, (b) All too busy for frivolity and (c) Too many versions of the Bible and if it is read in a different version to that used by the sender it usually falls very flat".

into power, thereby risking Iceland leaving NATO and the closure of the major airbase at Keflavík. These fears were exaggerated, however the CTG (Commodore Barry Anderson again) was reminded in a signal from the Admiralty on 5th June 1959 that ".. the Foreign Secretary has emphasized that this underlines need to do everything to avoid incidents before election". Commodore Anderson replied:

> *"1. Fully appreciated.*
>
> *My policy is:*
>
> • *Trawlers bristle with anti-boarding devices.*
>
> • *Trawlers take action for protection against gunfire as instructed. All trawlers on the coast know this now.*
>
> • *HM Ships ready to take firm action quickly.*
>
> • *Object is to show gunboats we are ready for them and mean business. This may be paying off as during last seven days gunboats have been much more docile and correct in behaviour.*
>
> *Our trawlermen up here at present are splendid and I could not wish for better co-operation."*

HMS *Apollo* was an odd ship to send on Icelandic patrol, but she was on patrol from the 6th June. She was a 16-year old, fast minelayer (40+ knots nominal max speed) and so was very lightly built. She also rode very high out of the water when not loaded with mines (her full load displacement was 4000 tons, as opposed to 2650 tons standard). However, there had been a mutiny[34] onboard and so, after the ensuing courts martial, with several of the ship's company under severe suspended sentences (never enforced)

HMS Apollo
(MoD/Crown Copyright)

[34] Although this breakdown in discipline was known to most of those involved as a 'mutiny', in fact there were only two courts martial and no one was charged with mutiny. This may have been because the charge of mutiny still carried the death penalty and Their Lordships felt that this sentence was completely inappropriate to the time and the circumstances.

and with quite a few new officers, it seems that Their Lordships decided that a good way to settle the ship back down, would be to send her off to sea. Equally, it may just have been that the Navy was, once again, short of hulls to fulfil all the tasks and aircraft had really taken on the ship's minelaying role.

Robert Moore, a sub-lieutenant onboard at the time, remembers:

> *'One general recollection concerns the state in which trawlers put to sea. 'Held together by rust' was one description used. We were certainly called to help repair radar equipment and, in one case, vital engine components. The skippers said that they knew about these defects before they put to sea but with ten skippers looking for every job it was more than their jobs were worth to report serious defects.*
>
> *I forget the exact claim and counter claim over Icelandic waters, but it was clear once we were there that British trawlers were doing everything the Icelandic authorities said. They fished inside the (undisputed) limits and we would chase them out - they feigned surprise and said they thought they were outside the limit. They were also fishing in the breeding grounds and, I suspect, doing a lot of damage there. The fishermen were too concerned for their incomes and the skippers for their jobs to be bothered with the niceties of international law or the preservation of fish stocks. The trawler owners (sitting safe at home) were plainly a rapacious and exploitative lot.*
>
> *We went off to find one trawler in which a crewman has broken his arm (we had a doctor embarked for the patrol). When we got to the trawler's alleged position, he was not to be found. After some exchanges on the radio, the trawler was located and he said the fish had moved! We asked about the casualty and the skipper said 'Oh, we've put him in his bunk with a bottle of whiskey, he's alright'*
>
> *Apparently the biggest crisis that could hit a trawler was to run out of vinegar - the crew lived on fish and chips soused in vinegar.*
>
> *We occasionally had a gift of fish from one of the trawlers. I shall never forget the wardroom table on those evenings - all the different types of fish, cooked in various ways. Cod fresh from Icelandic waters was one of the best things I ever tasted. Jack Vincent, our liaison skipper, said that many fishermen were so used to fresh fish that even the smell of a good fishmonger's shop made them feel ill, because the fish would be at least 14 days old.*
>
> *One abiding memory of the trawlers was to see a group of them lying to their nets, across the sea. The waves at that time (recently checked in the log) were 30 feet high with a wall of driven spray above. Little wonder that so many fishermen were killed or injured at sea, but a miracle that it was so few.*
>
> *Apollo was sixteen years old by this time. She was built for speed and constructed from very thin plates of wartime steel and lightly armed. She sat high in the water and without a full outfit of mines she was especially light. She really threw herself around off Iceland - my bunk was right at the waterline and so I had the most terrific noise alongside my pillow, but so rhythmic it put me to sleep in no time at all!*
>
> *The Commander (E)[35] suspected some damage to the ship from the pounding we took. On arrival in Rosyth we found that the foot of the ship had opened and that the bows were beginning to peel back. We had to make haste to Stavanger to embark the C-in-C, but once there the Engineer took a few lessons in shallow water diving and went down under the bows, in the freezing cold water. A Cox's Bolt Gun (?) was used to fire bolts between the plates, nuts were put on the threaded ends and tightened to close the plates. Concrete was then poured into the bow compartment.*
>
> *I was later told that on the next refit (after I left), one of the outer funnels was removed and it was found that there was only a thin skin of deeply rusted and holed steel between the inner and outer funnel. I gather a chip-*

[35] The Commander in charge of the ship's engineering department.

ping hammer would puncture it with one blow. Had this given way in high seas off Iceland there would probably have been a disaster. She was scrapped in 1963.
Sea time was not always easy to come by - even in those days. So this tour to Iceland was a godsend to the Sub-Lieutenants who, like me, were working for their watch-keeping tickets. We had very heavy watch-keeping duties - for which we were very glad. This was my first time on the bridge alone.
The bridge was open and when the weather was bad it was only a matter of minutes before one was soaked to the skin (literally). I remember going on watch at night with oil-skins over slightly damp clothing and a damp towel around my neck (no time to get properly dry between watches). The first wave over the bridge was rather a relief - one was properly wet.
We did not see much of the Icelandic gunboats and when we did, we shadowed them. Referring to these little gunboats as 'the enemy' amused me no end. Even Apollo could have blown them out of the water in an instant, so they were no threat. And, of course, they were protecting what was (and probably still is) their country's main source of income. British fishermen were trying to steal it. I rather felt we were there to support to Icelanders! If others onboard felt the same, they kept their thoughts to themselves.
We had quite a small patrol area and even when the weather was good there was still sufficient swell to roll the Apollo. So we mainly steamed very slowly into the wind/sea or downwind, sometimes so slowly, we were not actually moving over the ground - just stemming the sea (checked in log). The coastal scenery around that part of Iceland was very, very bleak and forbidding. I was glad to be in a nice warm ship. But I have always wanted to go back to Iceland, and when I do (not if) I will certainly try to get up to Isa Fjord.'

Vic Richards, an ERA[36] and ship's diver, remembers that their relief, HMS *Corunna*, had some problem and so they were delayed leaving the patrol. As a consequence it was decided to do a 48-hour full-power trial all the way back to Rosyth, not just to get back on time, but because they were about to take the CinC on an official visit to Norway. As noted above, the Commander (E) suspected that there might have been some damage done to the hull by the pounding she had taken and he was right - there was a 6-foot long, 18-inch wide split in the forefoot. Vic Richards was one of the team that dived to repair the split in the forefoot in Stavanger. When the hull was properly examined back in Rosyth, it was realised that they had all had a very lucky escape. *Apollo* was to do two more patrols.

So that *Apollo* could be relieved to go on the CinC's formal visit, HMS *Pellew*, of the Portland Squadron was given a 'pierhead jump' just before a visit to Londonderry and sent north. Dave Rogers was the Chippy (shipwright) onboard. He remembers the Chief Stoker, who had served up there on a previous ship saying:

> *"We wouldn't be able to move for fish"; anyway for a week we didn't see another ship let alone any fish!!! Then we were told we would be doing a dinghy jack stay transfer of a sick crewman from a trawler in the middle of the night. The 1st Lt said that I wouldn't be required, so I turned in, only to be rudely awakened some hours later with the news that a trawler had landed on the quarterdeck.*
> *I went aft to discover that we had sustained a split in the hull just below deck level in the stern compartment, port side; arming myself with wedges and hammer and secured by a life line I hung over the ships side, held my breath when it was all green and hammered in wedges when the green subsided. The following day the rough weather had abated and I was able to construct a cement box over the split inside the stern compartment. I can't remember now if we ever managed to get the trawlerman aboard, but we left the area soon afterwards to return to Portland still without fresh fish.'*

The Icelandic general election was held on 28th June 1959. The vote was held on one specific subject

[36] Engine Room Artificer.

- electoral reform - and the winners were committed to holding another election within six months. The Conservatives won a narrow victory, the Communists did badly and a centre/right coalition took power. The British government hoped that the new Icelandic government would, at least, be prepared to talk about the dispute. With another election due in 6 months, any inkling of concessions would have been political suicide, so this was not a realistic hope.

To the great surprise of all those actually involved, the UK Sunday papers ran a story on 5th July saying that relations between the Royal Navy and trawlermen were bad, protection was inadequate and there was not much fish. This was completely untrue as the summer had been quiet, with few attempted and no successful arrests and the fishing had been good. In fact, the CTG summarised on 15th July:

"Happily homeward our trawlers bold
Colossal catches in every hold
Frisky frigates frolic and play
Grumpy gunboats look on in dismay."

HMS *Vigo* was one of the 'frisky frigates ' (poetic licence, as she was actually a destroyer). Alfred Taylor, who was a Leading Seaman onboard, remembers some of this play 'it was flat calm, we lowered the seaboat and had pulling practice - the sun was shining, just like the tropics'. This may have been the British view, but it wasn't the Icelandic one. There can have been hardly a single Icelander who was not convinced of the justice of the 12-mile fishing limit and nearly a year of conflict had only hardened their resolve to win.

Commodore Barry Anderson was relieved as Captain, Fishery Protection Squadron on 29th July by Captain Hugo Bracken. As the CTG duties were now being more widely shared, it was not considered necessary to promote Captain Bracken to Commodore.[37] The autumn was quiet and there were only 11 attempted arrests in all of August, September, October and November.

On 31st August 1959, quite possibly to mark the anniversary of the 12-mile limit coming into force, *Thor* attempted two arrests - of *Cape Campbell* and *Man O'War*. The Haven Chief (and CTG), Captain Colin Madden, in HMS *Trafalgar* was refuelling at the time and broke away from the tanker on receiving

HMS Vigo *(MoD/Crown Copyright)*

[37] At the time, Commodore was not a substantive rank in the Royal Navy; it was a rank given to an officer whilst holding a specific appointment. On completion of that appointment, he would either be promoted to Rear Admiral or revert to Captain.

the report of *Thor's* action. Fortunately, *Thor's* boarding party had not reached either target by the time *Trafalgar* arrived and was withdrawn. The only other significant incident during this period concerned the 4-mile limit again and was, therefore, politically more sensitive.

The CTG (Capt Peter Howes at the time) in HMS *Venus*, carrying cadets from Dartmouth on their initial sea training, informed *Ægir* that he would be entering territorial waters to transfer medical supplies to two trawlers. *Ægir* did not object. Unfortunately, one of the trawlers, the *St Alcuin*, had not stowed her fishing gear on crossing the 4-mile limit and this caused *Ægir* to accuse her of the technical offence of being within 'undisputed' Icelandic fishing waters with gear ready for fishing. This may well have been right from the Icelandic perspective, but Britain had still not formally recognised the 4-mile limit. *Ægir's* demand to be allowed to arrest the *St Alcuin* was refused by *Venus*, however, *Ægir* was not to be dissuaded and she followed the trawler closely for the next two days. She was then relieved in the pursuit by *Albert* for another two days. The end result was that *St Alcuin* had to be escorted until she returned home on 1st October. The CTG's suggestion of putting a Royal Navy boarding party onboard her was rejected by the Admiralty. When *St Alcuin* returned to Icelandic waters 10 days later, she had been renamed *St Patrick*, but it was still considered prudent for her to remain outside 12 miles. The Navy was blamed for ordering *St Alcuin* to cross the 4-mile line and the CTG had to provide detailed explanations of what had happened and why. There were formal protests from Iceland, but fortunately no other repercussions.

HMS *Carron*, commanded by Lieutenant-Commander Peter Shaw and also with Dartmouth Cadets onboard, was on task at the same time. Her gunnery officer, Peter Miles, remembers the weather, the Liaison Skipper and, of course, the fresh cod:

> *'We were sent up to Iceland at the beginning of the Autumn Term in 1959, with a new batch of cadets onboard, for many of whom it was their first trip to sea. We got off to a bad start by hitting a gale in the North Sea soon after starting, and I remember many of the cadets hoping that this would not continue for the full thirty days of the patrol.*
>
> *We had a senior and experienced trawler skipper onboard, who acted as the Captain's technical adviser on fishing matters. This included advice on the locations for the fishing haven (called Butterscotch), which could be changed to cover better fishing grounds when required and requested by the trawlers. Skipper Fred would go on line to all ships morning and evening and ask how the fishing had gone. (It was always most impressive to hear him establish the net and get all trawlers on line within about 30 seconds. A squadron of four Royal Navy ships would take about half an hour to do the same). He would then decide where the best fishing was likely to be, and adjust the position of the haven accordingly. This haven was 9 miles wide, from the recognised 3-mile limit to the proposed, but disputed, 12 miles, and about 30 miles long, and our job was to prevent the Icelandic gunboats from interfering with our trawlers within the haven.*
>
> *We also provided medical help to any fishermen requiring it. The best time to send the doctor was when the trawler completed its trawl and stopped to recover the trawl and unload the fish. It was a fairly regular occurrence for the whaler to go alongside the trawler under the dripping trawl, and the coxswain would be offered some fish. If this offer was accepted, they would open the cod-end and fill the whaler with fish, which would make a welcome change to our diet onboard. I still maintain that the taste of a cod fillet, which had still been flapping when it was put in the pan, has few equals.*
>
> *Indeed, the fish was so popular with the Ship's Company that the Coxswain and the Buffer flashed up the emergency galley in the after superstructure and set up their own fish and chip shop, with profits going to charity.*
>
> *Skipper Fred was a splendid man, and was very popular with the ship's company, from the Captain down. It turned out to be his birthday on our last day at sea, and he was invited down to the Senior Rates' mess at tot-time (those were the days!), and then on to some of the Junior Rates' messes, after which he disappeared to his cabin and was unable*

to attend the farewell dinner that had been arranged in the wardroom that evening.'

Poetry was often exchanged between ships during the overnight watches. Peter Miles still has this offering from HMS *Carron's* resident poet:

When first we heard of 'Butterscotch'
We didn't think we'd like it much.
We'd heard a lot of salty tales
Of wind and storms and wintry gales.

But then we met our Skipper Fred,
And listened well to all he said.
He'd been at sea for years and years,
And very soon allayed our fears.

Now trawler men are often sick,
And need a doctor double quick.
When this is so, we send our Quack,
And usually we get him back.

But when he went to Wyre Gleaner,
To stay away he was much keener,
And gave us all an awful fright,
By staying there throughout the night.

The skipper of the great King Sol
Appeared to find this rather droll.
And like an ancient seadog's curse,
Sent us his comments, all in verse.

To match his wit, we haven't time,
But we've composed this little rhyme.
And so, until the dawn grows light,
Good fishing all, and so, good night.

The second Icelandic general election of the year was held on 20th November and the same centre/right coalition was returned to power. At the end of November, the northern and western havens were closed and two havens were established off the east coast. Based on the previous winter's experiences with trawler numbers and gunboat activity, the Royal Navy's patrol was reduced to two destroyers or frigates.

HMS *Duncan* was the Leader of the Fishery Protection Squadron and so was commanded by the Captain Fishery Protection Squadron (CFPS) Captain Hugo Bracken. She was another of the regulars, doing 9 patrols in all. John Hession was the Leading Writer onboard and has written a diary from the letters he sent home to his wife. A few of the extracts show what life onboard was like:

'6th November 59. I awoke to vague recollections of being tossed about a bit in the night, and sure enough my office was a shambles.

About 4am we rounded the northern tip of Iceland and the weatherman threw the book at us!

We're just about inside the Arctic Circle now, and it's incredibly cold. We're allowed to wear "Pirate Rig" whilst on patrol, which means we abandon conventional uniform and can wear any and every bit of warm clothing we can lay our hands on. Most of the lads

'Pirate Rig' onboard HMS Palliser
(Norman Robinson)

make the most of it and each tries to outdo his mates. We have the most wonderful display of headgear on display, from Andy Capps to fearsome looking Russian furs. Some of the sweaters are so colourful they hurt the eyes. One Petty Officer wears jodhpurs and riding boots, and another a Terry Thomas style waistcoat and a bowler hat!

It's a nice clean cold, though, if such a thing is possible. It absolutely bites into your body, cutting right through you. We are not yet far enough North to hit the ice pack, but we've been as close as 10 miles to it. Nor have we been close enough to Iceland to make out any definite characteristics - just a dark landmass on the horizon.

Now as I write some hours later it's been a lovely, calm featureless day, except when we have rounded Iceland at its highest latitude, which we do at regular intervals - up one side to just short of the ice, then back down the other side. The sea is gentle and although you couldn't feel the sun, it has been dazzling away just above the horizon.

The water is that brilliant pure blue you associate with the tropics. No snow yet, either. At the moment we're just going round to the various "havens". Our skipper, as Captain, Fishery Protection Squadron, wanders around haven to haven checking things are OK.

Tomorrow we point our bows north and plough into the vast emptiness of the ocean towards Bear Island, where the hardiest of fishermen go when the ice allows them.

This evening was wonderful. About 7pm the ship stopped and I braved the upper deck to see what was going on. About 250 yards away was a massive deep-sea trawler, and one of our seamen had been lowered in a large yellow dinghy to go over to her to swap mail for fish. The bridge searchlight beamed down on him as he paddled across the swell, now and then disappearing from view only to reappear again on the crest of a wave. The sea was black with millions of silver stars on it, stars of spray, which twinkled like diamonds as the sea whirled and eddied. The sky was black, no clouds were in sight, and the real stars were shining in all their glory. There was no moon. The searchlight lit up the by now tiny yellow speck on the ocean, and within its radius the sea was velvet blue. And overhead - the Northern Lights appeared! The sun was by now below the horizon, but its setting rays were directed onto the ice belt only a few miles away, and the reflection of the ice was in our piece of sky on our port side.

Long, vast, wide layers of what appeared to be dazzling white cloud, interspersed with purples and reds and greens and blues, with the stars shining through them, the whole twisting and weaving and spiralling, now closing, now spreading into several streams, as the icebergs heaved and pitched on the surface of the ocean.

Truly a memorable sight, which lasted for almost half an hour.

Eventually our dinghy returned, and I grabbed a rope and helped heave in four nets of fish, and finally the dinghy and the frozen matelot. (Apparently the same man always volunteers for the dodgy manoeuvre - I suspect the trawler skipper forces large quantities of whisky down his throat!)

There's been a wonderful smell of fresh cod and herring all night from the galley - fish so fresh it was probably still breathing when it hit the pan!

Tomorrow we're rendezvousing with another frigate, which has been up here for the statutory three weeks.

Later - Not a frigate, a destroyer, HMS Dunkirk. We were both stopped dead in the water, almost alone in a vast ocean, bobbing up and down, so clean looking and dashing and deadly. As she lowered a whaler for our mail I noticed a small hole in her starboard bow.

She'd just had a tussle with an Icelandic gunboat.

As we steamed away we saw a single trawler about 50 yards on her port quarter. This trawler had been buzzed by the Maria Júlia, which claimed she was fishing inside the 4 mile limit (which we do recognise, unlike the 12-mile one they're trying to impose) and told

HMS Palliser - a Run Ashore in Tromso. (Norman Robinson)

her to go with her to Iceland under arrest. Just then Dunkirk appeared on the horizon, like the US Cavalry, took a fix, and determined that the trawler was just a few yards outside the limit (how convenient!). The two warships then had a very hairy pushing and shoving match before the gunboat left, sending the usual warlike signals (they call us all the filth under the sun), and saying she was going to report Dunkirk for "threats of violence". Dunkirk remained in the area until we arrived and all has been quiet since then.

8th November 1959. The First Lieutenant announced that as the weather was too rough no special parade would be held, but the "still" would be sounded at 1100. All was indeed still then, as we thought of those we lost in the last war. When the "carry on" was piped the tannoy sounded the Last Post direct from the BBC.

We're headed for Bear Island, just under 1000 miles further north, and about 500 miles inside the Arctic Circle. What a vast, desolate place this is.

At the moment we're near Jan Mayen Island, about 260 miles inside. The skipper has just announced that Jan Mayen is twenty miles ahead, and has been picked up on radar, but due to the high winds and heavy seas over the last twelve hours, we will be too late to see it in daylight. We're due for a Storm Force 10 tomorrow. I am so lucky that I am never seasick, whilst all around me men, including our tough-looking veteran Captain, lead miserable existences.

Whew, we've just had a monstrous roll. The coxswain tells me we are rolling over 30 degrees each side, as well as the continuous pitching fore and aft. It's going to be another sleepless night for everybody. The Captain has just announced that no one is allowed on the upper decks at any time, even with a lifeline.

Next day - As predicted, the night was rough with winds freshening to Force 10-11. Breakfast was herrings swimming in oil (that chef is pushing his luck!). There's a very big swell. Now the wind has dropped the temperature is rising - 35F, wind Force 4-5 rising to 7 and Gale Force 8 tonight.

We're due some R&R soon - in Tromso, for heaven's sake - a little Norwegian town in the middle of nowhere.

12th November 1959. How wrong I was. Jack doesn't waste much time. Ten minutes after the gangway was thrown open the ship was deserted by nearly everybody but the duty watch.

This really is a beautiful place. The view from the upper deck is magnificent - snow capped mountains all around, a picturesque white bridge crossing the water, little boats

flitting about and the town nestling around the foot of the mountains. Everywhere has an air of grandeur.
The Norwegian Navy liaison officer, a Lieutenant, told us that they could not afford to lay on a dance for us. It's common knowledge that the Norwegian Navy is the poorest paid in the world.
So, the First Lieutenant asked me to whip round to the members of the ship's Welfare Committeeand ask them if they were prepared to subscribe £25 from the Welfare Fund for a dance tomorrow night. This was a very split vote, but eventually I got it through.
Nice music on the radio, but the Russians have just started jamming us again. When they do that with the official ship's radio and radar equipment it's a cat and mouse game - we change frequency, and see how long it takes them to find it. But with radio programmes there's nothing we can do about it, as we can't very well ask the BBC to shift to a fresh frequency every so often just for us! We receive BBC and Radio Luxembourg quite well when we are in harbour, but at sea so much depends on the ionospheric conditions. In really rough weather the aerials are bent nearly double, and reception is nil. Then the Russians (and, sometimes, the Danes) take it in their heads to jam us. And when the weather is rough and the ship is rolling a lot (and she usually is) the record players and tape-recorders are useless.
We are back to normal rig today. It felt so nice donning a white collar and shirt again. My boss has just come back aboard. He says you can buy a real polar-bear hearthrug for £2 10d.
13th November 1959. Once again the ship is almost deserted. Mind you, as well as the Duty Watch we have quite a few Open Arrests onboard. I've never seen so many men get so drunk as last night.
I thoroughly enjoyed the sightseeing tour this morning. We went over the town with a fine toothcomb. There are some magnificent sights. Half the population of Tromso make their living out of farming. I just can't see how they can make money out of this soil - though come to think of it, it's almost certainly volcanic and very rich. We stopped off at the cemetery and looked at the graves of those who lost their lives in the Tirpitz raid. So young, all of them. One inscription, on the headstone of a 15-year old boy seaman, was really tear jerking:

He called on some
To die, that others
In time to come
May have a song.

Poor little chap. The highlight of the tour was when the guide decided to pay a surprise visit on an old friend who had a huge place by the shore. This friend is an explorer/hunter. Periodically he takes off into the wilds of Bear Island and hunts seals and polar bears. He gave us a most interesting tour, showing us all his hunting equipment and his pelts. He breeds fish, and has them in large pools outside his house. Tunnels from these run under the house and come up into his living room, in one corner of which he has a beautiful fish tank. Well, maybe tank isn't the right word. It's a massive rectangular hole in the floor, tiled at the sides, into which the fish swim.
All over his ranch he has concealed microphones - built into dog-kennels, etc. - so that he is in constant communication with his wife in the house. He showed us his shed and his wonderful collection of parkas/anoraks. One beautiful example was made out of reindeer skin, but he dismissed it as being a cheap job. "But then I was only 14 when I killed this particular deer and made the coat". The best skins of all were husky dog ones.
His team of huskies was around the house, and of course we all fell for them right away. They are magnificent animals, and so friendly - with humans, but not with each other. Up they would jump and put their forepaws on your shoulders, as you dug your hands into their lovely fur. They stood about 6'6" on their hind legs, and weighed a ton! They were all chained up with a loose lead onto a long length of line giving them about 500

yards of free movement, but well separated from their brothers.
Chained up on a similar principle were two Arctic foxes. Like his dogs, they loved him, and bounded into his arms as he approached. They were afraid of us, though, but we stroked them when they were nestling in his arms. They, too, had wonderful warm fur.
He also kept 40 pigeons (for carrying messages back from the very far North), four cats and three children!
Later we found the famous Ale Hall and popped inside for a quick one. Quick it was, too. Dingy and dirty. You buy a ticket at the cash counter by the door, then present it to the barman at the other end of the room, and repeat the process if you want another. The beer was bottled light lager - disgusting.
Whaling and sealing is out of season, so we saw nothing of that.
17th December 59. At noon we were only 17 nautical miles away from HMS Russell, to whom we hoped to transfer mail. It's now 1950 and we still haven't reached her, which shows how bad the weather is. Nightmarish. Never have I seen seas like this, even after all this time on Arctic Patrol. My office is wrecked again.
It's awe-inspiring to see seas towering 80 feet above you when you're at the bottom of a trough, and next minute be on a pinnacle of water, with air all around you, the screw screaming round in space, and the sea eighty feet below.
One young lad was lifted up and flung 15 feet through the air, landing on a mess table. Both he and the table broke. The ship's carpenter mended the table, started walking away, the ship gave another bone-breaking lurch, the chippie took off onto the table and broke it again. I had no dinner tonight. I'd managed to slide a sausage, some boiled potatoes and a bit of onion gravy onto my plate. As I turned away I lost balance, shot along the deck at full speed, and ended up, food and all, on the doctor's lap. You should have seen Doc's bald pate glistening with thick brown onion gravy! However, he was too ill to take much notice.
Our engines are making 16 knots, but we're only actually making 2. It's cataclysmic weather. There is no way of getting aft in this ship without going on the upper deck, so the Stokers have to use the catwalks to get from their mess. When their messman collected 14 eggs and bacon from the galley this morning we had a sweepstake on how many he'd lose on the way back. The Watch on Deck tied a lifeline around him, and then he was gone. We couldn't see him for most of the way as he was completely under water. Later we found out that 14 Stokers shared 3 salt-water drenched eggs for breakfast.
The wind is still Storm Force 11. The skipper says that when we reach Icelandic waters, about 10pm, we may get a little lee, but it's only a maybe.
One nasty incident this morning. Sub Lieutenant Ainger was Officer of the Watch. At about 5am he left the enclosed bridge because the windscreen wipers couldn't cope with the hundreds of tons of water crashing over the screen, and he went onto the signal deck alongside it to look at a nearby fishing trawler which was in our path. Suddenly the ship gave a corkscrew turn; John took off, and was hanging onto the guardrail with one hand, over the ship's side. The lookout dragged him back in again. He came very very close to death.
Ainger has just come in to say that we're turning slightly to starboard to get the sea more friendlily orientated. He's bearing up surprisingly well considering his earlier adventure and his non-stop seasickness. But that's the thing about this mind-blowing weather - it's much too loftily superior for mere seasickness. You either live or you die in it - it's as simple as that. Things like eating, sleeping and so on are bonuses. I've got a tremendous admiration for our deep-sea fishermen. They spend up to 300 days a year at sea in their small boats. Every time I eat a bit of fish now I offer a silent thanks to those brave men.
There are now 9 fishing vessels up here - six in the haven, and the other three working independently. When they're in a haven and

'Roughers!' HMS Palliser, stern awash, off Icealnd.
(Norman Robinson)

come across a large school of fish, they pool information and decide, by ballot if necessary, which is the most favourable area and proceed to fish there.

So a haven is not what we think of as a haven - far from it, where the weather is worst, it seems, there are the fish.

21st December 59. We have had an abnormal amount of daylight today, even though there was little or no sun. It was light by 10am, the sun sort of bobbed up for a short while over the horizon at one, and it didn't go dark until about four-ish.

Incidentally, as we are at sea all the time we don't mess about with local times, we stick to GMT.

The First Lieutenant has warned us all not to get drunk on Christmas Day (fat chance). The Captain has received intelligence that the gunboats are going to make a sortie on the afternoon of the 25th, hoping to catch us with our pants down.

Plan A for Christmas Day is as follows. We each get 2 cans of beer at 1115. There is no set breakfast, but sausage and bacon rolls will be available for the early watchmen and anyone else with an appetite (me). A fat Engineer will dress up as Father Christmas and distribute beer and gifts donated by the fishermen. The First Lieutenant's friend the Archbishop of Lewes has tape-recorded a short service, which we hope to receive in tomorrow's mail. Our carol-singing efforts will be played back and judged.

We all look forward so much to the mail, and when none comes (because it can only be transferred in good weather) we get very low and depressed.

22nd December 59. Pitch black and bitterly cold. Sauté kidney and fried bread for breakfast, and eventually a cup of tea. The last storm smashed all but two of our cups, so we have to take it in turns and drink quickly so the next man can use the cup. All the rum glasses went too, so everyone shares a chipped jam jar.

9pm. Spent an hour watching aircraft. There were two of them, both Shackletons. The first one contained one Admiral, four Group Captains and our mail. The second was full of Press and TV cameramen, to photograph our brave lads and the unusual mail drop. We all lined the upper decks waving and cheering like mad.

In all nineteen canisters of mail were dropped for us and the Undine. Later on in the day we heard that a trawler had some mail for us, so we increased to 16 knots and raced towards her.

At 10am tomorrow we're refuelling from Wave Baron, which is fresh out of UK.

23rd December 59. We've been battling in the teeth of a fierce gale all day today. We fuelled from the Wave Baron at 10am. It was a long drawn out affair because she'd sailed with a scratch crew who kept getting the hoses all tangled up. They had three very sick men aboard, so we sent the Doctor over on the jackstay. On both the outboard and inboard journeys he was dipped into the water and I don't think it was entirely coincidental! The tanker had no mail for us, but then we were only half-expecting it. We had a lovely piece of roast pork for lunch today.

To compensate, supper was abominable - salt-spoiled bacon rolls.

Xmas Eve 1959. Our Quartermaster fell from top to bottom of the bridge ladder today. His right hand was badly ripped, blood everywhere, and his wrist is broken.

All day long signals of Yuletide fervour have been pouring in, many of them in rhyme. One from the "Daily Mirror" - presumably it was their cameramen in the aircraft.

We have had a medium-rough day today, and the same is forecast for tomorrow. Tonight at eight we had a Carol Service, consisting of 10 carols and 9 lessons. It was wonderful. We had about 120 people squashed down in the After Seamen's Messdeck. I had to read the 5th Lesson, the one about Scribes[38] *and Pharisees! Then we got a Skiffle Group going, with two guitars, a harmonica and numerous weird homemade instruments. I opened my last packet of cigarettes - it'll be a long time till I'm able to get more.*

Xmas Day 1959. A bizarre day today - especially on one of Her Majesty's Warships on operational duty! At eight o'clock the First Lieutenant staggered out onto the bridge to greet the morning. The first thing to meet his horror-stricken gaze was a hammock flying from the masthead. On it was drawn a perfect caricature of the skipper, complete with bushy black bread and huge red shiny conk. They had to disconnect the radar set for half an hour so someone could shin up and get the hammock down.

Then the announcement "The Wave Baron is six miles away and she has seven bags of mail for us". The crafty beggars hadn't given it to us when we refuelled, but saved it for today. What a wonderful surprise. Then we all got cracking on the messdeck. We put decorations up, with a shiningly clean white tablecloth (two sheets sewn together) and laid 13 places at table with crackers, cigars, dishes of fruit and nuts and a Christmas Cake in the centre - all saved up from various parcels from home.

Father Christmas visited, dishing out biscuits and chocolate. Then a visit from the "Captain", the youngest man aboard, a 16-year old signalman in Captain Bracken's best uniform!

We had a magnificent dinner - the Trawler Owners' Federation had really done us proud - followed by a mass conga around the ship.

11pm. Christmas doesn't last very long in the Navy - we're taking the decorations down to make way for hammocks. We are having a lovely display of Aurora Borealis tonight. I've just read that it isn't caused by the ice floes at all, but by something horribly technical to do with the diffusion of particles of dust thrown out by the sun. I prefer my original explanation!

Our signalman's hand is causing trouble - the Doc has just asked me to hold the X-ray machine steady for a few minutes while he has another look.

Boxing Day 1959. Yesterday was just the calm before the storm - and what a storm! It's really quite frightening, this little steel box being thrown around like a piece of tissue.

We managed to get mail off to a trawler about 11am, by liferaft transfer. AB Clark is a flipping hero for my money, taking that little dinghy out in gigantic seas. He lashes himself into it, and when the craft overturns, as it occasionally does, and he is sent under the icy waters, he calmly rocks back and forth until a wave catches him and rolls him upright again. He's done about 130 transfers to date, and has a well-earned decoration for bravery.

Another nasty incident today. The ship cartwheeled and as usual 5 Mess finished up in 4

[38] The Ship's Writer was often called 'Scribes'.

Mess, bodies, crockery, the lot. One man landed up with an awful smack 20 feet away from his original position. Another young lad came hurtling after him, and whilst in full flight smashed his windpipe against a metal edge. He went out like a light, right by my feet. I knew there was a good chance he'd broken his neck, so I told everyone not to touch him and sent someone off for the Doc. Fortunately young Wilson must have a very thick neck, and he was only concussed.'

HMS *Armada* (Commander Mark Kerr) was 'stand by ship for Iceland Patrol over Christmas', but as the ship's end-of-commission book notes:

'Once again it looked as though it was going to be too good to be true. But our luck held ... or perhaps changed for the better ... and a happy, if hectic, Christmas was held be all ... even the few who stayed behind to look after the ship in Portsmouth.
Only one thing marred the festivities of the Christmas leave and that was the news of the tragic loss of the trawler Red Falcon with all hands. We had seen a great deal of her up off Iceland, and had listened to the Radio Officer's poems over the Haven Net. We did what we could, and sent off a cheque for £50 to the Mayor of Fleetwood for the relief fund.'

With the new Icelandic government having a full mandate, once again, Britain hoped that negotiations might be possible, although there were still concerns that NATO membership and the Keflavík base might be brought into the argument. The Second UN Conference on the Law of the Sea (UNCLOS2) was due to open on 15th March 1960 and the British government was also worried that incidents off Iceland during the conference could damage its position. There were Icelandic hints that the charges that had accumulated against British trawlers fishing within 12 miles might be dropped in exchange for the withdrawal of naval protection. The British also had to get to grips with the reality that the international battle over a 12-mile limit was all but lost. The best that could be hoped for was an acceptance of 12 miles, with a phasing out period for those with 'historic rights'. Not surprisingly, whilst these very tentative talks were going on - no doubt they'd be spun as 'talks about talks' today - the CTG was told to keep things cool on the fishing grounds.

The NATO Secretary General, Paul Henri Spaak, and Halvard Lange of Norway reluctantly, having been misled once, if not twice, by the Icelanders' intransigence in 1958, became involved in secret mediation efforts. On 22nd January they produced a draft agreement under which the British would withdraw their patrols and cease all fishing within 12 miles; in exchange all poaching charges against British trawlers would be, irrevocably, dropped. Nothing in this agreement was to prejudice the positions of Britain or Iceland at UNCLOS2. Despite an almost complete surrender by the British, Iceland managed to find fault with these proposals - they would have to drop charges entirely, but the British could still reinstate their patrols!

The Icelandic Ambassador to NATO admitted to the two negotiators that 'frankly' the Icelandic authorities were not that keen to see the warships leave..... As the new British Ambassador in Reykjavik, Charles Stewart, noted, on hearing this, they 'might not be too displeased if there should be a small "incident" during or immediately before the … conference. They would then be able to pose as the innocent small nation being bullied by an imperialistic big brother'.

The British were less keen on the proposal because it did not allow any phasing out of 'historic rights' at all. The Icelandic Ambassador retorted that the 12-mile limit had assumed an 'almost religious importance' in Iceland and that any 'compromise' would have to involve a complete British withdrawal. There was no further attempt at reaching an agreement before UNCLOS.

The British are often seen as the villains, albeit for understandable historic reasons, of the whole Cod War saga, but I am once again indebted to Gudni Jóhannesson - this time for an Icelandic proverb:

'Rarely bears but one side blame when two fall foul.'

In February 1960, the Icelandic Coastguard was reinforced by the commissioning of the new 1000 ton, 20 knot *Ódinn*. The old *Ódinn*, built in 1938, was renamed *Gautur* and remained in Coastguard service.

HMS *Apollo* was back on patrol in February when

the birth of HRH Prince Andrew was announced. Captain Mike Lumby (a submariner, not a gunnery officer as it happens) decided to celebrate this event by firing a 21-gun salute. It was pretty rough and, no doubt, the gunnery officer was most embarrassed by the irregular timing of the salute, but the crew of the forward 4-inch gun (an open mounting) managed to complete their task and a signal was sent to Her Majesty congratulating her on the birth and claiming the most northerly gun salute in celebration. Vic Richards reports that, after this, the ship hit more heavy weather and the forward mounting was so badly damaged that water came into the mess deck below. In the same storm, the open bridge (on 02[39] deck) took a green wave and the water found it's way down 5 decks to the Stokers' Mess on 3 deck.

The winter was fairly quiet. The first incident of the New Year coming on 21st February when *Albert* fired warning shots 'near' the *James Barrie* in an attempt to arrest her. Bill Clark, the *James Barrie's* skipper, told the press when he returned to Hull:

> *'We were making our first run with the trawl down when the Albert came up at full speed. She went away but came back when we were hauling the first catch. Her boarding party of seven or eight men were lining her rails. She came up astern of us on our port side, hoping to nip in and board us while we were busy on the starboard side with our trawl. But I sent half the crew on to the boat deck with broom and mop handles and their bare fists to repel any boarding attempt, while the rest of us got on with clearing the trawl.*
>
> *To get up speed, I let the trawl run out behind us, but one of the two lines was cut by the propeller. We had radioed the Navy protection ship Palliser for help and had got up to about eight knots when the trawl fouled the bottom, and the second line snapped.*
>
> *While this was going on the gunboat banged off six shots from her two-pounder. Palliser came up fast and steamed between us and Albert and their two captains argued it out over the radio. Eventually Albert turned back.'*

Speaking in 2005, Skipper Bill Clark said that he will never forget this date:

45 years on....Now 84, Skipper Bill Clark points out the position that the ICGV Albert fired six warning shots at his trawler, James Barrie, in an attempt to arrest him. *(Ken Knox)*

[39] Decks are numbered down from the main (open) upper deck, which is 1 deck and up as 01, 02 etc. Hence the five decks between 02 and 3.

'They were shots supposed to be across the bow but the mate and I ended up on our knees and shaking on the bridge. I steamed all the way to the Norwegian coast.'

As the winter, which was as quiet as expected, moved into spring, the British Government considered how to improve their bargaining position for UNCLOS - one obvious way was to make a goodwill gesture by withdrawing from the 12-mile limit. The Admiralty was keen to stop the patrols, but the Foreign Secretary, Selwyn Lloyd, felt that a withdrawal would weaken Britain's case and the fishermen would see it as a 'betrayal of their interests'. The Foreign Office Legal Adviser's view, however, was that 'the maintenance of naval protection during the conference cannot fail to place us morally under a cloud, and to make it less likely that we shall achieve our aims'.

Eventually, the British Trawler Federation was persuaded by the British government to announce that British trawlers would be completely withdrawn from Icelandic waters during UNCLOS2 - just to have withdrawn outside 12 miles, might have been seen as recognition of the 12-mile limit. They probably also recognised that there would always be some skippers who would try to get away with fishing inside 12 miles and could then cause a very embarrassing incident during the conference. According to the Admiralty records, this concession seemed to spur the Coastguard into a flurry of attempted arrests, probably just to show that they weren't going to make any matching concessions. Contradictorily, the Icelandic records show that, in very early March (the report from the British Ambassador was sent on the 3rd), the Icelandic Minister of Justice, Bjarni Benediktsson, who had overall command of the Coastguard Service, secretly ordered his Captains to 'avoid incidents'. Both reports may, of course, have been true, as we have already seen that the Coastguard skippers were not always fully 'under command'.

At midnight on 14th March 1960, the day before UNCLOS2 opened in Geneva, the trawlers withdrew from Icelandic waters. Operation Whippet was suspended and *HM Ships Paladin* and *Undine* retired from the area.

A Summary of the first 18 months

By the time the British trawlers withdrew outside 12 miles, continuous Royal Navy protection had been given for 18 months, along with the medical and technical support necessary for the fishermen to operate without recourse to Icelandic ports. Fishing had continued almost normally, although catches were about 15% down on the years immediately before the dispute. There had been 71 serious attempts to arrest British trawlers and many incidents of harassment.

49 warships and 8 Royal Fleet Auxiliary tankers had shared the patrol, with the Fishery Protection Squadron and 3 RFAs taking most of the load. The details of the patrol stalwarts are:

	No of patrols	Days off Iceland
HMS *Palliser*	10	168
HMS *Russell*	9	167
HMS *Duncan*	9	139
HMS *Malcolm*	7	98
HMS *Lagos*	3	59
HMS *Trafalgar*	3	55
HMS *Dunkirk*	3	55
HMS *Hogue*	3	54
HMS *Jutland*	3	54
RFA *Wave Chief*		169
RFA *Wave Baron*		150
RFA *Wave Ruler*		136

Commodore Barry Anderson and his staff spent 180 days off Iceland, Lieutenant-Commander Peter Corson, in HMS *Russell*, logged 150 days, Commander 'Slug' Notley, in HMS *Malcolm* did 118 days, including a period as CTG in HMS *Russell* and Lieutenant-Commander Geoff Hammond in HMS *Palliser* did 110 days.

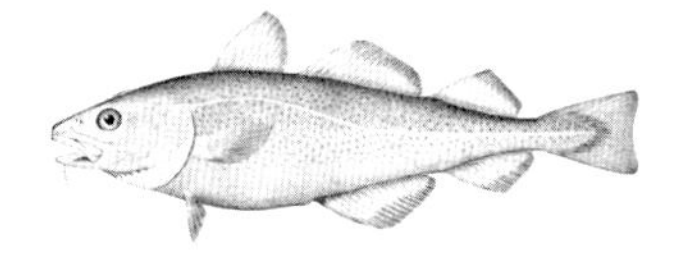

CHAPTER 7

THE FIRST COD WAR
MARCH 1960 - MARCH 1961

With British trawlers out of Icelandic waters and British warships withdrawn from the area, it was time for the diplomats to return to centre stage. The Second Law of the Sea Conference (UNCLOS2) opened in Geneva on 16th March 1960. It only needed to agree on one topic, the width of territorial seas. The British government was keen to settle the dispute, but without being accused by the fishermen of selling out. With the Icelanders intent on not giving an inch, these two objectives were incompatible.

The UK had proposed a 6-mile limit at the First Law of the Sea Conference in Geneva in 1958 and, just before the First Cod War started, had hinted heavily at a willingness to accept 12 miles, with some 'historic rights' between 6 and 12. By mid-1959, there was widespread agreement between the Whitehall departments that a 12-mile limit of some kind, hopefully with some flexibility, was inevitable. Britain was in discussions with both the US and Canada – hoping to have an agreed western position before the Conference started. The US was determined on 6 miles of territorial waters and was prepared to trade fishing limits and historic rights out to 12 miles to obtain them. The Canadian view was that a plain 6+6 (six territorial + six fishing with no historic rights) was the minimum that the West could sensibly hope for. Eventually, the US and Canada agreed on 6+6 with time-limited historic rights.

The British had great difficulty with this, but eventually accepted it. Macmillan even admitted that Britain might have to accept the plain 6+6 solution. The problem was that it was still believed that a blanket 12-mile limit would cause serious difficulties for the British deep-sea fishermen and a period would be needed for adjustment if significant unemployment was to be avoided. It was also feared that, if Britain gave in too easily, Iceland would extend her claimed limits sooner rather than later.

In Reykjavik, after a bit of internal discussion about the possibility of a minor compromise, limited short-term 'historic rights' inside 12 miles, coalition infighting meant that no party could be seen to be weakening on 12 miles. Domestic politics triumphed over international ones and Iceland entered the Conference committed to 12 miles, with no concessions and with a determination to stick with 12 miles, whatever UNCLOS2 decided.

Before the final session, the Americans, with British support, lobbied very hard, not just in Geneva, but also throughout the world for the proposed 12-mile limit with 10-year historic rights. They entered the final day with an assumed margin of five to six votes for this proposal. To their surprise, the proposal gained 54 votes, with 28 against (Iceland voted against) and 6 abstentions. As a two-thirds majority was required, the vote was lost by one vote. Ecuador, Chile, Japan and the Philippines had 'defected' at the last moment. One British delegate blamed the US for lobbying too aggressively - 'like a bull in a china shop'.

Whatever had caused this miscalculation, the net result was that, for the second time at a UN Law of the Sea Conference, no agreement was reached on the width of territorial waters. UNCLOS2 closed on 25th April 1960. The British view, in public, was that the legal limit remained 3 miles, but they were prepared to acknowledge four. The Icelanders thought that their 12-mile limit stood. However, the British privately acknowledged that any realistic limit would now be based on 12 miles, with or without some concessions.

In order to allow negotiations to continue after UNCLOS2, the British government persuaded the

British Trawler Federation to restrict fishing to outside 12 miles for three months and then announced that the Royal Navy would only patrol outside that limit. Fishing and naval protection resumed outside 12 miles on 28th April. Meanwhile, there was another skirmish to be fought over fishing limits.

EFTA and Norwegian Fish

EFTA, the European Free Trade Area (Austria, Britain, Denmark, Norway, Portugal, Sweden and Switzerland), had formally come into existence on 4th January 1960 - just before UNCLOS2. Although foodstuffs were specifically excluded from the EFTA agreement, Norway had negotiated an agreement over frozen fish fillets (an 'industrial product'!). Part of this agreement, allowing Scandinavian countries to import 24,000 tons of frozen fish into the UK tax-free, was that the agreement would be renegotiated if fishing limits were changed.

Almost as soon as UNCLOS2 was over, the Norwegian government came under strong domestic pressure to follow Iceland and announced the intention to declare a 12-mile limit on 13th May. However, no date for implementation was set because of the need to hold talks with interested parties - i.e. mainly the British government. The talk lasted several months, as these things do, but there was never much doubt that a mutually acceptable agreement would be reached, based upon the 6+6 proposal that had been only just lost at UNCLOS2. The 'historic rights' would be phased out over 10 years. Norwegian territorial waters were extended from 4 to 6 miles in April 1961 and on to 12 miles in September of the same year.

Any hope that this compromise agreement, reached between two countries that were close allies in so many senses, would influence the position in Iceland was completely unfounded.

The Patrols resume

Two warships and one Royal Fleet Auxiliary had been kept at 72 hours notice to resume the patrol throughout the Conference. On 26th April 1960, *HM Ships Delight* and *Palliser* were sailed, followed by *RFA Wave Ruler* on the 27th. HMS *Battleaxe* joined them off Iceland on the 31st. New instructions were signalled by the Admiralty, amplified by CFPS (Captain Hugo Bracken), Captain Fishery Protection Squadron, and issued as Operation MINT. The new mission was:

- *Primarily to support British trawlers in the fishing grounds off Iceland by giving them medical and mechanical assistance.*

HMS Battleaxe (MoD/Crown Copyright)

- *To protect trawlers if arrest is attempted outside the 12-mile limit.*

- *To protect trawlers between the 4 and 12 mile line if they disobey their owners' instructions regarding fishing inside the 12-mile limit, and arrest is attempted by an Icelandic gunboat in the vicinity of an HM ship.*

It was also emphasised that 'In the present very delicate diplomatic situation (May 1960), it is extremely important to avoid incidents.' The outline plan was to establish patrol areas along and outside the 12-mile limit. These areas would be based on the advice of the Liaison Skippers. The trawlers were to report in when they arrived in the area and when they left and to keep the warships informed of their general movements. Warships were to warn trawlers in or too near to the 12 mile limit, but no more. Only the owners could order them out. If, in spite, of the warnings and their owner's instructions, a trawler fishing inside 12 miles was threatened with arrest, then warships could enter the 12-mile limit to give protection. The skippers were not informed of this last instruction, in case they took deliberate advantage of it. It was hoped that they would obey their owner's instructions. The orders for the use of force were the same as they had been under Operation WHIPPET. Initially, HMS *Delight*, commanded by Captain Peter Dickens, patrolled off Stokksnes on the southeast coast, HMS *Palliser*, now commanded by Lieutenant-Commander the Honourable John Fremantle, was off the northwest coast and HMS *Battleaxe* was off Ingolfshöfdi, on the south coast. Very quickly about 100 trawlers had gathered for the spring fishing.

Surgeon Lieutenant John Curt was the 'Doc' in HMS *Battleaxe*. He remembers that, after four days of heavy weather, he was transferred to a trawler where the Radio Officer had a severe 'personal' problem. The transfer was done, as usual, in a rubber dinghy. The Coston gunline was fired from a .303 rifle, a line exchanged and the dinghy was pulled over to the trawler. There was no ladder; as the trawler rolled, he jumped and was grabbed by the crew. They heaved him up vertically and he arrived on deck head down.... It was quickly obvious that the man needed to be treated in *Battleaxe*. The skipper offered him a whisky whilst the radio officer packed his suitcase. He declined, but the skipper said that he's never met a non-drinking Scotsman before, so Doc felt he had to have one 'for the honour of Scotland'. This turned out to be a tumbler full of whisky. Back into the dinghy; patient first and doc last, followed by a 'gift' of fish heaped all over the dinghy's occupants.

Once the patient was safely in the sickbay, he reported to the Commanding Officer (Commander Jack Maidwell) who said 'well done Doc - I've poured you a large brandy .... One other thing that Doc Curt remembers is that the gunboats were referred to as 'man in grey' when reported by trawlers, although the Aberdonians called them the 'wee grey moose'.

The Icelanders were unable to see the decision to stay outside 12 miles as a gesture aimed at helping the fragile negotiations, but regarded it as a British acceptance of their position of 12 miles with no concessions. Whilst the British let it be known through foreign diplomats in London that a 12-mile limit with 2-3 years of 'historic rights' (as Iceland had offered in 1958) would be acceptable, Iceland said - to quote the *Navy News* in May 1960 'We are all right Jack, to **** with you.'

Nevertheless, as so often in Iceland's tangled political world, there was no 100% agreed position. There were those who felt that it would be better to get the dispute with Britain over and, on April 29th, the Justice Minister announced that all poaching charges against British trawlers would be dropped, so that they could enter Icelandic ports and take shelter in Icelandic waters (provided their fishing gear was completely stowed). The Aberdeen trawler *Alexander Bruce* was the first to risk going into port on 1st May and encountered no hostility in Reykjavik. Simultaneously, to the irritation of the Grimsby Trawler Officers' Guild, Icelandic trawlers re-started landing fresh fish in the UK.

The Icelandic concession removed some of the rationale for having the Royal Navy on patrol, but as the Foreign Office felt that a complete withdrawal would signal a clear surrender and 'evoke criticism from the trawler industry and in Parliament' the 3-ship patrol was, initially, maintained. The patrol was to be reduced to two ships about six weeks later, with the third ship at 24 hours notice to deploy.

HMS Crossbow.
(MoD/Crown Copyright)

Inside 12 miles again

As the Navy had suspected, and feared, there were many skippers who were not prepared to follow their owners' instructions and started fishing inside 12 miles - to the extent that about half of the British catch was coming from inside 12 miles. Initially, the Icelandic Coastguard just warned them (the Icelandic government had issued secret instructions to the gunboat skippers 'to use all discretion and avoid incidents wherever possible') and three or four trawlers would be reported to HM Ships by gunboats or the Catalina seaplane every day, with a peak of eleven on 9th June. The Admiralty's protests to the British Trawler Federation persuaded the owners to suspend repeat offenders, but it has to be remembered that most of the skipper's pay was based on the size of his catch - and owners benefited even more from a good catch. The disregard of the skippers for their owners' instructions put the warships into a very difficult position - the fishermen began to see the Royal Navy as doing the Icelandic Coastguard's job and keeping them from their favourite fishing grounds.

The job of preventing incidents whilst protecting 'sinning' skippers required a tightrope walker's skill and patience. On the 9th June 1960, the day when there were eleven sinning skippers, the CO of HMS *Crossbow* (Commander Donald Hay) was so provoked as to order one skipper to leave the 12-mile zone. This action produced a furious response from the fishermen, leading to a very embarrassing parliamentary question about the British government's position on the width of territorial waters.

Eventually, the Icelandic government stated that trawlers fishing 'illegally' inside 12 miles would be arrested. *Albert* made the first attempt against the trawler *Thuringia* on 22nd June when shots are said to have fallen only 9 feet from the trawler. In the next three weeks there were nine boarding attempts accompanied by the firing of blank and solid rounds or the dropping of flares from a Catalina.

On 28th June, *Thor* succeeded in getting a boarding party onboard the *Northern Queen.* The initial sighting report, at 1.8 miles inside the limit, had been made from a Catalina. HMS *Duncan* (with Captain 'Fish' - Hugo Bracken in command) had intercepted this report and challenged its accuracy. By the time *Thor* had caught up with the trawler, she was outside 12 miles. The skipper of *Northern Queen*, a well-known poacher in the Icelandic books, insisted that he had been outside 12 miles throughout and, when HMS *Duncan* sent her boarding party over, *Thor's* men withdrew under protest.

Things got more serious on 10th July, when, according to the Coastguard, *Grimsby Town* (another regular on their black list), tried to ram the *Ódinn*. *Ódinn* fired warning shots and ordered *Grimsby Town* to stop. When she failed to do so, *Ódinn* fired a solid round through her superstructure. According to Icelandic records, this was the first time that a shot had been fired at a poacher since 1954, when Belgian trawlers had been particularly difficult off the south coast. HMS *Palliser* arrived on the scene before the incident had escalated any further and *Ódinn* departed complaining that *Palliser* had interfered with his justified arrest of the *Grimsby Town*.

This was the only occasion during the whole two and a half years of the First Cod War that either side fired a shot intended to hit. The incident provoked demands from the trawlermen for more protection and spurred the two governments into greater efforts to find a solution before there was a really serious incident. In Iceland the left-wing leader Hermann Jónasson, called for the government to seek naval assistance from the United States under the terms of the 1951 Defence Agreement. The Socialists jumped on the bandwagon because they knew this would worry the Americans and increase the effectiveness of the 'close Keflavík - leave NATO' bogey. American concerns were real, because Bjarni Benediktsson of the Conservative Party had, back in May, warned them that, if Britain resumed patrols within 12 miles:

> *'Icelandic government with his support and on his initiative would withdraw from NATO. Benediktsson said, with considerable feeling, that this was not a threat but a statement of cold fact which he made despite the fact that he had always been, and was now, a whole-hearted supporter of NATO.'*

The British took this warning as seriously as the Americans, whilst believing that 'there must clearly be a large element of bluff and blackmail in such a statement.'

The British Trawler Federation's three-month 'truce' was due to end on 12th August 1960, but no negotiations had as yet started. There were threats of strikes by the fishermen and threats to re-impose the ban on the landing of Icelandic catches. In anticipation of the decision by the BTF to return to fishing inside 12 miles, the Admiralty had prepared a further Operation Order - for Operation BAILIFF. BAILIFF was based on protecting 3 fishing havens (to be called Pheasant, Partridge and Woodcock) between 6 miles and 12 for 5 years - the 6+6 proposal, with 'historic rights' that was very nearly agreed at UNCLOS2. The British government believed that this adherence to the 'almost' resolution of UNCLOS2 would give their action some international legitimacy.

The owners were prepared to accept this plan, but, whilst preparing for the worst, the government was working very hard to find a basis on which to start talks with Iceland. So, on 6th August, the Government persuaded the BTF to abide by the 12-mile limit for another two months. On 10th August, the Icelandic government announced that it was ready to start talks.

Meanwhile - back at sea ....

On the evening of 13th September 1960, the trawler *Lord Lloyd*, off the Whaleback on Iceland's southwest corner, reported an engine breakdown, a split in the hull and serious flooding. HMS *Saintes*, commanded by Commander Mike Porter, the CTG, proceeded to assist. Fred Deeks was one of the engine room artificers onboard. He remembers that:

> *'There was a considerable gale blowing and there were fears that the trawler would sink. We steamed off at as near maximum power as the weather would allow, to provide assistance. It was a hair-raising journey and many times we were grateful to the ship builders who had put Saintes together. As the propellers came out of the water, the vibration was terrific and often a large lump of rusty metal fell off the main engine and condenser bearings.'*

Saintes and arrived on the scene at 2150 to find *Lord Lloyd* abandoned, but not sinking. Her crew were in another trawler, the *Wyre Mariner*, whose crew with the assistance of a Belgian trawler, had succeeded in stopping the flooding, but had not been able to start the engine. With the owner's agreement, it was decided that *Wyre Mariner* would tow *Lord Lloyd* into Seydisfjord for repairs. The ETA was 1740 next day.

At 1600, the British Ambassador received an urgent call from the Ministry of Foreign Affairs asking that HMS *Saintes* tell *Wyre Mariner* not to enter harbour, but that another trawler or warship should take up the tow. Clearly there was still a 'black list of poachers' and because *Wyre Mariner* was on it, the Coastguard would feel obliged to arrest her if she entered harbour. The Ministry of Foreign Affairs was clearly trying to avoid an incident in the run up to talks, but unfortunately the Ambassador's message did not reach HMS *Saintes* in time. The skipper of the *Wyre Mariner* was arrested, charged with illegal fishing inside the 12 mile limit on 7th July 1960 and was fined £2000. The *Lord Lloyd* was swiftly repaired without any problems.

John Lawson, who was the Squadron Gunnery Officer in HMS *Daring*, on patrol during this period, remembers that watchkeepers had to be shaken 30 minutes early because it took so long to get into the foul-weather clothing necessary before you could spend 4 hours on watch on the open bridge.[40]

The second 'truce' was due to expire on 12th October and as this date approached there was no obvious progress towards talks. The Navy was making final preparations to start Operation BAILIFF when, on 1st October, talks finally started. The patrol's priority now became to ensure that there were no incidents on the fishing grounds. There was one attempted arrest when a gunboat (never identified) fired warning shots near the *William Wilberforce*. The gunboat had retired from the scene before HMS *Duncan* arrived. December 1960 was very quiet; both in terms of fishing and of gunboat activity. The last arrest attempt was by a Coastguard Catalina, which ordered the *Red Knight* to stop and await arrest. The trawler continued fishing and no gunboat appeared.

Talks at last

Having announced a willingness to talk (but note not to 'negotiate'), the Icelandic government then told the British that a pause would be needed so that the initial domestic political uproar could subside. Predictably, the left wing[41] parties condemned the move and numerous organisations, such as local councils and trades unions passed resolutions affirming that there must be no retreat from the 12-mile limit. The government also needed time to consult fully with its own supporters - once again the problem of coalition politics. Towards the end of August,

HMS Daring (MoD/Crown Copyright)

[40] At this time, almost all destroyers and frigates had open bridges. It was the Cold War nuclear, biological and chemical threat, with the need to be able to make the ship airtight that hastened the move towards enclosed bridges.

[41] In British political terms, the centre of Icelandic politics is to the left of centre. At this time, the Socialists & Progressives were the opposition & the Conservatives & Social Democrats were in power (but only just).

the Conservative leader confided in the British Ambassador that at least two of his MPs could not bring themselves to agree to any compromise on the 12-mile limit and so any deal would not get a majority in the *Althing* (the Icelandic parliament). The Social Democrat leader was a bit more optimistic. However on 23rd September 1960, the Prime Minister was warning that his government might fall. The British Ambassador, Charles Stewart, reported to London that Icelandic ministers would not be risking the charges of submitting to Britain unless they really wanted a settlement. In London, Christopher Soames, now the Fishery Minister, and his officials thought that the Icelanders were just playing for time. As is often the fate of Ambassadors when reporting unwanted views, Charles Stewart was accused of 'going native' - 'appears to be more Icelandic than the Icelanders'. Whilst the Fishery department wanted to stand firm, the Foreign Office were clear that a return to naval patrolling inside 12 miles was not a realistic option.

Both sides were having trouble with one of the five 'Ps'[42] - Prestige in this case. Britain was afraid of losing more and Iceland, having only been independent for 16 years, was determined to build some. His opponents were still taunting Ólafur Thors, the Prime Minister, over his failure to see any British Ministers during his visit to London as Fishery Minister in January 1952. He had made it quite clear to the British Embassy that 'he wouldn't talk to anyone except Macmillan'.

The British were very happy to bolster Ólafur Thors's prestige within Iceland, as it would make it easier for him to sell any agreement to his own people. Macmillan, who was a fan of 'summit diplomacy', readily agreed to play his part and, en route to the UN in New York on September 25th, he stopped off in Keflavík to have a working lunch with Ólafur Thors.

At this lunch, both set out their (predictable) cases. Macmillan emphasised the great respect in which trawlermen were held after their sacrifices in two world wars, how their very livelihood was at stake, that Britain would have to accept the principle of a 12-mile limit, but that a phasing out of fishing outside 6 miles was essential - over 5 years half the period agreed with Norway.

Thors responded that the 12-mile limit had become 'a national issue, almost obsessive'.[43] Macmillan said that there could be limits within the outer 6 miles and that Britain might be able to offer Iceland economic assistance. Thors said that 'it was too late, the Icelandic people believed that the 12-mile battle was already won.' Macmillan demurred and said that if Iceland attacked British fishermen fishing within international law, they would have to be defended. That would cause the Icelandic government to fall and Iceland would fall under Soviet control.

Macmillan left unimpressed with Thors - 'a nice old boy, but clearly a weak man in a weak position'. Thors's rattling of the communist skeleton had, inevitably, irritated Macmillan and Macmillan thought that, if pressed, Thors would give something. He was right and, shortly afterwards, Charles Stewart was able to report that Macmillan's visit had been a success 'if only because Mr Thors now realises, from the highest level, that Iceland too must make a contribution to an agreement'.

The logjam had been broken and on October 1st 1960, only 12 days before the BTF's second 'truce' was due to expire, formal negotiations began in Reykjavik. Sir Patrick Reilly, Head of the Economics Department in the Foreign Office, led the British team. The Socialists brought their supporters out onto the streets with the slogan 'No deal - no retreat - no surrender'. Even in the ruling coalition, there were some MPs unconvinced of the need for Iceland to make any concessions at all.

The talks were not easy. Iceland made it clear that they intended, in due course, to extend their fishing limits to 50 miles, the edge of their continental shelf. They also wanted restrictions outside 12 miles and longer baselines in exchange for any concessions inside - and those would be less than the British wanted, or believed that they could 'sell' on Humberside. The first round of talks ended with London less optimistic about reaching any kind of acceptable agreement. However, there was really no other option than to negotiate and the British government persuaded the BTF to extend their 'truce'.

The Soviet Premier, Khrushchev, was also, now playing the Icelandic card. As Sir Alec Douglas

[42] Pressure, Prestige, Principle, Precedent & Power. See Chapter 2 for more information.

[43] It was, of course, the politicians who had made it so.

Home, the Foreign Secretary commented 'Khrushchev was in a dangerous mood; he was trying throughout the world, for example in the Congo, Cuba and Laos, to bring countries into the Communist embrace and (at the UN) he had specifically named Iceland.' Sir Patrick Reilly, the leader of the British team at the Reykjavik talks and ex-British Ambassador in Moscow, felt that Khrushchev 'might jump at the chance to intervene in another colonialist affair .... by sending warships to Icelandic waters.' Unsurprisingly, these strategic issues were less important in Humberside than in Whitehall.

Talks resumed in London on 27th October. The Icelandic position was even more intransigent, with even longer baselines and more restrictions outside 12 miles. The leader of the Icelandic team, Hans G Anderson, admitted that he did not expect the British to be able to accept the Icelandic terms and the Fisheries Director, David Ólafsson, who was also on the team declared that they were influenced by the need to satisfy the selfish short-term needs of Iceland's inshore fishermen 'poorly educated and primitive people (who) were primarily concerned to get an eye for an eye, and a tooth for a tooth in terms of practical sea areas'. It was not only Britain whose national policy was being driven by parochial interests.

The talks continued intermittently over the winter, with Britain thinking that Iceland had agreed concessions, such as an agreement that any future dispute would be referred to the International Court of Justice (ICJ) in The Hague, only to find that, after consultations with the government in Reykjavik, they were withdrawn or amended. The British difficulties were compounded by the fact that there were simultaneous negotiations in progress with Norway and the Danes were reminding Britain that any terms agreed with Iceland would also apply off the Faeroes.

The subject of future recourse to the ICJ became the most difficult topic. On 1st December 1960 a British team flew to Iceland and insisted on meeting with Ministers, going over the head of Anderson, the leader of their negotiating team. They stressed that an 'assurance' on recourse to the ICJ was the key to an agreement. Benediktsson, the Conservative leader admitted that the British position was 'reasonable' but said that it was 'very difficult to present to Icelandic public opinion'. Eventually the Icelandic government accepted that, whilst Iceland would work towards sovereignty over the whole of their continental shelf, six month's notice would be given of any extension, which Britain could then refer to the ICJ. The Icelanders would not make this commitment a formal agreement - as Ambassador Stewart noted, referring to the Icelandic PM, 'the word "agreement" stuck audibly in his throat'. Any calls for more clarity only lead to a warning that 'Iceland might soon have to consider whether it should withdraw from NATO'.

The British were getting fed up with Iceland's unwillingness to engage in any kind of meaningful negotiations and, on December 16th, Macmillan wrote personally to Ólafur Thors saying that, should negotiations collapse, Britain would feel obliged to publish full details of the negotiations, so that the whole world could see that there was 'ample evidence that my government have been prepared to make very large concessions in order to secure a settlement.'

To be fair to the Icelanders, they realised that the British had already been pushed as far as they could go and both the leaders of the parties in the coalition government were genuinely pro-Western. They wanted to be seen as trustworthy allies, but could not resist the temptation of rattling the Soviet skeleton. Additionally, as Fisheries Director Ólafsson pointed out, 'we have got from the British more than we dared hope for'. Ólafur Thors wrote swiftly back to Macmillan saying that it was his 'sincere wish' to resolve the conflict and the Minister of Foreign Affairs arranged to meet the British Foreign Secretary in the margins of the North Atlantic Council.[44] After several sessions, the two Foreign Ministers hammered out an agreement that the 'assurance' about recourse to the ICJ would be separated from the rest of the agreement, but it would still constitute an 'agreement' and would be registered as such with the UN.

In Iceland, the ability to use domestic opinion as a weapon against the British now became the real problem of satisfying the coalition partners and the country that there really was no more to be gained in negotiations - and that the result was 'more than we dared hope for'. This was not easy - at one very difficult coalition meeting between the PM and some of 'his' MPs, a door was slammed so hard that the glass

[44] The North Atlantic Council is the top political forum within NATO.

shattered. In January, there was a fishermen's strike against the proposed agreement. As the spring fishing season approached, Macmillan put more pressure on Thors to announce the terms of the agreement.

Meanwhile, off Iceland, there were only 15-20 trawlers fishing, the patrol had been reduced to one frigate and the weather was very unpleasant. On 28th February 1961, the Icelandic government announced that a proposal to end the dispute would be put to the Althing. Trouble was expected and the police were put on alert to deal with Socialist-inspired riots. In the end, there was no trouble on the streets, but there were 9 days of lengthy and turbulent debate in the Althing. Accusations of 'treachery' and 'treason' were made over the concession that Iceland would not again extend her limits unilaterally. On 9th March, the government won the vote and defeated a vote of no confidence. On the 11th, both governments signed the agreement.

At 1100 that day Operation MINT was terminated. HM Ships *Rhyl* and *Malcolm* remained on patrol, with *RFA Tidepool* in support, but the First Cod War was over. During the two and a half years of the dispute, there had been 84 serious attempts to arrest British trawlers. None had succeeded. The conduct of both sides had been professional and reasonably restrained. No trawler, warship or gunboat had sustained significant damage and there had been no serious injuries to personnel. British trawlers had been able to go, without interruption, 'on the seas upon their lawful occasions'[45] and, overall, catches were only about 15% down on the best that could have been expected under normal conditions. The Royal Navy had deployed 63 warships and Royal Fleet Auxiliary ten tankers, with, on average, three warships and one tanker on task throughout the 2½ years.

[45] From the Naval Prayer.

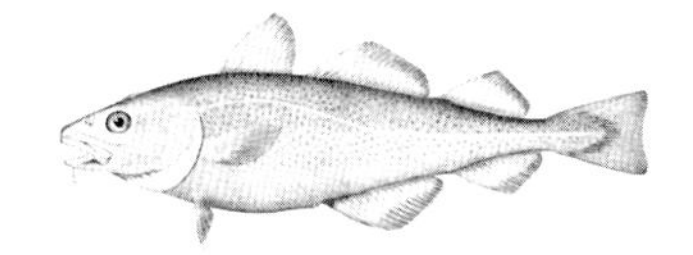

CHAPTER 8

TEN YEARS OF PEACE & THE COMMON FISHERIES POLICY 1961 - 1971

The First Cod War had been fought to bring Iceland to an agreement so that British trawlers could continue to fish up to the old limits for as long as possible and, at least, until new limits were internationally agreed. In August 1958, the British had been considering acceptance of a 12-mile limit, with historic rights of 10 years, if such a deal had been offered. At the time, Iceland was only offering an unqualified 12 miles. The agreement of 11th March 1961 stated:

a. The UK Government will no longer object to a 12 mile fishing zone .....

b. The base lines will be those set out in the Icelandic Regulation on 30 June 1958 ....

c. For a period of three years the Icelandic Government will not object to British trawlers fishing in the outer 6 miles of the fishing zone .... (there were certain specified areas and periods)

d. The Icelandic Government will continue to work for the implementation of the Althing resolution of May 5, 1959, regarding the extension of fisheries jurisdiction around Iceland, but shall give to the United Kingdom Government six months' notice of such extension and, in case of a dispute in relation to such extension, the matter shall, at the request of either party, be referred to the International Court of Justice.

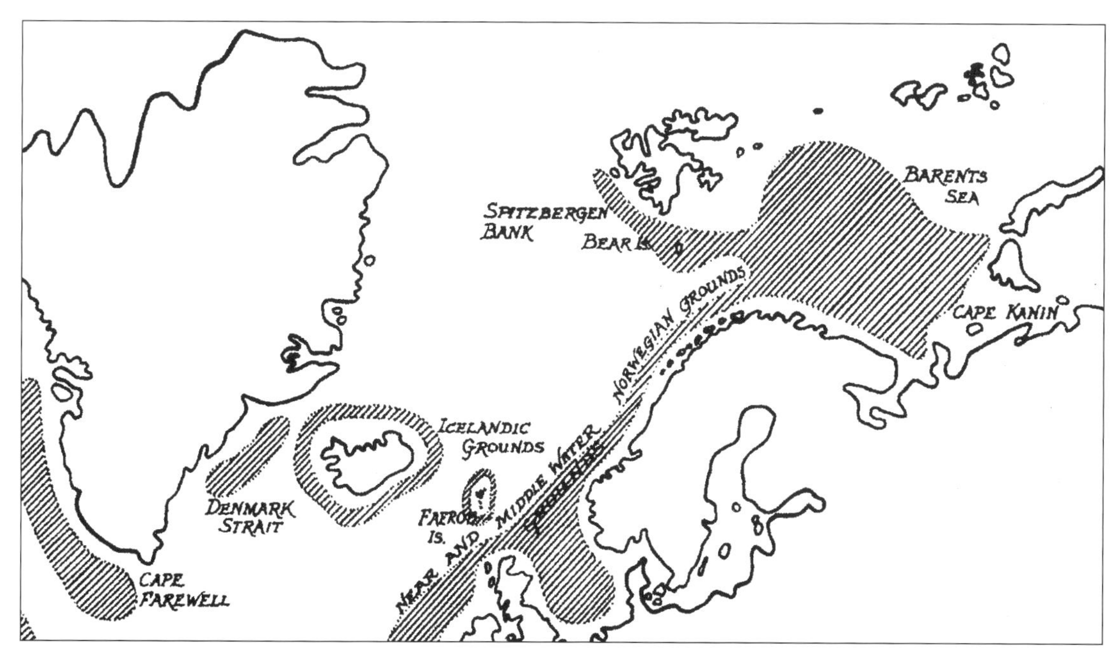

Britain's distant and middle water trawling grounds in the North Atlantic in the 1960s (Ross Group Publicity Brochure)

This agreement was not easy to sell in Iceland and the government emphasised the advantageous baseline changes, the closed areas and the short transitory period. The left wing parties were particularly vociferous about the reference to the International Court of Justice (ICJ) as they saw this as limiting their freedom of action. The authorities in Iceland were now trying hard to make amends. As a senior official at the Foreign Office observed 'The present Icelandic government is pro-NATO and basically pro-British' and 'They have had to exercise a good deal of political courage to come to terms with us.'

In Whitehall, the agreement was accepted as being the best that could have been achieved in the changed international atmosphere and the provision for any future dispute to be referred to the ICJ was seen as a particular success. Unsurprisingly, however, the trawlermen were not at all happy and their supporters in Parliament, from all sides of the House, condemned it as a sell-out. In Grimsby, the trawlermen went on strike and threats were made to ban Icelandic catch landings unless guarantees could be given that there would be no further extensions of limits within the next few years. When Commander Maurice Tibby of HMS *Malcolm* informed the trawlermen off Iceland of the agreement on 11th March 1961, one of the skippers replied 'Well what the bloody hell are you up here for then?'

Inevitably, others took advantage of the Icelandic agreement and, even before the formal signing, Russia revoked the 1956 UK-Soviet agreement allowing some fishing within 12 miles, giving the one year's notice as required. From March 1962, British trawlers would be banned from fishing inside Russian territorial waters. Negotiations over Faeroese limits took longer, but the end result was not in doubt after the precedent set by Iceland and Britain settled on historic rights within 12 miles that ended on 11th March 1964, the same day as off Iceland. The fishermen would not accept this agreement and banned landing of Faeroese catches. This ban lasted for a year.

In May 1962, Macmillan initiated a fundamental examination of Britain's position on her own territorial waters (still 3 miles). This was not a simple issue, partly because of the hope that Britain would shortly be joining the Common Market. Macmillan was no longer in power in January 1963, when President De Gaulle vetoed Britain's entry to the EEC and the complication of pan-European fishing limits was removed. However, as Macmillan had been the driving force behind the move to a 12-mile UK limit, the subject became less important. By March 1964, there was general agreement in Whitehall that Britain should announce a 12-mile limit, but then the Foreign Office legal team stated that enforcement of such a limit 'would be contrary to our international obligations and would be an unjustifiable encroachment on the rights of other countries to fish on the high seas'. Eventually, on 1st October 1964, the British limit was brought into line with what was by then the norm.

Fishery Protection continues...

After 11th March 1961, HM Ships *Rhyl* and *Malcolm* remained on patrol, with RFA *Tideflow* in support. Their initial task was to explain the agreement to the trawlers, most of whom were angry and did not understand some of the detailed restrictions. There were new problems of navigation to be worked through as well - because of the new extended baselines, in some places the 12-mile limit was nearly 30 miles out from a low lying coast. The Icelandic Coastguard were strict in policing the new limits and the Royal Navy were no longer there to protect, merely to help interpret the rules and, if necessary, to provide accurate navigational evidence.

On 29th May, Captain Hugo Bracken, Captain Fishery Protection Squadron (CFPS) flew into Reykjavik to rejoin HMS *Duncan* and made informal contact with the Icelandic Coastguard, and from July, HM Ships were invited to fuel in Icelandic ports. The Royal Fleet Auxiliary tanker was sent home and, for the first time in three years, there was no station tanker off Iceland. As normality was restored to the business of fishery protection, so the professional contacts between the Royal Navy and the Coastguard were also restored. During a refuelling visit in *Duncan* at the end of July, Captain George Leslie made official calls on the Foreign Minister and the Minister of Justice and was well received. The same evening, he dined with the Director of the Coastguard aboard *Ódinn*.

During this period, Ken Voller was the Petty Officer (PO) Radio Electrician in HMS *Russell* when visits were allowed again. His main memory of the first visit to Siglufordhur was '*the fact that young-*

sters would converse in perfect English'. His story continues:

> *'Anyway I was with my runashore buddy, the PO Chef and we did carry some "anti freeze" of the overproof variety, and being a very social minded person I offered a swig to one of the locals, who engaged us in conversation and invited us back to his trawler, where we proceeded to uphold our traditional role as 'Britain's Little Ambassadors', and not to refuse any offer of strong drink. This resulted in a late return to the ship, and afterwards a 'days pay and leave' were forfeited, whilst on patrol.*
>
> *We visited Reykjavik, where we did a 'culture' run. We being: Myself: the PO Chef and PO Electrician. Well we couldn't find an art gallery or museum, so we hailed a cab, and requested directions to a bar, and the Danish driver advised us that Iceland was 'DRY'. However, he did take us to a bar of sorts, where one had to spend a whole evening with a morsel of food to comply with regulations. It was not long before I started a conversation with another customer, and within minutes we were philosophically discussing the "Cod War", he then introduced himself as the Second Officer of the Thor. Actually it was a social success. He invited us to his home, which I swear was totally filled with booze. "Brenivin" I think it was called. We did manage to make the gangway of the Russell about thirty minutes late, and were observed by the First Lieutenant. When we appeared at "The Assizes", The CO (Lieutenant Commander John Lewis) was rather more interested in our political involvement than being adrift, so we were 'held over' until we continued on patrol so the days leave was not missed.'*

The West German government had been the only other government to take serious issue with Iceland's unilateral declaration of 12 miles and on 19th July 1961, they signed an identical agreement to the British one.

Until the end of the fishing season, in December 1961, two ships were kept on patrol. These were usually one of the Type 14 frigates from the Fishery Protection Squadron (FPS) and one destroyer or frigate from the Home Fleet. In March 1962 the patrol was resumed, but it was assessed that only one ship was now needed and the FPS Type 14s provided the permanent presence throughout the 1962 season as part of their distant-water patrol task. In 1963, the Iceland patrol was further eased to a 75% presence on the fishing grounds.

Then in April, there was a setback in the improving relations with the Icelanders. On 27th April 1963 the trawler *Millwood* was caught poaching by *Thor* inside the 6-mile limit. Skipper Smith decided to run for home at full speed, with *Thor* in hot pursuit. HMS *Palliser* (commanded by Lieutenant-Commander Nick Hunt) joined the chase to ensure fair play. Lieutenant Commander Hunt's instructions had included 'make sure International Law is obeyed' and it was very clear that *Millwood* had been poaching, so Lieutenant-Commander Hunt went across to *Millwood* with his Marine Engineering Officer (MEO) to try to persuade Skipper Smith to surrender.

Whilst Lieutenant Commander Hunt was on the bridge, his MEO disabled the *Millwood's* engines. Skipper Smith was furious and, still refusing to submit, was taken onboard *Palliser*. Whilst he was away from his ship, his crew allowed *Thor's* boarding party onboard and *Millwood* was arrested. Skipper Smith refused to return to his ship, Lieutenant Commander Hunt had no legal power to enforce him to do so and Smith was returned to the UK in *Palliser*.

This incident caused a public furore in Iceland, where the British were accused of preventing the lawful arrest of a poacher. Fuelling facilities were withdrawn from the Royal Navy and a Royal Fleet Auxiliary tanker had to be sailed to supply the patrol. The Coastguard became very difficult to deal with and a full Royal Navy fishery protection patrol had to be re-instated. It was two months before normal relations were restored and RN ships were once again allowed into Icelandic ports. Meanwhile Lieutenant Commander Hunt[46] had been summonsed to the MoD to explain his actions to Rear-Admiral Peter Hill-Norton, then Assistant Chief of the Naval Staff. Fortunately for Lieutenant Commander Hunt,

[46] Later Admiral Sir Nicholas Hunt GCB LVO

The two dramatic photographs on this page were taken by Michael Ellis, a junior seaman aboard HMS Duncan. The ship was on Fishery Protection duty off the South coast of Iceland in 1963 when it witnessed the underwater volcanic eruption which created the island of Surtsey. It has been claimed that the creation of this island gave the Icelanders the legal impetus to push for a 50-mile limit. (Michael Ellis)

Admiral Hill-Norton completely agreed with his actions.

John Armstrong, who was a Leading Stoker, in HMS *Battleaxe*, during this period has fond memories - *'Imagine - on watch (during the first) in the engine room. Under the fan with arctic cold air blowing in. One eye on the throttle and the other on a bit of battered cod with some chips. MAGIC.'* Christopher Parker, also a stoker onboard at the time, remembers that the weather was often so bad that both the ship's screws would sometimes be out of the water. And just remember, that this was in a 2,800-

ton destroyer - think what life was like in a 400-ton trawler.

Bryan 'Tiny' Height had the distinction of serving in HMS *Palliser* twice and so managed Icelandic patrols during both the period between 1st and 2nd Cod Wars and during the third. He also remembers how rugged life was in a Type 14 in the early 60s:

> *'The Patrols were up to six weeks duration ... The Russian Navy were doing exercises ... with their submarines. I think we used to do ... submarine listening; sonar buoys were dropped from Shackleton aircraft. I remember once we followed the Cruiser Sverdlov, as we could only do 22 knots, we lost her. On one of the patrols, we ventured as far as Jan Mayen, Spitzbergen and Bear Island, very bleak and remote, some of the roughest weather that I ever encountered during my career was in these waters. I have never been so seasick but it certainly cured me. I hated going up to the forward heads with the smell of sick and water wallowing all over the place plus the anchor cable clanging in the pipes down to the cable locker.*
>
> *These ships really pitched in heavy seas and to sit down on the heads was some experience, it was a good job you had these handles each side of you to hang onto. The crew only had to serve a year on the Type 14s; we received hard lying money for the poor living conditions. If you messed down aft, you had to go over the catwalks to get your dinner; in rough weather the upper deck was out of bounds, so you ate up forward in the 'jungle' - the Radar, TAS and Gunners mess.*
>
> *We had this Petty Officer Radar in his mid-thirties who used to make me laugh, great sense of humour - nutcase I would call him. He used to dangle a piece of raw bacon when the young lads were feeling seasick. He found out that I was in a kid's home before I joined the Navy and asked me to go and spend a weekend with his family; in Essex I think it was. I said I would love to.*
>
> *Anyway, we hit bad weather on this particular patrol, I think it was a hurricane, the ship was getting a right pounding and I was in the small ops room helping with the plot, when man overboard was piped. The waves were huge and I knew that something dreadful had happened. The Petty Officer who I have just mentioned went down to secure the life raft with a safety line, a huge wave snapped the line and he was washed over the side.*
>
> *The First Lieutenant wanted to go in after*

A liferaft about to be recovered after a transfer on a Type 14 Frigate. Note the low freeboard.
(Charles Dempsey)

him; he only lasted a few minutes in the freezing water and was lost in the darkness and heavy seas. A lot of the ship's company shed a tear that night; I did for a long time. He was a great Petty Officer.'

Another member of *Palliser's* ship's company in 1961 was Roger Smith (Ordinary Seaman UC[47] on joining) - who became the 'dinghy jockey'. He remembers the foul-weather clothing and the liferaft transfer procedures:

'Foul-weather clothing was a pair of oilskin trousers, a shortie-length belted oilskin jacket and sou'wester; cold-weather gear was a padded jacket and fur-lined hat with earflaps. These hats were in a variety of styles, some were leather Breton type, some a Russian fur type, but by far the best were the corded type, something like an air force cap, with black seal fur lining, a flap that protected the neck and another which came over the eyes.
Everyone agreed these were the warmest and most waterproof.
One of the first jobs after clearing the Forth Bridge (this was before the road bridge was built) was to prepare the dinghy. First a six-foot diameter iron ring was laid on the deck, then a heavy canvas insert was laced into it, a four-legged sling attached to the ring and lastly a six or eight man open liferaft lashed on top of the canvas.
Later in the year, I was made the dinghy jockey, which meant that I would prepare the dinghy prior to transfer, make sure that it was fully inflated, the warp was attached and ready to run free, the immersion suits were ready (if I remember rightly, they were shallow water divers' suits with a neoprene hood to pull over the head) and finally a couple of canvas sacks were in the dinghy. A dinghy transfer was usually done to take the doctor to treat a sick crewman or an artificer to sort out the radar or engine in a trawler.
The trawler would stop with the ship manoeuvring as close as possible, contact was established by Costin gunline; then the warp was passed. Meanwhile the dinghy would have been hoisted over the guard rail, the dinghy jockey and passenger would have donned immersion suits and climbed aboard, then been lowered to the waterline; the sling was tripped and the dinghy hauled across to the trawler. After the Doctor or Tiffy[48] had climbed aboard the trawler, the mail sacks were passed up in anticipation of a "fry", the free end of the warp was passed back and coiled in the bottom of the dinghy. Then the wait, trying to keep the dinghy clear of the monkey belting around the trawler's side.
The return trip was simple. The trawler would pull clear, the Captain would manoeuvre the ship as close as possible, contact would be established by heaving line, the dinghy hauled alongside, then once the hook was attached to the sling, up and onto the deck as quick as possible. The suits were hosed with clean water and the seals talc'ed before hanging up to dry.'

The End of (legal) Fishing within 12 miles

The three years of 'historic rights' up to 6 miles within Iceland's new 12-mile limit finished on 11th March 1964. This event passed without incident and fishing outside 12 miles continued to provide satisfactory, as the table (*Fig.1 opposite*) of catches[49] (in '000 tonnes) in Icelandic waters for 5 years either side of the First Cod War shows.

Whilst there was a dip of about 15% in 1959 and 1960, the two years when fishing was most affected by the Cod War, the catches soon recovered and the British Trawler Federation's claims that the industry would be ruined by a 12-mile limit were shown to be completely unfounded.

European Fishing Limits

Between December 1963 and March 1964, Britain hosted a European Fisheries Conference in London. All the northern European nations attended and, with the exception of Norway and Iceland, they agreed to

[47] UC = Underwater Control – the sub-branch who manned the submarine detection equipment.
[48] Short for Artificer - a Middle English term for craftsman, still in use in the Royal Navy.
[49] This chart shows the catches of demersal species, that is the bottom feeding types caught by trawlers. Most of the Icelandic demersal catch is cod.

establish a 12-mile limit, with 10-years reciprocal historic rights up to 6 miles. These new limits came into effect on 1st October 1964. Norway and Iceland insisted on maintaining their own 12-mile limit regulations. The British fishing industry was pleased to have an increase in their 'exclusive' zone from 3-6 miles, but would have preferred exclusivity in the whole 12-mile zone. They complained that the rights given to foreigners in British waters were not reciprocated elsewhere.

With a 12-mile limit around the UK, the need for fishery protection patrols in home waters increased. Simultaneously, the requirement decreased in distant-waters - not necessarily because there were fewer trawlers working there, but because the new limits were now well understood. In 1965, the Fishery Protection Squadron (FPS) was reduced from four to three Type 14 frigates. There were also five Ton class coastal minesweepers in the squadron. By 1966, only 18 weeks per annum were being spent on distant-water patrols and, ever short of frigates[50], the CinC Home Fleet, Admiral Sir John Frewen, questioned the need for Type 14s in the FPS, as they were spending most of their time in home waters.

On 1st February 1967, the FPS was reorganised. The Type 14s were transferred to general fleet duties and Captain FPS moved ashore into HMS *Lochinvar*, the small naval base on the south bank of the Firth of Forth. Captain FPS remained the main naval authority on fisheries; providing information, advice and extra seagoing staff for the Home Fleet frigates now used on deep-water fishery patrols. Peter Jones, who did two distant-water fishery patrols during the period mainly remembers the poor doctor:

> *'I was in HMS Grafton, a Type 14 tin-can frigate. In 1966-8 we did 2 Icelandic Patrols. I only have dim memories of them, it was so cold, rough and the ship seemed to be covered in ice most of the time. They were not pleasant experiences.*
> *However we could not feel sorry for ourselves, as the ship we relieved up there, I think Keppel, passed the naval Doc on to us having already been up there for 7 weeks,and when we left we passed him on to the next ship. I cannot remember his name, but he spent most of his time sewing up British fishermen's fingers and hands. He was pretty stoic about it.'*

Fig.1: Catches (in '000 tonnes) in Icelandic waters for 5 years either side of the First Cod War

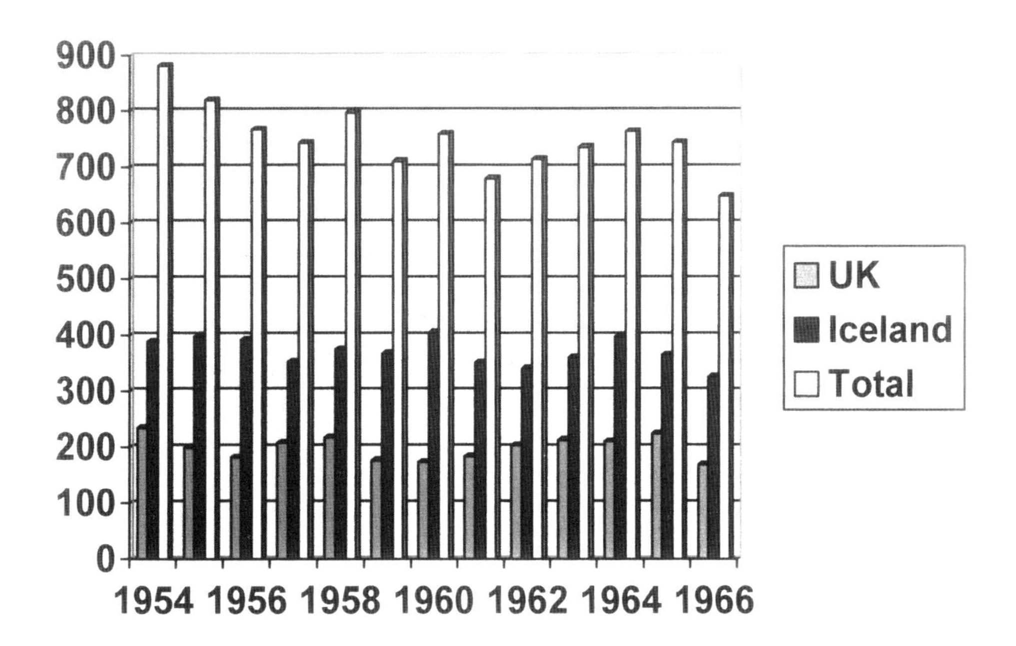

[50] As was Nelson. '"I am distressed for frigates" was his continual cry' to quote Mahan.

I am also grateful to Linda Roberts, the Archivist of the "*Grimsby Telegraph*", for the following story from this period:

HOW SKIPPER 'BUNNY' MADE ICELAND HOPPING MAD

"I'd love to stay... but I'm in a bit of a rush! Trawler skipper 'Bunny' Newton made world headlines in 1967 when he made a dash for freedom from Iceland - with two policemen locked in his cabin!

It was on 25 April that news reached Grimsby that the trawler Brandur had been arrested for alleged illegal fishing off Iceland. She had been apprehended by the most famous of gunboats, the Thor - which incidentally is now a well-patronised restaurant (she didn't last long as a restaurant). Four days later came the news that stunned Grimsby and intrigued the world. Bernard 'Bunny' Newton had broken out of Reykjavik Harbour and made a run for home. What was more astonishing was the fact he had two Icelandic policemen held "captive" on board. The escape bid lasted for 11 hours before Skipper Newton and his crew were back in custody. The Brandur had managed to get some 43 miles from Iceland. In a bid to avoid detection her number, GY 111 had been painted out and H52 painted in. Those hunting her had been ordered to use force if necessary. She had not been discovered missing until early the next morning when two policemen arrived at the quayside to relieve their colleagues. The trawler had slipped out under cover of darkness. Skipper Newton grinned later when he told how they had slipped past two Icelandic gunboats on duty at the dock entrance. Back in Iceland, a judge ruled that Skipper Newton should be kept in custody for the length of the case or 30 days. As the delay went on, the 1,000 kits of fish on board the Brandur was starting to deteriorate and tempers were fraying back in Grimsby. Fred Parkes, managing director of Boston Deep Sea Fisheries, was furious at the Icelanders' refusal to release the vessel. There were further problems as fire swept through the vessel as she lay in Reykjavik harbour. Several of the crew had to be taken off by police as the blaze was tackled. The fire, which was believed to have started in a liver boiling room or the paint store, gutted a two-man berth. Other berths were flooded by water from the hoses. Eventually Skipper Newton - who all along had denied illegal fishing - was found guilty of trying to escape with his arrested ship and obstructing the policemen with threats. He was given a

The Wreck of the Notts County (Bragi Gudmundsson)

three-month prison sentence and fined 300,000 crowns - about £2,400 - for fishing inside Iceland's 12-mile limit. 'Bunny' was freed when the vessel's owners immediately put up a £100,000 bond pending an appeal.

The Brandur left Reykjavik at 10pm on May 6 and three days later, she pulled into Aberdeen and landed her catch, grossing £2,500. Only three boxes of haddock were condemned by the port health officials, although the fish was said to be of poor quality. The story still had a few pages to turn. Nine crewmen said they were not leaving Aberdeen aboard the Brandur because, they claimed, there was no food on board. However they were eventually persuaded by Skipper Newton and the trawler sailed for Grimsby where she arrived a day later. It was some months later when the appeal court met in Iceland. And when they delivered their ruling, it caused quite a stir. They doubled the prison sentence to six months and increased the fine to just over £2,500. Skipper Newton was radioed on board the trawler Oratava and told to avoid the Icelandic fishing grounds. He headed for the Faeroes instead. The legal wranglings bounced back and forth and then, on December 19, 1968, came news that Skipper Newton had been granted a free pardon by the Icelandic authorities. Skipper Newton stayed away from Iceland for 15 years, but returned there in March 1982 to be greeted by one of the policemen he had locked up. Hilmar Porbjornsson had risen to become deputy sheriff of Reykjavik and he invited Skipper Newton to lunch!'

The winter of 1967/8 was particularly hard and four British trawlers - the *Ross Cleveland*, *Notts County*, *Kingston Peridot* and *St Romanus* foundered off Iceland due to a build up of ice on their superstructures. Captain Sigurdur Arnasson risked his ship and all his crew in the *Ódinn* to rescue the survivors of the *Notts County*. He was subsequently presented with the OBE for his gallantry. It is indicative of the tribal nature of the deep-water fishing community that, as one said to me, a Hull man will instinctively think of only three losses - the *Notts County* was a Grimsby trawler.

The loss of four trawlers in one winter led to a detailed investigation; one of the recommendations from which was that there should be better meteorological support off Iceland. As a result the Board of Trade chartered the Hull trawler *Orsino* as a support vessel. In addition to weather forecasting, she provided medical, technical and other general support services. A fisheries inspector from the Ministry of Agriculture, Fisheries and Food was embarked as Support Commander. The *Orsino's* presence further reduced the need for an Royal Navy deep-water fishery patrol.

In November 1970, the 10-year period of historic rights off Norway ended and the British trawler fleet was now excluded from a 12-mile zone in all their traditional deep-water fishing areas - Iceland, Russia, Norway and Greenland.

UNCLOS3

The developed world's increasing ability to find and exploit natural resources (oil, gas and mineral deposits) in deeper and deeper water, triggered regular discussions in the United Nations on the subject of the rights of coastal states. A 1967 Soviet/American proposal to hold a conference limited exclusively to agreeing that 12 miles was the maximum width of territorial waters was defeated and in 1970, the General Assembly adopted a resolution to convene a third Law of the Sea Conference in 1973. The intention was that this conference would produce an agreement on the age-old problems of territorial seas and fishing limits. However, it was also hoped to reach an agreement on the question of the ownership and use of seabed resources. There was already strong pressure from many Central and South American and African states for the international recognition of an Exclusive Economic Zone (EEZ) out to 200 miles. Iceland had sent observers to many of these meetings about a possible EEZ.

The Common Fisheries Policy

Under the Treaty of Rome, fish had been defined as an agricultural product and the fisheries policy, such as there was one, covered little more than the progressive reduction of tariffs between member states. The Commission produced a first draft of a Common Fisheries Policy (CFP) in 1966 and it was two years before substantive proposals were presented to the Council of Ministers. There was little real agreement and not much priority was given to the topic.

However, once Common Market membership for Britain, Denmark, Ireland and Norway became likely, the original six European Economic Community (EEC) members decided to establish a Common Fisheries Policy. It was hurriedly drawn up and agreed on 30th June 1970, the day before formal negotiations opened. The CFP established the principle of equality of access to the waters of all EEC countries for all EEC vessels.

The applicant countries, all with much bigger fishing industries than the original EEC members and with much richer fishing grounds, were all upset by this moving of the goal posts at the last moment. This feeling of a less-than-honest approach to the negotiations by the then EEC members was reinforced by the fact that, all the countries involved, with the exception of Norway, had been signatories only 6 years before to the London Convention on European fishery limits - agreeing 12-mile national limits.

It became clear during the negotiations that the original six members were not going to back down on this bonus for their own relatively small fishing industries. If there was one reason why the Norwegians voted against joining the EEC, it was over the terms of the CFP - 'though, no doubt, the way the CFP had materialised at the last moment may well have swelled the numbers of those who doubted the probity of the Common Market.

In Britain, the Conservative Government of Edward Heath was determined not to let this issue stand in the way of accession. The inshore fishermen were unhappy, but the deep-water sector was not that concerned - they had Iceland to fish off. The final accession agreement allowed a 10-year derogation for new members (Britain, Denmark and Ireland) from the principle of equal access within 12 miles - up to 31st December 1982. Until that date, new members could claim a 6-mile exclusive limit, with historic rights to be granted within 12 miles. In Britain's case, this protected 95% of the water within 12 miles and was claimed as a major concession by the government.

Sir David Hannay, who was one of Britain's negotiating team said in 1999:

> *'fisheries is a bit of a black spot in my view and I couldn't put my hand on my heart and say we did a brilliant job. ... One of the reasons why we didn't do terribly well is that we failed to spot that there were a whole number of developments in the fisheries field which were going to change all the rules of the game.'*

The consequences of this 'black spot' are best illustrated by the fact that when the 200-mile limit came into force in 1976, Britain 'donated' 75% of EEC waters, in exchange for 12.5% of the catch by value. Unsurprisingly, the CFP has continued to be a running sore[51] in Britain's relations with the rest of the European Community and, as fishermen become more and more enmeshed in rules that are driven mainly by politics in Brussels, this particular sore shows no sign of healing. However, the realisation of the reality of the disaster that the CFP was to become for British fishermen lay in the future.

The Second Cod War looms ...

The political situation over Iceland's fishing limits was stable from 1961 to 1971, but then there was a general election in Iceland, won by the Socialists and their Communist allies. The Left had never accepted the 1961 agreement with Britain to refer any agreements about future limit to the International Court of Justice and had campaigned, for the general election, on a promise to extend fishery limits to 50 miles, so covering almost all of the continental shelf. This was indeed the aim of the Icelandic 1948 'Conservation Law', as restated in 1959 in the 'Althing Resolution on Extension of Fisheries'. Another Cod War was imminent.

[51] The scale of interest in the subject can be gauged from the fact that 'Googling' 'Common Fisheries Policy' produced 1,260,000 pages!

CHAPTER 9

THE 50-MILE LIMIT 1971-72

The Icelandic General Election of 13th June 1971 produced a majority of left wing MPs for the first time since 1959 and so, on 14th July, a coalition government of socialists and communists was formed. The Prime Minister, Ólafur Jóhannesson, and his Foreign Minister, Einar Ágústsson, were socialists, but the Fisheries Minister, Lúdvík Jósepsson, was a communist. The left wing parties had campaigned specifically on the issue of extending the fishing limits and one of the new government's first acts was to cancel the 1961 agreements with Britain and West Germany and to declare a 50-mile fishing limit, to come into effect on 1st September 1972.

The Foreign Minister, Einar Ágústsson, made the following statement, which was reproduced and widely circulated in the Icelandic Government film '*The Living Sea*':

> *'The right of a coastal state to utilise the resources of the Continental Shelf, such as oil and shellfish, is recognised by international law and many states are utilising such resources well beyond the 50-mile limit. We think it therefore only fair that we should have the right to conserve, control and rationally utilise our only resource, the fisheries, up to the same distance.'*

And in the same film, the Fisheries Minister, Lúdvík Jósepsson, stated:

> *'The extension of the fishery limit to 50 miles is not based on our selfish interests but on our responsibility for the rational utilisation of fish stocks. We are trying to protect the resources of the sea around Iceland. It has been said that Iceland is breaking international law by extending the fishery limit to 50 miles, but which law? No international law prohibits such an extension. No specific limit is prescribed by international law. At least 10 different limits are enforced in different regions of the world varying from 3-200 miles.*
> *About 20 states have 200-mile limits now. We want to protect our livelihood and, at the same time, we are serving the long-term interests of all the fishing nations. Without our conservation measures, there will be neither good fishing for them nor for us in the future.'*

The announcement of the a 50-mile limit stated that it was necessary to preserve fish stocks, because Iceland's economy was so heavily dependent on fishing and because other nations were extending their limits for oil and gas exploration. The Prime Minister also announced his long-term intention of ridding Iceland of foreign military bases and personnel.

The battle lines were drawn once again and the 'Communist/Keflavík' bogeyman had been reawakened.

The 12-mile limit had had no significant effect upon British catches, but a 50-mile limit, covering almost all of Iceland's continental shelf, would have a dramatic effect on the deep-sea fishing business. The British Ambassador delivered a formal protest to the Icelandic government on 17th July, pointing out that the 1961 Agreement, which was not open to unilateral termination, made provision for reference to the International Court of Justice (ICJ). The aim of the British government was to secure a new agreement, working closely with the Germans, whilst preparing an appeal to the ICJ and making plans for naval protection, if all else failed.

The new Icelandic government ignored British

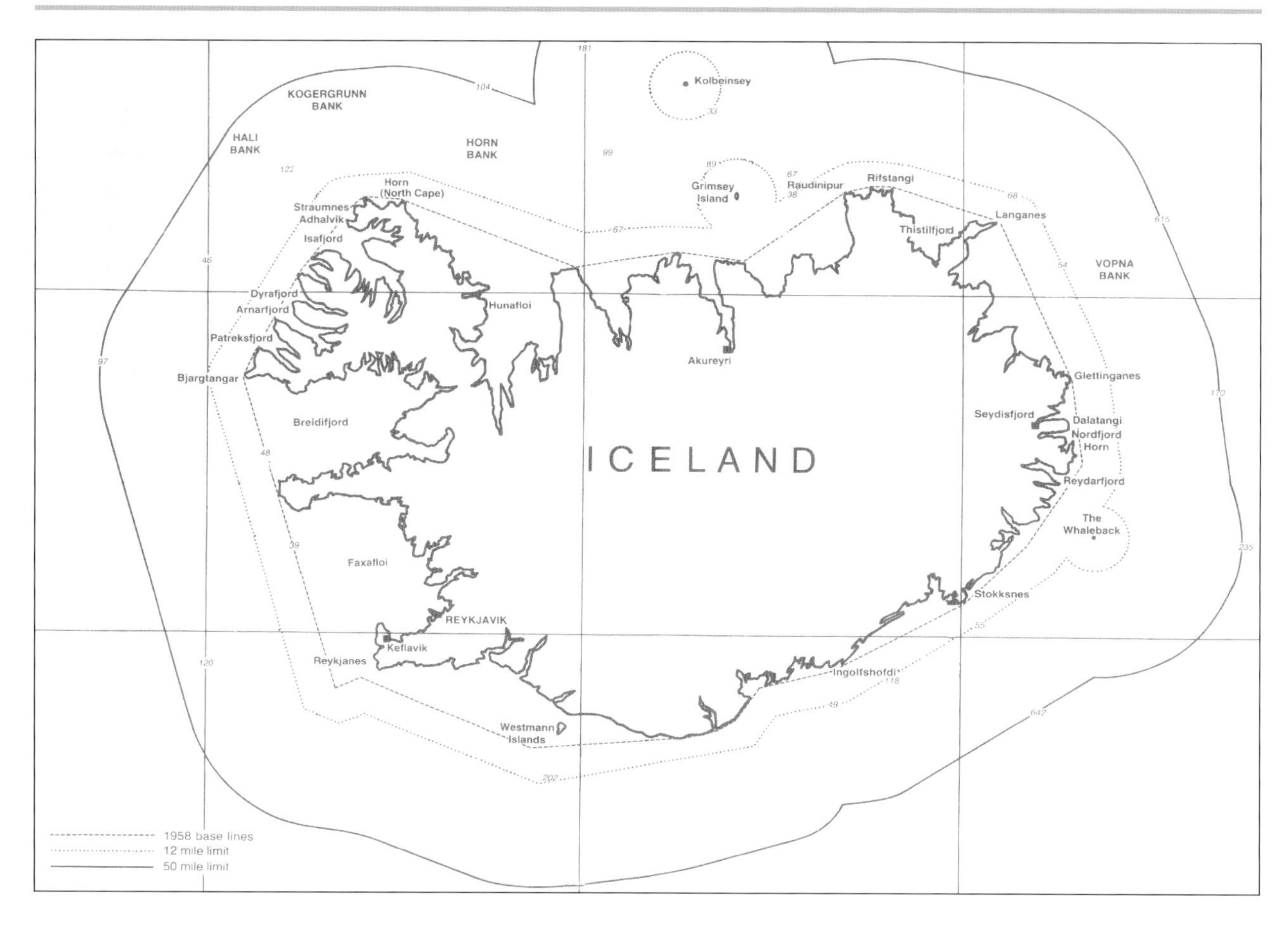

protests and rejected Britain's reference to the 1961 agreement. When asked by a *Guardian* journalist about Iceland's legal obligations, Lúdvík Jósepsson said 'What law? They don't exist'. Hannes Jónsson, in his book *Friends in Conflict*, makes one interesting point on this outright rejection of the inconvenient agreement:

> *'The condition that any future disputed extension could be taken to the International Court was accepted by the Icelandic Government not only under duress, but also on the basis of optimism. In their view, the evolution of international Law of the Sea on the width of the limit was so rapid towards a situation reflecting their main views that such restriction as was placed on Iceland in the Agreement would not in fact have halted further necessary extensions.'*

Iceland's optimism was unfounded, but only in terms of the speed of advance towards internationally agreed wider limits. The view that the Agreement had been reached 'under duress' (by a centre-right government) is more a reflection of the views of the left in Icelandic politics, than a serious statement of fact. It would be more balanced to see this minor concession to the British (and subsequently the West Germans) as part and parcel of the process of reaching an agreement that gave both sides some claim, however weak, to at least a partial victory. Nevertheless, this Agreement had been registered with the United Nations and so was International Law - as the International Court in The Hague was subsequently to decide.

Talks took place in London in August 1971, but there was no progress of any kind and on 31st August the Icelandic government formally terminated the 1961 Agreement with both Britain and West Germany. Further bilateral talks took place in London and Reykjavik; the Icelandic government refusing to negotiate trilaterally. Britain tried to persuade Iceland of the illegality of the proposed extension and offered, if the need for urgent conservation measures could be demonstrated, to limit the total British catch to the average of the years 1960-69 (i.e. 185,000 tonnes) as opposed to the expected catch in 1971 of 208,000 tonnes.

The Icelandic government was not prepared to negotiate on any of the British proposals and so, on 14th April 1972, the British government lodged an appeal with the International Court. Shortly afterwards, the West German government followed suit. Iceland's response to the Court was to declare the 1961 agreement invalid and to deny the ICJ's jurisdiction in this matter.

Further negotiations took place in May, June and July in both Reykjavik and London. Both sides agreed to set aside the subject of Iceland's right unilaterally to extend fishing limits and to concentrate on an interim agreement whilst the case was before the ICJ. The British re-proposed the 185,000 tonnes limit and Iceland insisted on a reduction in the size of the British fleet. The British counter-proposed a limit on the number of British fishing days, but this was rejected. Iceland then proposed a system of closed and open areas, provided the restrictions reduced the British catch by 25% (i.e. to 156,000 tonnes). However Iceland refused to discuss their own proposal in any detail and terminated negotiations on 12th July, claiming that they could no longer delay publishing the new regulations that would come into force on 1st September 1972.

The new regulations were issued on 14th July. The British government applied to the ICJ for interim measures of protection, as the full judgement was expected to take another year. The ICJ decided, by 14 votes to 1, that it did have jurisdiction and on 17th August issued an interim judgement enjoining Iceland not to enforce a 50-mile limit and instructing Britain to keep her annual catch to 170,000 tons and West Germany to 119,000 tons. Both sides were urged to take no steps of any kind which might aggravate the dispute.

Iceland's response was to reiterate that it did not recognise the ICJ's jurisdiction in this case and its intention to enforce a 50-mile limit from 1st September. The ICJ did not issue a full judgement until 25th July 1974, 8 months after the end of the Second Cod War. This final judgement stated that Iceland was not entitled, unilaterally, to exclude British and West German fishing vessels from the 12-50 mile zone. However, by this time UNCLOS3 was well underway, with a 200-mile fishing limit gaining support and Iceland was intent on jumping the gun, with a unilateral extension to the proposed 200 miles.

Naval Preparations

In Britain, no one was keen on providing protection for trawlers again. Memories of the First Cod War were still strong and it was believed that naval protection would only make the Icelanders more difficult and render the possibility of successful negotiations even more remote. The assumption in Whitehall was that, although the fishermen would not like it, a defended havens policy would be necessary. This would require 2 frigates per haven and would probably reduce the catch by 50%.

Although haven fishing had only reduced the catch by 15% in the First Cod War, much of the fishing had actually been outside havens and outside 12 miles. There was comparatively little fish outside 40 miles, hence the assumption that there would be a 50% reduction from haven fishing this time round. The other factor was that Iceland had modernised their Coastguard and now had much more capable fishery protection vessels. It was suggested that the catch might be greater if trawlers fished where they wanted to without naval protection.

One thing that was clear was that world opinion was moving in Iceland's direction and the forthcoming UNCLOS3 might well legitimise a 50-mile limit. There were elements within the deep-water fishing industry who believed that all of the traditional distant-water fishing grounds would be denied to British vessels within the short to medium term and who were pushing for the use of new areas (such as the Antarctic) and new technology (such as freezer trawlers). All were agreed that opposition to Iceland's claim was not going to succeed in the long term.

Nevertheless, Iceland was clearly in breach of international law and the 50-mile limit was not yet accepted worldwide. To have failed to oppose Iceland's unilateral moves would have been to abandon the Icelandic fishing grounds and the government, the industry, parliament, and the press were not prepared to countenance that. As a last resort, naval protection would be provided, but as before, Britain had the delicate task of keeping her NATO allies on side, especially with the future of the Keflavík airbase and even Icelandic membership of the Alliance at risk. It is interesting that even 'neutral' Sweden was concerned about Keflavík and in early March 1973, Olof Palme, the Swedish Prime Minister, not known for his support of US foreign policy, told Washington that it was 'absolutely essential' for Scandinavian security that US forces remained on guard in Iceland.

The Navy was, as always, short of escorts and examined the option of using naval manned armed trawlers for protection. The Royal Navy's Maritime Tactical School conducted a study into the subject in January 1972 and concluded that one frigate and two armed trawlers would be able to protect each haven. However, further investigations into the cost and practicalities of buying, converting and manning trawlers for naval use caused this idea to be shelved. The Naval Staff was very keen to avoid an open-ended commitment of a large number of frigates and proposed a short-term, overwhelming use of military power to force a solution to the dispute.

By the time this view was considered by the Cabinet on 14th March 1972, the proposal was that Her Majesty's Government should announce that any illegal action involving force by Icelandic authorities would be met with force. Furthermore, if a British trawler was interfered with outside the 12-mile limit, the Royal Navy would attempt to capture or immobilise as many Icelandic Coastguard vessels as possible.

This robust line did not find favour with any other government department and by May it had tentatively been agreed that one or two frigates should be off Iceland, but outside the 50-mile limit from 1st September. The idea was to 'show presence and act as a possible deterrent'.

Admiral Sir Edward Ashmore, the Commander-in-Chief, Fleet (CinC Fleet) and his staff were formally involved from May, when he was instructed to draw up plans for possible naval operations in Icelandic waters. As negotiations were still ongoing with Iceland, no firm guidance was available. However, it was assumed that, if no agreement could be reached, the two main threats to British trawlers were:

> *1. The arrest of trawlers entering Icelandic ports or territorial seas (i.e. within 12 miles) - assessed as virtually certain; and*
>
> *2. The attempted arrest of trawlers on the high seas within the 12-50 mile zone - assessed as possible.*

It was not suggested that the Royal Navy should plan against the first threat, but Ministers had not ruled out meeting the second. Whilst no firm decisions had been taken, the options, in descending order of priority were assessed as being:

> *a. Deploy two frigates to patrol off Iceland from 1st September, to act as a general deterrent until Icelandic intentions became clear - the hope being that an agreement of some kind could be reached, allowing the frigates to be withdrawn by mid-December at the latest;*
> *b. As a, but only deploying one frigate;*
> *c. Deploy two frigates from 1st September to cover one protected haven and to allow some, albeit reduced, fishing until mid-December;*
> *d. As a, b or c, but indefinitely*
> *e. Deploy four frigates to cover two havens from 1st September to mid-December*
> *f. As e. but cover to be provided, until further notice, for 8 months off northwest Iceland and throughout the year off the south-east coast.*

The Fleet could absorb options a, b and c without too much disruption to other planned tasks. Options d, e and f would require Ministerial approval, as other naval commitments would have to be cut. When Iceland pulled out of the negotiations on 12th July 1972, CinC Fleet called a meeting in Fleet Headquarters at Northwood at which the following tasks were allocated:

> *Ministry of Defence (MoD) - to provide a political directive for the task and to issue the necessary 'Rules of Engagement' (RoE). To arrange a meeting between the MoD, CinC Fleet, the British Trawler Federation (BTF) and other interested government departments.*
>
> *CinCFleet - to programme one or two*

The Civilian Support Vessel Miranda. (Nigel Hadley)

frigates to cover the period 1st September to 31st December 1972. To organise the logistic support.

Flag Officer Scotland and Northern Ireland (FOSNI) - to draft an Operation Order.

Whilst there was still some hope of further negotiations, the Cabinet continued to address the problems of protection and agreed that the civilian support ship stationed off Iceland, the *Miranda*[52], should be reinforced, so that there would always be two civilian support ships on task. This decision was taken so that sufficient medical and technical support could be provided to avoid trawlers having to call into Icelandic ports. Initially, the Ministry of Agriculture, Fisheries and Food (MAFF)'s 1600-ton research vessel *Cirolana* and the Department of Agriculture and Fisheries for Scotland (DAFS)'s research vessel *Scotia* were deployed.

They were later replaced by the converted trawlers *Othello* and *Ranger Briseis*. The civilian support ships took over the support tasks - technical and medical - that had been fulfilled by the Royal Navy in earlier times. *Ranger Briseis*, for example, carried a doctor and 4 radio officers; because she was a converted stern-trawler, the operating theatre was far from ideally placed - being right up in the bow.

The Defence and Overseas Policy Committee of the Cabinet met on 8th August and subsequently CinC Fleet was formally informed that one frigate would be required outside 50 miles from 1st September. HMS *Aurora* (Commander Guy Liardet) was the first ship on patrol, with RFA *Blue Rover* (Captain David Kindersley) in support. Commander Liardet remembers being briefed in Rosyth by a MoD official - the official line was to "provide reassurance to our fishermen by making presence known but not to do anything active - typical Whitehall." In order to disguise the fact that a naval patrol was being established, *Aurora's* sailing date was not changed and she sailed from Rosyth on 5th September.

Aurora's task was to set up a patrol in the Iceland-Faeroes gap and establish communications with the civilian support vessels, so that trawlers would hear that a British warship was in the area. They might also see the patrolling frigate whilst transiting to or from the fishing areas. *Aurora* was only permitted to enter the 50-mile limit to save life and no use of force was envisaged. Only the civilian support vessels would communicate with the Icelandic Coastguard. Flag Officer Scotland and Northern Ireland (FOSNI)

[52] *Miranda* was commanded by a British Coastguard Officer, usually 3 months on & 3 months off. All of these officers were ex-Royal Navy and at one stage one of them was Geoff Hammond, who had been Commanding Officer of HMS *Palliser* for much of the First Cod War and was the Director (Operations) for HM Coastguard during the Second.

had Operational Control over the ships on patrol and, from the meagre policy guidance available, he prepared the Operation Order for 'Operations in Support of British Trawlers off Iceland (Operation DEWEY)'. They were based on the assumption that two frigates and one Royal Fleet Auxiliary tanker would protect one haven. All the experience accumulated during the First Cod War and from regular fishery protection patrols was incorporated, as, in due course, were the Rules of Engagement issued by the MoD. The DEWEY Operation Order was issued at the end of August, but remained in abeyance until the Cabinet ordered naval protection to start.

The Icelandic Coastguard

The Icelandic Coastguard had been significantly modernised since the First Cod War. *Ódinn* and *Thor* had been joined by the new *Ægir* (1150 tons, 20 knots) and all three had had small helicopter decks fitted. *Arvakur* (380 tons, 12 knots) had joined the fleet in 1962 and in 1972 the whaler *Hvalur 9* (630 tons, 14 knots) was also added and renamed *Tyr*. The Coastguard also operated two Bell helicopters and a Fokker Friendship for longer-range surveillance.

The 50-mile Limit is Activated

As announced, the Icelandic Government activated the new 50-mile fishing limit on 1st September 1972. Ólafur Jóhannesson, the Prime Minister, declared:

> *'The extended fishery limit will be protected against foreign fishing vessels by all means at our disposal. The Coastguards will protect the limits firmly and resolutely, but with circumspection and by methods befitting good coastguards. Names and numbers of trawlers will be noted and those unmarked photographed from every angle, and although they may escape for a time, they will be punished later whenever, wherever and by whatever means they can be reached.'*

There were about 70 British trawlers on the fishing grounds on 1st September, mainly in two areas, one to the northwest and one to the east. *Miranda* and *Cirolana* were the two civilian support vessels on station, with *Aurora* and *Blue Rover* outside 50 miles. Another frigate was at 72 hours notice to join the patrol. Trawler skippers had been told that arrest attempts were likely and that they should attempt to evade capture, but were not to risk crew or vessel in doing so. Ministerial talks were due to start in Reykjavik on 5th September and the British plan was to wait and see what Iceland did next. The West German Government sent three tugs into the disputed area to prevent the arrest of West German trawlers. For the first few days of September, the Coastguard contented themselves with ordering 'offending' trawlers to haul their nets and move out of the 50-mile limit. Whilst under the direct gaze of the gunboats, the skippers did so. Some skippers had painted out their names and identification number, as well as hoisting the Jolly Roger. This provoked threats of arrest and the owners told the skippers to stop disguising their vessels, although, according to Icelandic reports, some skippers ignored these instructions.

An arrest attempt was expected daily, but the first

ICGV Crewman holding a warp cutter.
(Jón Páll Ásgeirsson)

incident was to be a surprise. The Coastguard had a secret weapon - the trawl cutter. This had been invented by Pétur Sigurdsson, the Director of the Coastguard and had been made by two blacksmiths, Fridrik Teitsson and Tómas Sigurdsson. The first trawl cutter had been made and tested in 1958, but it had never been used during the First Cod War.[53] By the time the Second Cod War broke out all the gunboats had been equipped with it and all the crews were fully trained in its use. The effects of this 'secret' weapon will be explored more thoroughly in the next chapter.

The first victim of the trawl cutter was to be the trawler *Peter Scott*, on 5th September, perhaps not coincidentally, the day Ministerial talks were due to start in Reykjavik. *Peter Scott* was one of those accused of covering up her identify and flying the pirate flag. The attempt by *Ægir* was only partially successful as only one trawl warp was cut. *Ódinn* attempted to cut the *Boston Explorer's* warps later the same day, but *Boston Explorer* hauled her trawl in before *Ódinn* could complete her cutting run.

The news spread quickly and the immediate reaction of the trawlermen was to threaten retaliation, both against the gunboats and against Icelandic fishermen. Fortunately *Miranda* was able to calm the situation down, whilst protesting strongly to *Ægir*.

During the rest of 1972, another eight British trawlers and one West German were to have their trawls cut.

[53] However, Geoff Hammond, who commanded HMS *Palliser* at the start of the First Cod War, remembers an incident in Toffeeapple (the southwestern haven) where in thick fog & with a flat calm, he was following one of the 'football team' trawlers. *Ægir* looked to be running in to interfere with the trawler's nets and so Geoff Hammond warned the Skipper of this possibility. The Skipper's reply was that he wasn't bothered about any 'f'ing gunboat' as his engineer was ready to put 40,000 volts into the warps if they tried to cut them. As this conversation was, as ever, on a voice circuit readily heard by *Ægir,* it is perhaps not surprising that *Ægir* turned hard to port and left the area. Geoff Hammond believes that this may well have been an early attempt to prove the warp cutter.

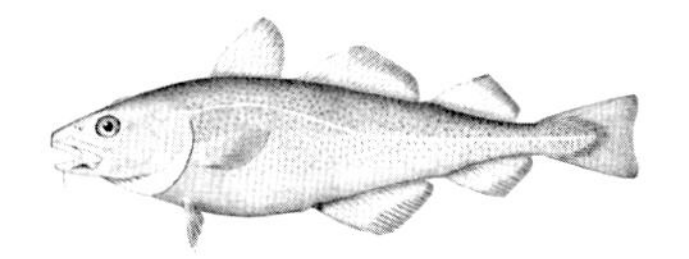

CHAPTER 10

THE SECOND COD WAR SEPTEMBER 1972 - MAY 1973

It was to be eight months before naval protection was authorised. During this period, the Ministry of Agriculture, Fisheries and Food (MAFF), with their civilian support ships, tried to minimise Icelandic interference with British trawlers. The British aim was still to find a solution by diplomatic means and, in order to ease this process, naval forces were kept in the background, outside 50 miles. Initially, the Coastguard used the warp cutter sparingly, presumably in the hope that, once the capability had been demonstrated, fishermen would put pressure on the British government to settle the dispute. This did not happen.

The Warp Cutter

As has been said, the Coastguard had developed the warp cutter in 1958, but had decided not to use it until 1972. The warp cutter was very simple and very effective, just a pair of jaws with a cutter in the throat - akin in many ways to the paravanes of the First World War or to minesweeping gear before the advent of the explosive cutter. The gunboat towed the cutter on a wire so that the cutter would catch one, or both, of the trawl warps. With the momentum involved, this action would force the warp into the cutter and so sever the wire. A successful cutting run required very close-quarters manoeuvring by the gunboat, with a definite risk of collision and every chance for the participants to hurl insults, and whatever else came to hand, at each other. British accusations of dangerous and unseamanlike manoeuvres led to Icelandic counter-accusations of aggressive action by trawlers.

The British Government complained formally every time this 'dangerous and illegal' tactic was used. There was great concern that the severed warp would whip back onboard and cause severe injury, but in fact, there is no record of this ever happening, probably because the trawl was always so deep that the tension in the warp was absorbed by the water. There are even reports of the trawler's crew being unsure if a warp had been cut or not. There are no full records as to how many successful warp cutting runs actually cut both warps, the best estimate seems to be about two-thirds. If only one warp was cut, the repairs were much quicker and more straightforward as very little gear had to be replaced.

Skipper Ken Knox recounts that:

> *'Most trawlers, especially the side towing ones (Sidewinders) only carried a limited amount of fishing gear; two full sets, the luckier ones maybe three sets. By cutting both warps, the skipper would lose:*
>
> *2 x lengths of trawl warp*
> *2 x trawl doors (otter boards)*
> *2 x bridles (cables)*
> *1 x full set of ground bobbins (24)*
> *5 x ground ropes (to hold the bobbins)*
> *2 x Dan Leno bobbins*
> *1 x full trawl (wings, square, bellies, leathers, cod ends)*
> *8 x cod end protectors (cow hides)*
>
> *When a trawler's warps were cut, it resulted in great stress on the crew as well as the captain. A full set of gear could take up to 18 hours to replace and skippers would often stop the watch below and work all hands. Trawl doors, heavy ground gear and full sets of bobbins had to be replaced, the trawl itself and the cod-ends to prepare with protective cowhides etc, warps to splice and ropes and cables. All this work affected crews both physically and mentally. Lots of work with no fish, resulting in tiredness and less earnings.*

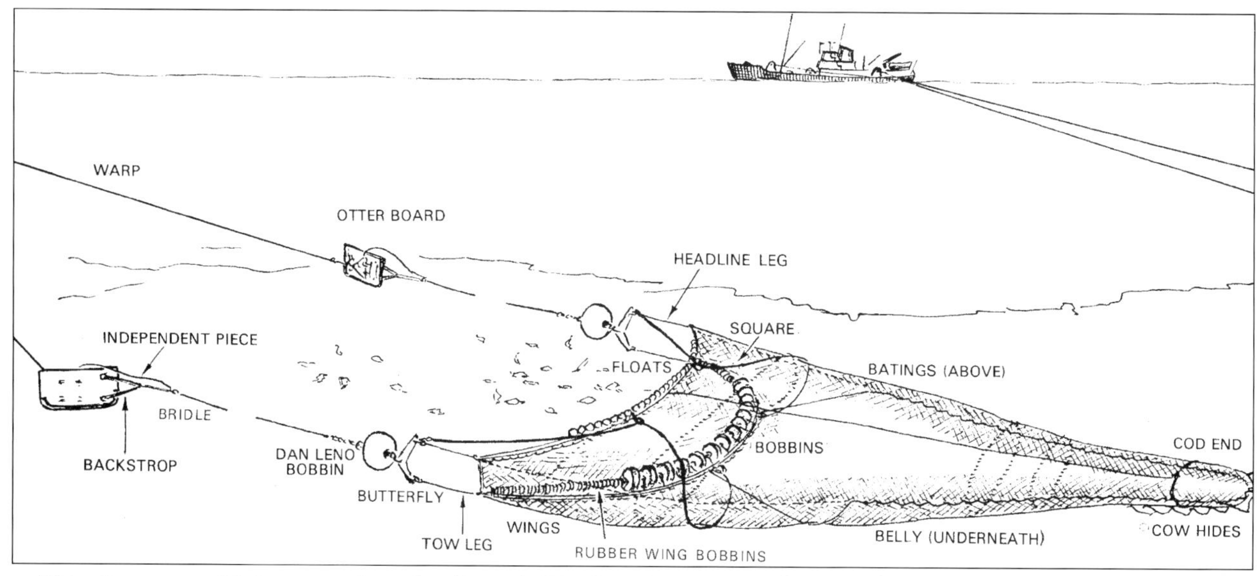

This diagram, which comes from the Bosun's Watch website (www.fleetwood-trawlers.connectfree.co.uk) courtesy of Jim Porter, shows how the trawl was made up and illustrates the specific parts mentioned in the section above.

Many trawlers had far less replacement gear, so became very restricted in their fishing. It is important to realise that losing a full set of gear didn't just result in long hours of hard work and loss of valuable fishing time, but also of skipper's and crew's earnings. The nets, wires, doors and all ancillary equipment cost thousands of pounds. At the end of the voyage, and after the fish had been sold, all costs of gear, fuel and victuals etc were deducted from the catch sale. After these expenses had been deducted, then the officers' and crew's earnings would be worked out. So the ICG gunboat captain sweeping across the warps of a trawler and successfully cutting both warps could quite easily be the reason for the trawler's seamen to end up "settling in debt" or a very low amount of money in their pockets for three week's hard work.'

Ægir cut *Lucinda* and *Wyre Victory's* warps on 12th September 1972 and *Ódinn* cut *Kennedy* and *Wyre Captain's* 10 days later. HMS *Aurora* (Commander Guy Liardet) was on patrol, outside the 50-mile limit, over this period and so could only observe from a distance. It was whilst on patrol on the 19th September that *Aurora* heard a distress call from the 100-ton wooden Icelandic fishing boat *Jón Eiríksson*, on fire about 80 miles northwest of the Faeroes. *Aurora* immediately closed *Jón Eiríksson's* position, transiting through the 50-mile limit to do so. As soon as she was within range, her Wasp rescued the five survivors from their dinghy. Once on the scene, *Aurora* got the fire out and took the *Jón Eiríksson* in tow towards the Faeroes. Unfortunately *Jón Eiríksson* sank before she could be towed to safety and, after discussions with Whitehall and the Icelandic Authorities, *Aurora* returned *Jón Eiríksson's* crew to their homes in Hornafjördur, in southeast Iceland. Commander Guy Liardet remembers that the only thing that was new or worked onboard *Jón Eiríksson* were the liferafts and 'the crew were absolutely delighted when she sank. Lovely weather, frigate and Royal Fleet Auxiliary quite close - no probs. You can quote the Captain of *Aurora* saying he believed it was an insurance scam.'

Negotiations, in both Reykjavik and Whitehall

The third phase of negotiations opened in Reykjavik on 5th October 1972 and, despite the continued harassment of fishermen by the Coastguard, sufficient progress was made for the officials involved to agree to set-up a ministerial meeting in November.

In Whitehall, the pros and cons of naval protection continued to be actively debated. The MoD was still of the opinion that, if warships were to be sent in to give protection, they must be given robust Rules of Engagement (RoE). The fear was that the Coastguard was not likely to be deterred by the mere presence of a frigate. Decisive action to prevent warp cutting would involve the risk of damage and injury, possibly death.

The Foreign and Commonwealth Office (FCO) and MAFF would not accept this basic military premise and, in due course, neither did Ministers. Purely defensive naval protection, using minimum force, was to be the Government's bargaining position both internationally (with the Icelanders, the International Court of Justice and NATO) and internally (with parliament and the fishing industry). Any suggestion of an aggressive posture in order to force an early resolution of the dispute was, again, ruled out.

On 24th October, Edward Heath, the Prime Minister, decided that if negotiations were unsuccessful and harassment continued, the Royal Navy would provide protection and it would probably be necessary to establish havens. However, a simple demonstration of presence by a British warship might suffice. The Secretary of State for Defence was, meanwhile, invited to give further consideration to suitable RoE if ships were to be ordered to give direct protection.

There had already been much discussion of RoE between CinC Fleet, FOSNI and the MoD. Three options had been prepared for different levels of escalation:

Option A: simple demonstration of presence.

Option B: to attempt to deter and frustrate harassment without using gunfire or any other kind of force; to prevent arrest by the selective intervention of one or more frigates.

Option C: to attempt to frustrate harassment, allowing the use of force up to certain levels. These included placing armed parties onboard trawlers to prevent arrest and physically obstructing gunboats attempting to get to a trawler. Gunfire was only to be permitted in self-defence.

Since the First Cod War, RoE had come of age as a tool for explaining to politicians exactly what they were asking the Services to do and detailing how much force and of what sort they could use to do it. The Fleet Operational and Tactical Instructions (FOTI) contained detailed RoE for every possible scenario and the Navy was well practised at operating under RoE.

So, it was a comparatively straightforward job to

HMS Aurora rescues the Icelandic fishing boat Jón Eiríksson. (Mike McAllister)

extract the necessary RoE from the Fleet Operational and Tactical Instructions (FOTI) and to attach a list of authorised RoE to each of the three Options. Ships would initially operate under Option A and since no use of force was authorised until Option C, which would require Ministerial approval, agreement on the RoE package was easily achieved. MoD formally issued the Rules to CinC Fleet and FOSNI; FOSNI then incorporated them into the DEWEY Operation Order (OpOrder).

Escalation and then the Winter 'Calm'

Whilst the politicians were deciding what they would, or rather would not, let the Navy do to fulfilling the aim of the mission, life was continuing at sea. Bryan 'Tiny' Height, who had served in HMS *Palliser* during the First Cod War, was back in her again for the Second.

> *'I thought it was all very costly and should have been sorted out years ago. After all it was their livelihood and in their waters, as we now know, fish stocks are dwindling. We did our stint up there. We did have a mishap. We were doing a RAS up forward for fuel in high seas. It was lucky for the team, if that lifeline had not been rigged quite a few of us would have been lost overboard. A wave came over the bows, as we dipped we were all on our backs clinging to guardrails soaking wet. The RAS was aborted.'*

Although there had been five warp cuttings in September, the first serious incidents involving warp-cutting attempts did not take place until 17th and 18th October. Over these two days, *Ægir* cut *Wyre Corsair* and *Aldershot's* warps and *Ódinn*, in pursuit of *Wyre Vanguard*, fired blank rounds. It was claimed, in Iceland, that the trawler *Aldershot* had rammed the *Ægir*. The British version of the incident is rather different and more plausible. *Ægir* attempted to cut *Aldershot's* warps and the two collided during the attempt. The *Ægir* sustained rippled plating, whilst *Aldershot* was seriously damaged in the stern. Unless *Aldershot* was going astern (with her trawl down…) it is difficult to see how she could have rammed *Ægir*, as the Icelandic propagandists claimed. It is much more likely that *Ægir* miscalculated her warp cutting run.

Although the hole in *Aldershot's* hull was above the waterline, the wash from her screw was causing water to come in through the damaged plates. The crew effected temporary repairs with mattresses and matting, whilst heading to the Faeroes. After an initially unfriendly reception from a group of young demonstrators, the hole was fixed and the damage patched with cement. *Aldershot* was back fishing within 36 hours of the incident.

As a result of these incidents, the second frigate was brought forward and HMS *Phoebe* joined HMS *Achilles* outside the 50-mile limit. On 25th October 1972, Edward Heath also wrote personally to his opposite number, Ólafur Jóhannesson, deploring the deterioration in relations between the two countries, emphasising the advantage of early talks and suggestion that further harassment at sea was inappropriate. He added that, if harassment continued, naval protection was inevitable. Ólafur Jóhannesson responded immediately, noting that he shared the concern and agreeing to continue talks on the basis of reduced British fishing. No mention was made of harassment and interruption to fishing, which continued. On 4th November, the second frigate, HMS *Falmouth* by this stage, was withdrawn.

Meanwhile, the search for a defence against the warp-cutter was underway. As an immediate antidote, trawlers were instructed to work in pairs or larger groups, with non-fishing vessels guarding the sterns and quarters of those actually trawling. This tactic had some success, but as the Icelanders gleefully pointed out, it reduced the active trawling fleet by 50%. There was only one successful warp cut in November and FOSNI was cautiously optimistic in a signal on 23rd September that a combination of trawler self-defence measures and civilian support vessel assistance would be sufficient.

Ministerial talks were held in Iceland on 27th and 28th November and, whilst inconclusive, the two sides were still talking, even though the British made it clear that naval protection would be provided if necessary to allow fishing to continue. As winter drew on, the northern and northwestern fishing areas were closed and overall trawler numbers reduced to about 20. The respective Foreign Ministers met at a NATO meeting and agreed to resume talks in early 1973. There was much less harassment in December and only one warp cutting; despite all the Icelandic actions 1972's catches were normal and there was hope that talks would produce a compromise without the Royal Navy having to enter the 50-mile limit.

This was a boring period for the frigate on patrol and all that Tony McManus, in HMS *Rhyl* can remember of the entire 3 week patrol over Christmas that year is watching *Paint your Wagon* wedged into a corner of the Senior Rate's Mess on a very rough Christmas Day.

1973 - Escalation again

On 1st January 1973, Britain joined the European Economic Community (EEC) and the Common Fisheries Policy (as amended for the first 10 years) came into effect. Whilst the process of joining the EEC and signing up to the CFP had no direct effect on the dispute with Iceland, the difficult negotiations over coastal fishing rights had reinforced the view that distant-water fishing must be protected.

The only minor effect was that Britain could join Germany in refusing Iceland the special import duty reductions to all EEC states that she would normally have been entitled to. These economic sanctions had no noticeable effect in persuading Iceland to settle the dispute with Britain and Germany. The Germans, whose distant-water fleet was about one-third the size of the British one, were treated in exactly the same way. An agreement had been reached that both countries civilian support vessels, of which the Germans had one or two on task, would provide help to both fishing fleets. At no stage did the Germans consider the use of naval protection. After the first week's lull, the harassment and warp cutting recommenced. The *Westella* and *Boston Blenheim* both had their warps cut on 7th January.

The Support Commander in *Ranger Briseis* was heard by the Coastguard advising trawlers to work in pairs and so give mutual protection. This produced a complaint that he was encouraging illegal fishing and there were fears that the civilian support vessels might be denied access to Icelandic ports or might even be arrested. Thereafter, he was ordered to be more discrete and communications with the Royal Navy frigates outside 50 miles were kept to a minimum.

Harassment escalated markedly during January 1973 and there were seven successful warp cuttings by *Ægir*, *Ódinn* and the new *Tyr* between 7th and 23rd. These incidents produced the normal crop of accusations and counter-accusations. By now the trawler skipper were demanding naval protection, but the British Trawler Federation (BTF) and the fishing port unions took a more measured view. They

Built in 1960 Ódinn was one of the larger 'gunboats'. (David Mathias)

believed that naval protection would probably mean less fish in the short term and less likelihood of a reasonable settlement in the longer term. Patience was urged upon the skippers and then, as one of the gunboat captain's later put it 'The Devil rescued them'.[54]

The Heimaey Volcanic Eruption

In the early morning of 23rd January 1973, the Helgafell volcano on Heimaey Island, in the Westmann Islands group off the south west of Iceland, erupted, after having been dormant for at least 5000 years. The Surtsey Island volcano, in the same group, had appeared out of the sea nearby only 10 years before and then continued to erupt for 4 years, but the reawakening of Helgafell was still a shock to Vestmannaeyjar's 5,300 population - especially as the volcano was only 200 metres from the edge of town.

Fortunately, the prevailing wind blew all the fumes straight out to sea and the fishing fleet was in harbour that night, so it was a comparatively simple job to evacuate the island without any loss of life. All the Coastguard vessels were withdrawn from fishery protection duties and sent to help with the relief operations - leaving the British and West German fishermen free to continue fishing unhindered.

Britain offered assistance, but the Icelandic Government politely declined the offer. There was, however, one occasion just after the relief work finished, when help was again offered and accepted. On 15th March the Icelandic fishing vessel *Sjoestjarnan* was lost and *Ægir* took charge of the search and rescue operation, assisted by a Royal Air Force Nimrod maritime patrol aircraft, HMS *Caprice*, *RFA Wave Chief*, the defence tugs *Statesman* and *Englishman*, the civilian support ship *Ranger Briseis* and some British trawlers. Sadly no survivors were found. Before this joint search and rescue (SAR) operation, in early March, the Heimaey relief operations had finished and the Coastguard had returned to their patrols on the fishing ground.

The Search for a Defence against Warp Cutting

After the first warp-cutting incident on 5th September 1972, some trawlers had tried towing ropes and wires astern to foul the gunboat's screws. *Ódinn* was successfully snared using this tactic, but thereafter it had no effect - probably because the Coastguard fitted some kind of propeller guard. In January, February and March 1973 extensive trials were conducted with a double sweep wire fitted with diverters, floats, snag-lines and static cutters. The final trial proved that this rig would work, but it became unstable above 6 knots. It was also very cumbersome to stream and recover each time a trawler hauled and shifted, so this rig was abandoned in favour of a simple towed cutter (similar to the Icelandic one) with a suspension float. The Navy gave a dozen to the BTF and the owners were encouraged to produce more themselves. There is no evi-

The American owned tug Statesman, on long-term charter to the United Towing Company of Hull, was one of several tugs chartered by MAFF as Civilian Defence Vessels. To avoid potential political considerations, she was transferred to the British Register.
(David Mathias)

[54] Quote from the 3-part Icelandic TV documentary '*The Last Waltz*' shown in the spring of 2000 and, later, in an abridged one-part programme on BBC.

Consideration was given to deploying Royal Maritime Auxiliary Service salvage tugs, such as Roysterer, seen here, however, they were no faster than the civilian vessels and as naval auxiliaries were likely to be portrayed as "military' units in the international propaganda war. *(Tim Meredith)*

dence that any were ever used in anger.

The production of a counter-warp-cutter was difficult as no one was sure exactly what a warp-cutter looked like. In fact it consisted of a cheap, simple, robust, cast-iron four-pronged grapnel with sharp internal surfaces. The whole was about 5ft long and weighed about 30lbs. It was towed on a 3½-inch wire with a length of chain shackled to the cutter to help stability and depth keeping. There were no floats or diverters and the whole rig could be streamed in about one minute. Even with this knowledge, the British were never able to produce an effective counter-measure. The advantage always lay with the aggressor.

However, in response to the trawler skippers' pressure for more protection, it was decided to deploy civilian tugs. This idea of placing a large robust vessel between the gunboats and their quarry had first been mooted during discussions in late 1972 between MAFF and the industry. Once Ministerial approval had been obtained, the 1,166 ton, 16 knot ocean-going tug *Statesman* was placed on a long-term charter and she sailed from Leith on 20th January. *Statesman* was American owned, Liberian registered, British crewed and on long-term charter to the United Towing Company of Hull (UTC). To avoid the potential international political complications, she was transferred to the British Register. Another smaller UTC tug, the *Englishman* (573 tons, 15 knots), joined the *Statesman* on 15th February.

Each defence tug, as they were called, carried a Support Commander, who was either a fisheries officer or a retired naval officer. The Support Commander was responsible to the MAFF for the employment of the tug. Their instructions were to support and assist British trawlers in their defensive efforts to counter Icelandic harassment, whilst remaining within the International Regulations for the Prevention of Collisions at Sea and acting in accordance with the usual seamanlike customs.

The defence tugs were always intended to be neutral and, to clarify the issue, in March the Support Commanders were redesignated Defence Commanders and the title Support Commander was reserved for the Fisheries Officers in the Civilian Support Ships. Meanwhile, a search was underway for more tugs, preferably faster and more manoeuvrable.

The problem was that the *Statesman* was really not fast enough and the *Englishman* was too small and too slow. The Royal Maritime Auxiliary Service (RMAS) tugs were considered, but even the fastest, *RMAS Roysterer* was no faster than the *Englishman* and the RMAS, as naval auxiliaries, would undoubtedly be portrayed as 'military' units in the international propaganda war. UTC's 2000 ton, 18 knot tug *Lloydsman* would have been ideal, but she was committed to a long-term commercial contract. There were suitable foreign (German, Dutch, US and Japanese) tugs on the market, but expense and international/political sensitivities prevented them from being chartered.

Within the 50-mile limit, the defence tugs devel-

Irishman was the third tug to be chartered by the MAFF.
(United Towing Company)

oped two main tactics. The gunboats had an advantage of up to five knots, but one tactic was to trail the gunboat until she had to slow down to stream the warp-cutter and then remain at a lower speed to allow the cutter to stabilise at the required depth. Whilst this was going on, the tug could catch up and interpose herself between the gunboat and her target. On several occasions this caused gunboats to move on and so abandon that target or to start the cutting run too early - before the cutter had settled - so missing either one or both warps. As noted earlier, if only one warp was cut, it was a comparatively simple job to repair the trawl.

The second main tactic was not popular with the trawler skippers, as it required them to trawl in echelon, keeping station carefully on each other's quarter, with the defence tug protecting the quarter of the rearmost trawler. Even allowing for the co-ordination problems of station keeping, there were only so many fishing grounds suitable for echelon fishing.

After a month of the tugs being on station, MAFF's assessment was that they were useful, but not the full answer. If (a big if) the trawlers would do what they were asked to, it was possible for a tug to limit a gunboat's warp-cutting activities, but not to eliminate them. Additionally, one tug could only protect one small group of trawlers; the gunboats could transit from one group to another faster than the tugs and the tugs did not have the equipment or the personnel to be able to run an intelligence picture of the gunboats movements. As for the skippers' opinions - they were disappointed that the tugs were not faster, but content that, once in company, the tug could usually keep a gunboat at arm's length.

A third tug, the *Englishman's* sister ship *Irishman*, was chartered from early May and an option was taken on *Lloydsman*, as soon as she was free. The defence tugs remained on task for about a month at a time, before returning to a UK port for maintenance and crew rotation. By May 1973, there were three defence tugs on task, with the fourth expected shortly, as well as the two civilian support ships.

Back in Whitehall, the naval staff had also been re-examining the protection policy. No one was keen on protected havens - the fishermen because of the restrictions on their freedom and the likelihood of reduced catches and the Navy because of the number of frigates that would be needed - at least two per haven. One alternative was to locate and mark the gunboats, so allowing the fishermen the freedom they wanted. Assuming that, as experience had shown, the Coastguard could usually only deploy three gunboats at any one time, only three frigates would be needed for this option.

The frigates would have their integral surveillance assets - electronic support measures (ESM[54]), radar and Wasp helicopter, but, to be able to track the gunboats effectively, extra surveillance assets, such as Royal Air Force long-range maritime patrol aircraft (MPA) would be needed. On 7th March, Ministers agreed with this new protection policy. CinC Fleet and FOSNI were instructed to implement it; a third frigate was brought to 72 hours notice to deploy northwards and the Royal Air Force made plans to provide Nimrod surveillance.

The risk of using Nimrods in the dispute was that the Icelanders would then deny use of the NATO base at Keflavík to all Royal Air Force aircraft, but this was judged to be manageable. The were also potential air traffic control problems, but on-balance the mounting of daily, or twice-daily, patrols over the disputed area was considered to be feasible, even if they might use up most of the Nimrod's peacetime flying hours. The task - mainly compiling and maintaining a picture of every surface contact around Iceland - was good basic training for the Nimrod force and, with Soviet submarines having to transit the area to get out into the Atlantic, the was always the chance of some 'live' anti-submarine training as well.

The Foreign and Commonwealth Office advice was that aircraft should not fly inside the 12-mile limit. Apart from the occasional need for a positive visual identification, this was not a major problem as the Nimrod's other sensors could detect and track any contacts within Iceland's territorial waters.

Another factor that had been considered in Whitehall was the need to improve co-ordination between the different players, both off Iceland and back in the UK. Once naval protection was authorised, the chain of command would be much clearer and effective command and control would be much easier, but until then the defence tugs and the civilian support vessels were under MAFF's control, whilst the naval units (still outside 50 miles) were under FOSNI's. In addition, the naval operations room in the MoD had a role to play.

In order to improve the liaison and information flow, MAFF's Chief Inspector of Fisheries visited FOSNI's maritime[55] headquarters (MHQ) at Pitreavie near Edinburgh, in March 1973. This visit succeeded in improving the immediate situation as well as agreeing how command and control would be exercised once the Royal Navy and the Royal Air Force were committed to protection within 50 miles - as seemed to be very likely, if not quite inevitable yet.

Back to 'Normal' Business...

Early in March 1973 the Westmann Islands relief operations were completed and the Coastguard returned to patrolling the fishing grounds. This coincided with the opening of the northwestern fishing areas, the improved spring weather and an increase in the number of British trawlers in Icelandic waters. Almost as if they had a quota to catch up on, the gunboats set about warp cutting in the next month with gusto, as the following table shows:

5 Mar	*Ægir* cut *Ross Resolution's* and *Port Vale's* warps.
5 Mar	*Ódinn* cut *William Wilberforce's* warps.
6 Mar	*Ódinn* cut *Real Madrid's* warps.
6 Mar	*Ægir* cut *Ross Kelvin's*, *Brucella's* and *Vanessa's* warps.
7 Mar	*Ægir* cut *Spurs's* warps.
7 Mar	*Thor* cut *Grimsby Town's* warps.
8 Mar	*Ægir* cut *Real Madrid's* warps.
10 Mar	*Ægir* cut *Newby Wyke's* warps.
11 Mar	*Ægir* cut *Ross Canaveral's* warps.
13 Mar	*Thor* cut *Irvana's* warps.
14 Mar	*Thor* cut *Boston Explorer's*, *Northern Sceptre's*, *Boston Blenheim's* and *Benvolio's* warps.
17 Mar	*Ódinn* cut *Robert Hewitt's* warps.
25 Mar	*Ægir* cut *Wyre Defence's* warps.
26 Mar	*Ægir* cut *St Leger's* warps.
2 Apr	*Ægir* cut *Kingston Emerald's*

[55] Apologies to the non-naval readers for the increasing density of the 'alphabet soup'. I shall try to minimise it, but writing about military operations without using any of the jargon becomes impossibly long-winded. For the purposes of this story, Electronic Warfare (EW) is divided into the passive (listening to the 'enemy's' signals) – called Electronic Support Measures (ESM) and the active (jamming, spoofing etc) – called Electronic Counter Measures (ECM).

[56] Pitreavie was a joint Royal Navy-Royal Air Force headquarters under overall naval command.

The Icelandic Coastguard Vessel Arvakur was typical of the smaller 'gunboats'. (Jón Páll Ásgeirsson)

and *Ross Resolution's* warps.

3 Apr *Tyr* cut *St Leger's* warps.

23 successful (or partially so) warp cutting runs. What was more alarming was that there were also four firing incidents in the same period:

18 Mar	Shooting incident - *Ódinn/CDV Statesman.*
25 Mar	Shooting incident - *Ægir/ Brucella.*
26 Mar	Shooting incident - *Ægir/ St Leger.*
2 Apr	Shooting incident - *Ægir /CDV Englishman.*

The first firing incident took place after *Statesman* had successfully thwarted repeated warp-cutting attempts by *Ódinn*. The Icelandic claim was that *Statesman* had repeatedly tried to ram *Ódinn*. This type of incident was to be repeated and shows how tense and dangerous close-quarters manoeuvring was to become.

In the midst of this month of intense activity, and hence in a somewhat strained atmosphere, British and Icelandic officials met in Reykjavik to prepare for the next round of ministerial talks. Officials agreed, in principle, to a further reduction in the annual British catch, with the numbers being left to Ministers to agree in May.

There was no let up in the level of aggression as April continued. There were ten more successful warp cuttings in the rest of April and six firing incidents. The increase in firings by the Coastguard was probably an indication of the increased effectiveness of the defence tugs. The most dangerous incident occurred on 23rd April when *Arvakur* successfully cut a German trawler's warps. *Arvakur*, one of the smaller gunboats and not fitted with a gun, had not been recognised as she approached and so no defensive measures had been taken. Once she was recognised, three British trawlers boxed her in and 'ran' her back inside the 12-mile limit. During this process tempers ran very high; threats and abuse were being exchanged and eventually *Arvakur* fired about ten rifle shots directly at the trawler *Brucella*, hitting her lifeboat and bridge. She also fired at and hit the *Portia*.

Later, when fishing had been resumed, *Thor* arrived on the scene, cut *SSAFA's* warps, collided with *St Leger* and fired blank warning rounds from her 57mm gun. The British trawler skippers reacted by taking up very close station on an Icelandic trawler fishing nearby, in what the Icelanders claimed was a 'dangerous and provocative' manner (not that *Thor* actions were not dangerous and provocative). The final act was when *Thor* threatened, chased and fired blanks at *Macbeth*. Fortunately no one was hurt in these exchanges.

David Robinson, who was a trawlerman for most of his working life, was present this day - in what came to be known as the 'Battle of the Islands'.

'I was onboard the Robert Hewitt, a Fleetwood one-sided trawler. She was one of the largest vessels in the port and, on this day, we were fishing at the islands off the south west coast of Iceland. A smaller gunboat, the Arvakur, had been stopping us fishing and making runs at us when we tried to commence again.

Understandably, our skipper (Alfie Blackburn[57]) had finally had enough and decided to take the fight to the enemy. At the time there was no protection near us. We chased the gunboat and he took flight, slightly hampered by the fact that his paravanes cutting gear had a problem, as it was streaming out astern of him as the winch mechanism wouldn't haul it in. Eventually they almost got it out of the water and, by that time, we were less than a cable from his stern. We had our anchor ready on the slip to release it as soon as we could get close enough to drop it on his stern.

By now, we were actually looking down on his stern and this chap emerged from the port side bridge door. I vividly remember he wore a peaked cap and a white, rolled neck, submarine type sweater. He carried what looked like a .303 rifle with a shoulder strap. We laughed and shouted at him, asking him what he was going to do with the gun, all convinced that no way would he dare fire it. Unfortunately he did! Fortunately into the air! And the bullets whistled past our forestay. I would not have thought that it was possible to hide behind a rivet, but it is! Most amazingly, three deckhands took shelter behind the bosun, possibly thinking that he was on more money and should take more risk!

By now, the chap had had enough and retreated back to the bridge, and we were almost ready to slip the anchor. The cluster of men on Arvakur's stern had given up with the paravanes and had momentarily disappeared in a housing at the stern, only to emerge with a mooring rope, which they threw over the stern. As both ships were going full speed, everything seemed to happen in a flash. The rope, with floats along it, streamed along our starboard side and our skipper suddenly realised what their game was! But it was too late to take action.

The gunboat skipper went hard to port and crossed our bows. His idea was to have us run over the rope, which would foul our screws. It was amazing that we didn't hit him - there couldn't have been more than a couple

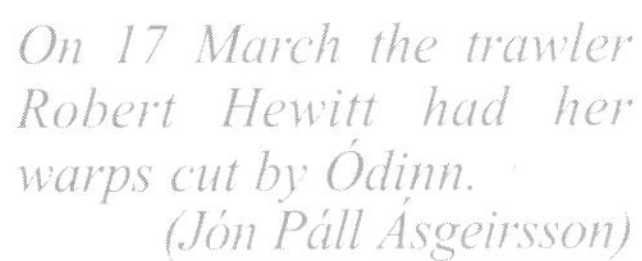

On 17 March the trawler Robert Hewitt had her warps cut by Óðinn.
(Jón Páll Ásgeirsson)

[57] Skipper Alfie Blackburn was punished by his owners by being relieved of his command and given a smaller (therefore less profitable) trawler instead.

of fathoms between us as his stern crossed our bows. If his plan had succeeded, we would have been dead in the water, there for the taking. It was a brilliant piece of seamanship by the Icelandic skipper, but could have resulted in a high-speed collision with the resulting consequences.
Following this incident, after complaints lodged by the Icelanders, our skipper lost his command. Seemingly they could do whatever they wanted, but in no way could we retaliate. Today, we would say a level playing field was needed. Basically, we were not even allowed to kick the ball.
That evening, at least three gunboats caused havoc among the fishing fleet, which comprised trawlers from Hull and Grimsby, as well as Fleetwood. Shellfire, as well as rifle fire, was heard that night, during what some of us fishermen called the 'Battle of the Islands'. Some damage was caused to one trawler's radio room and we saw a trawler having a tug of war with a trawler after actually throwing a grapple over the headline as he tried to scramble his trawl aboard.'

Both governments protested very strongly about each other's behaviour on 23rd April 1973. The next talks were due to be held, at Ministerial level in Reykjavik, on 3rd and 4th May. It was clearly vital to reach a settlement before lives were lost.

More Talks, but no Negotiations

The talks opened with cautious optimism - the agenda had been well prepared by both countries' officials and there was reasonable hope of reaching an interim agreement. The principle of a substantially reduced British catch had been agreed in advance and the British opened by proposing a total of 1000 tons less than the 156,000 tons proposed by Icelandic Ministers in July 1972 - which was itself a 25% reduction on the 1971 catch. However, the Icelandic Minister counter-proposed a further reduction to 117,000 tons. The British believed that this size of a reduction would have a very serious effect on the fishing industry and the ports that supported it. They offered a cut to 145,000 tons, but the Icelandic Minister was not prepared to discuss any total other than 117,000 tons.

To sour these, so-called, negotiations further, *Tyr* cut *Wyre Victory's* warps on their second day. This tactic of cutting warps during actual negotiations was to be repeated, so it has to be assumed that it was either Icelandic Government policy to up the pressure or another 'independent' gunboat Captain implementing his own harder-line policy, as had happened at the opening of the First Cod War. In this strained atmosphere, the negotiations broke up with the British details proposals for a 145,000-ton catch still on the table and Iceland agreeing to study them.

Back to Whitehall and Westminster

Whilst accepting that naval protection was now almost inevitable, there remained an unwillingness to take this step because to do so would close the door on any further negotiations. The naval staff considered arming the defence tugs, but this proposal foundered on the legality of arming contracted merchant ships, the difficulties of command and control and the fact that, if it came to shooting, the gunboats would probably still have the advantage. Overflights of the disputed areas by Royal Air Force Nimrods or ships' helicopters were also ruled out because they would be widely perceived as military interference, whilst adding little to the tugs' ability to intervene effectively. Another proposal was to deploy coastal minesweepers or HMS *Endurance* - both being seen as less of an escalation that using frigates in defence. The former proposal was turned down on weather grounds and the latter because *Endurance's* role in the South Atlantic was seen to be of higher importance.

From the beginning of the 50-mile dispute, Parliament and the press had been supportive of the Government's line, which was to negotiate, whilst accepting that, ultimately, naval protection might be necessary. The fishing industry was also, in general, content to put up with the harassment and warp-cutting, knowing that naval protection would be provided if there was no other solution. The rhetoric (clearly for Icelandic, as well as British, consumption) became less emollient as the dispute progressed.

On 6th March 1972, a Foreign Office Minister had told Parliament:

'I cannot say that we would in no circumstances resort to naval protection for

our fishing vessels, but I hope that protection will not prove necessary.'

By 19th October 1972, the line was:

> *'The British Government reserve the right in the event of further interference to take without notice such measures as we may think appropriate to protect our vessels.'*

On 1st November 1972, the Ministry of Defence said:

> *'The Royal Navy accepts the commitment to assist our trawlermen and naval forces are available in case of need.'*

And on 22nd January 1973, the Foreign Secretary said:

> *'We will if necessary send the Navy to the support of our vessels, but I think that everybody in the industry is conscious of how dangerous it would be to start another 'Cod War'. There may be no alternative, but we must avoid it if we can.'*

Fortunately, the British press had also taken a moderate and helpful line. So when the talks broke down on 4th May 1973, the British government felt that it had shown utmost patience in attempting to negotiate a settlement with Iceland, especially bearing in mind the International Court of Justice's ruling in Britain's favour. Mindful of the lessons of the First Cod War, Britain was keen to avoid being seen as the aggressor and was equally keen to maintain the quiet sympathy, if not the support, of her allies.

The crux of the matter, as it was to be in all of Britain's fishing disputes with Iceland, was that Britain believed she had international law on her side and Iceland believed she was morally right. There is no doubt in my mind that international law is, in reality, a political construct and not a legal one, by which I mean that international law is what countries agree to be bound by. Short of the UN Security Council authorising an invasion (and we've seen where that leads to), there is no 'legal' way of enforcing the judgements of the international court against a country that is not prepared to accept its wrong doing. The other factor in all three disputes was that Iceland believed, rightly, that international law was moving in her favour; she just wasn't prepared to wait. Britain, on the other hand, was hoping to slow the move towards the increasing restrictions on the traditional freedom of the high seas. There were many reasons for this desire, but in the fishing context, the hope was to preserve employment or, at the least, to buy time to permit a manageable decline.

With the other side in this standoff not prepared to negotiate in any meaningful way, Britain had no option, other than complete surrender, but to up the ante. The hope remained that any recourse to naval protection would be of very limited duration and that meaningful negotiations would swiftly follow. The issue was to be forced by the events of 12th -15th May.

The End of 'Civilian' Protection

On 12th May 1973, both *Englishman* and *Irishman* managed to foil warp-cutting attempts by *Thor*, who consequently fired warning shots at them. On the afternoon of 14th, there was a group of about ten British trawlers fishing off the northeast coast. Without their knowledge, and with no forewarning, this area had been declared a conservation area.

When *Thor* and *Tyr* appeared in the area, the trawlers stopped fishing, but did not clear the area, as ordered. According to the trawler *Lord Alexander*, *Tyr* ordered him to stop and was about to board him. The Coastguard denied this and counter-claimed that several trawlers had tried to ram *Thor* and *Tyr*. The trawlers, in their turn, denied this accusation and claimed that they were just 'chasing off' *Tyr*, who fired live rounds across the bows of *Macbeth* and another trawler.

Next morning, in the same area, *Arvakur* attempted, unsuccessfully, several warp-cutting runs. Throughout the rest of the 15th, the skippers, angrily, debated this series of incidents and, finally, that evening sent the following ultimatum was sent by the skipper of the *Northern Sky* to their owners:

> *'From All British Trawlers. It is now impossible to fish off Iceland due to continuous gunboat action. If naval protection is not forthcoming by 0400Z 17 May, it is the unanimous decision of all trawlers to leave Icelandic waters.'*

HMS Plymouth *(MoD/Crown Copyright)*

Over the 16th and 17th, the trawlers, about 40 in total, congregated off the east coast outside 50 miles.

Meanwhile, HMS *Plymouth* was diverted from another task to join HMS *Cleopatra* just outside the 50-mile line off the southeast coast. At 1800 on the 16th, the Commanding Officer of *Plymouth*, Commander Mike Rawlinson, assumed command of both ships, as Officer in Tactical Command, or OTC. HMS *Lincoln* was sailed from Portland, with dispatch, next morning to join the patrol force, and RFA *Wave Chief* was also sent north to relieve RFA *Brown Ranger*.

Whilst the Navy was getting all the necessary units into place, the owners were still wavering about the desirability of naval protection. Despite the 50 warp-cuttings and 20 shooting incidents since the coming-into-force of the 50-mile limit, there were many who still believed that the restrictions that would be necessary under a naval protection regime would be commercially disadvantageous. For three days the owners tried to persuade the skippers to return to the fishing grounds. The gunboats sat inside 50 miles and listened to the skippers' debate.

Whilst the industry was still debating, the Royal Navy and the Royal Air Force were getting ready. The first Nimrod sortie, aimed at starting to build the surface picture, started at 0400 on the 17th. Later that day, both *Plymouth* and *Cleopatra's* Wasp[58] helicopters conducted surveillance flights inside 50 miles.

By the morning of the 19th, it was clear that the owners had failed to persuade the skippers to resume fishing and at midday, the skippers sent a second ultimatum, threatening to leave Icelandic waters for the Faeroese fishing grounds or their home ports unless naval protection was provided by 1600 that day.

Having already decided that it could not surrender to harassment, the British government authorised naval protection from 1500. The trawlermen heard of this decision before it was formally transmitted to the frigates and at 1430, cheering and a recording of '*Land of Hope and Glory*' was heard on the trawler

[58] The Wasp was a fairly primitive helicopter in terms of sensor fit – it only had the pilot's and the aircrewman's 'Mk1' eyeballs, augmented by the x10 magnification, stabilised optical aiming sight, which was part of the AS12 missile system. Nevertheless, in good visibility, it was possible to identify a contact as a gunboat at 18 miles.

net. At 1450, the OTC was informed that Operation DEWEY was to start at 1500.

That morning, the British Ambassador in Reykjavik, John MacKenzie, informed the Secretary General of the Ministry of Foreign Affairs of Her Majesty's Government's intentions. That evening, the Ambassador was summonsed to the Prime Minister's Office and given the following statement:

> '*The Government of Iceland strongly protests against this aggression of Great Britain against an Ally in the North Atlantic Treaty Organisation who is defending its vital interests by protecting its main natural resources and reserves its right to take any necessary countermeasures.*'

At 1535 on 19th May 1973, HMS *Plymout*h led HMS *Cleopatra*, RFA *Wave Chief*, the tugs *Englishman*, *Irishman* and *Statesman* (now under naval command) and about 30 trawlers back inside the 50-mile limit off Seydisfjord.

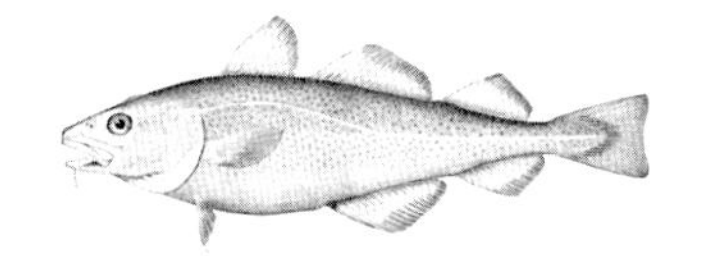

CHAPTER 11

THE SECOND COD WAR
MAY 1973 - JUNE 1973

The first part of the 50-mile Cod War - under civilian protection - lasted 8½ months. The second phase - up to an interim agreement - was to take 4½ more, followed by a final six-week period of negotiations, whilst fishing continued inside 50 miles and the warships and tugs remained on patrol just outside 50 miles.

I have already mentioned Tactical Command - in effect local command, which is usually exercised by the senior officer on the patrol - called the OTC (Officer in Tactical Command). The next level of command up is called Operational Command, which during all the naval protection operations off Iceland, was exercised by Flag Officer Scotland and Northern Ireland (FOSNI) from his Maritime Headquarters (MHQ) at Pitreavie, just north of Edinburgh. On 19th May 1973, FOSNI was Rear Admiral Mike Lucey CB DSC.

The Commander-in-Chief Fleet (CinC Fleet) allocated the necessary forces to FOSNI and FOSNI was responsible through CinC Fleet to the Ministry of Defence (MoD) for the conduct of operations; he was allowed to deal directly with the British Trawler Federation (the 'owners'), but only over fishing matters.

After the first ten days, the OTC was always a Captain (i.e. in at least his second sea command) or a Captain (F) (i.e. Captain of a Frigate Squadron, as well as being in command of his own ship and therefore usually in at least his third sea command). Officers of this seniority would invariably have served in the Ministry at some stage in their career and so would have an awareness of MoD and Whitehall politics. The OTC had command of the warships, fleet auxiliaries and the defence tugs. The civilian support vessels remained under MAFF's command, but the OTC would regularly seek fishing advice from the Support Commanders embarked in the MAFF vessels and deal with the fishermen either via them or via the Defence Commanders in the tugs.

Neither the OTC nor indeed the British Government had any authority over the trawlermen. All they could do was advise and hope that the owners would insist on compliance with the Navy's requirements.

The British Preparations

Her Majesty's Government's aim, as laid down in the OpOrder for Operation DEWEY was to maintain the legal rights of UK fishing vessels on the high seas between 12 and 50 miles off Iceland. Prime Minister Edward Heath laid out his views in the TV documentary *The Last Waltz*:

> *'We believed that we'd had these rights for so long and that we were entitled to have them, and there was no sound explanation as to why we shouldn't have them. Now we knew about the internal political situation in Iceland, which was that you'd got a communist minister there who was trying to run the show and he wanted to get rid of everybody in every respect. He wanted to get out of NATO. We knew that, but that wasn't our view.*
> *.....Don't make me laugh, there was no problem of conservation there. And all the fishermen knew it.'*

The naval mission was to maintain this aim, whilst exercising the minimum force necessary. FOSNI's amplifying instructions included the following:

> *a. Employ HM Ships to mark*[59] *gunboats*

[59] 'Mark' has a specific meaning in this context - it means to be in position to be able to stop a gunboat from completing her mission - i.e. be able to stop a warp cutting run.

once located.
b. Employ defence tugs in either their well-proven role in giving close protection to trawlers, or to assist in marking gunboats.
c. Deploy all available forces to match the concentrations of trawlers within the designated fishing areas; 'Havens' or 'Fishing Boxes' are not to be instituted.
d. Operate helicopters to locate gunboats and to assist in maintaining a trawler plot.
e. Reconnaissance will be available from daily (or more frequent) maritime patrol aircraft sorties.
f. Provide medical and material aid to British trawlers when support ships are not available for these services.
g. The twice-daily trawler round up (the reporting of positions) remains the responsibility of Support Commanders.
h. Avoid all involvement with foreign trawlers. No protection is to be provided to other nationalities.

The Designated Fishing Areas (DFAs) were approximately 100 miles long on the inner (12 mile) edge and were agreed between the MAFF and the BTF as likely to be the best fishing areas. The idea was that, within these areas, the trawlers could fish as and where they wished. Although most of the trawlers had gathered to the east whilst awaiting a resolution of the protection issue, the initial DFAs were to the northwest and southeast of Iceland.

The BTF had issued instructions to their skippers, which included the following:

a. Only fish within a DFA or fish outside 50 miles.
b. Fish well clear of the 12-mile limit.
c. When on transit within the 50-mile limit, keep in groups for mutual protection and have all gear stowed.
d. Report arrival, departure and position (twice daily) to the Support Commander.
e. Report gunboat sightings.
f. Take every precaution and action to avoid being boarded, short of endangering life.
g. Cooperate fully with the Royal Navy ships, defence tugs and civilian support ships.

FOSNI's signal initiating Operation DEWEY instructed the OTC to operate under Rules of Engagement (RoE) Option Charlie. These were the least restrictive of the three options agreed in Whitehall in October 1972 and would permit the physical obstruction (riding off) of gunboats attempting to cut a trawlers warps; the use of searchlights and the jamming of both radar and radio; buzzing by helicopters, the placing of armed parties in trawlers and the counterboarding of arrested trawlers. Military units (frigates, helicopters and maritime patrol aircraft) were not permitted to enter the 12-mile limit except for lifesaving purposes.

The use of gunfire was only permitted in self-defence. Option Delta, which did lay down the rules for gunfire had been promulgated in April 1973. The principles were clear warning and slow escalation to the minimum use of force necessary to disable a gunboat's weapons. Control of Option Delta was retained in Whitehall, but release could be requested by FOSNI, the OTC or an individual commanding officer if he felt the situation justified it.

Icelandic Preparations

On 19th May 1973, the three larger Icelandic gunboats, *Ægir*, *Ódinn* and *Thor* were all available, as was the smaller, unarmed *Arvakur*. *Albert* was considered to be too small and too slow and was rarely deployed against the British trawling fleet. *Tyr* (*Hvalur 9*) was due to be returned to her owners for whaling. Captain Gudmundur Kjærnested of *Ægir* was the Senior Coastguard Officer afloat - in effect the Icelandic OTC. Political control over the gunboats activities was nominally in the Justice Minister's hands, in consultation with the Fisheries minister. The Prime Minister was consulted over major issues.

The Icelandic Government wished to gain world sympathy for its cause and was to fight the propaganda war much more effectively than the British. The Icelandic Government set up a dedicated link between their Coastguard HQ and their Embassy in London, so ensuring that every incident was reported initially by Icelandic sources and the British invariably found themselves trying to correct the Icelandic version. As is the media's wont, measured corrections never get the same exposure as the original story, especially when the original story is more sensational.

FOSNI's assessment, subsequently proved to be correct, was that the Icelandic aim was to arrest British trawlers within the 50 mile limit, with a secondary objective of harassment in order to restrict the British ability to fish or, maybe, to make the fishermen withdraw completely.

On the evening of the arrival of the British frigates, Prime Minister Ólafur Jóhannesson appeared on Icelandic national television declaring that Iceland would ask for help against the aggressor at the UN Security Council or within NATO. He observed that, under the NATO treaty, 'an attack on one was considered an attack on all' and subsequently he asked the US Ambassador Frederick Irving (at 0700 on Sunday morning) to send the American aircraft based at Keflavík to fly out and 'bomb' the British warships. He did not expect his request to be followed up, but was just making it very clear that NATO's use of Keflavík and the fishing dispute with Britain were inextricably linked.

Fishing Recommences

The OTC's initial intention was to keep the trawlers in one loose group so that it was easier to give protection until the Coastguard's tactics became clearer. HM Ships *Plymouth* (OTC) and *Cleopatra*, with the three tugs *Englishman*, *Irishman* and *Statesman* formed a screen to cover the north, west and south of the trawlers. RFA *Wave Chief* was stationed to the east. For two days, nothing happened and at 0700 on the 20th May 1973, HMS *Lincoln* joined the patrol.

The first Icelandic reaction to the start of naval protection came that afternoon, when an Royal Air Force Belfast transport aircraft en route to Gander, in Newfoundland, was refused permission to land at Keflavík and the Icelandic Ministry of foreign Affairs announced that British military aircraft would no longer be permitted to use Icelandic airfields.

In May, June and July this far north, twilight lasts all night. At 0645 next day, the 21st May, the Nimrod on task detected a gunboat about 25 miles southwest of the trawler group. *Cleopatra's* Wasp was launched and identified the contact as *Thor*, whereupon the OTC detached *Cleopatra* to mark.

Thor's first action was to harass a group of German trawlers fishing about 15 miles south of the British. At 1730 she then approached to within 5 miles of the British group, before turning off to the southwest. HMS *Lincoln* shadowed her up to the 12-mile limit, after which *Cleopatra's* Wasp, also from outside the 12-mile limit, tracked her until she was well clear.

At 0100 on the 22nd, RFA *Blue Rover* relieved RFA *Wave Chief*. Later that morning, the Icelandic trawler *Steinunn*, with a full complement of British and Icelandic pressmen, approached the British group. Commander Mike Rawlinson, the OTC, gave a brief interview by loudhailer and the *Steinunn* took her journalists on a tour of the whole group.

Ódinn appeared from the shore just before lunchtime; she was marked by both *Plymouth* and *Lincoln* and just observed the fishing, no doubt noting the names of the 'poachers' for future use. *Lincoln*, having been taken off another task to augment the patrol at short notice, was relieved by HMS *Jupiter* at 1500 and returned to her other duties. *Ódinn* remained in the vicinity, making an unsuccessful warp cutting run on the evening of the 23rd. He was headed off by HMS *Plymouth*. *Ægir*, who had been located to the southwest by HMS *Cleopatra*, joined the group shortly afterwards.

Early next morning, both gunboats separately attempted to get in amongst the trawlers. *Ægir* was ridden off by *Plymouth* and *Cleopatra* and *Jupiter* kept *Ódinn* at bay. The tugs formed a second line of defence between the trawlers and the gunboats. Further harassment attempts were made and thwarted that afternoon. That evening, ashore, an angry crowd coming from a trade union rally, stoned the British Embassy in Reykjavik. Some windows were broken, but the police contained the violence and no one was injured.

At 0300 on the 25th May, *Ægir* headed north and was lost from the plot; *Ódinn* remained in company. The first three days of close marking and riding off had proved that three frigates and three tugs were well capable of protecting a group of trawlers, even one spread out over 30 miles. No warps had been cut and fishing had not been interrupted. However, one of the factors leading to this initial success had been the weather, which had allowed early detection of the approaching gunboats and so pre-positioning of the defending forces.

The First Shots

Although the policy of keeping all the trawlers in a loose group had been agreed by the skippers and was

The Trawler Everton – one of the regular 'poachers' in the view of the Icelandic Coastguard.
(Unknown Origin)

supported by the Support Commanders, there were soon calls for more freedom. Commander Mike Rawlinson, the OTC met with the two Support Commanders in HMS *Plymouth* on 23rd May 1973 and they agreed that the skippers who wished to move north should be advised to do so in a group at an agreed time, so that protection could be provided both during the transit and in the new fishing area.

When this advice was passed to the skippers, there was much debate and disagreement on the trawler net - monitored, of course, by *Ægir* and *Ódinn*. On the morning of the 25th, trawlers started to move north (following *Ægir…*) in little groups and at different times. Four, with the support ship *Miranda* in company, were escorted by the *Statesman* and ten set off later, escorted by *Jupiter*. Unknown to the Navy, another four had set off independently earlier.

A group of about fifteen, supported by the *Othello*, stayed in the southeast with *Plymouth*, *Cleopatra*, *Englishman* and *Irishman* defending them. *Ódinn* remained in the southeast, where she was being marked by *Cleopatra,* commanded by Commander Tony Wavish. *Ægir* was found by a Nimrod off the northerly point of eastern Iceland - Rifstangi; she was directly in the transiting trawlers path. However, it was one of the four who had slipped away without telling anyone whom *Ægir* found first.

At 1245 HMS *Jupiter*, commanded by Commander Jock Slater, heard the trawler *Everton* calling on trawler net. She was fishing alone about 15 miles north of Grimsey Island - *Ægir* was threatening to fire on her if she did not stop and submit to arrest. There were no other British vessels in the vicinity - the other three who had sailed independently were 40 miles to the east, *Statesman* was 120 miles away and *Jupiter* 250. The sea was calm and *Everton* hauled her nets as soon as she sighted *Ægir*, then headed east.

The two skippers were in clear VHF communication and *Ægir* told *Everton* that her instructions were to stop and arrest her by whatever means necessary. When *Everton* refused to stop, *Ægir* fired blanks and then 57mm solid shot across the bow. This was followed by a solid shot, from very close range, into *Everton's* bow above the waterline. A crewman was allowed forward to inspect the damage and the skipper told to report when he was safely back aft, before a second shot was fired into the bow. Over the next two hours, interspersed with orders to stop, *Ægir* fired seven shots into *Everton*, the most dangerous of which caused a 4-in x 10-in hole below the waterline and started to flood the lower hold.

Ægir refused to allow anyone forward to inspect the damage to *Everton*, but offered to send assistance if *Everton* stopped. *Everton* continued eastwards and at about 1500, she reached the position of the other three independents, *C S Forester*, *Arctic Warrior* and *Northern Sky*. Ministers ashore had been controlling the incident carefully and at this juncture *Ægir* was called off.

Everton's pumps were defective and it was not until *Statesman* arrived at 1900 and transferred two portable pumps that the rate of flooding was slowed down. *Statesman's* pumps were not powerful enough to reduce the flooding and by the time HMS *Jupiter's* Wasp started to transfer divers and a repair party at 2100, *Everton's* lower hold was completely flooded and there were 4ft of water in the hold above. There were also two press boats on the scene by this stage. Overnight *Jupiter's* repair party saved *Everton*, to the apparent complete lack of interest of her skipper and crew. By next morning the holes had been plugged and a cement box was in place. *Everton's* skipper was briefed that his ship was only fit to steam at slow speed in low sea states; he returned immediately to the fishing grounds.

The Icelandic plan had been to arrest a UK trawler fishing within 50 miles. *Ægir* had been instructed to avoid casualties, so when faced with a courageous and obstinate skipper, the arrival of reinforcements and the imminent arrival of a warship, he had to withdraw. Once again, the difficulties of arresting a trawler determined to resist, had been clearly demonstrated.

Fortunately no one was hurt in this incident, but it was clear that the comparatively restrained operations of the First Cod War were to be replaced by much rougher and more dangerous ones. In recognition of this escalation, FOSNI had, at 1445, requested a change in the Rules of Engagement to Option Delta (firing permitted) in case *Ægir* was still actively harassing or attempting an arrest when *Jupiter* arrived at the scene of action. The MoD turned this request down at 1830. At 1744, *Jupiter* had to ask for permission to enter the 12-mile limit as *Everton* was now inside it. This request was also refused, although her Wasp helicopter and the *Statesman* were allowed in.

Slightly surprisingly, considering their earlier decisions, that evening the British Cabinet gave serious thought to responding aggressively to *Ægir's* actions, by capturing *Ægir* herself. On being advised that this was not a simple operation, that lives would definitely be at risk and that it would be very hard to justify legally, the idea was dropped.

The *Everton* incident certainly concentrated minds. Rear Admiral Lucey (FOSNI) met the BTF on 29th May 1973 and the owners agreed to impress on their skippers the vital importance of obeying the BTF's Instructions to Skippers, especially with respect to reporting positions and movements, transiting in groups and only fishing in designated areas (the DFAs). The BTF published a scale of varying periods of suspension for skippers who failed to comply.

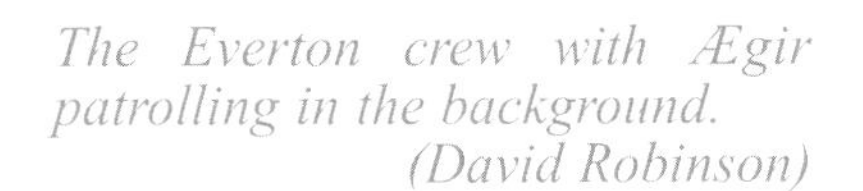

The Everton crew with Ægir patrolling in the background. (David Robinson)

HMS Juno on protection duties.
(Jón Páll Ásgeirsson)

The skippers declared their intention to follow the *Everton's* lead in resisting arrest and to ram gunboats if necessary. The positions of the DFAs were reissued and a system put in place so that skippers could request, via the Support Commanders, changes to the DFAs.

FOSNI approved the OTC's policy of gunboat marking and local protection, with the emphasis being put on the marking. In order to keep a better handle on gunboat (and trawler) movements, Nimrod flights were increased to two a day from 26th May and for several days after 28th May to three. Additionally, the British Embassy in Reykjavik was asked to send daily reports of gunboat movements into and out of harbour, as had been done during the First Cod War. A formal request for naval and air force units to be allowed into the 4 to 12 mile zone was turned down on the grounds that it would strengthen the Icelandic ability to accuse the UK of taking offensive military action.

The British Government formally protested over the shelling of the *Everton* on 27th May. The Icelandic Government responded that the action was a normal Coastguard response to an offending vessel that failed to stop when ordered. On 28th May both sides put their case to the UN Security Council and the next day Iceland presented a formal demand to NATO asking the Alliance to arrange for the withdrawal of British warships from 'inside the fisheries jurisdiction of Iceland. …. Furthermore, it is pointed out that Iceland considers the extension of its fishery jurisdiction as an Icelandic internal affair '. The UK agreed to withdraw its warship as soon as Iceland ceased harassment. Dr Joseph Luns, the Secretary General of NATO, visited London and explained to Edward Heath that NATO's view was 'that Britain was paying much too much attention to fishing and that it didn't matter'. Edward Heath told him that 'it did matter, a great deal'. There were no more diplomatic moves for the next four months.

As the dust settled on the *Everton* incident, the trawlers gathered, as instructed, into one DFA or the other. About two-thirds were in the northwestern area, where *Cleopatra*, *Jupiter* and *Statesman* provided the defences. HMS *Jaguar* relieved HMS *Cleopatra* on 31st May. The remainder were in the southeastern DFA, where HMS *Plymouth* was relieved on 28th by HMS *Scylla*. Captain Ollie Sutton, the Captain of the Seventh Frigate Squadron (aka Captain F7) took over as OTC from Commander Mike Rawlinson. From then onwards, as envisaged when naval protection commenced, the OTC was always to be a senior Captain.

Arvakur joins in

At 0600 on 1st June 1973, the 380-ton *Arvakur* made a rare appearance in the southeasterly DFA. HMS *Scylla* and the tug *Irishman* were on patrol. At 0620 *Arvakur* attempted to cut the *Vivaria's* warps, but was ridden off by the 1166-ton *Irishman*, whose bow struck the gunboat's port quarter. Fortunately it looked as if the *Arvakur* was only superficially damaged.

Vivaria, having hauled her nets, joined *Irishman* and both 'sandwiched' *Arvakur*, attempting to force her away from the group of trawlers. At 0753, *Arvakur* again streamed her cutter; *Irishman* tried to hook it, but in the process collided with the gunboat's quarter. *Arvakur* then stopped for about an hour, watched carefully from close range by both *Irishman* and *Vivaria*. *Arvakur* was suddenly off again and, this time, succeeded in cutting the warps of one of the nearest trawlers, *Gavina*. *Irishman* and *Vivaria* set off in pursuit and, once again, came in close on either side of *Arvakur*. *Arvakur* collided with *Vivaria* and the 'backed into' *Irishman's* bow. Tempers were very high all round by this stage.

The OTC, Captain Ollie Sutton in HMS *Scylla*, detected *Thor* joining from the north and steamed to meet her. Captain Sutton told *Thor* what had happened and suggested that *Arvakur* might be called off before there was a more serious incident. The captain of *Thor* ignored Captain Sutton's suggestion and closed the group with his gun uncovered and manned. At 1023, Captain Sutton signalled a request for RoE Option Delta (approval to use gunfire) and manned his own close range weapons. Once *Thor* had joined *Arvakur*, they both opened to the north.

The MoD turned down the OTC's request for the ROE change, but did authorise him to warn the gunboats that he had authority to fire if they used direct gunfire against any British ship. Captain Sutton decided not to exercise this option and signalled that he saw it as a very high trump and would only use it in particularly threatening circumstances. Whilst this was going on, *Óðinn*, in the northwest DFA made four warp-cutting attempts, but was ridden off by HMS *Jaguar's* close marking every time.

Arvakur needed three weeks in Akureyri for repairs after these incidents. Thereafter she was mainly employed on lighthouse supply work and only made one further appearance on the fishing grounds; even then she did not attempt harassment or warp-cutting. *Irishman* was concerned that he might come under attack and proposed withdrawing outside 50 miles until *Englishman*, in Lerwick for a crew change, rejoined. The OTC did not wish to lose *Irishman* and signalled his intention to put an armed protection party onboard; an action that was already authorised by the RoE. FOSNI overruled the OTC, but did confirm that *Irishman* should remain on task. The owners and the OTC warned the skippers that, whilst mutual support was one thing, ramming and other acts of provocation were quite another.

On 4th June, HMS *Ashanti,* commanded by Commander Neil Blair, relieved *Scylla* in the southeast DFA, allowing Captain Ollie Sutton to take his ship up to the northwestern area and relieve Commander John Caughey in *Jaguar*, who then returned home. This was the preferred deployment - the OTC + 1 in the busier, more important northwest and the other frigate in the southeast. The OTC's ship and the southeasterly frigate would always be Wasp helicopter equipped. *Statesman*, the more powerful tug, was to the northwest and the two slower ones, *Irishman* and *Englishman*, were in the southeast. *Lloydsman*, a much bigger and more powerful vessel, was to join the OTC's team shortly. Two of the Civilian support vessels, *Miranda*, *Othello* and *Ranger Briseis*, were always on station. Finally, there was always one, sometimes two, Royal Fleet Auxiliary tankers in support of the patrol. This allowed the OTC to refuel his ships every three days - so ensuring that they were always ready for action. As the protection routine became more settled, trawler numbers increased - by 4th June there were 53 and by 6th, 59 - 53 of them in the northwest DFA.

On 4th June 1973, *Jupiter* caught *St Leger* fishing on her own 10 miles off the Icelandic coast. This sort of independent action made a mockery of the efforts to provide protection and *St Leger's* skipper was reported to her owners so that disciplinary action could be taken.

Every day one of the three main gunboats (*Ægir*, *Óðinn* and *Thor*) would appear on the fishing grounds and probe the defences, sometimes attempting a warp-cutting run or trying to engineer a close-quarters situation where they could claim that the frigates had broken the Rule of the Road[60]. *Ægir* was the most belligerent and collided with *Scylla* on 7th June.

At 0920, *Ægir* was heading north at 14 knots towards a lone trawler. *Scylla* was overtaking at 18 knots, about one cable[61] to port. When *Scylla* was on *Ægir's* port beam at about 150 yards, *Ægir* sounded

[60] More formally, The International Regulations for Preventing Collisions at Sea.
[61] 200 yards; one tenth of a nautical mile. The Rule of the Road does say that 'any vessel overtaking any other shall keep out of the way of the vessel being overtaken'.
[62] The formal signal for 'your movements are not understood', but often used to mean - 'get out of my way'.

six short blasts[62] and turned hard to port, seconds later she struck *Scylla's* starboard quarter with her bow. Neither ship was seriously damaged by this collision. Captain Sutton's protest was not acknowledged.

Three days later, *Ægir* approached HMS *Jaguar* from 25 degrees abaft her starboard beam - this made *Ægir*, this time, the overtaking vessel and so legally obliged, by the Rule of the Road, to keep clear of *Jaguar*. *Jaguar* was on a steady course, between *Ægir* and a group of trawlers. At about 50 feet off *Jaguar's* beam, *Ægir* came hard to port and passed 20 feet astern of *Jaguar*, who had meanwhile gone to full ahead.

The Long Term Plans

The large tug *Lloydsman* (2,000 tons and 18 knots) joined the patrol on the 10th June 1973. After brief discussions with the Support and Defence Commanders in the southeasterly DFA, she joined the OTC in his area. To complete the available protection forces, two liaison skippers (senior experienced trawler skippers) arrived in theatre. Skipper Ken Hames joined HMS *Ashanti* on 12th June, having taken passage up in the trawler *Gavina* and Skipper R Blyth, who came up in the *Vanessa*, transferred to HMS *Scylla* on the 14th. Thereafter, there was always one liaison skipper, who provided fishery advice and acted as the BTF's representative, in each DFA. They were especially useful in dealing with skippers who wished to act independently.

Norway continued to be very concerned about these hostilities on her doorstep and even informed the British delegation in NATO HQ that they were considering sending a Norwegian warship to keep peace on the fishing grounds. A minute prepared for the Norwegian Foreign Minister said:

> *In practice, this would take the form of unarmed Norwegian vessels replacing the frigates. These Norwegian inspection vessels would not take over the functions of the frigates but they would patrol the grounds in order to:*
>
> *a. Prevent the British trawlers from fishing in areas where the Icelanders have imposed a total ban on fishing, and*
> *b. Prevent the Icelandic Coastguard vessels from harassing British trawlers (cut trawl-wires etc.)'*

This briefing paper acknowledged that the British might be willing to accept this proposal, but the Icelanders might find it difficult. Unsurprisingly, nothing further was heard of this idea.

As it became clear that there was not likely to be any movement on the diplomatic front for some time, the navy, having assembled all the necessary forces, had to plan for their rotation. The usual training and deployment programme for the frigate force was already suffering from serious disruption, so the CinC Fleet decided to allocate FOSNI seven or eight frigates to form a Cod War group for three months. FOSNI then became responsible for filling the patrol slots, whilst keeping the 'off-watch' frigates fully trained and ready for Cod War operations in Scottish waters or ports. The point of this group was that the rest of the frigate force could then be used on normal Fleet business without fear of disruption to their programmes. Programme stability is always of great concern to the CinC, affecting, as it does, the operational effectiveness of his ships and the morale of his ships' companies - an important factor in the retention of manpower in an all-volunteer navy. The first group, to be on-task from mid-September to mid-December, was nominated on 14th June 1973.

By the 14th, almost all the 50 trawlers on station were fishing in the northwest DFA. It was decided, however, not to close the southeast DFA, as newly arrived trawlers often checked out their gear there and departing ones sometimes tried for a final top-up. Additionally, the fish might move and with the routine now in place and known by the fishermen, it was deemed better not to change it - just in case confusion was caused, or even maybe confusion was used as an 'excuse' for fishing outside an established DFA. One frigate and two tugs were kept in the southeast, although the second on-task support ship, *Othello* at this stage, was sent round to join *Ranger Briseis* in the northwest DFA.

The southeast frigate (HMS *Ashanti*) took over the task of the twice-daily round up. This in itself was no bad thing, as the trawlers transiting through were all reminded that the Navy was there to protect them and what the Navy expected the trawlers to do in their own defence. As well as the British trawlers, there were between 12 and 20 West German vessels, accompanied by one or two support ships, on the fishing grounds. The West German Government having decided that it could not protect its fishermen, they were subject to noticeably more harassment, warp-cutting and warning shots than the British. There were, inevitably, times when the two nationalities would get mixed up, making the MoD's instructions not to give protection to foreigners difficult to obey.

HMS *Leopard* relieved her sister-ship *Jaguar* on the 15th June and Captain Geoffrey Lloyd, in HMS *Charybdis*, took over as OTC on 20th. HMS *Scylla* returned home. Naval Protection had been in force for a month and the only serious attempt at arrest (the *Everton*) had been thwarted. Only one warp had been cut and the fishing had been excellent, with the only interruptions being trawlers who had had to haul early when a gunboat had appeared. The weather had also been kind and it looked as if the International Court of Justice's limit of 170,000 tons might be reached.

The ships' Wasp helicopters were all double-manned, so nearly doubling the available flying hours. The combination of the Wasp acting as a probe to identify positively contacts found by the Nimrod plus the use of electronic warfare to identify the gunboat's radars had enabled an adequate surface picture to be maintained. Once the gunboats had been found, they could be marked and, so far, there had been no attempt to swamp the defences by deploying all three large gunboats simultaneously.

All was not completely satisfactory however. There were still some skippers who were prepared to fish alone and who would send in false positions so as to keep the fish to themselves. Secondly, the gathering of intelligence was not 100%. The ban on helicopters entering the 12-mile zone, though sometimes knowingly broken by Commanding Officers, closed off vast areas of Icelandic waters and so allowed the gunboats to transit close inshore undetected. Additionally the intelligence of gunboats movements into and out of port provided by the Embassy was neither comprehensive nor timely enough to be of much use. Whilst the Embassy reporting did improve significantly, the 12-mile entry ban was never lifted.

Although the first month had seen comparatively little damage, the next nine weeks were to see several rammings, four shooting incidents and the only attributable death in all three Cod Wars.

CHAPTER 12

THE SECOND COD WAR
JUNE - AUGUST 1973

The first month of naval protection may have been a comparative success from the British perspective, but the Icelandic belief was that more of the same harassment and warp cutting would, over time, drive the British to surrender. They believed that time was on their side for two reasons - the cost of the British protection operation, not just financially, but in international political terms, and the fact that the movement towards wider fishing limits was continuing to gather strength.

Surprisingly, from the British perspective, the Coastguard did not seem to learn the most 'obvious' lesson of the first month; had they concentrated their forces and attacked a British group with all available gunboats simultaneously, they would have been able to inflict considerable damage upon the trawlers. This no doubt, would have led to a violent counter-attack from the fishermen, but there is no evidence that the Coastguard ever considered that their actions might produce a violent counter-reaction.

On 21st June 1973, the defence tug *Lloydsman* collided with the gunboat *Ódinn* 25 miles north of The Horn (North Cape). This was one occasion where there was no doubt in either country as to who was to blame.

Ódinn appeared out of Adhalvik Bay at 0600 and headed 020° at 12 knots, with HMS *Leopard* marking from three cables astern soon after she cleared the 12-mile limit. *Lloydsman* had been with a group of trawlers and on being advised of *Ódinn's* approach came south, (course approximately 150°) to put herself on the gunboat's port bow, whilst covering the trawlers. At about a mile, when she was Red 45° from *Ódinn*, *Lloydsman* came to port and steadied on 070°, right across *Ódinn's* bow.

Although *Lloydsman* disputes the final moves, the facts are that, despite going full astern, *Ódinn* struck *Lloydsman's* port quarter. There was negligible damage to *Lloydsman*, but *Ódinn's* bow was stove in and she was holed at the waterline. *Ódinn* refused offers of help and retired to Isafjord for repairs.

Both *Leopard* and the OTC in *Charybdis* witnessed the incident and both were in no doubt that *Lloydsman* was at fault for deliberately turning across *Ódinn's* bow. Inevitably, there were protests from Iceland where the press was able, for once honestly, to talk of 'deliberate attempts to ram and sink our Coastguard vessels'. The British press was reasonably sympathetic to *Lloydsman*, pointing out that, sooner or later, the gunboat's harassment was bound to lead to misunderstandings and collisions. The British government was also fairly relaxed about this incident and *Lloydsman's* robust actions were very good for the trawlermen's morale.

In his Report of Proceedings[63] (RoP) dated 4th July, FOSNI said:

> *'It will be a brave gunboat who does not give way to her (Lloydsman), as the incident with Ódinn on 21 June indicated. Even if Lloydsman was not entirely blameless, the fact is that Ódinn has not been seen at sea since...'*

In fact *Ódinn* was under repair in Akureyri until 3rd July and *Ægir* was also on the slip in Reykjavik until 2nd July as a result of her 7th June collision with *Scylla*. This left the Coastguard temporarily short of ships, but in fact the one operational gunboat, *Thor*, did manage to outwit HMS *Charybdis* on the 27th June and cut *Arctic Vandal's* warps.

Both the weather and *Arctic Vandal* conspired against the protection forces. The latter because she was fishing alone and was not in her reported position - hence her radar echo was presumed to be an Icelandic trawler. *Charybdis* had been following

[63] A formal report up the command chain - in this case from FOSNI to CinC Fleet.

and/or marking *Thor* all day. The visibility had been poor since dawn and *Thor* was regularly slipping inside the 12-mile limit, altering her course and speed, as well as cleverly using other contacts, presumably Icelandic fishermen, to mask her movements. At the time she slipped out of *Charybdis's* grasp and cut *Arctic Vandal's* warps, the visibility was under a mile. This incident illustrated, once again, the importance of fishermen obeying the rules and the difficulty in maintaining a constant coherent surface picture.

Next evening, *Charybdis* and *Thor* locked horns again when *Charybdis* was protecting a group of seven trawlers. Captain Lloyd's RoP says:

> *'Close marking on Thor's beam was adopted when she was 2 miles from the group, and the gunboat was headed off. A close quarters melee ensued for over an hour during which time Charybdis successfully held the inner ring, turning inside Thor. Violent engine movements and helm alterations were required, the machinery responding at all times. Even when Thor went full astern from 19 knots, Charybdis was able to match her deceleration and prevent her breaking through. At no time during this encounter was Thor further away than one cable and on several occasions the distance was down to 60 feet. Finally Thor withdrew, being marked from the quarter at two cables. No further problems were encountered with Thor at subsequent meetings.'*

Unsurprisingly, after this very tense encounter, *Thor* withdrew and *Charybdis* took station on her port quarter at a more relaxing distance.

By this stage tension was getting high on the fishing grounds and it seemed to be almost inevitable that there would be a major incident before long. On 1st July, in the northwest DFA, HMS *Leopard* was marking *Thor*; *Lloydsman* was also in the vicinity. The Captain of *Leopard*, Commander M J Harvey, takes up the story in his RoP:

> *'...during the afternoon Thor returned to the fishing grounds escorted by* HMS *Leopard. Additional cover was being given by Lloydsman when a similar situation to that leading to the Lloydsman/Ódinn collision began to develop, and Thor gave a clear warning to Lloydsman on VHF that if he continued his aggressive approach Thor would take defensive measures. At this warning the gunboat uncovered his guns and apparently closed up at action stations. I immediately matched his act for act and moved to a station one cable on Thor's beam*

HMS Leopard (MoD/Crown Copyright)

from where I was able to observe his actions. Lloydsman reduced speed and took station two cables astern of Thor, and progressively the tension relaxed with Thor re-covering his guns and Lloydsman marking from a longer range. Thor carried out a stop-go policy of remaining dead in the water for unpredictable periods and then suddenly making a run towards the nearest group of trawlers. He appeared particularly restless overnight and made several aggressive approaches to various British trawlers, but by timely warnings on the radio all attempts were thwarted. Thor returned to Hunafloi at about 0830.'

This exchange did not escalate, but the day after, *Ægir*, just back at sea after three weeks under post-collision repairs, fired shots towards *Leopard*, who was marking her from a distance of a mile or so. *Ægir* was harassing a group of West German trawlers, including warp-cutting and attempting boarding. At 1515 she fired two warning shots in *Leopard's* direction; *Leopard* responded by going to action stations, asking MoD for a release of RoE Option Delta and warning *Ægir* that if she continued to fire in *Leopard's* direction, fire would be returned. *Ægir* did not acknowledge this warning.

At 1559, Captain Geoffrey Lloyd, the OTC in HMS *Charybdis* (in the southwest DFA), signalled FOSNI asking for permission to give assistance to the Germans 'on humanitarian grounds, up to Option Charlie', which would have allowed *Leopard* to ride off *Ægir*. Shortly afterwards, *Ægir*, with her gun still manned, left the Germans in peace and closed *Leopard* at 20 knots. The two ships then circled each other with their guns, including both Leopard's 4.5"-inch turrets (which were manned but not loaded), trained on each other for a few minutes. *Ægir* then covered her guns and cleared the area to the south.

An hour later, FOSNI replied to *Leopard's* RoE request signal, pointing out that the DEWEY OpOrder only allowed assistance to foreign trawlers for lifesaving/safety reasons and not in order to thwart the Icelandic Coastguard. Similarly the MoD, at 1735, turned down the OTC's request for Option Delta, noting that the existing RoE already allowed gunfire in self-defence and warnings that any direct fire would be returned.

As the Coastguard continued to concentrate on the undefended Germans, this became a sensitive topic - Britain was very keen not to be seen to be supporting one NATO ally against another. *Charybdis* who was, a couple of days later, watching *Ægir* harassing more German trawlers was told by FOSNI to move further away as even two miles might give the impression of supporting the Germans.

And so it continued, day by day. In the south, whilst *Leopard* was scrapping with *Ægir*, *Charybdis* was closing on *Thor* at 24 knots when it looked as if she was about to try and board the trawler *St Leger*. Even the Royal Fleet Auxiliary managed to get into the game - Captain Dick Thorn in RFA *Olwen* (a 20 knot 33,000 tons full load steam turbine tanker) reported that he had been able to block *Ægir* from getting to groups of trawlers several times. The MoD invited him to desist, observing that whilst RFAs should certainly be used for locating, shadowing and reporting, they were not suitable for close marking.

As can be seen from the diary of the Second Cod War at the end of the book, these incidents are fairly typical for the period. During the following week, things were quiet for the British as *Ægir* was involved in a Danish State Visit and the Germans, easier targets, kept *Óдinn* and *Thor* occupied. Even *Albert* had a go, firing warning shots at some German trawlers in the southeastern DFA, but keeping away from the British.

Ægir was back on duty in the northwest on the 11th July 1973 and, having failed to cut *Ross Kashmir's* warps, was kept at bay for an hour by *Charybdis's* close manoeuvring. Eventually, she managed to slip past *Charybdis* and ran down towards the *Boston Explorer* at 19 knots, with *Charybdis* holding position 60-120 feet on her bow. *Boston Explorer* had been ordered to haul his nets by the Liaison Skipper when *Ægir* was still at 6 miles, but failed to complete in time. As *Boston Explorer* was on *Ægir's* port bow, *Charybdis* was to thwart the attack without a high risk of collision and so the Liaison Skipper told *Boston Explorer* to go astern, so as to bring the warp up and down. *Ægir* missed on the first run, but cut one warp on the second; however *Boston Explorer* did recover and repair her gear.

Ægir now transited to the southeastern DFA, where fishing had been uninterrupted for over a month. *Charybdis* handed over *Ægir* to the, recently arrived, *Lincoln*, who in turn passed her on to *Gurkha*, the

HMS Charybdis on patrol (MoD/Crown Copyright)

southeastern frigate. *Lincoln* returned to the northwest to rejoin *Charybdis*; *Ódinn* and *Thor* were still in the area.

One of the geographical features of southeast Iceland is the Hvalsbakur, or Whaleback Rock. The significance of the Whaleback is that it is about 14 miles southeast of the coast and so it extends the Icelandic 12-mile limit much further out to sea. The gunboats had the option of transiting inside or outside the Whaleback and, if going inside would always be lost to the frigate's radar at some stage. The frigate then had to guess whether the gunboat would reappear from the north or the south and either position herself to north or south, with a 50% chance of getting it wrong, or linger to seaward and be committed to a stern chase once the gunboat reappeared. When fog was present as well, the frigate's problem was compounded. The same difficulties applied to Grimsey Island, off Iceland's north coast, when the northwesterly DFA came that far round.

The Summer Season

By early July 1973, the summer fishing season was in full swing and there were about 80 British trawlers off Iceland - split approximately 50/50 between the southeast and the northwest DFAs. *Ægir* had been shadowed by Captain Vincent Howard in *Gurkha* as she came down from the north and, on the afternoon of 13th July, she slipped inshore inside the Whaleback. When she reappeared, she was six miles ahead of *Gurkha*, heading southwest towards a group of trawlers. *Ægir's* lead was too great and despite warnings from both the frigate and the defence tug, two trawlers, *Wyre Vanguard* and *Peter Fleming*, had their warps cut.

Gurkha managed to keep *Ægir* away from her prey for the next couple of days, but fishing was severely disrupted. Although the owners (and the Royal Navy) realised that naval protection was never going to be 100% effective, some skippers felt that the Navy had let them down if there was even one successful warp-cutting. Overnight on the 13th/14th July, two or three of the skippers decided to take revenge by harassing Icelandic fishermen within the 12-mile limit.

Fortunately more words than action resulted and, with the assistance of the Defence Commander, the situation was calmed and the trawlers returned outside 12 miles. On FOSNI's advice, the British Trawler Federation (BTF) issued (one could almost say, re-issued..) the following:

> *'To all Trawlers: Nothing is to be gained by hot-headed action in revenge for action by Icelandic gunboats. Skippers must adhere to advice of Naval and Defence Commanders. In particular, instructions relating to fishing outside DFA must be followed. Disciplinary action will be taken against offenders.'*

The search for weapons, short of lethal force, that

could be used against the gunboats was a continuous one and on 12th July, Captain Lloyd asked for approval to use fire hoses and foam against a gunboat's bridge when attempting to ride her off. The MoD rejected this suggestion as likely to be ineffective[64] and escalatory, although the British Ambassador in Reykjavik (who saw almost all the signals between the ships on patrol and the UK authorities) thought that 'the longer HM Ships can avoid using force, the better.'

In the Naval Staff in MoD, a small group, known as the 'Ice Bucket', had been formed to look into every option. They considered everything from high-pressure water hoses, foam, paint, sand, smoke, CS gas, rubber bullets and the use of chain cable to catch the gunboats' cutters. Ultimately, none of these proposals were deemed likely to be effective and several, such as CS gas and rubber bullets were dismissed as being counter-productive on public relations grounds. As FOSNI summed it up:

> *'The plain facts of the situation are that, if the bluff of a warship's presence is called, and she is not fitted with a ram, there is little she can do except to use explosives. And we must be very careful in thinking up funnies short of firing, that they will really be effective, or we shall be laughed at and our last state will be worse than our first.'*

A Change of Watch

On the 14th July 1973, HMS *Arethusa* (Captain Tony Skinner) arrived in the southeastern DFA and took over marking *Ægir* whilst HMS *Gurkha* refuelled. Then *Arethusa* headed north to relieve HMS *Charybdis* and for Captain Skinner to relieve Captain Lloyd as OTC. Two days later, HMS *Gurkha* was relieved by HMS *Berwick*.

Ægir clearly decided to test the mettle of the newcomers and within the hour, Commander Peter Dingemans found himself, assisted by *Englishman* and *Irishman*, close marking her. At her sixth attempt, *Ægir* managed to slip past *Berwick* and cut both *Boston Blenheim's* warps. It was during these close encounters that Lieutenant Matthew Fyfe remembers a well-aimed potato, thrown by one of the chefs, breaking one of *Ægir*'s bridge windows. This does illustrate how close the ships were to each other.

Despite the BTF's warning, a few skippers, once again, decided to head inside the 12-mile limit in order to take revenge on Icelandic fishermen. They were quickly headed-off, before they got to the 12-mile limit, and the OTC decided to send HMS *Lincoln* round to reinforce[65] the southern DFA.

En route along the north coast, *Lincoln* met *Ægir* for the first time and, as usual, the gunboat decided to 'test the new kid on the block'. Commander David Howard remembers[66] that he was towing a length of cable that just reached under the water, so that it looked as if he had a towed body astern and he hoped that this would encourage gunboats to keep well astern. In the event, *Lincoln* stood on as *Ægir* closed to approximately 30 feet on her starboard side. As the waves built up in the gap between the two ships, *Ægir* shipped a bigger than average one and lost her port ship's nameplate. First blood to *Lincoln*, which might explain what came next - especially as *Ægir* had Press onboard.

Before relieving *Berwick*, *Lincoln* refuelled from *RFA Olwen* to the north of the southern DFA. Listening to the trawler net, it became apparent that *Ægir* had already arrived in the DFA and was giving the defending forces a very hard time. The trawlers were unhappy with *Ægir's* attention and so were giving the defending forces an equally hard time on the radio.

That afternoon, the 17th of July, *Lincoln* relieved *Berwick* in the marking position on *Ægir* from two cables on her port beam. There was a group of trawlers five miles ahead, fine on the port bow. It was calm and both ships were making 8 knots as *Lincoln* eased *Ægir* round to the southeast and clear of the trawlers. *Ægir* seemed to be content with this gentle riding off and started to drop back, probably to take a closer look at the length of chain still hanging from *Lincoln's* stern. *Ægir* closed to within a few feet and then seems to have misjudged the distance,

---

[64] It is difficult to see that the MoD were in a better position to judge the 'effectiveness' of this proposal than the OTC who, by this stage, had three weeks of hard-won practical experience. However such decisions, which are inevitably (and probably rightly) tinged with politics, rather than just operational effectiveness, are the prerogative of 'Head Office'.

[65] 'Reinforce' is the term used in the Naval Staff History, but there must have been a subsidiary requirement of 'try to keep the trawlers in order'. Commander Howard states that he was actually ordered south to relieve *Berwick*.

[66] I am grateful to Commander Howard for all the detailed descriptions of this and his next patrol in HMS *Lincoln*.

ICGV Aegir from HMS Lincoln (MoD/Crown Copyright)

because she struck *Lincoln's* stern, breaking a guardrail stanchion, damaging a fairlead and making a small hole[67].

From the photographs published at the time it could be seen how the British version could be disputed and the claim could be (indeed was) made that HMS *Lincoln* had cut across *Ægir*'s bow. Undeterred by this event, *Ægir* made several further attempts to break through to the group of trawlers, one of whose nets was caught on the seabed. Commander Howard recollects:

> *'I moved into a close mark on his port beam, holding him off from being able to make a direct run at his intended trawler victim. At about 17 knots I passed the trawler at approximately 30ft on my port side with the wheel hard a port, half astern on the port engine, full ahead on the starboard*[68]*. Lincoln spun around that trawler keeping the gunboat outboard throughout and safely clear. Ægir then backed off.*
> *This incident had several repercussions:*
>
> *1. The trawlers went from being a surly uncooperative bunch to suddenly showing a lot of respect for Lincoln. The first sign came over the trawler net immediately "Chr....ist, I didn't know an effing frigate could effing turn like that".*
>
> *2. I was subsequently offered shedloads of fresh fish; on one occasion we were unable to hoist the seaboat until we'd unloaded most of the fish, which had been above thwart level! The donating trawler had had no baskets to spare and had simply emptied several of them down into the seaboat.*
>
> *3. When I returned on patrol in September, Ægir was very wary of Lincoln during our first 5-hour brush on 19 September, 4 hours in thick fog. I don't attribute his caution to my railway lines!*[69]
>
> *I had a specially embarked photographer who filmed the whole of this incident. The film was dispatched to MoD and was never seen again. I was later informed that it had been "lost"'.*

Simultaneously in the northwestern DFA, *Ódinn* was testing the newly arrived *Arethusa's* resolve in a 90-minute period of very close manoeuvring - 'right down to barge-pole distance'. *Arethusa* prevailed and *Ódinn* was unable to cut any warps on this occa-

[67] One of HMS *Lincoln's* traditions was that her spurnwater (the wooden lip on the deck edge) was painted in 'Lincoln Green', which was in fact, red. The ship ran a running battle with assorted staff officers who directed that the spurnwater be painted in the regulation sand colour. It was, but as soon as the Staff had gone, it was repainted in Lincoln Green.

[68] HMS *Lincoln* was a diesel-powered frigate, one of only eight in the Royal Navy, with the consequence that she had variable pitch propellers, allowing her to vary her speed more quickly than the more common steam-powered frigates.

[69] See below for more on 'defensive railway lines'!

sion. Two days later, on 19th July, *Ódinn* and *Arethusa* once again found themselves in very close company, as close as 15 feet, for seven and a half hours - between 1700 and 0030.[69]

Finally, *Ódinn* from 40 foot on *Arethusa's* starboard beam, sounded two short blasts (meaning 'I am turning to port'), put her wheel to port and hit *Arethusa* amidships. *Ódinn* rolled heavily to starboard, but appeared to suffer no significant damage. *Arethusa* lost her accommodation ladder and several guardrail stanchions. Having bounced off, *Ódinn* immediately tried to cut the nearest trawler's warps. She was again baulked.

There was much discussion during both the Second and Third Cod Wars as to how much the Icelandic Coastguard understood about the pressure and suction effects between ships in close company. The problem is that ships have bow and stern pressure zones, with a low-pressure zone in between. If another ship gets her bow into the low-pressure zone, she can be sucked in and will collide before being able to take avoiding action. The Royal Navy, through its experience in replenishing at sea, was well practised at managing this effect, but the Coastguard seem to have been less aware of it and there were occasions when this probably caused a collision. However, it is difficult to see this incident as anything other than the first deliberate ramming of a frigate by a gunboat.

Taking Stock

On July 20th 1973, FOSNI summarised the position as follows:

'1. Icelandic Policy now seems to be intensified gunboat activity by:
- Maintaining long and dangerous close quarters situations with frigates.
- Angering trawlers by interfering with their fishing and thus driving a wedge between the militant skippers and the protecting forces.

2. However, ultimate Icelandic aim is still to capture a trawler.

3. Consider we must maintain the high standard of marking already being achieved by frigates. The risk of collision is great but it will have to be accepted and a high damage control state maintained whenever in company with gunboats.

4. The majority of skippers seem to be cooperating but every effort will be made to convince the more vocal and volatile skippers that they do not help their cause.'

The technique of marking had evolved by this stage. Generally, whilst well away from any British trawlers, the frigate would try to remain near, but clear astern of, the gunboat. Once trawlers were deemed to be at risk, the frigate would move up onto, or maybe just ahead of, the gunboat's beam, between the gunboat and the trawlers. The aim was to stop the gunboat from getting either across the frigate's bow or around her stern. Remaining in this position, sometimes only feet from the gunboat, often involved engine orders such as 'full ahead' or 'full astern', which, in the Royal Navy, are usually only used in an emergency as they mean 'give me full power as quickly as possible, accepting that damage to the machinery may occur (although injury to personnel is not acceptable)[70]'.

If the gunboat managed to slip past the frigate, it might become necessary to get back onto the gunboat's 'up-threat' beam and then 'ease her over' by altering a degree or so towards her at a time. The frigates always had a speed advantage over the gunboats, but usually the gunboats, by virtue of their diesel/controllable pitch screw could react more quickly.

The International Regulations for Preventing Collisions at Sea 1960 (usually just called the 'Rule of the Road') were to be used by both sides in justification of their actions, but in reality both sides disregarded the Rules. The three Rules most often quoted in defence of ship's actions during close quarters situations were Rules 21, 27 and 29.

Rule 21 - Where by any of these Rules one of

[70] One major difference between the Second and Third Cod Wars was that the Second was fought in the long days of summer (May to October), whilst the Third (November to June) started in the long winter. To use the year 2005 as an example, the longest day (18th June) has sunrise at 0257 and sunset at midnight - on 22nd December, sunrise is at 1122 with sunset 4 hours later at 1531.

[71] Formally, responsibility for any machinery damage passes from the Engineering Officer of the watch (in the Machinery Control Room) to the Officer of the Watch on the bridge.

two vessels is to keep out of the way, the other shall keep her course and speed. When, from any cause, the latter vessel finds herself so close that collision cannot be avoided by the action of the giving-way vessel alone, she also shall take such action as will best aid to avert collision.

Rule 27 - In obeying and construing these Rules due regard shall be had to all dangers of navigation and collision, and to any special circumstances, including the limitations of the craft involved, which may render a departure from the above Rules necessary in order to avoid immediate danger.

Rule 29 - Nothing in these Rules shall exonerate any vessel, or the owner, master or crew thereof, from the consequences of any neglect to carry lights or signals, or of any neglect to keep a proper look-out, or the neglect of any precaution which may be required by the ordinary practice of seamen, or by the special circumstances of the case.'

The Royal Navy view was that ships had to operate under Rule 27 (special circumstances), with Rules 21 and 29 being the only manoeuvring rules that applied. The dangers inherent in very close quarters manoeuvring were recognised, but there was no effective alternative short of gunfire. As Hannes Jónsson says in his book '*Friends in Conflict*' when discussing the balance of power between the Royal Navy and the Coastguard:

'But most important of all, one has to bear in mind the restraint which the British Government placed on the Royal Navy and their protective flotilla, forbidding them to use their guns and armour against their NATO ally in the Cod Wars. Consequently, the Cod Wars were never a test of military strength but, due to the strategy and tactics applied, first and foremost a delicate test of excellence in seamanship.'

Successful close marking enabled fishing to continue undisturbed. If a gunboat slipped through, trawlers would be ordered to haul their nets. This would take at least 12 minutes in a depth of 80 fathoms - enough time for a gunboat to cover 4 miles. Hauling caused significant disruption to fishing, 'though not as much as a warp-cutting.

Whilst close marking provided the exciting '5% terror' part of the Cod Wars, the '95% boredom' bit was the OTC's main concern - keeping constant tabs on the gunboats' movements. The Embassy team were now a reliable source of gunboat movements into and out of Reykjavik, but there was only occasional reporting from other ports. Electronic Warfare (EW) was the most important sensor, 'though there was evidence that the Coastguard had realised how much they were giving away and they were beginning to operate an intermittently or sometimes silent radar policy.

Air reconnaissance, by the Nimrod and Wasp, was invaluable for maintaining the trawler plot as all the trawlers were (usually!) outside the 12-mile limit, but was less useful in tracking the gunboats inside 12 miles, especially in the frequent poor visibility. The result of this weakness was that gunboats could sometimes appear unexpectedly. Accordingly, the OTC had to deploy his forces to cover the gunboats' most dangerous moves, which sometimes meant moving the third frigate from one DFA to the other as well as rotating the defence tugs to cover their off-patrol periods for maintenance and crew changes. One of the Royal Navy's major fears - of a coordinated operation by the entire Coastguard fleet, so swamping the defences - was, surprisingly, never realised.

Lofty Lofthouse was one of the LRO(G)s[72] onboard HMS *Arethusa*; he remembers that there was much banter between the trawlers and the protecting frigates on the marine VHF circuits - such as requests from a skipper to 'lend him the fxxxing great gun for a couple of hours. He'd do the rest'. And, as in the First Cod War, these exchanges, sometimes edited, were replayed on Icelandic TV and radio. His other, perhaps surprising, memory is that the gunboats still had no understanding of electronic warfare. If they

[72] Leading Radio Operator (General) – usually known as a 'killick sparker'. The RO(T) was a Tactical Operator, who specialised in visual signalling. They were known as 'buntings' from their signal flags. The third kind of radio operator was the (W) and they were the Electronic Warfare operators – known as 'Gollies'. There is some dispute about how they got this name, but the most likely is that when the branch was formed initial promotion was so rapid that it was believed that all a Golly had to do to be promoted was to collect the labels off the Robertson's jam jars.

RAF Britannia long-range transport aircraft, used as a maritime patrol aircraft from time to time to save flying hours on the Nimrod fleet. (David Berry)

were transmitting on their radar (as they had to in low visibility), the Gollies (see footnote[72]) would detect them. Additionally two of the Leander class frigates (*Ariadne* and *Apollo*) were fitted with a device called UA13 that could detect and direction-find VHF voice transmissions.

After an initial flurry, the British press quickly lost interest in the operation, although a variety of press facilities - from flights in Nimrod reconnaissance aircraft to trips in frigates - was always on offer. This is understandable because, apart from the occasional ramming or firing incident, there was little 'front page' news and to keep a reporter off Iceland for a couple of weeks on the off-chance of being there during an incident was not worthwhile.

The net result of this was that the Icelanders always had the upper hand in the media war. They could offer a day trip out in a gunboat, ensure that there was an incident and have the journalists and their photos back ashore with the Icelandic version long before the UK version was available[73]. In retrospect, this mattered less than was thought at the time. The Icelandic population was 100% behind their government's actions and so were not interested in truth or balance in the reporting - a collision was always a 'ramming by the British' etc. The lack of contemporary British material did mean that Icelandic pictures would be used, often uncritically, on British TV, but on the whole the British press took a similarly nationalistic view of events. The international press tended to print the first (almost always Icelandic) version, but as Britain's friends were, on the whole, understanding and her enemies were delighted that there was an ongoing dispute between two NATO allies, the international press had little influence on events.

Back at Sea

After the 17th/19th July 1973 collisions between *Ægir*/*Lincoln* and *Ódinn*/*Arethusa*, there was a fortnight of comparative peace. *Thor* had entered Akureyri for repairs and maintenance on the 10th July, although the OTC did not know this until the 2nd August, and she did not sail again until 19th August. *Ægir* and *Ódinn* were around, but seemed to be less aggressive and were not keen to tangle with the frigates. There were between 70 and 85 British trawlers enjoying good uninterrupted fishing and, with the gunboats quiescent, some skippers were, yet again, beginning to stray from the DFAs.

The defence tug *Irishman*, whose charter had expired, departed on the 19th to be relieved by her

[73] A scheme to install a photo transmission system in the OTC's ship was initiated in September 1973, but was not ready when the Second Cod War ended.

sister-ship *Welshman* in the southeastern DFA on the 24th July and the Nimrod patrols were supplemented by Britannias for a couple of months from 10th July. The Britannia was a long-range transport aircraft and their contribution to the Second Cod War is best illustrated by an extract from David Berry's book '*The Whispering Giant in Uniform*':

> *'The Britannias of 99 and 511 Squadrons were called upon to support a great variety of tasks throughout the world. One of the strangest of these occurred in 1973. Britain was in dispute with Iceland over territorial waters and the associated fishing rights. This resulted in many skirmishes between British fishing vessels and Icelandic gunboats; the Royal Navy attempted to police the area. Airborne surveillance provided vital intelligence and the maritime Nimrod aircraft were hard pressed to keep up the constant watch. This reached a point in July when it was decided that the Britannias could ease the situation by flying some of the patrols. Aircraft were detached to Royal Air Force Station Kinloss. A Nimrod captain and navigator and four observers supplemented the normal Britannia crew. Flight Lieutenant Derek Oldham, then one of a new Britannia breed, a first tour co-pilot, remembers:*
>
> *"Both our flights took 10½ hours and included one hour of night flying which was no mean feat at that time of year in North Scotland. We flew up to Iceland at high level, let down off the coast and flew anti-clockwise around Iceland at 1000 feet, returning to Kinloss at high level. The plan was to note any British fishing boats approaching the disputed waters and call in the Royal Navy to warn them off before they were intercepted by one of the Icelandic gunboats."*

It was said that the results obtained were far better than expected. The task continued into August resulting in a very busy month. 2,517 hours were flown. Amongst navigator, Flight Lieutenant Tony Bennett's 1973 memories is this recollection of the 'War':

> *"At the end of August both squadrons were involved in what was one of the more unusual tasks ever undertaken, and became known as 'The Cod War'. This led to skirmishes between seaborne forces with airborne surveillance provided by Nimrod aircraft. Some of these tasks were to be undertaken by the ubiquitous Britannias based at Kinloss, with each crew increased by a Nimrod captain and navigator. We also carried an extra Britannia navigator. The idea was to transit high level to and from Iceland letting down to patrol at 500ft, weather permitting, to track, identify, and report the movements of British and Icelandic vessels, particularly the gunboats.*
> *Fuel planning, to give the optimum time on patrol and an appropriate position to return, was the first consideration and whilst on patrol an accurate update of position was necessary. The nature of the task gave rise for some improvisation by the two Britannia navs and we discovered that, in our case, one nav would operate as normal and the other would be a nav radar. The only 'comfortable' position to operate the CCWR (Cloud Collision Warning Radar) was to perch on the cylindrical life jacket container. Not very satisfactory, but successful, changing roles every 1½ hours or so. On my radar watch I picked up a very strong return as we flew anti-clockwise on the north side of Iceland at a range of 120 miles. One of the strongest returns I can recall. It was large, slow moving and on our track.*
> *For the next 100 miles we speculated, and decided that it was on the surface. At 20 miles it was as strong as ever, but nothing was seen with five pairs of eyes, and a pair of maritime binoculars - until about five miles away, there it was - a huge whale lying on the surface. After that I certainly had a greater respect for the CCWR but the rest of the patrol was an anticlimax!*
> *The most rewarding of the three sorties we flew, was ironically in the worst weather. Just as we levelled off at 1500 feet after descent to commence our patrol, right beneath us through a hole in the cloud was the Icelandic Gunboat Thor in pretty rough seas. This was particularly pleasing, as she had not been*

seen for two to three days. And then for us a remarkable week was over. Three sorties in seven days each of 10 hours 15 minutes, operating in a totally different environment. What next?
Three days later we were on our way to Nairobi via Masirah carrying some units of the army on exercise ...'"'

On 2nd August 1973 the 200-ton gunboat *Albert* made her first appearance at 1500 and attempted, with gun manned and trained on the trawler, to cut the *Ian Fleming's* warps. The OTC, Captain Alec Weir in HMS *Andromeda*, was 25 miles away, at the eastern end of the northwestern DFA. He immediately launched his Wasp helicopter, whilst closing *Albert* at speed. Meanwhile, the 2000-ton *Lloydsman* interposed herself between *Albert* and *Ian Fleming*, nudging *Albert* in the process (mind you, in a 200-ton ship, a 2000-ton 'nudge' can seem quite forceful); *Albert* seemed to be undamaged and fortunately the sea was calm. *Ian Fleming's* skipper also threatened to ram *Albert*.

Andromeda was at the incident by 1600, but by then tempers had cooled, *Ian Fleming* had been persuaded to return to fishing and *Albert* had covered her gun. The OTC, fearing that the incident was a ploy to draw all the defence forces to the western end of the DFA whilst one of the larger gunboats got in amongst the main body of trawlers at the other end, recovered his helicopter and returned to the east.

Lloydsman was left to mark *Albert* until she departed at 1930. *Lloydsman* reported a press party onboard *Albert*, but this was denied by the Coastguard; nevertheless, claims were made that *Lloydsman* had deliberately rammed 'little *Albert*' and attempted warp-cutting, manning and training of the gun were denied.

Again, there was a quiet period of just over a week until *Ódinn* reappeared off Iceland's northwest corner. She was detected by the on task Nimrod at 2230 on 10th August. *Andromeda* closed at 24 knots and took up a marking position at 5 cables[74] at 2315. As both ships approached a group of trawlers, *Andromeda* moved into a close marking position and the usual period of tense manoeuvring started. *Ódinn* tried all the usual tactics of violent speed changes to slip past *Andromeda* and at 0046, when she was actually stationary, *Ódinn* clipped *Andromeda's* portside aft whilst attempting to cross her stern. The only damage to *Andromeda* was the buckling of the flight-deck netting stanchions.

At 0230, *Lloydsman* joined *Andromeda* and both ships marked *Ódinn*; 30 minutes later, *Ódinn* retired inshore. At no time had she got within 2 miles of a trawler.

At the other end of Iceland, HMS *Sirius* had also had a quiet spell, but on the 12th August at 0430 *Ægir* came out of the 12-mile limit and headed for a small group of British trawlers. *Sirius* took up station and her Commanding Officer, Commander Peter Coward, recounts in his Report of Proceedings (RoP):

'took up a close marking position at 5 cables on her starboard side. Ægir had her cutting

ICGV Albert (Norman Dempsey)

[74] A cable is 200 yards, therefore 5 cables is half of a nautical mile.

gear streamed. The ensuing foray was an interesting experience. Ægir selected her target and I interposed myself along her line of attack. We then continued at high speed and at close distance for some 50 minutes during which Ægir made lunges at five trawlers. She was thwarted on all occasions although on one run she managed to manoeuvre under my stern and cross astern of the trawler Luneda. Luckily I had warned the trawler to haul and she in fact reversed her engines to make a sternboard towards Ægir. There was no collision, and Ægir failed to cut the trawl. At 0745 Ægir headed off to the north and re-entered the 12 mile limit.'

Another Major Incident

Later on the 12th August 1973, HMS *Sirius* was south of the Whaleback and HMS *Plymouth*, recently returned to the area, was to the north. The defence tugs *Englishman*, *Statesman* and *Welshman* were all in company. The northern area was being guarded by the OTC, in *Andromeda*, and *Lloydsman*. *Thor* was known to be on the slip in Akureyri and *Ódinn* was somewhere in the northwest. *Ægir* had last been seen that morning, entering Reydarfjord, north of the Whaleback - hence the positions of *Sirius* and *Plymouth* - ready to mark her as she reappeared. The weather was stable - overcast, visibility 3 miles with some fog patches, wind 20 knots from the south and sea state 4 to 5.

At 2230 *Ægir* found the Hull trawler *Lord St Vincent*, fishing alone, allegedly 2 miles inside the limit. *Ægir* ordered the *Lord St Vincent*, who denied being inside the limit, to stop and await arrest, upon which the trawler hauled his nets and made off to seaward. *Ægir* fired three blank warning rounds and set off in pursuit. *Sirius*, 10 miles to the southwest and *Englishman*, to the east, closed *Lord St Vincent*. Both were in agreement that, from their radars, the trawler had been at least 1½ miles inside the limit.

At 2300, *Sirius* started a series of reports on the situation as it developed. Forty minutes later, after discussions with both parties on VHF, Commander Coward persuaded *Lord St Vincent's* skipper to come onboard for discussions, whilst *Ægir* agreed not to take any action and to lie a mile off. Meanwhile, *Plymouth*, *Statesman* and *Englishman* had joined and there was a group of ten trawlers hurrying down from the north. These skippers were forcibly declaring their intention to defend *Lord St Vincent* against all comers - including the Royal Navy if necessary.

Onboard *Sirius*, the skipper's navigational evidence was not convincing, however, he was adamant that he was not going to submit to arrest and that he was taking his trawler full of fish home - preferably with the Royal Navy's protection, but if not, with that of his friends. By 0045, *Sirius* had the MoD's instructions - not to interfere and to allow the arrest to take place, whilst establishing as many of the facts surrounding the incident as possible.

It was clear to Commander Coward that any arrest attempt would be resisted - certainly by *Lord St Vincent* and her crew; probably also by the ten other trawlers. *Ægir* might well, then, resort to gunfire and life could be endangered. *Plymouth* and the three tugs were deployed to keep the approaching 'posse' of trawlers away from the immediate scene of the event and the Defence Commander warned the other trawlers to keep clear.

Unfortunately it was not possible to establish a private (i.e. one that could not be overheard) circuit between *Sirius* and *Ægir*, so all communications had to be by light. At 0150, Commander Coward told *Ægir* that 'he proposed not to interfere, but that he could not accept any action that would endanger life'. The Captain of *Ægir* responded that he was 'ready to make the arrest but had no wish to endanger life or limb.'

At 0220, having been clearly told that he was judged to have been fishing inside 12 miles, the skipper was returned to *Lord St Vincent*. He was also told that the Royal Navy would not intervene to prevent his arrest and that, if lives were at risk, he should submit. He immediately set off southeast at 12 knots, with *Ægir* following at 7-10 cables and *Sirius* and *Plymouth* at a mile on each quarter. By the International Law of the Sea, *Ægir* was entitled to make an arrest on the High Seas (up to territorial waters - British, or in this specific case, Faeroese) as long as he remained in company with the offender. This is called being in 'Hot Pursuit'. The tugs remained in the DFA and only one trawler, the *Kingston Emerald*, followed the little convoy.

At 0250 *Ægir* signalled 'I shall do nothing drastic for 6 hours. You may relax.' This was a courteous action and there were probably several reasons for it. It allowed time for political reflection in Reykjavik, as well as an opportunity for both captains to stand-down for a while. It was also dark by now and it was safer to attempt an opposed boarding in the day. Commander Coward's dilemma was how to balance his instructions to defend British lives with those not to interfere with a lawful arrest.

Accordingly, at 0336, he signalled to MoD, FOSNI and the OTC that, should *Ægir* fire on the *Lord St Vincent*, his intention was to warn *Ægir* that he had authority to return fire, to place *Sirius* between *Ægir* and *Lord St Vincent* and, if *Ægir* continued to fire, to return fire in self-defence. At 0501, the OTC, Captain Alec Weir in *Andromeda*, responded that he did not agree with this interpretation - that the order not to interfere with a legal arrest was paramount - and that fire should not be opened pending the MoD response. MoD responded at 0700 saying that, pending Ministerial guidance, the OTC's instructions were to be complied with. It was to be 1730 that afternoon before MoD finally signalled the considered Ministerial guidance - which was that *Sirius's* intentions were approved.

At 0430, HMS *Lynx*, on her way north to relieve HMS *Sirius*, joined the convoy and *Plymouth* was released to return to the southeastern DFA. The group continued southeast at 12 knots, *Kingston Emerald* having caught up and joined *Lord St Vincent*. Once the six hours were up, *Ægir* informed *Lord St Vincent* that he was awaiting instructions from his government and that he could not be held responsible for any damage or danger to the trawler should the trawler fail to comply with his instructions.

Meanwhile ashore, the diplomats were turning to. The British Ambassador was instructed to propose an agreement whereby hot pursuit would be called off, the skipper be disciplined and financial reparations be paid, if investigations proved the skipper to have been fishing illegally. The Icelandic Prime Minister rejected this and demanded the calling off of the frigate escort and the immediate return of the trawler to an Icelandic port. The British reply was that the frigates were not preventing arrest and that the British government had no legal authority over the trawler.

Whilst this diplomatic exchange was going on, the Icelandic Coastguard[75] had rightly concluded that there was little chance of an unopposed arrest and that, in the event of the use of force by *Ægir*, the frigates would intervene. The Prime Minister reluctantly ordered that pursuit was to be discontinued on reaching Faeroese territorial waters. At 1800, *Ægir* ceased her pursuit; HMS *Lynx* followed her back north and HMS *Sirius* continued southeast in company with *Lord St Vincent*, who resumed fishing, for another 12 hours.

The Political Fallout

There were two immediate consequences from this incident. The trawlermen accused the Royal Navy of failing to support them - despite the 'fact' (still disputed by her skipper) that *Lord St Vincent* had broken the BTF instructions by both fishing alone and was within the 12-mile limit. *Lord St Vincent's* skipper was suspended for six months, but this was too late to placate the Icelanders, or make the news, whilst being soon enough to reinforce the trawlermen's irritation with the Navy. Meanwhile Iceland had gained much good free publicity - 'Britain had used frigates to prevent a lawful arrest' and the British response, quoting the strict legal position, gained little sympathy.

This incident well illustrates the problems in defending fishermen who, sometimes, didn't want to be defended, or at least, didn't until they were caught poaching. The whole crew's income was dependent upon the size of the catch and so, not surprisingly, these hunters of the sea tried to follow the fish whenever possible and, once good fishing had been found, tried to avoid sharing it. The owners, whilst instructing their skippers to follow the Navy's instructions, also had major financial incentives to be ambivalent about their skipper's 'independence'. Navigation off some areas of the coast was difficult - in defence of the *Lord St Vincent's* skipper, the Whaleback is only 16 feet above the water and makes a very dubious fixing point (but as he shouldn't have been alone near there in the first place....). Neither Her Majesty's Government nor the Royal Navy had any legal authority over the trawlers and finally, the Navy was caught between allowing (accepted) Icelandic Law to

[75] It should be remembered that the Icelandic Prime Minister was also the Minister of Justice and the Commander in Chief of the Coastguard.

be upheld and protecting British fishermen.

In the TV documentary "*The Last Waltz*", Captain Gudmundur Kjænested noted wryly:

'They fished up to the three mile limit, and preferably inside it. To the British skippers, and actually to the Icelandic skippers as well, it became a kind of sport to fish within the limits. Anyone who wanted to be anybody fished inside.'

Skipper Dickie Taylor, who had a 'record' with the Icelandic courts contended that:

'It wasn't out of badness; it was more for what we call "the crack". If you thought there was more fish inside, you'd go for it. Just to have a little game of cat and mouse with the Icelandic Coastguard. They used to love me, I used to love them'.

Later in this documentary, Gudmundur Kjænested declared:

'I found it most enjoyable to deal with the British. At the beginning they fought like lions, but when they realised that the game was up, they simply gave in. I recall that Commander Eiríkur Kristófersson (the captain of Thor in the 1st Cod War) was very cunning in getting them to admit their guilt since this would result in a shorter trial and a reduced fine. ..... Fishermen of other nationalities, the Belgians for instance, especially the Belgians, were so soft that they began to cry. That was my worst experience in my career at sea, to have a crying skipper in my cabin, threatening him with a jail sentence and a steep fine.'

And the final word on being arrested from one of those with more experience than most, Richard Taylor again:

'I've got to be honest and say, in every court case I was involved in, I never ever knew one of the Icelandic Coastguard officers to tell a lie. They always stated the facts as they was. I wanted to congratulate them on their navigation and their chartwork, but I daren't, else I'd be dropping myself in it, but they were very fair in that respect.'

The Royal Navy was being used by politicians, who were not prepared to acknowledge that they were fighting a losing battle in order to buy time in the hope that some other solution would appear. This was not a new situation and, to be fair to British politicians, the obdurate determination of the Icelandic leftwing politicians to force the issue, in advance of International opinion, had left them with almost no manoeuvring space. The British were going to have to surrender again, but not quite yet.

In the *Ægir*/*Lord St Vincent* incident, Commander Coward's view had been, ultimately, supported and FOSNI was content that the incident could not have been handled better. The RoE covering attempted arrest and hot pursuit of a recognised 'poacher' were reviewed in Whitehall and a clarifying signal was issued on 6th September 1973. The main message was not to interfere, but to remain in the near distance but close enough to be able to intervene if the situation warranted. A Cabinet committee discussed the subject on 20th September and concluded that, whatever the strict legal position, it was not possible for it to look as if the Royal Navy was more concerned with legal niceties than with the lives and livelihood of British trawlermen. CinC Fleet, by now Admiral Sir Terence Lewin, had stated that 'hot pursuit cannot excuse inactivity by one of HM Ships in the presence of murderous action'.

The line taken by Commander Peter Coward of HMS *Sirius* was now the approved doctrine and was clearly laid out in the DEWEY OpOrder. Commanding Officers were to make every effort to avoid interference, including telling the skipper not to risk the lives of his crew, preventing other trawlers from interfering, keeping out of the immediate vicinity of the incident and not allowing the skipper onboard one of HM Ships, but in the last resort, they were to take action in defence of the trawler if they considered that unnecessary or unreasonable force was being used.

Fortunately, there was now a lull before the final six weeks of hectic action inside 50 miles.

CHAPTER 13

THE SECOND COD WAR - A SHORT LULL BEFORE THE STORM AND THEN WITHDRAWAL TO OUTSIDE 50 MILES 14th AUGUST TO 3rd OCTOBER 1973

After the *Lord St Vincent* incident, the Royal Navy expected the Icelandic Coastguard to step up harassment, but in fact there followed a 10-day lull. The four-week period from 24th August 1973 produced two collisions with frigates, seven warp-cuttings and a break in the diplomatic logjam.

Thor emerged from her refit on 19th August and was sighted by HMS *Andromeda*, commanded by the OTC, Captain Alec Weir. *Thor's* return to sea brought the gunboat fleet up to full strength. Apart from a half-hearted run towards the trawler *Kennedy*, the captain of *Thor* was friendly and forthcoming - the two ships even conducted a mutual radar calibration exercise[76].

On the evening of 22nd August, a Coastguard Fokker Friendship (the Catalina had been pensioned off) sighted two British trawlers, the *Zonia* and the *Luneda*, fishing on their own outside the DFA 35 miles northwest of North Cape. The Friendship vectored *Thor* and *Ægir* towards the two trawlers and by 0200 *Thor* had arrived and ordered them both to stop. The skippers hauled their nets and *Thor* and *Ægir* concentrated their efforts on *Zonia*, the northerly of the two.

The two gunboats attempted to force *Zonia* to stop, with one close stationed on each beam and, at 0307, *Ægir* fired three shots across her bow. The OTC ordered *Zonia* to steam east at her best speed, zigzagging violently to make boarding impossible, whilst *Andromeda* closed at his best speed. *Andromeda's* Wasp was on the scene by 0400 and at 0430, *Andromeda* herself arrived. Recognising that an unopposed arrest was no longer possible, *Thor* retired to Isafjord, but *Ægir* remained in company attempting to cut warps and manoeuvring aggressively in close company with *Andromeda* and later HMS *Lynx*.

Coastguard Operational Policy

This combined operation by *Thor* and *Ægir* was assumed to herald much greater co-ordination of the gunboats' activities, but fortunately for the Royal Navy this was not to be. Coastguard Headquarters continued to give each of the three major gunboat Commanding Officers an area, based on the main trawler concentrations. Within their area, the Commanding Officers made their own decisions, with headquarters just supplying intelligence about trawler movements. No authority was required for warp-cutting, but the headquarters would be asked for approval before boarding or opening fire. It appears that the Coastguard had neither the training nor the inclination to mount the kind of co-ordinated military operations that the Royal Navy were expecting.

The Navy were also surprised that *Tyr* was not retained in service after May 1973 and that no efforts were made to speed up *Thor*'s six week refit (for example by funding overtime working), at a time when fishermen were busiest. This failure to return the *Thor* to service early was criticised in the Icelandic left-wing press, at the time.

In retrospect, it looks as if the Icelandic Government was intent on showing that it was 'business as usual' in their fishery protection activity, whilst they could accuse the British of deploying warships against their lightly-armed gunboats. They hoped that constant pressure, intermittent warp-cutting, trawler indiscipline, Royal Navy frustration and

[76] An exercise when both ships steam on exactly parallel courses and use the range of the other vessel, often determined by an optical range finder, to check the accuracy of their radar.

international pressure would force the British Government to back-down.

It is not believed that the Icelandic Government ever ordered their gunboats to cause collisions, but there was little doubt that some of the collisions were deliberate, as has now been admitted by the gunboat captains. Some may have been caused by a mistake whilst manoeuvring at very close quarters or by a misunderstanding of the pressure and suction effects, but undoubtedly frustration at being outmanoeuvred whilst attempting to get at a trawler caused some captains to ram their opponents.

Nevertheless, in the Icelandic media, every collision was portrayed as a deliberate ramming by the British and no one in Iceland wanted to believe anything else. The Icelandic Government may not have ordered the collisions, but was very happy that they happened and made the most of the resulting publicity.

The British Position

FOSNI had another meeting with the BTF in Hull on 23rd August 1973. The owners accepted that there was a need for better discipline and more co-operation from their skippers; improved ways of moving the DFAs were agreed and the Navy successfully resisted suggestions that the liaison skippers should be withdrawn. With an average of 70 trawlers on the fishing grounds, the first anniversary of the 50-mile limit approaching and catches at nearly 160,000 tons, a figure that could never have been achieved without naval protection, the owners expressed themselves to be well pleased with the Navy's actions.

The next UN Conference on the Law of the Sea (UNCLOS) was less than a year away, when wider fishing limits were bound to be agreed, and so the British Government needed to restart negotiations. With the Icelandic offer of 145,000 tons believed to be still on the table, the British hoped that their proven ability to catch over 160,000 tons under naval protection might persuade the Icelandic Government to negotiate. The truth of the matter was that the Icelandic Prime Minister was not politically strong enough to be able to enter any kind of real (i.e. those were both sides make concessions) negotiations.

Both Britain's and Iceland's allies were, meanwhile, getting rather fed up with this dispute - especially Dr Joseph Luns, the Secretary General of NATO who was very keen to help resolve the dispute.

Another Collision and a Death

On 24th August 1973, Captain Dickie Fitch in HMS *Apollo* took over as OTC. As noted above, he was to have a very busy period in command of the patrol. Initially, he had HM Ships *Plymouth* and *Lynx* under his command. RFA *Green Rover* took over from RFA *Olna* on the 26th as the station tanker. All three major gunboats were active, sometimes in the same DFA and there was a lot of thick fog - for about 50% of the time in August and September. The first incident came on 27th when *Ægir* slipped, undetected in the fog, into the eastern end of the northern DFA and succeeded in cutting both *Ella Hewitt's* and *Wyre Corsair's* warps.

On 29th August, the northern DFA was centred on Grimsey Island. *Óðinn*, to the east of the DFA, was being watched by *Green Rover*, *Lloydsman* and *Apollo's* Wasp. She subsequently retired to the south. *Thor* appeared at the western end of the DFA and then also retired inshore. *Ægir* was to the north, being marked by *Lynx*. At 1125, *Apollo* took over marking *Ægir*, who was then 17 miles north of her and heading southwest at 20 knots towards a group of British trawlers.

Ægir passed through the 12-mile limit around Kolbeinsey, whilst *Apollo* remained over 12-miles south of the island, remaining between *Ægir* and the trawlers. Captain Fitch takes up the story in his collision report:

> *'Ægir crossed the (12-mile) limit (around Kolbeinsey) at 1256Z, with HMS Apollo on a westerly course at 15 knots, and Ægir steaming 230° at a similar speed. Visibility was poor and Ægir was not sighted until 1259Z, at a range of about 7 cables 60 degrees on the starboard bow.*
> *I was deliberately steering a course of 270° in order to place myself on the track between Ægir and the British trawler concentration some 15 miles to the southwest. I thus hoped to deter him from approaching this concentration. I appreciated that Ægir could alter course under my stern if he so desired in order to proceed to the south of me. In this case I intended to turn to the southward myself and mark him from astern until he became a direct threat to the trawlers. In the*

ICGV Aegir just before the collision with HMS Apollo on 29th August 1973. (Chas Gillespie)

event, Ægir held her course and the range continued to close rapidly to about half a cable. She made no attempt to pass astern of HMS Apollo, and it became quite clear that she herself intended to take up a very close marking station on my starboard beam, in order to test my resolve in preventing her from reaching the trawlers as she and other Icelandic gunboats had done with previous HM Ships in close quarters situations.

At about 1303Z, Ægir accelerated, sounded 2 short blasts (I am altering my course to port), and made to cut across HMS Apollo's bows. I held on and she altered back to starboard. I hoped she had learnt her lesson. HMS Apollo at this time had engine revolutions for 26 knots rung on[77] *and was accelerating rapidly. Almost immediately after the first attempt to force HMS Apollo to port, Ægir sounded 6 short blasts (Your movements are not understood - but often used to mean 'get out of my way') and again put her wheel over to port. This time Ægir held on. In order to avoid running her down, I was obliged to alter course violently to port, and with the ships in such close proximity Ægir's port quarter came into contact with HMS Apollo's starboard side by the forward end of the flight deck.*

Undoubtedly I could have avoided the close quarters situation by altering to port, under her stern to starboard, or by reducing speed before Ægir took station on me, thus enabling her to continue on her course to the southwest and the British trawlers. However, to have done so would have shown a lack of resolve on my part to screen the threatened fishing trawlers from harassment. Such action from me was clearly just what Ægir was hoping for and to have taken it would have resulted in the loss of HMS Apollo's deterrent capability in any future encounter.'

In his Report of Proceedings, Captain Fitch wrote:

'I am however convinced that my resolute stand against Ægir on 29 August resulting in minor collision, stood myself and the trawlers in very good stead for the remaining 23 days of my patrol. Subsequent to this incident, no warp cutting was seriously attempted whenever HMS Apollo was anywhere near the vicinity.'

[77] This means that power for 26 knots had been ordered, but the steam turbines were not yet providing all the necessary power - hence *Apollo* was accelerating.

The view from FOSNI, CinC Fleet and the MoD was that, although *Apollo* was the giving-way vessel (under the International Regulations for Preventing Collisions at Sea), Captain Fitch's actions were completely justified and entirely in accordance with the Rules of Engagement (RoE) in force, which required him to screen threatened fishing vessels from harassment. This balancing of the requirements of the International Regulations with the National RoE illustrates the sort of decision that Commanding Officers frequently had to make. In his personal briefings of COs, FOSNI always encouraged a robust and determined posture. This policy was to be proved correct time and again - the gunboats would often 'test' a new CO soon after his arrival and once he had proved himself resolute in protecting the trawlers, the gunboats would act more circumspectly.

Both *Ægir* and *Apollo* suffered minor damage in this collision. *Ægir* stopped whilst immediate repairs were carried out and about $2\frac{1}{2}$ hours later, observed by the tug *Statesman* from a mile away, headed south towards Grimsey Island at 18 knots. *Apollo* had moved away to the west where *Thor* was reported to be active. As *Ægir* moved south, an engineer, Halldór Hallfredsson, who had been welding the damaged section was electrocuted, when a wave came inboard and he never regained consciousness.

At 1617, *Apollo* returned to mark *Ægir*, having decided that *Thor* was not presently a threat. Then minutes later, the Captain Sigtryggsson of *Ægir* called Captain Fitch on VHF to tell him of the death of his engineer. *Ægir* withdrew to Grimsey Island and on the 30th went into Akureyri, not reappearing until the 5th of September.

The first Coastguard statements, whilst (legally justifiably) blaming *Apollo* for the collision, were reasonably restrained about the engineer's death, which was surprisingly the only death directly attributed to Cod War activity in any of the three disputes. However the subsequent press reporting was violent and exaggerated - 'the first death of the Cod War' 'directly attributed to the British policy of deliberate ramming' etc. *Statesman* (not having been within a mile) was accused of having pursued *Ægir* and even of having caused the fatal wave.

Whilst this regrettable fatality could not be directly attributed to British action, the Coastguard statements, perhaps in self-justification, became wilder; media and public pressure mounted and, for the first time, the Icelandic Government considered breaking off diplomatic relations with Britain. On 1st September 1973, John McKenzie, the British Ambassador, described one of the Coastguard statements as 'a mixture of self-deceit and wilful misrepresentation.'

The View from a Defence Tug

Roddy Jardine was the First Mate in *Lloydsman* at this time and he had no previous experience of either tugs or fishery protection. He had a rude introduction:

Defence Tug Lloydsman (David Mathias)

'August 1973 and I had just returned from a voyage, as 2nd Mate, on a rather large and cumbersome Ore/Bulk/Oil carrier. 3 cargoes and no shore leave in 6 months, together with an assurance from the company that this was the future of the industry and that I was well placed for advancement in this class of vessel, was enough to ensure regular visits to the local library to peruse the situations vacant in Lloyds List.
During one such visit I spotted an ad from United Towing of Hull, seeking Navigators to serve on ocean tugs, and duly put pen to paper, noting interest in an industry that I had previously only read about. Thus started a long association with the towing industry.
On 24th of August 1973, I joined Lloydsman as 1st Mate, for a two-month tour of duty, the requirement for Ocean Navigators having been superseded by the Cod War charters.
Despite being some 77,000 gross tonnes smaller than my previous vessel, and with a wheelhouse that was alarmingly near the forecastle, Lloydsman was larger than I had anticipated, and certainly as well fitted out as any of the merchant ships I had previously served on.
After an uneventful 2 day passage we arrived off SW Iceland and took up station, and I have vivid memories of being rudely awakened from a post lunch siesta, by the duty watch, who shouted "action stations" and promptly disappeared to round up the rest of the off duty bridge team.
Arriving on the bridge I found us in near proximity to an Icelandic gunboat, possibly Ægir, steaming at around 18 knots, and attempting some form of pincer movement with a British Warship (Apollo?) which was in close attendance on the other side of Ægir. I am not sure what I really expected, such manoeuvres were well outside my previous experience and certainly did not fit in with my understanding of the regulations for preventing collisions at sea, as explained to the Examiner for Masters and Mates.
After much twisting and turning, but no physical contact, Ægir dropped back, possibly in an attempt to initiate a collision between the tug and the frigate, which was thankfully avoided, and slunk off to harass another section of the fleet, with as I recollect a certain degree of success as several trawlers had warps cut around this time.
During the whole of this close marking "exercise" Captain Jack Golden, on Lloydsman exhibited amazing ship handling skills, and was completely unflappable, treating the whole thing as a normal afternoons work.
I do remember the Ægir/Apollo collision and the Ægir's welder being electrocuted during subsequent emergency repairs. There were allegations that shipwash caused a short circuit but I don't recall any further investigation.
Various other events occurred on a fairly regular basis, and we were kept busy carrying out a close patrol of the fishing fleet while the warships circled further out to try and ensure early warning of the approach of a gunboat.
Helicopter operations were, unlike today, a fairly rare event for merchant seamen, and I remember being left in command whilst Captain Jack was picked up to attend a Masters' Briefing on the command frigate. My only instructions were to ensure that the lift off was captured on cine camera, as his grandchildren would never believe the story otherwise. (I am not sure that he had any grandchildren at that time but he was always a forward thinker!).
Much later in the day (what did go on at these briefings?), he ordered us to close the frigate and carry out a boat transfer, as he would not be utilising the helicopter for the return journey. He subsequently revealed that it was only after arrival on board that he found out about the emergency release mechanism on the winch, and that following a quick risk assessment over a G&T decided to return by sea.
The twice-daily round up, where the trawlers reported their positions, could often have been prepared by Hans Christian Anderson, as despite the inherent danger from the Icelandic gunboats, many skippers were extremely wary of letting others know where

they were actually fishing. Indeed from the VHF chatter one might have been excused for believing the fishing grounds were already barren.

All the tugs were fitted with a UHF system, code named uckers, to speak directly and discreetly to the Navy. It was spectacularly unsuccessful and only worked at extremely close range if at all.

Direct Bridge to Bridge VHF comms worked well between the tugs and the trawlers, but less so with the warships, where we strongly suspected the OOW and the VHF set were not in the same part of the ship and there always seemed to be a time lapse whilst the watch officer was summoned. This issue was resolved during the 1975-76 conflict and comms were much improved.

The tugs and many of the trawlers had "private" VHF channels for company business in home port or when operating in consort, and through use of these channels were able to speak directly without being overheard by the Icelanders.

The trawler skippers seemed able to speak continuously on the VHF whilst carrying out a fairly complex operation. Deep water trawling is not for the faint hearted, and they were amazing in their ability to trawl in close company without either collision or entanglement of nets which, after all, were some distance astern most of the time.

I have recollection of modifying the navigation and deck lighting on Lloydsman, to make her look like a stern trawler, and then steaming slowly at the edge of the pack as if fishing. Around six o'clock one murky morning I swung the vessel round, just to go the other way for a change, and was confronted by Thor, which had crept up in our radar blind spot, and was in the process of cutting our non-existent fishing gear. I don't know who was more surprised as we entered into the obligatory game of cat and mouse.

I also remember the Euroman, under command of Captain Charlie Noble, being engaged in a particularly extended period of intercept and counter intercept. Charlie eventually called up the gunboat on VHF, was answered, and following an exchange of pleasantries a 30 minute truce was negotiated, with both vessels drifting, whilst the respective masters went for lunch. Exactly 30 minutes later pursuit was resumed!

I was on leave during the final few weeks of the conflict, and rejoined Lloydsman in Hull, on her return. She was heavily iced during November 73 and suffered a lot of superficial damage, mainly due to the enthusiasm of the crew in getting rid of the unwanted top weight.

Escalation

On 4th September 1973, *Albert* made her final ineffective appearance in the dispute. She approached a group of trawlers through the fog in the southeastern DFA and attempted to cut the *St Alcuin's* warps. The cutter caught in the trawls doors and when Albert desperately manoeuvred to attempt to free it, the heavy trawl door swung dangerously across *St Alcuin's* deck. Eventually the wire parted and *St Alcuin* kept the cutter as a souvenir, whilst *Englishman* ushered *Albert* back to the 12-mile limit.

A couple of days later, on the 6th and 7th of September, HMS *Lynx* had a couple of very near misses with *Ægir* and then *Thor*. At 0730 on the 6th, after an hour's close marking in amongst the trawlers, *Ægir*, from 100 yards on *Lynx's* starboard beam, sounded six short blasts and turned hard to port. At the last moment, both ships put their wheels hard over and they steadied bridge-to-bridge at 5-10 feet.

At 1240 on the next day, the tug *Welshman*, protecting the trawler *Glenmoriston*, was threatened with gunfire by *Thor* if she tried to ram. *Lynx* closed to support *Welshman* and reported as follows:

> *'Both Thor's guns were uncovered and at one stage a man wearing a crash helmet closed up by his after gun. Lynx's armament was manned, but not visibly so, and the guns were not cleared away. After a short period of very close manoeuvring, Thor headed north at 12 knots, marked by Lynx at 2 miles.*
>
> *At 1635 Thor altered course towards two British trawlers fishing apart from the main group, and Lynx began close-marking. Thor streamed his cutting gear. At 1648, with Lynx*

half a cable on Thor's starboard beam and both ships doing 18 knots, Thor altered to starboard. Lynx held on, and twice a collision was averted by approximately one foot. Thor then opened again to port (firing a few salvoes of potatoes). He was then marked in to the 12-mile limit, and later stopped in the mouth of Seydisfjord.'

In his RoP, Commander Kit Layman of HMS *Lynx* reflected on these events:

'I had three extremely close near misses. These were not caused by riding off, but were, I am sure, deliberate attempts by thwarted gunboats to achieve a minor collision with a small amount of damage.'

'If a trawler is in a group, as they are always supposed to be, the gunboat must be ridden off in good time. I would start to do this as soon as the gunboat declared a hostile intent by altering course towards, increasing speed, and streaming his cutter. This usually happened at about three miles.'

At any stage during a riding off situation the gunboat can hold his course and speed and accept the subsequent collision. However, I found in practice that they never did this, but invariably sheered away at about 50 to 100 feet when confronted with a collision on our terms. From the point of view of the frigate's captain, this required one to hold on long after one's seamanlike instincts told one to turn away, and felt most uncomfortable; but I can think of no other way to ride off a captain who is determined not to be ridden off, other than to exhibit a greater determination than his.'

'Once the gunboat had been turned off his originals course by this dangerous practice a period of violent manoeuvring began, when the gunboat tried every trick of wheel and engine movement to evade the frigate and close the trawlers. Slightly to my surprise I found that Lynx could match Ægir, Thor and Ódinn provided one used plenty of revolutions and the occasional "full ahead/full astern", keeping the ship inside the gunboat's turning circle and roughly parallel.'

'Certain ground rules emerged during this manoeuvring phase. If the distance between gunboat and trawlers was closing, I would offer to ride off and the gunboat would turn away. If the distance was opening, I would drop back to about one cable or more, remaining parallel. At all times I would try to keep exactly between gunboat and trawlers.'

'All three gunboats seemed to accept the rough justice of these ground rules, and would not disregard them until they had exhausted their repertoire of tricks. After that, no doubt feeling thwarted and exasperated, on three occasions (Ægir once, Thor twice), they attempted a minor collision on their own terms. The technique here was to steady on course at about 18 knots with the frigate close and parallel, and then alter course towards so that the ships should touch broadside on, bridge to bridge. Ægir did this with great panache, sounding six short blasts as he did so, and in spite of Lynx putting the wheel hard over and back again, closed to between 5 and 10 feet. Thor's attempts were less spectacular but very nearly successful; twice he came in to an unbelievable one foot before a lucky wave or our guardian angel pushed him away.'

One of the direct consequences of the heightened tension after the death of *Ægir's* Engineer was that, on 7th September, the Icelandic Prime Minister instructed the Foreign Ministry to inform the British Government that, from 20th September 1973, Icelandic authorities would only accept sick or injured persons from the fishing or naval fleets if they were brought ashore in the ships in which they were registered and employed at the time of being taken ill or being injured. One consequence of this was that any claimed 'poacher' would be arrested if he had to take an injured crewmember inshore.

This rule had been applied in the First Cod War, when there had been no support ships, and had resulted in emergency treatment, including an appendectomy, being carried out onboard one of HM Ships. As it happened, once the announcement had been made public, a softer private line was taken and the Icelandic Prime Minister agreed that each case would be considered on its merits (quite possibly dependent upon the 'poaching status' of the injured man's vessel). The policy of landing emergency cases in support ships was therefore continued, permission being sought from the Icelandic authorities on each occasion.

The British were keen to avoid any further escalation and on 7th September, FOSNI sent the following personal signal to Commanding Officers:

'Diplomatic relations between the UK and Iceland are now in a delicate state. It is essential that for the immediate future all maritime action within the 50-mile zone off Iceland should be strictly within the rules. While there is no criticism of HM ships actions to date collisions can always be argued both ways. Therefore until further orders you are to avoid close quarters situations with Icelandic gunboats which might lead to a collision.'

That evening, *Ódinn* entered the western end of the northwesterly DFA undetected and managed to cut one of the *Kingston Sapphire's* warps. At the time, HMS *Apollo* was at the other end of the DFA and *Jaguar* and *Lynx* were with the majority of the trawlers in the southeastern area. *Thor* followed this, early next morning, by a successful cutting-run against the *Northern Isles* in the southeast DFA. This was despite timely warnings from Commander John Caughey in *Jaguar* and the presence of *Lloydsman* close to the trawlers.

Captain Dickie Fitch, the OTC in HMS *Apollo*, found FOSNI's, somewhat Delphic, signal difficult to interpret and on 9th September responded:

'During this latest incident Ægir probably with press embarked steamed through a group of 11 British trawlers all of whom disrupted their fishing by hauling their gear at my suggestion on Ægir's approach. Apollo marked at 2 miles throughout and Lloydsman stood by trawlers and showed no sign of aggression. This has provoked much discontent among trawler skippers.
Request early amplification to clarify whether HM Ships and defence tugs are to stand by and condone this disruption to fishing while advising trawlers to recover their gear on the approach of gunboats, or whether it is still intended that HM Ships and defence tugs should interpose themselves between trawlers and gunboats and encourage fishing to proceed. This latter desirable action is likely to lead to close quarters situations and perhaps collisions.'

FOSNI replied with:

'Cancel my (previous signal). Your good sense is relied on not to mix it unnecessarily.'

During the night of 7th/8th September there were two further warp-cuttings. Late on the 7th, *Ódinn* slipped undetected into the western end of the northwestern DFA. *Apollo* was 80 miles to the east and *Jaguar* and *Lynx* were in the southeastern area. *Ódinn* succeeded in cutting one warp of the *Kingston Sapphire*. In the other area at about 0400, *Thor* managed to evade *Englishman*, who was in company with the trawlers and, despite timely warnings from *Jaguar*, managed to cut both *Northern Isle's* warps.

Improved Helicopter Support

Helicopters had proved to be very useful in locating and identifying the gunboats, but only the more modern Leander and Tribal class frigates carried their own helicopters. Accordingly, it was decided to embark a frigate Wasp flight in the larger ('O' and Tide class) Royal Fleet Auxiliary tankers when there was only one helicopter-equipped frigate on the patrol. The aim was to have one helicopter available in each DFA. The first tanker on station to carry a Wasp was RFA *Olna* on 1st September.

From 10th September 1973, when *Olna* returned to the patrol, a Wessex 3 Flight, from one of the County class destroyers was added to the Wasp Flight. The Wessex 3 was a larger and much more capable aircraft than the Wasp, carrying a crew of three and being equipped with radar. The OTCs reported that the Wessexes provided 'significant advantages' and were 'invaluable'. Thereafter all the larger tankers carried a Wessex 3.

There was another minor collision in calm weather on 10th September, between *Jaguar* and *Thor*. This took place in the southeastern DFA where Jaguar was marking *Thor*, initially from about 2 miles. *Thor* was

A Wessex 3 anti-submarine helicopter, as carried in the larger RFA tankers after September 1973. The dome contains the helicopter's radar. The badge was made for the embarked helicopter flights as a memento of their Cod War deployments and would have been sewn to the flying overalls of all those involved.
(Alan Paterson/Jón Páll Ásgeirsson)

making for the trawler *Volesus*, about 11 miles away, and *Jaguar* was steering to maintain position between the two with the trawler on her starboard bow and the gunboat on her port beam. By 5 miles, *Thor* was in to a mile on the beam and *Jaguar* eased over to starboard a couple of times as *Thor* closed in. Michael Boydon, who was one of *Jaguar's* cooks, remembers *Thor* sending the following message to *Jaguar* - 'Beware *Jaguar* you are a long way from home.' This kind of exchange was not unusual.

By the time *Volesus* was at 3 cables, *Thor*, with cutter streamed, was only 30 feet to port and doing 18 knots. Finally, *Jaguar* could go no further to starboard with out colliding with *Volesus* and so steadied up. *Thor* reacted too late (if at all) and hit *Jaguar* under the flare on her port bow. Fortunately damage to both ships was superficial, although *Jaguar* was put into dry dock on return to Rosyth, where 114 holes were reputedly found in her hull.

Diplomatic Reaction

The Icelandic Cabinet met on 11th September 1973 and decided on further diplomatic action. The following resolution was given to the British Ambassador for forwarding to London:

> *1. The British Government be informed that if their warships or tug-boats continue ramming Icelandic ships, the Icelandic Government will be compelled to demand the breaking of diplomatic relations between the two countries in such a way that the British Embassy in Reykjavik be closed and its diplomatic personnel returned back home.*
>
> *2. The Icelandic air traffic control authorities be instructed to stop communicating with the British Nimrod jet planes.'*

The British Government, not wishing the tension to increase any further, proposed that an international commission of enquiry be convened to establish the facts in cases of alleged ramming. The Icelandic Government did not, unsurprisingly, take up this offer.

On 12th September 1973, FOSNI reiterated the policy on marking and protection:

> *'Current diplomatic pressures in Iceland increase the burden on Commanding Officers in this politico-military operation.*
> *The conduct of defence forces must continue to demonstrate to both Icelandic gunboats and UK trawlers our resolve to prevent arrest and minimise harassment of UK trawlers.*

Commanding Officers are to be guided by the following principles when marking gunboats:

- Mark gunboats at a discrete distance when they are not actively threatening a British trawler. The distance must remain at the discretion of the Commanding Officer and will vary with geographical position, weather and visibility, proximity of trawlers (Icelandic and others as well as British).

- Mark gunboats at a decreasing distance as they approach UK trawlers retaining bearing advantage where possible.

- Close mark gunboats in close manoeuvring operations when it is clear that gunboat directly threatens trawlers.'

There were two more warp-cuttings on 14th September. At 0545 *Thor*, in poor visibility, entered the southern end of the southeastern DFA (unusually) from seaward and, showing fishing lights, successfully closed with the *St Giles* and cut both her warps. That same morning, in the northern area, *Ódinn* succeeded in cutting one of *Boston Concord's* warps.

Apollo and *Whitby* had been watching *Ódinn*, and *Whitby* was closing to mark, when *Ódinn* took off at full speed towards the *Boston Concord* four miles away and just beat *Whitby* to it. Part of the reason for this failure was that *Boston Concord* was a foreign built trawler and so had been assumed to be German or Icelandic, not British, until it was too late. This assumption had been reinforced by the fact that she was fishing on her own, contrary to the oft-repeated Instructions to Skippers.

After his collision with *Thor*, Commander John Caughey of HMS *Jaguar* had concluded that some kind of cutter fitted to a frigate's bow would, in some circumstances, enable the frigate to cut a gunboat's warp-cutter. He signalled FOSNI with the proposal that frigates and defence tugs should be fitted with a bow-cutter. FOSNI supported this idea, but the MoD had their reservations. Eventually, it was agreed that *Jaguar* should be fitted as a trial before her next patrol (she was due off patrol on 16th September and back on 12th October). Rosyth dockyard made and fitted the device at the foot of *Jaguar's* stem, but by the time she was back on patrol, the naval protection forces had been withdrawn outside 50 miles and it was never tested in action. A trial with the tug *Sea Giant* in November did prove that the bow-cutter would have worked.

The, very tentative, beginning of a Settlement

Dr Joseph Luns, the Secretary-General of NATO, had long been concerned about this dispute between two NATO allies. On 17th and 18th September 1973

HMS Whitby laeving Portsmouth for Fishery Protection duties. Note FPS pennant on funnel. *(Tim Meredith)*

he visited Reykjavik to discuss Iceland's position in NATO, her geographic and basing importance to the Alliance, as well as the benefits that Iceland herself accrued through membership. Inevitably the fishing dispute was discussed and Dr Luns, no doubt briefed on the British Government's position, asked the Icelandic Prime Minister for an assurance that, pending negotiations, harassment would cease if British naval forces were to be withdrawn outside 50 miles. No assurance was forthcoming, but Dr Luns felt that he detected some movement and he visited London on his way back to Brussels to apprise the British Government of his hopes.

On 16th, HMS *Lincoln* had relieved HMS *Jaguar* in the southeastern area. HM Ships *Apollo* (OTC) and *Whitby* remained on patrol in the northwest. On the 19th, *Lincoln* found herself in company with *Ægir*, three months after *Ægir* had collided with *Lincoln's* stern. *Lincoln* had been repaired in Chatham dockyard, but to allow Commander David Howard to resume his story:

'Chatham dockyard seemed to be strewn with old railway lines and it occurred to me that, were we to meet again, a pair sticking out through my after fairleads would at least keep Ægir away from my stern. Apart from his strengthened stem, I assessed that the rest of his ship's plating would be vulnerable if he were rash enough to risk impacting what was purely a defensive measure. I was also particularly anxious to protect my rudder and my variable pitch propellers. The latter had been invaluable during July's riding off affair.

When I was detailed for my next patrol, I had a pair of lines smuggled onboard, cleaned up, wrapped in canvas, painted ship's side grey and stowed as unobtrusively as it's possible to stow a package that large in a relatively small frigate. En route to Iceland, we refuelled in Loch Striven and rigged the railway lines, buttressed against the anti-submarine mortar on the quarterdeck and fanned out through the after fairleads: the "porcupine look", as it came to be known.'

On the afternoon of 19 September, I had arranged a rendezvous with Ranger Briseis to transfer mail for the trawler fleet in the southeast DFA. We were to meet up north of the Whaleback bulge. The whole area was in thick fog. As we approached the rendezvous, we got a report from the Wessex (Olna's helicopter) of a fast moving contact heading northeast towards us. We had trawlers fishing fairly close, east of us, and I decided to lie up 'in the grain' and behave like a trawler while I waited for Ranger Briseis. The fog delayed Briseis getting to the rendezvous, which happened to be in the only small clear patch in the fog.

When the contact was still some way off, I got a request to come down to the ops room: a Wasp pilot wanted to talk to me personally. The pilot was an old chum of mine, Dick Ward, and he told me he could see, just above the layer of fog, the yardarm and topmast of what he took to be a gunboat, but he couldn't see her hull and wondered if I could identify her from his sparse description. It was Ægir. Back on the bridge, it became touch and go whether Ægir got to me before Ranger Briseis. I couldn't let Briseis know that Ægir was coming up fast. It would have given the game away. I had to watch Briseis lower her inflatable, which started crossing the clear patch towards me. Exactly half way across, Ægir broke out of the fog. I've never seen a hastier retreat but, to my relief, the inflatable reversed course and got back to mother safely. The gunboat realised she'd been duped and made off for the nearby trawlers.'

For the next 5 hours, 4 of them in thick fog, *Ægir* and *Lincoln* manoeuvred in close company - *Ægir* attempting to get at the trawlers and *Lincoln* thwarting her every move. Twice *Ægir* came within a few feet of *Lincoln*, intent, so it seemed, on causing a collision. As David Howard remarks:

'he did very nearly hit me. Only my starboard 30 prevented him from raking down my starboard side after he'd deliberately turned into me from close range on my starboard beam.'

Ægir had a press party and a Swedish TV team

onboard and this may well have been the reason for her desire for close-quarters manoeuvres in fog. However, the immediate effect of the media's presence was that UK shore authorities became aware of the railway track defences. FOSNI approved of this initiative and arranged for other ships to embark railway track before joining the patrol, with the intention of ships being able to rig beam as well as stern defences. The MoD however, were more cautious and expressed concern that these defences could be portrayed by the Icelanders as being offensive - fitted to allow frigates to collide with gunboats and cause more damage and, possibly, injuries to the gunboats. There were also concerns that the frigates themselves might sustain worse damage and casualties in a collision. In the event, although HMS *Ariadne* arrived on patrol on 24th September with railway lines embarked, she was not allowed to rig them and they were all subsequently landed.

Next evening, the 20th September 1973, HMS *Charybdis* joined the patrol to relieve HMS *Apollo* and Captain Geoffrey Lloyd took over as OTC on the 21st. On the way to the northwestern area, *Charybdis* was passing through the southeastern DFA when she detected a suspicious contact amongst a group of trawlers 5 miles to the south. On investigating, this turned out to be the *Ægir*, who had already succeeded in cutting the *Ross Aquila's* warps.

The Naval Staff History states 'For nearly an hour the *Ægir* was marked at distances between 100 yards and fifty feet at violently varying speeds, and was prevented from approaching any other trawlers.' I was the newly joined junior officer of the watch in *Charybdis* during this incident and, as so often, the official prose disguises the drama of events. The ship was, in effect, at Action Stations, without all the weapon systems being manned. I forget what this modified Action Stations was called - probably something like Gunboat Stations or maybe even Ramming Stations!

We were ready for a collision, with all the damage control personnel at their stations and all the ship's watertight doors closed. Special Sea Dutymen[78] were closed up - meaning that the No1 team were on watch in the machinery control room (MCR), the engine room and boiler room were both manned, as was the tiller flat (so that emergency steering could be connected immediately if necessary). The wheelhouse was also manned by the most experienced helmsman.

On the bridge, I was the Specials Officer of the Watch, but the Captain had the con[79] whenever we were in close company. The Navigating Officer was also on the bridge, keeping an eye on the ship's position (it would, after all, have been most unfortunate if whilst contending with a gunboat, the ship had entered Iceland's 12-mile limit) and feeding back to the Captain the consequences of his conning orders - i.e. the ship's actual speed, the rudders' actual position etc.

One of the ploys we expected *Ægir*, who was close on our port side, to use was to go full astern suddenly, so that she could slip around our stern and get at the trawlers on our starboard side. In attempting this she had the technical advantage in that her diesel engines with controllable pitch screws could react much more quickly that our steam turbines. So we had to 'anticipate' her moves. The First Lieutenant[80], an ex-submariner, had briefed the bridge team that ships have two bow waves and that the first indication of a reduction in speed is the second bow wave closing up on the first. This indicates forward power coming off seconds before stern power is applied. Another sign, but slightly later in the process, is a plume of exhaust as the engines suddenly come off-load, before coming straight back on-load as stern power is applied.

The Squadron Marine Engineer Officer (as *Charybdis* was a 'Leader', we had Squadron Staff onboard) and his team in the MCR were briefed to be ready for a 'full-astern' order - 'full-astern' is an emergency engine order and, in effect, means override the safety valves etc - just get full power on as quickly as possible. We were bridge to bridge with *Ægir* and my task, as the junior officer on the bridge, was to watch her bow waves.

As soon as we saw the second bow wave moving forward, the order to go full astern was given. *Ægir*'s response was, as expected, faster than ours and she was just beginning to turn across our stern as the ship started to gather sternway. It may take a few seconds to get stern power onto a steam turbine plant, but once on, it builds up quickly. *Ægir* was not going

---

[78] SSD - usually just known as 'Specials'

[79] Another archaic naval expression – to con, according to the OED, is to direct the steering of a ship.

[80] The Second in Command

to make it across our stern before we hit her, with the probable consequences that we would have rolled her over, losing both our screws and rudders in the process. There would undoubtedly have been very serious casualties onboard *Ægir*.

As it was, both Captains realised what was about to happened and *Ægir* went full astern as we went full ahead. The official record may say that the closest we got was 50 feet; I remember it as looking like much less. I am sure that our experiences that evening were typical of many during throughout both the Second and Third Cod Wars - serious incidents and casualties were only avoided by superb seamanship and ship handling, plus, to quote Commander Kit Layman of HMS *Lynx* 'a lucky wave or our guardian angel..'.

Another Search and Rescue and then two very public collisions

At 0945 next morning - 21st September 1973 - Captain Lloyd assumed the duties of OTC and was immediately involved in a search for a small Icelandic fishing vessel that was 48 hours overdue. *Óðinn* accepted *Charybdis's* offer of help and *Charybdis*, her Wasp and the support ship *Othello* joined *Óðinn* in the search. I said in a letter home on 23rd September:

> *'The Northern Lights*[81] *have just made a faint appearance - quite spectacular. Nothing much has happened - we were helping in the search for a missing Icelandic fisherman - very pally with the gunboats whilst it happened, then back to war as soon as the search was called off.'*

The truce was very short lived - next day, *Lincoln* and *Ægir* clashed once more - and once more the press and TV were present. Who can say which is cause and which effect, but in this much more media-savvy age, we expect a certain degree of 'acting up' for the cameras. Even at the time there was a strong belief that *Ægir* was seeking to construct an incident that could be portrayed advantageously, both to garner international support and to heighten the domestic pressure on the Icelandic government.

HMS *Lincoln* was in charge of the southeastern DFA and was patrolling the southern end of the area, with HMS *Whitby* to the north. The weather was good, as was the visibility, and about 50 trawlers were enjoying rich fishing with *Englishman* and *Welshman* in close company. *Ægir* was first detected on radar by *Olna's* Wessex 3 and then, at 0830, identified coming out from Nordfjord by a Wasp helicopter.

She stopped and appeared to be waiting for *Lincoln* to join her, then at 0915 headed north towards some trawlers, with *Lincoln* marking. As they neared the first trawlers, *Lincoln* took up a defensive position and, for 45 minutes, kept *Ægir* at bay. When clear of the trawlers, *Ægir* continued to close on *Lincoln's* port beam until, from about 30 feet, accelerated ahead and, either intentionally or because of a lack of understanding of the pressure and suction effects, despite emergency engine and helm orders in *Lincoln*, just caught one of her guardrails on *Lincoln's* port anchor. *Ægir* then retired, presumably to brief the media, feed them and prepare for the afternoon session.

At 1445, the performance resumed, with *Whitby* now also in company. *Ægir* made for the nearest trawler and *Lincoln* marked from the up-threat bow. *Ægir* came up on Lincoln's starboard beam, slowed down and *Lincoln* sounded 'Uniform' (the International Code for 'you are coming into danger'). At about 50 feet, *Ægir* turned to port and hit a nearly stationary *Lincoln* hard amidships at 1504. An hour later, after another session of close marking and riding-off, a similar situation developed with *Ægir* on *Lincoln's* port beam at about 100 feet. Both ships had just altered to port at 12 knots, when, *Ægir* having steadied up first, she suddenly turned to starboard and hit *Lincoln* amidships. Harassment attempts and riding-off by both frigates continued for another two hours.

As so often during both the Second and Third Cod Wars, both sides could argue that they had right of way, but in reality the Rule of the Road was irrelevant because no professional seaman would have got himself into such close quarters in the first place, unless he had very good reason to. Plainly both could have avoided collisions had they given up on their aim - in *Ægir*'s case to harass trawlers and gain good publicity and in *Lincoln's* to protect the trawlers from warp cutting.

[81] The Aurora Borealis – that spectacular display of light that occasionally fills the northern sky.

The TV crews were busy throughout; there was a second crew overhead in a Coastguard Fokker Friendship from 1445-1630, surely further indication that this was a deliberate attempt to garner publicity, in which it succeeded. The airborne film, grainy and disjointed as it was, was shown on Icelandic television where it demonstrated, to those who were already wishful believers, 'proof of the British frigates' policy of ramming gunboats'.

Olna was relieved by *Olmeda* on the evening of the 22nd. *Olmeda* had HMS *Norfolk's* Wessex 3 Flight embarked and Sub-Lieutenant David Snelson was the helicopter controller. His saga well illustrates how the Cod War was causing disruption throughout the Royal Navy.

> *'I had been appointed to HMS Norfolk as the ship's Fighter Controller and Helicopter Control Officer. I had been married on 21st July, but had lost my honeymoon because my helicopter controller's course at RNAS Portland had had to be reorganised – the Cod War was causing chaos in the Fleet's frigates' programmes and a frigate was needed for the final section of the course. In the end, my honeymoon 'leave' was filled by my wife driving me to Portland Dockyard every day for me to embark in a ship of the 2nd Frigate Squadron to complete the live control part of my course.*
>
> *Then I joined Norfolk in Portsmouth. I had been onboard about three weeks; it was a Friday night & I was at home in my married quarter when the Duty Engineer turned up at my door. He had a barchit, signed by the Commander[82]. He also had a First Class Rail Warrant (which a Sub-Lieutenant was not entitled to). The barchit said:*
>
> *"Join Olmeda in Rosyth before she sails at 1100 tomorrow. Sorry. Commander".*
>
> *I rang the station, to find that I had just one hour to catch my train. My wife was in tears, but she drove me to Portsmouth & Southsea Station & I caught the train. I joined up with the rest of the ship's flight & the Wessex 3 helicopter onboard Olmeda in Rosyth.*
>
> *I remember two particular incidents from our fortnight on patrol. We had been conducting a stern refuelling. The hoses were being recovered along the whole of the ship's length, but the winchman was unable to see all the way aft. A line parted and one of the Royal Fleet Auxiliary crewmen was very badly injured. The Icelandic Coastguard was informed and they immediately offered full assistance. The Wessex was given immediate clearance to land the crewman in Iceland, but sadly he died.*
>
> *The other incident concerned one of the gunboats that was harassing Olmeda. Captain Colin Barker lowered all the RAS rigs[83] & the gunboat quickly cleared off.'*

Tension was now high at sea and there was beginning to be action on the politico-diplomatic front as well. On 23rd September a deep depression (the result of tropical storm Ellen[84]) brought the first severe autumn gale, with force 10 to 11 winds off eastern Iceland. Some trawlers entered the 12-mile limit to find shelter and the defence tugs *Englishman* and *Welshman* sheltered overnight off Langanes[85].

Next morning, at 1100, the worst of the weather had passed, but it was still very rough, when *Ódinn* found the two tugs still 5 miles inside the claimed 12-mile limit. *Ódinn* approached and, when it appeared that they were not about to clear outside 12 miles (there being no reason under international law why they should), fired two blank warning shots in their vicinity. *Ódinn* subsequently accused *Englishman* of trying to ram him.

At 1137 the OTC in HMS *Charybdis* received *Englishman's* report and dispatched Commander Jim Flindell in *Whitby* to cover from just outside the 12-mile line. *Whitby* arrived at 1245 and *Ódinn* and the tugs were still only 8 miles from the coast. The situation cooled as the tugs joined *Whitby* and then proceeded to their protective duties in the southeastern DFA. *Whitby* remained to mark *Ódinn*. The Master

[82] The ship's Executive Officer or Second-in-Command

[83] The gantries that hung out from the ship's side to support the hoses during a replenishment.

[84] This is, of course, the pre-PC age, when all tropical storms, hurricanes etc were female.

[85] Instructions for Defence Commanders (i.e. the tugs) stated that '...unless extraordinary circumstances involving safety at sea or other humanitarian purposes obtain, these vessels should as far as practicable keep clear of the 12-mile limit.'

of *Englishman* stated that he was inside 12 miles, sheltering from the weather to ensure the safety of his ship, which was his prime duty and that he would do so again if necessary.

On 26th, at about midday in the northwestern DFA, *Charybdis* had a very close encounter with *Thor*. *Charybdis* was marking from about half a cable on *Thor's* port beam, with a group of trawlers over to port. *Thor* tried to get across her bow, failed and then sounded two short blasts, turned and managed to clear *Charybdis's* stern by 30 feet. *Lloydsman* took over the mark and kept *Thor* away from the trawlers.

Diplomatic Repercussions

The more serious consequences of the two collisions between HMS *Lincoln* and *Ægir* were that the Icelandic authorities, on 25th September 1973, opened a court of enquiry to looking into the evidence for breaking off diplomatic relations with Britain. Simultaneously the British Ambassador was approaching Icelandic Cabinet Ministers in an attempt to see if there was now an opportunity for peace talks. As a result, Edward Heath, the British Prime Minister, wrote to his opposite number, Ólafur Jóhannesson, expressing his deep concern at the way in which the fisheries dispute had developed and at the damage it was doing to the longstanding friendly relations between their two countries. He then proposed a modus vivendi whereby, either for a fixed or an indefinite period, the frigates and tugs would be withdrawn, the Icelandic Coastguard would cease to interfere with fishing and the British Government and fishing industry would agree to a voluntary reduction of the British fishing effort. No catch figure was mentioned, but something between 130,000 and 150,000 tons was envisaged.

The hope was both to open a path towards negotiations, 'talks about talks' we would call them in these days of spin-doctors, and to forestall Icelandic moves towards breaking off diplomatic relations. However, when the Cabinet met on 27th September to consider the results of the enquiry into the *Lincoln*/*Ægir* collisions (at which only Icelandic evidence had been taken, despite the British Ambassador having supplied HMS *Lincoln's* signalled report of the incidents), Ólafur Jóhannesson was unable to persuade his left-wing colleagues to consider Edward Heath's offer. As his coalition government was dependent upon communist support he was unwilling to follow his own, more conciliatory instincts, and the Cabinet decision was that 'a ramming by the frigate had taken place'. The following Cabinet resolution was consequently passed on 27th September:

> *'The Government agrees to inform the British Government, that should the British warships and tug-boats not have left the 50-mile fisheries limit before Wednesday 3 October 1973, then the breaking of diplomatic relations with Britain will become effective in accordance with the Government's resolution from 11 September.'*

As in the Third Cod War, when the French would provide the diplomatic cover for the 'British Interests Section' in Reykjavik, the French agreed to take the rump of the British Embassy under their wing. In London, the Norwegians would have 'adopted' the Icelandic Embassy. When Sir Alec Douglas-Home, the British Foreign Secretary was advised of this possibility, he commented that he would be perfectly happy with Norwegian care of Iceland's interests and that 'Iceland would then for once be properly represented in Britain.'

Later on the afternoon of 27th, after the Cabinet decision, but before the issuing of the ultimatum to the British, another collision occurred. As was now the pattern, this one was arranged with full media attendance. In calm weather off the northeast coast, *Thor*, with cutter streamed, was attempting to get at a trawler whilst *Whitby* marked from 50 yards on her starboard beam at 16 knots. *Thor* sounded two short blasts, but turned to starboard[86]; *Whitby* went hard to starboard and then hard over to port to parallel up with *Thor*. The ships were now 10 feet apart, when *Thor* again turned to starboard so that the flare on her starboard bow hit *Whitby* a glancing blow on the port boatdeck aft; there was no significant damage. It is possible that the actual collision was caused by pressure-and-suction interaction between the two ships. Inevitably, claims were made to the media that *Whitby* had failed to act in accordance with the Rule of the Road.

Bearing in mind that the Prime Minister was nominally in command of the Coastguard, it is interesting

[86] For which the correct sound signal is one short blast.

to speculate if, as happened at the beginning of the First Cod War, this collision was staged for domestic reasons - to strengthen the hand of the far left in the coalition government and to prevent any compromise, or if the reason was to maintain the pressure on the British. Either way, the result was the ultimatum on breaking off diplomatic relations.

Ólafur Jóhannesson replied to Edward Heath's letter on 28th September, agreeing with the concerns expressed on the damage to the long-standing good relations between the two countries and laying out the Icelandic position in full. He declined Heath's offer of a modus vivendi, as even if the protection forces were to be withdrawn, 'enforcement of Icelandic law within the Icelandic fisheries jurisdiction cannot be discontinued'. He did however admit to a 'true and deep interest to find an interim solution to the fisheries dispute'.

Also on the 28th, FOSNI signalled to the forces on patrol:

> *'High level national and NATO moves are in the air and therefore the next few days are most important if we are to meet the immediate political aim of a truce on the (fishing) grounds.*
> *While continuing to conduct operations with determination, Commanding Officers must avoid being drawn into the trap of a stage-managed close marking situation from which they can be rammed by a gunboat. There is evidence that Ægir and Thor's primary aim recently has been to collide with frigates while feinting to harass trawlers.*
> *All this calls for even more care by Commanding Officers in their conduct of operations. Frivolous actions and exchanges are counterproductive and should not be indulged in.'*

The final warp cutting took place on 30th September 1973 when *Thor* used the geographical advantage of the Whaleback bulge in the 12-mile limit to enter the southeastern DFA undetected and successfully cut both *Arctic Warrior's* warps.

After further diplomatic exchanges, and despite his Cabinet's decision, on 30th September Ólafur Jóhannesson agreed that he would be prepared to accept an invitation to London to discuss the British modus vivendi proposal.

Edward Heath's formal letter of invitation to talks, whilst disagreeing with the Icelandic version of events in Ólafur Jóhannesson's letter of 28th September, also offered to withdraw British frigates and tugs from the disputed area at 1500GMT on 3rd October. This offer was caveated that they would return if Icelandic Authorities took 'any measures against British trawlers fishing, or which have fished, in the disputed area.'

Ólafur Jóhannesson's reply of 2nd October welcomed the British withdrawal but repeated his statement that the 'enforcement of Icelandic law within the Icelandic fisheries jurisdiction cannot be discontinued'.

Endgame

From the 30th September 1973, the gunboats still patrolled the fishing grounds and the frigates continued to mark them from a distance, but Icelandic orders were to avoid incidents and there was no harassment. On 2nd October the British Trawler Federation told their skippers about the peace moves and on the morning of the 3rd October, the final Royal Air Force Nimrod sortie was flown.

That afternoon, *HM Ships Charybdis* (Captain Geoffrey Lloyd as OTC), *Ariadne* and *Leopard*, with the defence tugs *Lloydsman* and *Welshman* left the 50-mile area and took up patrols adjacent to the two DFAs. Sixty-six trawlers, supported by the *Miranda* and *Othello* remained fishing inside the disputed area.

It was to be another 6 weeks before the negotiations were concluded and the protecting forces were withdrawn.

CHAPTER 14

UNCLOS3 AND THE 200-MILE LIMIT OCTOBER 1973 TO JULY 1975

The British forces were to spend six more weeks on patrol off Iceland before the peace deal was finally signed, although for the last month of this period, there was provisional inter-governmental agreement. This month was spent in internal politicking in Iceland. The mission of the protecting forces was to maintain a presence whilst being ready to return to full protection duties within the 50-mile limit if required. Force levels were maintained at three frigates, with one Royal Fleet Auxiliary tanker in support and two or three defence tugs. Two civilian defence vessels continued to support the 50 or so trawlers still fishing inside the disputed area.

The Royal Air Force fishery protection flights were suspended and, to ensure no misunderstandings, regular Royal Air Force Nimrod submarine surveillance sorties were kept outside 50 miles from Iceland. Ships and helicopters were, similarly, not allowed inside 50 miles except to save life. This restriction forced the ships into rougher weather than was necessary or seamanlike, as will be seen below.

Despite Prime Minister Ólafur Jóhannesson's reiterated warnings that the 'enforcement of Icelandic law within the Icelandic fisheries jurisdiction cannot be discontinued', all was fairly quiet on the fishing grounds. From time to time a gunboat would order a trawler to haul and move further out to sea. On the advice of the Support Commander, they did so. Tempers remained under control and there was little disruption to fishing. The Support Commanders also organised DFA changes and dealt with the Icelandic Coastguard when required.

Peace Talks

Prime Minister Ólafur Jóhannesson's travelled to London for talks with his opposite number, Edward Heath, on 15th and 16th October 1973. The talks built on the work already conducted through the normal diplomatic channels and, as there were no unpleasant surprises for either side, a tentative agreement was provisionally agreed, although the details, especially the agreed tonnage, were not made public.

The statement released to the press said it all, or rather said nothing:

> *'The two Prime Ministers exchanged views and proposals with regard to an interim solution of the dispute. The Prime Minister of Iceland will report to his Government.'*

The provisional agreement, which was to run for two years, allowed for a British catch within the 50-mile limit of 130,000 tons per annum, plus a reduction of the permitted fishing areas. It should be remembered that Iceland had offered Britain an annual catch of 156,000 tons in July 1972, before the Second Cod War started. The reduction in areas was to be achieved by a combination of closed conservation areas, small boat only areas and a division of the remainder into six areas, of which one would always be closed to the British. Many of the richest areas were now to be closed to British trawlers.

Only 139 named British trawlers would be allowed to fish in the 50-mile zone; 71 of these were to be under 180 feet long. Any trawler on the list found poaching would be struck off and no replacement would be allowed. Three trawlers had been struck off the list by May 1974. No factory or freezer trawlers were to be allowed; this clause was preventative rather than prohibitive, as very few British factory or freezer trawlers had ever been deployed to Icelandic waters.

It took Ólafur Jóhannesson a month to clear this deal domestically, a process that was greatly complicated because his (communist) Fisheries Minister, Lúdvík Jósepsson, regarded the proposed deal as a 'breach of trust'. Apart from the communists, he achieved agreement and, with a very few minor changes, the package was put to the Icelandic Parliament, the Althing, on 11th November 1973. It was voted through with a large majority (54-6), diplomatic notes were exchanged between governments and at 1800 that same day, HM Ships *Phoebe* (OTC), *Danae*, *Ariadne*, RFA *Grey Rover* and the defence tugs *Lloydsman*, *Statesman* and *Welshman* headed back towards UK waters.

However, the final six weeks on 'presence patrol' - over 50-miles off the coast in October and November - had not been without incident for the warships and their supporting tankers ….

At the end of October 1973, the winter storms arrived to keep the patrolling forces on their toes. The best fishing was to the northwest and there were still about 50 trawlers working inside the 50-mile limit. The patrolling forces were sandwiched between the 50-mile limit and the encroaching ice line[87] in the Denmark Strait. This made finding a safe course in storm and icing conditions difficult and eventually caused unnecessary danger to the ships. The seamanlike action would have been to run for shelter in the lee of the land. For political reasons, initially, this was not permitted.

On the night of 26th/27th October, *HMS Jaguar* spent a very difficult night in winds up to force 11, temperatures down to -8.5ºC and with an estimated 50-60 tons of ice, up to 18-ins thick, forming on the forward upper deck and superstructure. On the night of 2nd/3rd November, off the northwest again, *HMS Yarmouth* (Commander Ian Powe) and RFA *Tidepool* (Captain John Moffat) suffered substantial storm damage in hurricane force winds, very high seas and severe icing conditions. *Yarmouth* was actually pooped[88], her hangar door was stove in and the rear of the funnel was cracked open, allowing the sea to enter and put out one of her boilers.

During this storm, ships were permitted to shelter within the 50-mile limit and thereafter, as the clear

[87] The Arctic Pilot shows that the maximum southerly ice edge overlaps the 50-mile limit from the end of October onwards.

[88] Being 'pooped' is where a large wave breaks right over the stern of a vessel.

WINTER NORTH ATLANTIC....

Such were the conditions encountered by HMS *Yarmouth*, RFA *Tidepool* and CDV*Lloydsman*, that the following account was used in the national press to accompany a Royal Navy recruiting campaign:

For a November day in the Denmark Strait, the weather forecast was normal enough:

NE wind force eight; air temperature minus 2.5ºC.

Little indication really that HMS Yarmouth was about to experience conditions no naval ship had seen since the War.

At fairly short notice, green waves, swollen to 50 feet, began coming over the fo'c'sle, packing ice on the superstructure to an average thickness of 12 inches.

Chunks of ice started hitting the bridge windows at 70 mph.

Looking after Yarmouth was challenge enough for Cdr Powe and his Officers.

But added to his concern were two other vessels: the Fleet Tanker RFA Tidepool and the Defence Tug Lloydsman.

Normal practice would be to steer clear of such conditions.

But Yarmouth and the other two ships had an operational requirement to stay on patrol. Over one shoulder lay the Icelandic coast. Over the other was an ice shelf, now closing in with some encouragement from the wind.

The channel left in between wasn't exactly vast leeway.

To make matters even more interesting, Yarmouth's Loran aerial became iced up and finally carried away. Radar froze too, leaving sonar the only remaining navigation aid.

But "growlers" - large icebergs grinding together - and the general noise of a sea strewn with "bergy bits" produced false sonar echoes.

Executive Officer, Lt Cdr Robins, and the other Officers of the Watch were obliged to rely on dead reckoning; a time-honoured system of estimating position by direction, distance and speed.

Turning downwind would help clear the ice. But to turn Tidepool, with her single screw and high freeboard, across a stormy sea at night seemed an unacceptable risk.

The decision was made to continue north until daylight.

At 0500 an overgrown wave engulfed Yarmouth, delivering sufficient water down the funnel to extinguish one boiler.

She hove to and stayed that way until dawn.

At first light, with the boiler re-ignited, the turn was started.

The experience showed that indeed the manoeuvre should not have been attempted in darkness.

Tidepool took 25 minutes, a two mile circle and 180 tons of water into her hold while reversing course.

Yarmouth's top heaviness, caused by the build up of ice, made broaching a real prospect.

But she rode the turn with great credit to her designers, It then took all available hands 4 hours to chip the ice to a safe level.

Yarmouth made it through the storm, but not before the sea's final coup de grace: a freak 70-foot wave that pooped her, making spaghetti of the flight deck guard rails and fittings.

Ice build up can be seen on Tidepool's upperdeck, while below Yarmouth's crew work to clear debris from the flight deck after she was pooped by a 70-foot wave.

(Alan Paterson)

water between Iceland and the ice line narrowed and the winter gales looked set to continue, the OTC was authorised to withdraw his forces to the south and east of Iceland. Even there, it was difficult to keep the frigates fully fuelled - I remember conducting a stern-replenishment for real, as opposed to for training purposes. Eventually, the tanker was moved south towards the Faeroes and refuelling operations were conducted in the, slightly, calmer waters there. HMS *Charybdis*, in which I was serving, was sailed on 6th November to relieve HMS *Yarmouth*. We had initially gone a day earlier, but during a practice 4.5-inch gun firing with the target on the bow, we had damaged one of the mushroom ventilators on the focsle and, it being pretty rough off Scotland too, water was pouring in up forward, so we had to return to Rosyth to have the ventilator welded up. As did all the frigates, we sailed with anti-icing paste smeared all over the superstructure. This nasty brown gungy stuff was designed to stop ice sticking, not forming and it was quite effective, but very difficult to remove afterwards.

We took other anti-icing precautions. The Leander class had a very seaworthy hull - sometimes dangerously so as the large flared raised focsle would ride above almost every sea and this could give one a false sense of security. Once the sea came green over the bow, it would sweep on down and break against the bridge screen. They also had very large reserves of buoyancy and, again if I remember correctly, positive buoyancy only disappeared when the ship had heeled to 93°; this was because of the buoyancy provided by the raised focsle.

To add to this inherent buoyancy, for this winter patrol, we took the precaution of winding explosive cord (Cordtex) around the base of the Type 965 long-range warning radar (the big bedstead aerial) at the masthead.

This aerial weighed five or six tons and had icing become severe, we were ready to blow it off and over the side - on the down-roll of course. One of the squadron staff officers had been a junior seaman in the Arctic Convoys during the Second World War, so he was more aware of the dangers of icing and the difficulties of ice-removal than most.

The patrols during this period were not, however, all conducted in bad weather and this period of calm was used for training and relaxation. During one training serial, I remember the ship practising direct (i.e visual) shore bombardment with the ship's 4.5-inch guns against an iceberg.

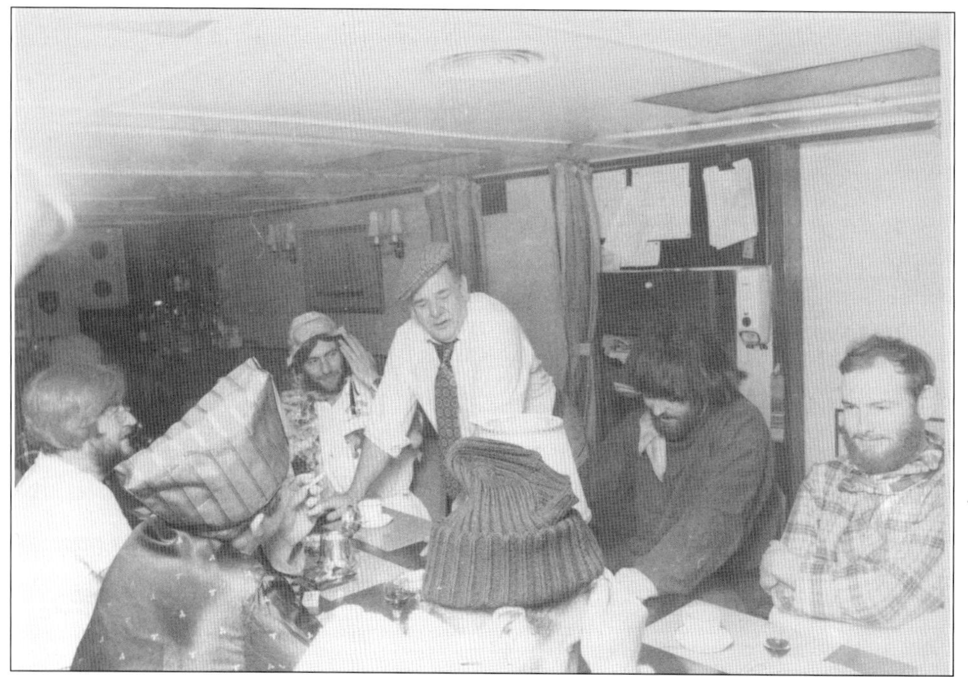

The photograph shows the wardroom of HMS Charybdis dining in 'fancy dress' on 6th October 1973. The gentleman addressing the assembled officers is our Liaison Skipper, Eric Thundercliff. The author is seated on the far right.

(Andrew Welch)

Wider Events

Surprisingly, no agreement was reached with the West German government until November 1975, a couple of weeks into the Third Cod War. The German-Icelandic dispute never reached the status of being called a 'war', partly because the West German Government never used their armed forces to protect their trawlers. All the action was between the Icelandic Coastguard and West German trawlers. One trawler had her warps cut in 1972 and fourteen in 1973, with six to come in 1974 and nine in 1975. In contrast, nine British trawlers lost their warps in 1972 and forty-one in 1973. The other reasons were the smaller number of German trawlers (about 25% of British numbers) and the fact that they usually fished further from the coast and, also, they fished for ocean perch, saithe and other red fish, rather than cod.

A landing ban on Icelandic-caught fish had been imposed in both Britain and West Germany. This was lifted in Britain after the agreement of 13th November, but remained in force in Germany until November 1975 (by which date the Third Cod War was underway). One of the consequences of this was that Iceland was denied special import duty reductions to EEC markets that she would normally have been entitled to until the final settlement with the British after the Third Cod War.

A week after the signing of the agreement, the Royal Air Force was once again using Keflavík airbase and conducting normal national and NATO surveillance flights with Icelandic air traffic control support. Simultaneously talks started between the Icelandic and US Governments on the future of Keflavík. Ólafur Jóhannesson's government had promised, on being elected, to renegotiate the defence agreement and to have no foreign military personnel permanently based in Iceland. A series of meeting were held between December 1973 and April 1974, with the Icelandic delegation proposing that all American personnel be withdrawn by mid-1976.

They proposed to fulfil their NATO obligations by permitting temporary military and air force deployments, with the airfield and the radar facilities being run by Icelanders, assisted by NATO civilians. This proposal was operationally totally unacceptable to NATO, let alone the Americans. It also seemed very likely that Ólafur Jóhannesson's government's proposals were not widely supported outside his narrow political circle. The matter was never put to the test as his government fell in June 1974 over its handling of the economy and a more broadly based coalition was elected on 30th June. It is indicative of the nature of Icelandic coalition politics that Ólafur Jóhannesson became the Minister of Justice in the new government.

One of the outgoing left-wing government's final acts was to amend the 1948 Conservation Law. This law gave the Fisheries Minister authority to make regulations concerning '... conservation zones within the limits of the continental shelf ... wherein all fisheries shall be subject to Icelandic rules and control'. The amendment added after 'continental shelf' 'or in the sea to 200 nautical miles measured from baselines.'

Geir Hallgrímsson, the incoming Prime Minister, made two important policy statements on taking office - the first was to declare that the defence agreement was satisfactory and would not be changed. The second was that his government supported the previous administration's aim of a 200-mile fisheries limit and that it intended 'to extend the fishery jurisdiction of Iceland to 200 miles during 1975 and start practical preparations for the extension at once.' NATO was relieved; the British Government was not.

And the British Domestic Reaction

Slightly surprisingly, the November 13th 1973 agreement was universally welcomed in Britain. The Navy had protected trawlers inside the 50-mile limit for 4½ months, with three frigates, one or two RFAs and three or four defence tugs on station at all times. There had been nine gunboat collisions with frigates and three with tugs, six arrest attempts or shootings and 14 warp cuttings. This last compared with 34 warp-cuttings in the 2½ months before the Navy was sent in. Fortunately there had only been one casualty and his death was not directly attributable to frigate/gunboat activity. Overall the annual catch had nearly reached the 170,000 tons ordained by the International Court.

A British Trawler Federation spokesman called the agreement 'astonishingly good - better than the most optimistic of us thought possible'. However, this initial reaction disguised the realisation that this was only a two-year agreement. The UN were gearing up towards the Third UN Conference on the Law of the Sea (UNCLOS3), at which it was expected that a 200-mile fishing limit would be agreed. Iceland had assumed that an international agreement would be in place within two years; in fact UNCLOS 3 was to drag on for ten years. As will be seen shortly, domestic politics in Iceland were not prepared to wait until UNCLOS3 reached agreement - hence the Third Cod War was already looming. This possibility was always recognised in Whitehall.

UNCLOS 3

Preparation work for UNCLOS3 started in Geneva in July and August 1973; the first meeting of the Conference was in New York from 3rd-15th December 1973. The British Government position was to agree with the concept of a 200-mile Exclusive Economic Zone (EEZ), as this would give it control over oil and gas resources around the UK. There was an acceptance that a 200-mile fishing limit would inevitably follow and that, therefore, the UK distant-water fishing industry was doomed. The British Government's aim was to secure a long transitional agreement with Iceland so that the end of British distant-water fishing could be a gentle, rather than an abrupt, process. There were also hopes, equally unfounded, that an agreement could be reached to limit the opening up of all British waters to her European partners under the Common Fisheries Policy (CFP).

The final act of the Second Cod War was not until 25th July 1974, when the International Court of Justice at last issued their judgement on the UK and West Germany's application of April 1972. The ICJ declared that Iceland was not entitled to exclude foreign fishing vessels from the waters between 12 and 50 miles. Whilst this legal confirmation of Britain's stand was welcome, it was meaningless as Iceland had made it clear that they rejected the ICJ's jurisdiction and international opinion had moved on.

The court's decision was actually announced on 25th July, during the 1974 UNCLOS3 session in Caracas. At this stage of the conference, the principle of a 200-mile EEZ had already been accepted and agreement on an identical fishing limit was expected to follow. The 1974 UNCLOS3 session closed on 29th August 1974 and the 1975 session was expected to see the Convention signed. This was to prove to be a highly over-optimistic view of the negotiations to come.

The 1975 UNCLOS3 session was held in Geneva from March to May 1975. There was general agreement on the 200-mile EEZ and fisheries limits, but lengthy arguments on subjects such as High Seas, Straits and Archipelagos - 'Freedom of the High Seas' issues. Consequently, there was no agreement and plans were made for a fourth session in 1976.

Iceland was not prepared to wait. The main conservation argument was that stocks were already diminishing - a 1975 Icelandic White Paper stated that since 1954, when the total cod catch was 546,000 tons and, 'in spite of ever-increasing fishing effort, catches have been decreasing since then on the average by about 8000 tons annually. The estimated catch in 1976 is only 350,000 tons.[89]' In addition there was evidence that the mortality amongst the breeding population was unsustainable - between 1945-9, the average cod spawned 2.5 times, by 1970-4, this was down to 1.3 times. Needless to say, these Icelandic figures were not universally accepted. Allied to the disagreement between scientists over the facts was the, perhaps unsurprising, Icelandic belief that all the reduction in catches 'needed' for conservation reasons should be borne by foreigners.

Declaration of a 200-mile limit

On 15th July 1975, Iceland declared that a 200-mile fishing limit would come into effect three months later, on 15th October 1975. Because of the agreement of 13th November 1973, British trawlers would be permitted to fish inside 200 miles until 14th November 1975. The Icelandic Government did indicate a willingness to enter into discussions (not negotiations) with other Governments whose interests might be affected.

Serious contingency planning for a third Cod War started immediately.

[89] The 'British' figures, taken from the post 2nd Cod War White paper for 1954 and the French Bulletin Statistique des Peches Maritimes for 1976 are a total demersal (i.e. mostly cod) catch in 1954 of 881,000 tonnes and 1,071,400 tonnes in 1976. It is difficult to reconcile these with the Icelandic White Paper of December 1975.

CHAPTER 15

THE RUN UP TO THE THIRD COD WAR
JULY - NOVEMBER 1975

Declaration of a 200-mile limit

The Icelandic declaration of a 200-mile limit was not unexpected in London and the possibility of a Third Cod War had been recognised almost as soon as the Second was over. The British Government's immediate aim was to negotiate an extension of the interim agreement allowing a total catch of 130,000 tons. There was a realisation however that, in the longer term, the British distant-water fishing fleet was going to be denied any access to Icelandic waters out to 200 miles. The tentative agreements already negotiated at UNCLOS3 made this clear. Nevertheless, it was hoped to negotiate a gradual reduction so that the inevitable job losses could be spread over a few years. As before, the British concept of negotiations as a bit of 'give and take' and the Icelandic one of 'no surrender' were going to make any discussions difficult, to put it no more strongly.

The British Embassy in Reykjavik summed up the Icelandic position, as edited for the Naval Staff History:

> *'The Icelanders saw this as the final step in the realisation of the central aim of their national policy. Control of the fisheries of the continental shelf was viewed as the correlative of independence, an essential safeguard for the future existence of the nation, and a matter of natural right. It engaged the fundamental patriotic emotions and did not admit of discussion on a merely technical, statistical or legal basis.*
> *According to the Icelandic view of history, their Danish rulers in 1901 divested Icelandic fisheries of the protection they had traditionally enjoyed just when the threat from foreign fishermen and 20th century fishing techniques made protection more than ever necessary. Independence was therefore soon consummated with the Law of 1948 on the Scientific Conservation of the Continental Shelf Fisheries, which was the bedrock on which all subsequent policy had been based. In pressing for the enlargement of the rights to control her maritime resources, and in moving out to 12, 50 and now 200 miles, Iceland sought to interpret international opinion, in the knowledge that international law would soon catch up with her position in the current climate of widening coastal jurisdictions.'*

Faced with such a position, it was evident that a Third Cod War was more likely than not. The civil and military protection plans, refined during the Second Cod War, could easily be reintroduced, although both the Royal Navy and the Royal Air Force would not be able to protect British trawlers in the new enlarged limits without other important commitments being affected. But first, the diplomats had to try to reach an agreement.

Talks

The initial British reaction to the 15th July 1975 declaration was a rejection of the claim and a request for early talks. These did not start until 11th September when a ministerial team of Roy Hattersley from the FCO, and Ted Bishop from MAFF, went to Reykjavik. Their Foreign Minister, Einar Ágústsson, who, in diplomatic terms, significantly outranked Roy Hattersley, led the Icelandic side. As in the First Cod War, the British failure to recognise the status of the leader of the Icelandic delegation caused additional strain. The British team's assumption was that these 'negotiations' would follow the normal 'Brussels' patterns - start from a position that everyone recognises, privately, as unachievable and then barter towards the middle ground. This process had never worked with Iceland before and would not do so now.

Icelandic officials told the Norwegian Ambassador, Olav Lydvo, that Roy Hattersley had been advised, right at the start of the talks, that the Icelanders would not move and that were a 'compromise' to be found, it would have to involve an almost unconditional British acceptance of the Icelandic position. Ambassador Lydvo reported to his Foreign Ministry that, however faulty Hattersley may have been in his conduct, he was not to blame for the failure of the talks.

Roy Hattersley's team claimed a need and a legal right to continue fishing between 12 and 50 miles; the 50-200 mile belt being dismissed as irrelevant because it contained almost no fish. However, in recognition of the way international opinion was moving, concessions were offered over catch totals, trawler numbers, closed areas etc. No specifics were tabled at this stage.

Einar Ágústsson, aware of local sensitivities, that he only really represented his faction in the coalition government and of the promises that had been made in the recent election, offered nothing, but agreed to consider any British proposals. A tentative date was set for further talks in October and the Icelanders emphasised that the new limits would affect British trawlers from 14th November.

Ministers met again in London on 23rd and 24th October 1975. The British, after consultation with the fishing industry, had decided that they could accept a total catch of 100,000 tons; their opening bid was to be 130,000 tons, with an indication that they would accept a lower catch. This total was, according to some industry sources, quite unrealistic in that the trawlers no longer existed to catch this total, but Don Lister, the Grimsby trawler skipper advising the British team, was told by Roy Hattersley that Harold Wilson had decided on this figure and that was that.

Just before these talks, the Icelandic Marine Research Institute issued a report, the so-called '*Black Report*', claiming to show an immediate need for drastically lower catches. The British Ambassador, Kenneth East, managed to get it translated and tried to get it circulated to the British side over the weekend before the talks. Unfortunately, no one had studied it over the weekend and the British fishery scientists had not even seen a copy before the meeting opened.

The British, failing to appreciate that the Icelanders actually believed the report, took it to be no more than a negotiating ploy and commissioned their own scientists to refute the more dramatic Icelandic figures. The Icelandic side half-heartedly proposed a catch limit of 50,000 tons, but the status of this 'offer' was unclear, because of party-politics within their delegation. In the absence of a clear figure to bid against, the British side were unable to suggest a realistic catch total and the meeting broke up with no agreement, except that there should be another meeting, if possible, before 14th November.

The British fishing industry and the distant-water fishing ports were still heavily dependant on Icelandic waters and an end to distant-water fishing would have a disastrous effect on employment in traditionally Socialist areas. Harold Wilson's Labour government, elected in October 1974, only had an overall majority of four, so there were strong domestic political reasons for supporting the fishermen. The Government made it clear, both in parliament and in its public statements, that the fishermen would get naval protection if they needed it.

An intelligence assessment on 2nd October correctly concluded that there was little chance of a negotiated settlement and that, in Iceland, public opinion and calculations of domestic political advantage would push the government into an early display of their determination to enforce the new limits. If the British Government was going to fulfil its promises, naval protection would be needed very shortly after 14th November.

Naval Preparations

By the end of October 1975, CinC Fleet had earmarked three frigates and a Royal Fleet Auxiliary tanker (with an embarked Wessex 3 helicopter) to be at seven days notice for Icelandic operations from early November and the Royal Air Force were ready to reactivate the Nimrod fishery protection flights. FOSNI was updating and re-issuing the Operation DEWEY OpOrder and making arrangements for liaison with the British Trawler Federation (BTF), issuing of special stores, briefings etc etc. Instructions to Skippers and Support and Defence Commanders were being reissued. The MoD had checked the charter market and *Lloydsman* and three oil rig support

The Civilian Defence Vessel Star Polaris.
(United Towing/Adsteam Towage)

vessels - *Star Aquarius*, *Star Polaris* and *Star Sirius* had been earmarked. The MoD had also checked, and slightly amended, the Rules of Engagement (RoE) from the Second Cod War.

The Intelligence dossier on the Icelandic Coastguard was updated. A new gunboat, the *Tyr*, had been commissioned in 1975. *Tyr* was 25 feet longer than *Ægir* and 2 knots faster, but otherwise a sister ship. The main difference for recognition purposes was that *Ægir* had two derricks at the forward end of her flight deck and *Tyr* only had one on the port side. The Icelandic Coastguard Fleet now consisted of four modern gunboats[90], *Ægir*, *Òdinn*, *Thor* and *Tyr*. In addition there were the two slower and smaller vessels *Albert* and *Árvakur*, plus a chartered stern trawler, the *Baldur*.

The one area in which the British had been constantly outflanked during the Second Cod War had been public relations (PR), as they were then called, or media operations, as the present jargon has it. Journalists and TV crews were to be encouraged to go to sea in frigates and to fly in Royal Air Force patrol aircraft on Cod War sorties. Interviews with Commanding Officers at sea would be arranged and there would always be a 'naval spokesman' available ashore. The picture transmission system that had been under consideration in September 1973 was now under trial and, if successful, would be fitted in frigates. On the political side, a Foreign Office Minister was appointed to be in personal charge of day-to-day Icelandic PR matters; he would have the authority to release the detailed facts and provide the British perspective on any incidents. There was a determination that the British case should be rapidly, fully and sympathetically explained both at home and abroad.

The final chance for Diplomacy …

The deadline of 14th November 1975 approached all too quickly. The Royal Navy and Royal Air Force were ready to do the Government's bidding, but there was still a faint hope that diplomacy might succeed. However, the Wilson Government had made very explicit promises to the fishing industry, and bearing in mind that it had a parliamentary majority of only four, was going to have to honour them unless a satisfactory settlement could be reached. There was a clear momentum developing towards naval protection.

The government's political difficulties were compounded by the fact that there were several other contradictory factors. A 200-mile fisheries limit would 'soon' ('though this was to take much longer than

[90] It is at about this period that the official records start to talk about ICGVs – Icelandic Coastguard Vessels – rather than gunboats. I shall continue to use the latter except when quoting official documents.

either side expected) become accepted international law - but it was not so yet and there was no doubt that Icelandic actions were in defiance of the existing law. The BTF had acknowledged that British distant-water fishing was a dying industry. The Icelandic government were proving to be the usual perverse and intransigent negotiators. The West Germans were very near to a settlement, which would, in effect, leave the decision about granting Iceland EEC tariff privileges to the British. However no effort was being made to persuade the British fisherman to continue fishing without naval protection.

The Icelandic Political Scientist Albert Jónsson assessed that Britain started the Third Cod War 'not to protect their future interests, but to buy time to renegotiate the Common Fisheries Policy.'

On 5th November, Foreign Minister Einar Ágústsson, in a private conversation with Ambassador Kenneth East, said that 50,000 tons was not a fixed figure and that 60,000 or even 65,000 might be possible. Back in Britain, the Industry (Owners, Unions and Skippers' Representatives) told MAFF Ministers on 7th November that they would accept 90,000 tons and maybe even 80,000. As a consequence, the Minister of Agriculture wrote to the Prime Minister, Harold Wilson that the industry:

> *'... while they naturally wanted the largest catch quota possible, would prefer, if necessary, to take a lower figure than fish under protection in the absence of an agreement, and indeed would give their support to the Government for an agreement at any figure from 80,000 tons upwards.'*

This statement, combined with the fact that a West German settlement was imminent, leaving Britain capable of offering Iceland the EEC tariff reductions, produced a touch of optimism over the next round of talks. A meeting was arranged in Reykjavik for 16th November 1975 and private diplomatic soundings, at the highest level, indicated that, although this was two days after the 200-mile limit came into force for British trawlers, nothing would be done to jeopardise the negotiations.

As on several earlier occasions, it became clear that the Icelandic government was not necessarily fully in charge of their own forces. When the British Ministerial party arrived at Reykjavik on the evening of 15th November, Roy Hattersley was 'bounced' on air, by Larry Harris[91] of the BBC, with the news that two trawlers, the *Primella* and the *Boston Marauder* had had their warps cut by *Thor* and *Tyr* respectively. *Ægir* was also in amongst the British trawlers and so with three gunboats harassing them, fishing had ceased.

Interestingly, the Naval Staff History has an unexpectedly sympathetic view of *Thor* and *Tyr's* actions:

> *'The Coastguard was instructed to avoid serious incidents, while still giving the impression of being appropriately active. Such ambivalent orders proved difficult to carry out. Instructions to trawlers to haul, if obeyed, meant unacceptable interruptions to fishing, and if disobeyed, as they not unexpectedly sometimes were, meant loss of credibility for the Icelandic Coastguard Vessels (ICGVs), particularly when Icelandic trawlers were also present. It was left to the Coastguard officers themselves to interpret their orders, and it was on their initiative that warnings gave way to warp-cutting.'*

Roy Hattersley had to make the difficult decision as to whether to break off negotiations and to return to London immediately. In the event, he decided to make a strong protest and to make a final attempt at negotiations. The talks proved to be fruitless. An Icelandic offer of 65,000 tons was made, and even possibly, 65,000 tons of cod, which was approximately equivalent to a total catch of 70,000 tons. Britain's counter-offer came down to 110,000 tons, but there were no further negotiations and the British team returned home. Their final statement made it clear that Britain believed that she had a right, under the terms of the old agreement, to fish up to 12 miles and that, if British trawlers were prevented from exercising this legal right, they would receive protection.

The Third Cod War was underway. It was to last for only six and a half months, but was much tougher and was to result in 55 collisions.

[91] Larry Harris was actually in Iceland to report on the World Monopoly Championship.

CHAPTER 16

THE THIRD COD WAR
NOVEMBER 1975 - JANUARY 1976

The Third, and final, Cod War lasted from 15th November 1975 to 1st June 1976. There was to be a brief pause (on the British side at least) for negotiations between 20th January and 6th February. The British tactics were very similar to those used during the Second Cod War - a combination of protection by frigates and tugs, with the addition, for the first three weeks, of three oil rig support vessels. Surveillance would be provided by Royal Air Force Nimrod Maritime Patrol Aircraft, supplemented by Wessex 3 helicopters embarked in the Royal Fleet Auxiliary (RFA) tankers and the frigate's own Wasp helicopters.

The Icelandic Coastguard had four larger, more capable gunboats, two smaller ones that took little part in the hostilities, and the chartered trawler *Baldur*. One of the difficulties in assessing the likely actions of the Coastguard from the British (and maybe also the Icelandic) point of view was that, to quote an unnamed Foreign Office official:

> *'Part of the problem was the difficulty already noticed of identifying the source of the orders and the chain of command. The Coastguard skippers quickly became popular heroes and were tempted to Nelsonian tactics.'*

Baldur, strongly built, was to prove to be one of the most aggressive of the gunboats, but in the coming contest, it was to be Captain Gudmundur Kjærnested of *Tyr* who won the accolade of the *Mad Axeman* and even had a T-shirt produced in his honour - a common enough tribute now, but rare in 1976.

The Royal Navy returns

On the 17th November 1975, the gunboats failed to cut any warps because the trawler skippers provided

The BBC's veteran Cod War Reporter Larry Harris with his 'Mad Axeman' T-shirt. Larry Harris spent many days reporting from onboard Tyr. (Andrew Welch)

mutual protection, but in so doing, they had to stop fishing. Next day, *Tyr* succeeded in cutting *St Giles's* warps and on the 19th the skippers told their owners that they would pull out in three days time unless the Navy provided protection. They were told that civilian protection vessels were on their way and that they should be given a week to prove their effectiveness. Despite this move, there was no serious belief that civilian protection would suffice and the fishermen had made it clear that they expected the Government to stand by their promises to provide naval protection.

Three oil rig support ships, the *Star Aquarius*, *Star Polaris* and *Star Sirius* had been chartered on 11th November, fitted with extra radio equipment and given a short period of training by the Fishery Protection Squadron staff. These ships displaced approximately 800 tons, were highly manoeuvrable and seaworthy and capable of 14 knots. Initially they were pre-positioned to the Shetlands and then, on 17th November, they were ordered to Icelandic waters in company with the tug *Lloydsman*, a veteran of the Second Cod War.

On 19th November a Defended Fishing Area (DFA) was once again established in Icelandic-claimed waters. The initial DFA, set up by the Defence Commander in *Star Aquarius*, was 70 miles long inside the 12 to 50-mile zone off the east coast, which is where the majority of the British trawlers (about 30) were at the time. There were another dozen trawlers off the northwest coast and all trawlers were advised to make for the DFA if they were having problems with the gunboats. That day *Benella* became the fourth trawler to lose her warps - to *Tyr* again.

The West Germans Settle

On 20th November 1975, the West German government reached a two-year agreement with Iceland. Since the end of the Second Cod War, they had suffered six warp cuts in 1974 and nine in 1975. Their agreement allowed forty licensed trawlers to take an annual catch of 60,000 tons, of which only 5,000 tons could be cod. The majority of the German catch was ocean perch and saithe. This agreement expired after two years and was not renewed. Belgium, Norway and the Faeroes, the only other countries interested in fishing off Iceland, had in 1972 and 1973 reached annually renewable agreements for small catches. Britain was now the only country holding out against Iceland's unilateral extension of fishing rights.

Out at sea, there were frequent interruptions to the fishing. The support ship *Othello* was present, but she remained strictly neutral, dealing only with repairs, casualties, weather forecasting and fishing matters unconnected with the dispute. *Tyr* was busy - cutting *Real Madrid's* warps on the 21st and *Ross Sirius's* on the 22nd. The skippers issued their owners with a second ultimatum on the 23rd November, threatening to leave the area on the 25th unless the Navy had been sent to protect them by then. HMS *Leopard*, one of the three frigates on patrol on 3rd October 1973 when the final negotiations to settle the Second Cod War started, had been briefed on the Icelandic situation before leaving the UK to take up a distant-water fishery patrol off Norway. She was then dispatched to Icelandic waters, but told to remain outside 200 miles.

The British Ambassador, Kenneth East, made a final appeal to the Icelandic Prime Minister, Geir Hallgrímsson, for harassment to stop whilst a solution was negotiated, but in vain. *Leopard*, commanded by Commander Hugh Whyte-Melville-Jackson (known as Tack-Tack-Jack), was ordered into the disputed area on 24th November and next day Kenneth East gave the following statement to the Icelandic Ministry of Foreign Affairs:

> *'Her Majesty's Government have decided to provide naval protection to enable British trawlers to continue fishing off Iceland in the face of efforts by Icelandic Coastguard vessels to stop them.*
> *HMS Leopard, which is already on its way to the area, will reach the fishing grounds later today. She will assume control of the civilian protection vessels and organise operations on the fishing grounds so that effective naval protection can be provided, once she is joined by two other frigates, on Saturday 29th of November.'*

Naval Protection is dispatched

In fact the first British military presence in the disputed area was a Royal Air Force Nimrod on a surveillance flight at first light on 24th November 1975.

The objectives of this flight were to start to build up the surface plot - which trawlers (British and Icelandic) were where - and to demonstrate, both to the trawlers and the Icelandic Government, that Britain was going to defend her right to fish in the disputed area. There were daily Nimrod sorties thereafter. HMS *Leopard* was, meanwhile, waiting 3 to 4 hours steaming from the DFA. She had been instructed to avoid attracting attention and not to let the fishermen know that she was there.

On the 25th, *HM Ships Falmouth* and *Brighton*, with the tanker RFA *Tidepool* in support, were ordered to Rosyth for briefings and to embark specialist stores, a Liaison Skipper and the press. Captain John Tait, the Captain of the Third Frigate Squadron and Commanding Officer of HMS *Leander*, was ordered to embark in HMS *Falmouth* as the OTC (Officer in Tactical Command). The plan was to provide two frigates on station, with a third on stand-by in Rosyth. The frigates would be supported by an Royal Fleet Auxiliary tanker with a Wessex 3 helicopter embarked. There were normally two RFA tankers allocated to the patrol, of whom one would be on station. The station tanker was often resupplied by an RFA Leaf class freighting tanker halfway through her patrol. Shaun Jones, who was a Deck Cadet in RFA *Tidepool*, remembers the refuelling rig being pulled out of RFA *Plumleaf* during a particularly rough mid-patrol pump-over. Initially, at least during the winter months, only one DFA would be established.

Operation DEWEY was reactivated at 1101 on 25th November 1975 when Vice Admiral Sir Anthony Troup, Flag Officer Scotland and Northern Ireland (FOSNI) ordered Commander R H Whyte-Melville-Jackson in HMS *Leopard* to take over the protection of British trawlers from the Defence Commander in *Star Aquarius*. His mission and the RoE under which he was to operate were exactly the same as they had been on the 2nd October 1973, just before the frigates had been withdrawn to sit outside the 50-mile limit during the peace negotiations that ended the Second Cod War. Essentially the task was to provide protection outside 12 miles and to attempt to frustrate harassment by the use of force up to certain levels but, except in self-defence, not including gunfire.

A copy of the updated DEWEY OpOrder was dropped to HMS *Leopard* by a Royal Air Force Nimrod and at 1530 she was in the DFA amongst the trawlers. The weather was calm, with fog patches and dusk was falling. As if awaiting *Leopard's* arrival, *Ægir*, being marked by *Star Aquarius* and *Star Polaris*, accelerated away from her 'minders' and cut *William Wilberforce's* warps. Over the next

HMS Falmouth (Jón Páll Ásgeirsson)

DOMUS

Demonstrations outside the British Embassy in Reykjavik at the start of the Third Cod War - 26th November 1975.

(Reykjavik Museum of Photography)

four days, the weather worsened, fishing was poor and both *Tyr* and *Ægir* were around. There were no warp cuttings.

Reaction in Iceland

On 25th November 1975, *Othello* entered harbour, with Icelandic Coastguard approval, to land an injured man. Her boat's crew were abused and had stones thrown at them. As one FCO source put it:

> *'The advent of Royal Naval frigates raised the emotional temperature. This was bullying. What was NATO for, if not to protect Iceland from external aggression? No Icelander could have entertained the notion that NATO had an equal obligation to protect British vessels from aggression on the high seas.'*

Next day, Iceland reintroduced the same restrictions on British activity as during the Second Cod War. Royal Air Force aircraft were forbidden to land at Keflavík, except in an emergency, and port visits were banned except for humanitarian reasons. The threat to withhold air traffic control services was made but never acted upon. The next afternoon, a crowd of about 5000 demonstrated noisily outside the British Embassy. Stones were thrown and two windows were broken, but the police acted firmly and after a couple of hours the crowd dispersed.

With a view to keeping the possibility of negotiations open and in the hope that positions would not become too entrenched, Harold Wilson sent his opposite number a personal message on 28th November. As part of this initiative the trawlers were told not to break the terms of the interim agreement and not to fish in conservation, small boat or rotating closed areas. The industry was unhappy with this ruling, as they had hoped to make up for the inevitable losses incurred in protected fishing by having unrestricted use of the whole of the 12 to 50-mile zone.

The Initial Dispositions

Captain John Tait arrived on station, in a typical Icelandic gale, on the 29th November 1975 in HMS *Falmouth*, with HMS *Brighton* and RFA *Tidepool* in company. This group was designated Task Group 600.1 and as the Task Group Commander, Captain Tait became CTG 600.1[92]. HMS *Leopard* was detached to return to her other duties on the 30th and

[92] In effect CTG and OTC are one and the same.

The Defence Tug Lloydsman as seen from the ICGV Baldur (Jón Páll Ásgeirsson)

the other two frigates, accompanied by *Lloydsman* and the three Star class defence vessels took up where HM Ships *Charybdis, Ariadne* and *Leopard*, RFA *Olmeda* plus the defence tugs *Lloydsman*, *Statesman* and *Welshman* had left off on 3rd October 1973, just over two years previously. The DFA was centred on the Whaleback, off Iceland's southeast coast. There were 30 trawlers fishing, with the civilian support vessels *Othello* and *Miranda* in company.

The Royal Air Force operation, in support of the naval protection forces was called HELIOTROPE. To ease the load on the Nimrod force, the Royal Air Force planned to use Hastings and Hercules transport aircraft, together with Vulcan bombers for some patrols. In the end, the Hastings flew 20 sorties to the Nimrod's 158. Normal NATO procedures were used in filing flight plans and, despite their threats, Iceland was punctilious in providing air traffic control services.

The Handley Page Hastings was originally a long-range transport and, as such, played a significant role in the Berlin Airlift. A number were subsequently converted to radar training aircraft, the T5s, and it was T5s of 230 Operational Conversion Unit, also known unofficially as 1066 Squadron, who flew the Third Cod War surveillance sorties.

According to the Naval Staff History, there were no Vulcan sorties in the Cod Wars, but according to Alan Croskill, there were some 'very boring' ones out of Royal Air Force Station Scampton. Alan remembers this well, because Colin, a Vulcan pilot, fell out with the local constabulary:

'Returning from a sortie in the early hours the crew quickly debriefed and hastened to their beds. After changing from uniform into civilian sweater and slacks, Colin was annoyed to find his car would not start and accepted the loan of a friend's dilapidated old Ford Consul to get him to his rented home off station in the local Market Town. Suffice to say he wasted no time and pushed the old car to its limits.
Unfortunately for him the only other vehicle on the deserted roads was a police patrol car, which flagged him down shortly after entering the restricted outskirts of the town.
The Constable approached Colin with the ominous question of "Are you aware you were doing 38 mph in the 30 limit?" Colin apologised and confessed he was not. The next question: "Is this your car Sir?"
Colin said it was not. What is the registration was met with a negative. The question "where are you going" meeting with the reply of

"home to bed" was clearly another black. When asked; "Where have you been?" Colin, without thinking, responded "Iceland." This resulted in the hapless Flight Lieutenant being asked to step from the car and accompany the police to the local station.

It was an older and wiser Colin who finally reached home with his speeding ticket.'

Under the 1973 Interim Agreement, 139 named British trawlers were allowed to fish inside the 50-mile limit. By the beginning of the Third Cod War, the increasing difficulty of making a profit from a trawler had meant that over 40 of the named vessels had been paid off. As the Icelanders were unwilling to accept additions to the list, British fishing off Iceland was clearly already in terminal decline. One consequence of this was that numbers of trawlers off Iceland varied between 10 and 50. This compared with 30 to 90 during the Second Cod War (albeit those are summer season figures) and 10 to 110 during the First.

Catches were also in decline - from 154,500 tonnes in 1973 to an estimated 116,000 tonnes in 1975 and it was important for the British to be able to demonstrate that more than 65,000 tonnes could be caught under naval protection. In order to bolster the catch, the BTF were keen to reverse the Government's decision to respect the catch limitation measures, such as rotating closed areas and the named vessel list. They also tried to persuade their members to fish in Icelandic waters, even if there was better fishing elsewhere and to persuade the Government to open up a second DFA to the northwest, where the fishing was usually best in December. This last request was turned down because of the assets required to protect two DFAs and because of the difficulties that might arise if trawlers, defence tugs and/or warships needed to shelter from the weather within territorial waters. Warships could be put into a very difficult position if they were to try to protect trawlers, perceived by the Icelanders as being poachers, within Icelandic territorial waters. To have done so would probably have been against international law, not to have done so would have produced much adverse publicity in Britain.

The Coastguard seemed to have learnt some of the lessons of the Second Cod War - certainly as far as electronic warfare was concerned, for they were to be more circumspect in their use of radar. The warp-cutter remained their most effective weapon, to which they knew that the Royal Navy could only respond by attempting to ride them off. The counter to being ridden off was just to keep going and to accept, even at times cause, the subsequent collisions. The British continued to wonder who exactly was in charge of the Coastguard. Political control seemed to be tenuous and the Coastguard Captains were well aware that 'if they were rammed', they would receive both political and public support. The real power to influence the timing, level and scale of actions on the fishing grounds was therefore in the hands of the individual gunboat captains and possibly the Chief Coastguard; certainly not with Ministers.

The other major factor that was different the third time around was the weather - the Third Cod War started in the winter, which meant gales, icing and shorter days. The first two affected the safety of fishing and protection operations, the last diminished the effectiveness of the Wasp helicopter as a surveillance and identification resource.

The OTC's primary objective was to obtain early detection, identification and interception of the gunboats. To achieve this, the Royal Air Force Nimrods and Hastings provided area search, supported by the radar-equipped Wessex 3 helicopters (known as 'Oscar Flight') based in the Royal Fleet Auxiliary tankers and the frigates' own Wasp helicopters, which were restricted to visual search and identification. Ships' Electronic Warfare (EW) listening equipment could detect gunboats' radar transmissions and ships were positioned to cover fjords where gunboats might wait up and other likely approaches to the DFA. The civilian defence vessels were kept closer to the trawlers as the final line of defence. Every ship (including the Royal Fleet Auxiliary tanker and the trawlers, but not the civilian support vessels, who remained firmly 'neutral') was instructed to report all suspicious radar contacts to one of the frigates.

The aim was detect any gunboats early enough for them to be marked before they got within range of the trawlers, so that fishing was not disrupted. If this failed, at least it was hoped to be able to give the trawlers enough notice of the threat so that they could haul their nets before their warps were cut. As in the Second Cod War, it was assumed that the gunboats would coordinate their efforts and aim to overwhelm the defences.

A Wasp helicopter hovering off the stern of the Fleetwood trawler Boston Kestrel.
(Jón Páll Ásgeirsson)

The First Six Weeks

The weather was the determining factor for the first few days and up to 1st December 1975 there was almost no fishing and no sign of the gunboats. On the evening of 30th November, whilst refuelling from *Tidepool*, *Falmouth,* commanded by Commander Gordon Walwyn, sustained five injuries when two large waves broke right over her fo'c'sle. She broke off from the replenishment and headed to the Faeroes to land her casualties and to complete fuelling. This left *Brighton,* commanded by Commander Nick Kettlewell, as the only frigate on station for 36 hours.

During this period, on the night of 1st/2nd December, 250 miles north of the DFA, the trawler *Port Vale* had both her warps cut by the *Árvakur*. The *Port Vale* then made best speed towards the DFA. On the 2nd, the weather improved and there was good, uninterrupted fishing. That afternoon the newly chartered Defence tug *Euroman* arrived and in the evening *Falmouth* was back in the DFA.

The first incident occurred on the 3rd December. It was pretty rough and there were 48 trawlers in the 120-mile long DFA. *Òdinn* was detected leaving Reydarfjord, north of the Whaleback, at 0400 and was marked by *Brighton*. *Òdinn*, who may have been acting as a decoy to draw the frigates south, remained close to the inner edge of the DFA. Meanwhile *Ægir*, undetected, entered the DFA from the northeast and, despite the presence of civilian defence vessels, managed to cut one of *Boston Comanche's* warps. An attempt on *William Wilberforce's* gear was unsuccessful and *Boston Comanche*, having recovered her trawl, was back fishing within a few hours. Nevertheless, fishing was disrupted and Captain Tait reported:

> *'this night's action must be given as round one to the Icelandic Coastguard but will serve as a sharpener to the defence forces.'*

Ægir returned to Reydarfjord at 0525, followed by *Òdinn* at 0830. For the next three weeks of rough to very rough weather (with winds up to 90 knots on two occasions), there were two or three gunboats active on the east coast. As weather permitted, they would come out to the trawlers and attempt to disrupt the fishing. The press were often embarked and usually a Coastguard Fokker Friendship would be overhead, passing positional information and filming any incidents. Marking and riding off gunboats became routine, almost daily, tasks for the defending frigates.

The second major confrontation was in the early morning of 5th December 1975 when there were 52 trawlers in the DFA, 47 of them within a 30-mile circle. At 0100 *Òdinn* appeared to the south of the group and was marked, from about a mile, by *Falmouth*. A couple of hours later, *Thor* came down from the northwest and was detected by *Star Aquarius*. *Brighton*, *Euroman* and *Lloydsman* all closed her and took up close marking stations, *Brighton* between ahead and on the beam at a cable and one of the tugs on each quarter. *Thor* spent the next three hours attempting to break away from her 'escorts'. She did manage to cut one of *Ross Ramilles's* warps, but was headed off on several other cutting runs.

During this period of close manoeuvring, the ships' speeds varied between stopped and full ahead, four times. Whilst trying to slip astern of *Brighton*, *Thor* came within 24 feet of the frigate and once within six feet of *Lloydsman*. The wind was force 8 and the visibility was three miles at the best, reducing to a thousand yards in snow showers. At one stage *Brighton* used her 15-inch signal lantern as a searchlight on *Thor's* bridge and this produced an acrimonious exchange on VHF[93]. All three British captains agreed that *Thor* was acting rashly and seemed intent on causing a collision. Fortunately a collision was avoided and *Thor* was escorted back to the 12-mile limit at 0600. Later in the forenoon[94], *Ægir* relieved *Òdinn*, to the south of the main group of trawlers, She was marked by *Falmouth* without much difficulty, only making a few half-hearted efforts to get at the trawlers and never coming within 2 cables of the frigate.

More of *Thor*

Thor was detected again by *Tidepool's* Wessex 3 at 0850 next morning (6th December 1975). *Euroman* headed to intercept her and at 0915 they collided. According to *Euroman*, *Thor* crossed her bow whilst she was taking up her marking position. According to *Thor*, she was deliberately rammed by *Euroman*. Either way, the gunboat was struck on her port side, sustaining minor damage to her flight deck guardrails. By 0935, *Brighton* and *Lloydsman* were also on the scene, taking up the same marking positions, at about a cable's distance, as on the day before. *Thor* broadcast a warning that if the British came any closer, she would open fire and then pro-

ICGV Aegir (Isaac Newton)

[93] The usual title for the international voice circuit enabling ships to talk bridge to bridge.
[94] The 0800-1200 watch.

The Defence Tug Euroman 'in action'.
(Jón Páll Ásgeirsson)

ceeded to try to get in amongst the trawlers. One trawler, the *Northern Reward*, lost her nets and others hauled theirs as a precaution. Thereafter, the three defending ships managed to keep *Thor* away from her prey, despite some very aggressive manoeuvring. At one stage, *Thor* appeared to be about to uncover and man her after gun. After authorisation from the OTC, the Commanding Officer of HMS *Brighton* warned *Thor* that, if she opened fire on any British vessel, he had authority to return fire. *Thor's* gun was left unmanned. This declaration was in accordance with the RoE change that came into effect on 1st June 1973, during the Second Cod War, after *Thor* had been harassing trawlers with her gun both uncovered and manned in the presence of HMS *Scylla*. HMS *Brighton* had embarked a minesweeping cutter before sailing for the patrol and towards the end of this confrontation she streamed it, hoping to catch and cut *Thor's* cutter-wire. Several frigates had embarked cutters; this is the only instance of one actually being used.

Commander Nic Kettlewell, the Commanding Officer of *Brighton*, reported:

> *The chances of getting a gunboat's cutter wire are slim, as one would need to set up a situation where the gunboat was streamed at speed and the frigate slow. However, the threat has been posed and they have watched my stern warily since. Thor certainly was distracted from at least one trawler on the occasion I streamed.'*

The use of cutters by frigates was forbidden after this one attempt on the reasonable grounds that it led to additional and unnecessary close quarters situations and it was unlikely to be effective. Whilst *Thor* and *Brighton* were sparring in the north of the DFA, *Ægir* had entered the area to the south and caught the trawler *Kingston Jacinth*, fishing alone. *Ægir* managed to cut one warp before *Falmouth* arrived on the scene and prevented any further harassment. As a result of all the gunboat activity on 5th and 6th December, the stand-by frigate, HMS *Galatea*, commanded by Captain Willie Gueterbock, was sailed from Faslane to reinforce *Falmouth* and *Brighton*.

The 9th of December was clear and very cold, with force 5 to 6 winds and seas of 10 to 12 feet. Three gunboats were to be deployed in the DFA during the day. *Thor* appeared first and was initially detected by the trawler *Ross Altair* at 0930. *Ross Altair* and the small group of trawlers around her hauled their nets and awaited support. *Brighton* arrived at 1308, with *Lloydsman* panting along behind. Trawling recommenced as *Brighton* moved in to mark *Thor*, successfully preventing any further interference with the fishing.

At 1415, *Brighton* detected another gunboat, *Tyr* and, unable to mark both gunboats, advised all the trawlers in the vicinity to haul their nets and close on the frigate in case a boarding was attempted. Unfortunately, the skipper of *St Giles* decided to ignore this advice and *Tyr* succeeded in cutting both his warps. *Lloydsman* finally arrived on the scene at 1450 and about half an hour later, *Thor* headed south towards the main group of 36 trawlers, followed by *Lloydsman*. *Brighton* stayed to mark *Tyr*, who made a couple of tentative lunges towards the trawlers, was easily headed off and then retired inside the 12-mile limit at 1730.

Thor was far more determined to get at the trawlers and caused *Falmouth* to have an energetic couple of hours, during which collision was very narrowly avoided several times. Captain John Tait, the OTC in HMS *Falmouth*, reported that *Thor* was extremely aggressive, with the ships from 6 to 10 feet apart, at speeds from zero to 26 knots, in the pitch dark with only the flash of photographers' bulbs and *Thor's* searchlight providing any light. At 1900, *Thor* retired inshore to the west, having failed to cut any warps in the 9½ hours she had spent in the DFA.

Fifty miles to the south of the main group, *Ægir* had approached a small group of four trawlers but was detected by *Wyre Defence* in time for them all to haul and save their nets. Fishing remained suspended until HMS *Galatea* arrived at 1215, directly from UK waters and started to mark *Ægir.* As fishing recommenced, *Ægir* made tentative attempts to reach the trawlers, but was easily ridden off by *Galatea* until she retired inshore at 1710.

This busy day, described by Captain Tait as 'the most hectic day so far', had seen the welcome reinforcement of the patrol by HMS *Galatea* and uninterrupted fishing by the main body of trawlers. One trawler, the *St Giles*, had lost her gear and about a dozen others, operating away from the main group, had been prevented from fishing for greater or lesser periods. Although three of the four larger modern gunboats had been deployed, there was no evidence that their attacks had been, in any way, coordinated and only *Thor* had shown any real persistence. The OTC later reported:

> *'one feels that these craft manned by Royal Navy officers would make a much better job of evading frigates and cutting wires.'*

The First Shots are fired

A gale blew up on the night of 10th December 1975 and the *Star Aquarius* and *Star Polaris* took shelter near Seydisfjord. Next forenoon, *Lloydsman* joined them to take water from *Star Aquarius* because the tug had an evaporator defect. The water transfer took place two miles off shore. At 1230, *Thor* appeared out of Seydisfjord flying flag Lima ('stop your vessel instantly') and flashing Limas on her signal lamp. He also ordered the British ships by radio and loudhailer 'stop or I fire'. Assuming that *Thor* intended to board and arrest them, the three ships headed for International water at their best speed[95].

Thor, probably trying to get alongside *Star Aquarius*, struck her starboard quarter. *Lloydsman* then tried to insert herself between the two and in the subsequent manoeuvring, collided with *Thor* when the gunboat tried to cross her bows. *Thor* then opened away and fired a shot across *Lloydsman's* bow. A second attempt to cross *Lloydsman's* bow to get to *Star Aquarius* produced another collision and this time *Thor* fired two warning shots, before returning towards Seydisfjord, threatening future reprisals. As soon as the OTC became aware of this incident, he ordered the three ships to clear outside the 12-mile limit at their best speed and sent *Galatea* to support them from just outside 12 miles. The two Star vessels and *Lloydsman* were legally 'Government vessels on non-commercial service' and so were both fully entitled to shelter from the weather inside territorial waters and were also outside Icelandic jurisdiction. *Thor* had no legal right to try and arrest them.

The British ships sustained no damage, but *Thor* needed 10 days of repairs to her flight deck, funnel and derrick. Needless to say, the Captain of *Thor* claimed that he had been deliberately and repeatedly rammed and no Icelander would have believed anything else. It is also worth remembering that the Icelandic Coastguard were insured with Lloyds of London, so it was the British who were paying for the repairs to the gunboats.

[95] The Icelandic version is that the ships were ordered by *Thor* to leave Icelandic territorial waters immediately and did not, initially, do so. Without access to both side's log books, it is impossible to know exactly what happened, where and in what sequence.

HMS Galatea crosses the bow of an Icelandic gunboat. *(Jón Páll Ásgeirsson)*

Politics and 'Spin'[96]

The Icelandic Government was determined to extract the maximum political advantage from these incidents and raised the issue with both the UN Security Council and at the NATO ministerial meeting in Brussels on 12th December 1975. The report from the British Ambassador to the UN in New York stated that their protest alleged:

> *'British auxiliary vessels operating under instructions of British naval units repeatedly rammed an Icelandic Coastguard vessel with the obvious intent of inflicting serious damage in which they succeeded ... This attack took place 1.9 miles off the east coast of Iceland, i.e. far inside the undisputed territorial waters of Iceland. The Icelandic Government views this attack as a flagrant violation of Iceland's sovereignty endangering peace and security.'*

In New York, both the Nordic and the United States representatives pointed out that many nations might not view an incident with three British tugboats as that serious, especially when compared with some of the bloody conflicts that were raging elsewhere in the world at the time. The US representative asked the Norwegian to point out gently to his Icelandic colleague, the episode could hardly be called 'a threat to international peace and security' as was usual for resolution addressed by the UN Security Council. The Icelandic delegation, rightly, concluded that it would be unwise to force a debate on this issue. That they had ever considered it worthy of the UN Security Council's attention demonstrated 'the extreme emo-

[96] 'Spin' was unknown in its present meaning in the 1970s, but the process of news management and manipulation is nearly as old as the printed word.

tions and even irrationalism which often influenced Icelandic thinking during the Cod Wars.'[97]

In both the UN and NATO, public acrimony was avoided and in discussions the British case received reasonable sympathy. The British were able to show that they were keen to negotiate, whereas the Icelandic side was becoming less and less willing, or perhaps able, to do so. The Prime Minister, Geir Hallgrímsson, was aware that, since the frigates had arrived off Iceland, not only his coalition partners, but also many of his own party were determined that there should be no concessions. Both the Fisheries Minister, Lúdvík Jósepsson, and the Justice Minister were from the hard left, the latter, Ólafur Jóhannesson, having been the Prime Minister who had been so difficult for the British to deal with in 1973 and had tried to evict NATO from Keflavík. As Ólafur Jóhannesson was now the Minister, nominally at least, in charge of the Coastguard he should have had some influence over the gunboat operating policy, which was not conducive to peacemaking or opening negotiations. Geir Hallgrímsson was not master in his own house and was not politically strong enough to respond to any peace overtures. In fact, he felt that he had to move in the other direction and the 65,000 tons offer was withdrawn.

The solidarity and single-mindedness of the Icelanders, both politicians and the general population, in pursuit of the aim of getting total control of 'their' waters was a great strength in all three Cod Wars. However the rest of the World did have some sympathy for the British who were, at least, trying to negotiate.

On 13th December, HMS *Leander* relieved HMS *Galatea* and allowed the OTC, Captain Tait, to return to his own ship. Trawler numbers were, as usual running down (there were only about 20 on 14th December) as they returned home to catch the last of the pre-Christmas markets, but they would be up again by Christmas. The frigates were managing to keep the gunboats at bay and the trawlermen's morale was, consequently, high. Fishing had been good since the frigates arrived; more fish being landed than in the same period in 1974.

Under pressure from the industry, the British Government agreed that, if there were no sign of negotiations by the end of the year, the terms of the 1973 interim agreement would be allowed to lapse from 1st January 1976. Conservation and small boat areas would continue to be respected, but rotating closed areas and the licence list would be ignored.

Back at Sea

The three Star vessels were withdrawn on 16th December 1975 after continued doubts about their seaworthiness and effectiveness in the rough seas off Iceland. HMS *Falmouth* also had to leave the patrol two days early to land a seriously sick man in the Faeroes. With *Lloydsman* off task for a week's maintenance, this left only two frigates and one tug to cover the 17 trawlers still fishing. The Coastguard's Fokker Friendship soon noticed this reduction in the defence forces, but the levels were considered adequate for the 48-hour period until HMS *Lowestoft* arrived to relieve *Falmouth*.

Urgent consideration was, however, given to replacing the Stars and the tug *Statesman*, another veteran of the Second Cod War, was hired from the New Year. Additionally, it was decided to deploy, also from January, *RMAS Roysterer*, the Admiralty tug stationed in Scottish waters. Although she was considered to be a bit too slow and not robust enough for protection duties, she would be another hull in the area in case of need and could act as an additional detection and reporting platform.

Lowestoft, commanded by Commander Richard Carpendale, arrived on 18th December, bringing the frigate numbers back to three. As she arrived, business was 'normal', *Leander* was marking *Tyr*, who had appeared from the east and *Brighton* was covering the south. *Òdinn* appeared from the northwest at 1000 and, in spite of warnings to the trawlers and the dispatch of *Euroman*, managed to cut one of *Crystal Palace's* bridles[98] as she was hauling. *Tyr* and *Òdinn* remained in the DFA for the next two days. Fishing continued and the few attempt to reach the trawlers were successfully defeated by the frigates, although not without some drama. *Leander* and *Tyr* came within 6 feet of a collision during one close marking phase. As already noted, this sort of activity was becoming routine.

The OTC changed on 20th December when Captain Bob Gerken in HMS *Andromeda* took over

[97] Another quote from Gudni Jóhannesson in *Sympathy and Self-Interest.*

[98] The bridle is a short length of wire between the warp and the net ground chain. It is easier and quicker to renew than when a warp is cut.

The defence tug Statesman 'in action'.
(Jón Páll Ásgeirsson)

from Captain John Tait. *Andromeda* had come straight from Gibraltar, where she had just completed a deployment with NATO's NAVOCFORMED[99]. There had been rumours that the ship might not get home for Christmas and Captain Gerken remembers that, within 4 hours of his broadcast breaking the news to his ship's company, the Petty Officers Mess, en bloc, were coming back onboard having scoured Gibraltar for Christmas presents and decorations. David Jones was in another of the frigates returning from the NAVOCFORMED Exercise and remembers hearing that one of the frigates was not going to be home for Christmas:

> *'Fortunately it wasn't us, and the Captain, when he made the announcement, named the unfortunate ship that would be returning to the Cod War. He also added that, unlike us, the crew of this frigate would only have the one night ashore in Gibraltar before returning to Iceland and he reminded us that it could have been us, and to be sympathetic to any of their crew that we might meet ashore. The following morning, I (Dave Jones was the Chief Radio Supervisor) was called for by the Master at Arms[100] to discuss the circumstances under which one of my lads had been arrested and locked up the night before. It appeared that he had been the instigator of a huge punch-up with the crew of the unfortunate frigate nominated to return to Iceland.*
> *"Stan" I said to him later that morning "you were specifically told not to wind them up you b****r."*
> *"I didn't Chief," he answered. We were in the bar with them and we told them they didn't have to pay,for any of their booze 'cos we'd pick up the tab".*
> *"That sounds pretty generous to me," I said, "so how did you end up in a punch-up with them?"*
> *"Well I dunno Chief" he answered, "'cept they got a bit miffed when I asked them if they'd like some ice in their drinks." He paused "I don't remember much more."*

That story rings true!

As *Andromeda* arrived, both *Leander* and *Brighton* departed for Christmas at home, leaving two frigates and one tug to cover the Christmas period. Fortunately the MoD's assessment that the Christmas period would be quiet was correct and from 21st December 1975 there was a week of comparative

[99] NAVal On Call FORce MEDiterranean.
[100] The ship's policeman.

peace, but not before both *Ægir* and *Òdinn* had spent the 20th harassing trawlers and, in all likelihood, assessing the new OTC's robustness.

Trawler numbers were back up to about 30 over the Christmas week, during which there was only one incident. Early on the 22nd, *Ægir's* radar was detected off Reydarfjord and the Wessex 3 was launched to locate her, which she did at 0815. The Nimrod on patrol subsequently re-identified her at 1045. Visibility was good, the sea was rough and the winds force 6 to 7. *Ægir* was seen to be heading towards two trawlers, the *Falstaff* and *Ross Leonis*, fishing on their own about 60 miles south of the main group.

The Nimrod was able to warn the two trawlers who hauled in time and *Andromeda* headed south to give protection, launching her Wasp helicopter at 1403. At 1407, the Coastguard Fokker Friendship joined the Royal Air Force Nimrod over the two trawlers and *Ægir* arrived 5 minutes later. By 1430, *Andromeda's* Wasp was also on the scene and by 1520 *Andromeda* herself was there. *Andromeda* escorted the two trawlers back towards the main group, followed by *Ægir* until 2300. The Nimrod's early warning had prevented any warp cutting and with the defence forces gathering, *Ægir* had made no attempt to board or arrest the trawlers.

Nearly four weeks after it had been sent, on 24th December, Geir Hallgrímsson replied to Prime Minister Harold Wilson's conciliatory letter of 29th November. He opened by deploring recent events on the fishing grounds, particularly the incidents of 11th December 'when three British tugboats attacked an Icelandic coastguard vessel and rammed it repeatedly 1 to 2 nautical miles from shore.' He repeated the arguments on conservation, Iceland's dependence on fishing and the expectations of international agreement on a 200-mile limit. He refused to negotiate unless the frigates were withdrawn and withdrew the 65,000-ton offer. This was not an encouraging message.

On 27th December 1975, the support vessel *Hausa* and the trawler *Volesus* closed Seydisfjord to look for shelter in order to transfer an injured man from the trawler. Commander Richard Carpendale in *Lowestoft* provided support from the 12-mile limit. It was too rough, even a mile offshore, and the two vessels moved further north looking for a lee. At 0530 *Hausa* reported that they had not managed to find anywhere calm enough for the transfer and that both vessels were now clear of territorial waters (4 miles wide at the time). As was usual when dealing with humanitarian cases, the Support Commander in *Hausa* had kept the Icelandic coastguard and the British Embassy informed of all movements into and out of territorial waters.

At 0635 *Andromeda* detected *Try's* radar moving

The support vessel Hausa.
(Jón Páll Ásgeirsson)

north from Reydarfjord and at 0935, when it looked as if *Tyr* was closing on *Hausa* and *Volesus*, Captain Bob Gerken signalled FOSNI asking for permission for a frigate to enter the 12-mile fishing limit. His intention was not to enter the 12-mile limit immediately, but to be able to do so if *Tyr* continued to close *Hausa* so that the frigate would arrive in *Hausa's* vicinity at the same time as *Tyr*. Captain Gerken hoped to prevent *Hausa* from being boarded, rather than to have to persuade *Try's* boarding party to leave.

In the event, Captain Gerken's request was refused and *Tyr* retired to Nordfjord without approaching the two British vessels. The British policy of not entering the Icelandic 12-mile limit had been in force since 1973, in spite of the problems that this caused. To have broken this self-imposed limit now would have been seen as an escalatory move which would only be authorised in response to actual, rather than possible, Icelandic aggression.

The First Collision

The 28th December 1975 was calm; there were 28 trawlers fishing in the DFA, which was still off the east coast. At about 0600, both *Tyr* and *Thor* were detected and the OTC made his defensive dispositions. *Andromeda* marked *Tyr*, *Lowestoft* marked *Thor*, *Lloydsman* stood by the main group of trawlers and all the skippers were warned of the approaching gunboats. The tanker, *RFA Olwen* was sent south to replenish HMS *Gurkha*, due to join the patrol at midnight.

By 0915, *Tyr* was within 10 miles of three trawlers, with *Andromeda* marking on her beam. Two of the trawlers hauled their nets as advised and *Tyr*, trying to get at the third who was still hauling, closed to 60 feet on *Andromeda's* beam. From this position, she three times rapidly reduced speed and cut very close across *Andromeda's* stern. On the third occasion, by now possibly in frustration that she would not be able to show the embarked press a trawler having her nets cut, she tried again. This time, from a position about 100 feet away on parallel courses, with both ships at 19 knots, she seemed to miscalculate and closed in on *Andromeda* before dropping astern. Her bow swung rapidly in towards *Andromeda's* starboard side as she dropped back and she struck the frigate amidships with her port bow, before scraping down the side and dropping astern.

There was a small dent in *Andromeda's* ship's side, she lost her starboard accommodation ladder and suffered some damage to her guardrails and the rocket flare launcher sponson. *Tyr* also suffered minor damage, but this did not dissuade her from repeating the manoeuvre an hour later, when she missed *Andromeda's* stern by 10 feet.

Captain Gerken's assessment was that the collision occurred because:

> *'the use of astern power by Tyr in order to drop rapidly astern caused her to lose steering control in a critical position such that she was unable to steer out of Andromeda's midships suction zone.'*

He also judged that:

> *'the manoeuvre, which she had successfully if dangerously completed twice earlier, was probably for the benefit of her many embarked photographers to get photographs which would appear to show Andromeda crossing her bow.'*

In a statement released by the MoD before his return to the UK, Captain Gerken described the final stage of his encounter with *Tyr*:

> *'On the third occasion, she turned in too soon and appeared to lose control as her bow rode over my guardrails. At the time she drove into my starboard side I was on a steady course and speed and had a trawler I was protecting on my port bow inside one mile.*
> *From the number of photographs taken from Tyr she seemed to be making a last bid for the 1975 Photograph of the Year competition and I was the anything but smiling subject.*
> *I still wonder whether the proper captain was on leave and an inexperienced ship handler had the control since she lost steering control by using astern power and being sucked in by interaction between the ships, the danger of which should be well known to an experienced man.'*

This was Captain Gudmundur Kjærnested's first collision in his new ship, the *Tyr*, and in *The Last Waltz*, he comments:

> *'When the 200 mile limit was declared, I was commanding Tyr, which was brand new at the time, and some silly novice rubbed his ship against mine and I hurt terribly. Had I commanded a bigger ship I would have shot at him, but he was well armed.'*

Though still fairly dark at the time of the collisions, by the fourth occasion there was good daylight for photography[101]. *Tyr* remained in the vicinity until about 1700. *Thor*, with *Lowestoft* marking, remained in the vicinity of the trawlers until the evening, but made no serious attempt at harassment. However, the close proximity of the two gunboats caused many trawlers to suspend fishing for up to 6 or 7 hours.

Naturally, both sides made diplomatic protests. The MoD rejected the Icelandic claim that *Andromeda* had rammed *Tyr* as 'absolutely laughable. It would be like a mini trying to ram a tank.' After this successful day disrupting the fishing, the gunboats seem to have retired for the New Year holiday and onboard HMS *Andromeda* the New Year's Eve 'Sods Opera'[102] production had been '*Codspell*' in which the 'Fairy Codmother' *Andromeda* was attacked by the wicked fairy 'Thor'. This turned out to be unfortunately perceptive, as the events of 7th January 1976 were to show.

British adherence to the interim agreement ceased on 1st January and this opened up new areas for fishing, so permitting more flexibility in the location of the DFA. The Liaison Skipper, an experienced trawler skipper attached to the OTC's staff, took a vote amongst the skippers and the location of the DFA was adjusted accordingly.

Perhaps surprisingly, there were still some skippers who perceived that they would get better catches by going off on their own. The dangers inherent in this independent stance were well illustrated on 3rd January when *Prince Philip* and *Ross Resolution*, both fishing well outside the DFA, had their warps cut by *Ægir*. According to Ken Yates, the skipper of *Prince Philip*, *Ægir* had lights rigged to make her look like a merchant ship. She lost her cutting gear on this occasion and so had to return immediately to port to replace it. The OTC judged that the recent peaceful fishing conditions had led to overconfidence and asked that the owners reiterate their instructions to skippers to remain within the DFA.

RMAS *Roysterer* arrived on task on 3rd January 1976. Thereafter, she, *Rollicker* and *Typhoon* would share the patrol. The newly chartered tug *Statesman* joined on 4th January. Roddy Jardine, her Captain, notes that she was properly called *Statesman 1*, as there was already a *Statesman* on the UK ship register. She had almost yacht-like lines, having been

ICGV Ægir *(Bob Turner)*

built in Japan as the flagship for Moran Towing of New York, but was deceptively heavily built and highly manoeuvrable.

On 4th January the December catch figures were published. They showed that, if the catch rate was maintained, the annual catch, under protection, would exceed 100,000 tons. The Icelandic reaction was to maintain the pressure at sea and to look for

---

101 In latitude 66°N in late December, there is only 2½ hours of light between sunrise and sunset.
101 'Ship's Onboard Dramatic Society'

further diplomatic moves. The Cabinet considered severing diplomatic relations with Britain, a new approach within NATO and, once again, threatening to withdraw the use of the Keflavík base. The British hoped that the realisation that fishing could continue successfully under Royal Navy protection might encourage Iceland to negotiate. However, they recognised that this was a slim hope and an extra frigate was ordered to join the patrol to cope with the coordinated assault that was expected.

The Expected Assault

On 7th January 1976, there were 39 trawlers in the DFA with three frigates and three tugs in defence; there were also three gunboats in and around the area. HMS *Naiad*, under Captain Tony Casdagli's command and newly arrived that day, was thoroughly tested by *Tyr* even though they were both outside the DFA and there were no trawlers anywhere in the vicinity. *Thor*, marked by *Andromeda*, made a determined attempt at 1215 to cut the warps of *Ross Resolution* and *Portia*. In keeping her away from the former, *Andromeda* was nearly forced onto the trawler.

Ten minutes later, approaching the *Portia*, with both ships on a steady course, 100 feet apart at 19 knots, *Thor* altered to starboard and hit the frigate aft. The port quarter bollard and fairlead took the main impact and Captain Gerken judged that, had he not gone full ahead when *Thor* started her turn, *Andromeda* would have been hit hard amidships with a real danger of major damage and loss of life. *Thor's* action seemed to be quite deliberate. Perhaps unsurprisingly, there was a television crew onboard. Despite the *Thor's* press guests, this was one occasion when the British won the media battle. *Andromeda* had a converted Mufax weather machine onboard which allowed the Navy's photographs to be transmitted to London before the press, including an ITN crew, embarked in *Thor* were ashore in Iceland. *Thor* had a 3 foot by 2 foot hole in her bow, well above the waterline. Within minutes of the collision, a drawing was circulating onboard *Andromeda* showing a soccer goal with the scoreboard behind reading '*Andromeda* 2 Iceland 0'. It takes a lot to separate the sailor from his sense of humour.

Andromeda offered *Thor* assistance, but this was declined and after *Tyr* had joined to inspect the damage from outboard, the two gunboats left the area together. At a press conference on return to the UK, Captain Gerken said of this collision:

> *'To my horror, I saw Thor well up on the port side of this ship (a British trawler) and turning towards us. I reckoned she was going to turn back again and I could not believe she was going to run into the port side. But that*

HMS Lowestoft with fenders out. *(Peter Harrison)*

HMS Bacchante on guard. Note the old car tyres being used as defensive fenders. *(Jón Páll Ásgeirsson)*

was what happened. I ordered an emergency movement at the risk of damaging machinery as she closed in.
Fortunately we took the blow on our bollards ...We took a very considerable shock and were fortunate not to suffer severe damage. If we had taken the blow further forward then we must have been holed.'
'The sea water temperature is near freezing and the life expectancy of anyone going overboard is three minutes. It is hard for me to see into the mind of someone who would deliberately ram their bow into someone else's ship. It could be that having been thwarted with one trawler, perhaps reasoning was beginning to slip a bit.'

In the same interview, Captain Gerken said of the captain of *Thor*, Helgi Hallvardsson, 'He is a very aggressive man' but of *Ægir's* captain, Throstur Sigtryggsson, he said 'He is my sort of captain and uses the wide open spaces, making it very hard for us to fight him. He bides his time and is not one of the blood and thunder merchants.' Captain Gerken's opinion of the man who had just rammed his ship is not surprising, but his overall appreciation of the gunboat captains, given to the press, shows the respect that the Royal Navy generally had for the Icelandic Coastguard:

'They are extremely fine seamen with extremely fine ships. I admire them and have no animosity towards the captains. I see them as executing a policy they have been ordered to do.'

Ægir made an appearance that afternoon, approaching a group of trawlers in the northwest of the DFA. She was detected in good time and the trawlers were able to haul, but fishing was interrupted for several hours before *Lowestoft* and *Roysterer* arrived to offer protection. Next day, *Ægir* was still around, *Thor* and *Tyr* were both in Seydisfjord. HMS *Bacchante,* commanded by Captain Tony Dunn, joined the protecting force, bringing the frigate numbers up to four. That evening, *Andromeda* was relieved by the returning HMS *Leander*.

On the 9th, *Bacchante* was marking *Ægir* in the north, when *Tyr* and *Thor*, still with a hole in her bow, reappeared on the fishing grounds. The frigates managed to get into marking positions in time to prevent any warp cutting, but not before several trawlers had had to haul their nets. *Tyr* and *Naiad* had several very close encounters, as did *Bacchante* and *Ægir*, but fortunately there were no collisions. As soon as he had taken over as OTC again, Captain John Tait in *Leander* was involved in close marking *Thor*. Ian Daniels, a Leading Seaman onboard, remembers:

'Every time it looked as though we were about to collide the Captain (who seemed to live on the bridge) gave the order to man the

> *fenders Port or Starboard side. It was our job to run out on deck and push the rattan fenders over the guard rails and try to keep hold of them as the gunboats scrapped along side and bounced off,'*

After an hour's successful prevention of warp cutting, *Thor* and *Leander* collided at 1420. *Leander* had been keeping *Thor* just ahead of the beam on the side away from the threatened trawlers and *Thor* had been trying to force *Leander* off her course by slowly altering towards her. Finally, *Thor* came too close and even an order of full astern was insufficient to prevent *Thor's* port quarter and *Leander's* starboard bow from meeting. There was little apparent damage to either ship, although *Leander* did leave patrol early because of concern over the crack in her bow. As was now expected, Captain Tait assessed that *Thor's* aim had been to provide dramatic film crew for the embarked ITN crew.

Genuine Diplomatic Moves

On 9th of December 1975, Iceland had announced new diplomatic moves, intended to both reinforce and publicise their case, to involve NATO, in the person of Dr Joseph Luns, the organisation's Secretary-General, directly in the negotiations and to threaten a breaking-off of diplomatic relations. The press release from the Prime Minister's office stated that:

> *'.. the Icelandic Government considers it inevitable that a continuation of deliberate rammings by British warships on Icelandic Coastguard vessels will lead to severing of diplomatic relations with Great Britain.'*

Dr Luns's efforts led to a withdrawal of British naval protection from 20th January and a period of, ultimately unsuccessful, negotiations lasting through to the 5th of February 1976.

CHAPTER 17

THE THIRD COD WAR
JANUARY - FEBRUARY 1976

The Icelandic diplomatic moves of 9th January 1976 were aimed at hastening the withdrawal of British trawlers and their protecting forces from 'Icelandic' waters. Firstly, special briefing visits were planned to the capitals of all NATO and UN Security Council states in order to enlist support for the condemnation of 'British aggression' at subsequent Security Council and North Atlantic Council meetings. Secondly, Dr Luns, the Secretary General of NATO, would be invited to Iceland – presumably so that he could see the 'self-evident truths' of the Icelandic case and would therefore put more pressure on the British. Finally, the British Ambassador in Reykjavik was told that:

> *'if deliberate rammings by British warships of Icelandic Coastguard vessels did not cease, a severing of diplomatic relations would be inevitable'.*

In his report, forwarding this message, the Ambassador added that there was a total credibility gap in Iceland over opposing versions of events at sea, all Icelanders regarding it as self-evident that the British were bent on securing control of the fishing grounds by disabling the coastguard vessels. The UK press were taking a more (but not completely) balanced view and abroad, where both versions were reported, the main theme was impatience that a commercial dispute between NATO allies could not be quickly and peacefully settled.

On 12th January, Dr Luns accepted the Icelandic invitation and, before leaving Brussels, asked both the British and Icelandic representatives to consider instructing their ships to be as 'passive' as possible during his visit. In Iceland, he managed to extract from the reluctant Prime Minister, Geir Hallgrímsson, an agreement that the British Government should be informed that:

> *'while the Icelandic Government could not give any guarantee to desist from the exercise of its rights within the 200-mile zone, it was the personal belief of the Secretary General that withdrawal would probably result in the absence of incidents'.*

There was some evidence that Ólafur Jóhannesson, the Minister of Justice, rather than Prime Minister Hallgrímsson, was actually in charge, but nevertheless based on this very fragile assurance, the British Foreign Secretary, Jim Callaghan, and Dr Luns met in Brussels on the 19th January and decided to announce the withdraw of the frigates and the Royal Air Force surveillance aircraft. The faintest possibility of compromise was clearly too much for some and on the same day, *Ægir* attempted to cut a warp and collided with the trawler *Lord Jellicoe*. To compound this, almost simultaneously, the Ministry of Foreign Affairs informed the British Ambassador that:

> *'... should British warships and Nimrod aircraft still be operating within the Icelandic 200 miles fisheries limits by 12 o'clock midnight GMT on January 24th 1976, the Government of Iceland will consider diplomatic relations between Iceland and Great Britain to be severed and the British Embassy in Reykjavik must be closed and its diplomatic personnel recalled.'*

This ultimatum caused considerable annoyance to Dr Luns, who had given Mr Callaghan his agreed personal assurance about Icelandic behaviour. Jim

Callaghan, who was getting very fed up with the undiplomatic behaviour of the Icelandic Government, commented to the Norwegian Foreign Minister:

> *'There is a limit to how often one can turn the other cheek. Truly enough the Bible said that one should turn the other cheek, but there was nothing about the need to do it 17 times. There is a limit to the number of insults which the British cabinet could accept.'*

The British announcement had to be reworded to make it clear that the withdrawal was taking place in spite of and not in response to this threat.

Also on the nineteenth, it was decided that *Leander* should return to Devonport because of concerns about the damage to her bow after the collision with *Thór*. Lieutenant Commander Chris Pink, the Executive Officer took command of *Leander* and Captain John Tait, as the OTC, transferred to *Falmouth* again. *Bacchante* relieved *Leander* on the patrol. *Leander's*[103] website, courtesy of Joe Fraser (RO1(T) onboard at the time), tells the story of the return home:

> *'With only one boiler, which made effective marking of the gunboats impossible, HMS Leander was detached from the Cod War on Monday 19th of January 1976. ... All looked well for a quiet passage to Guzz and a few extra days alongside the wall. Storms were forecast, and how right the Met. Man was! Rough weather was nothing new to ships involved in the Cod War although the storm coming from the west, did make our southerly passage very uncomfortable in the absence of stabilizers. By midday on Tuesday Leander was experiencing winds of 60 knots and a sea state of nine. Superficial damage began to mount up. The flight deck guardrails were a mess, three liferafts were missing, the port accommodation ladder had been ripped off (it weighs two tons), and several focsle guardrails had been buckled. Despite this Leander was once again demonstrating the superb sea-keeping qualities of this class of ship. To avoid further damage, the frigate hove to heading 270 at six knots. This effectively reduced much of the rolling motion, which had been as much as 45 degrees to port. Events were now to take a nasty turn. Able Seamen Paddy McNulty and George Jefferson were in the tiller flat when the emergency hatch into the flat from the variable depth sonar (VDS) well sprang open, admitting a vast amount of water. The alarm was raised and, working in about 3ft of extremely cold water, which soon reduced efficiency, Lieutenant Ben Vernon-Rogers, Fleet Chief MEA Mick Targett, PO Graham Platts and two Able Seamen secured the hatch with tackles. It looked as though a very nasty situation had been avoided by this prompt action. Pumping out operations were started. Twenty minutes later the port steering motor went. Despite the closing of the hatch, water was still pouring into the tiller flat and the large after messdeck through the ventilation trunking. Most serious was the water getting into the tiller flat. The pumps were only just about holding their own and water was splashing around the remaining steering motor.*
>
> *A look at the ship's drawings revealed that the offending fan flap was in the VDS well, which was continuously being pooped and filled with water. The flap was closed, stopping the entry of water into the tiller flat. But the damage had already been done. The second steering motor stopped soon after. Leander was now in trouble. She could be held head to wind only by use of the main engines. In the next three days, no less than 2,300 engine orders were to be given by the officers of the watch, working half an hour on at a time. The Stokers did a magnificent job in responding to these orders, for not only was Leander down to one boiler, but that boiler was beginning to show the strain.*
>
> *Meanwhile, the after messdeck was still in something approaching chaos. Water was coming in, with the result that bedding and gear was soaked. A bucket chain was formed*

103 www.hmsleander.co.uk

to the after showers, and kept going for hours. So successful was it that the water was never deep enough to necessitate the use of pumps. The cheerfulness of the sailors was remarkable, especially as many of the 50 men who lived on this messdeck had lost their kit. To stop the water entering, another flap had to be closed in the VDS well.

Even this was not enough. The whole air treatment unit compartment was full of water to a depth of 18 inches, and this had to be pumped out from the mortar well before the flow finally stopped. By 2130 the ship was watertight once more and mopping-up operations were in full swing. The after messdeck was evacuated and its 50 former occupants found pits[104] wherever there was space in the ship. The tiller flat was nearly dry, and the "Greenies[105]" had started to dry out the steering motors. Rocket (now called WD40), methylated spirits, heaters and air blowers were pressed into action, a process that was eventually to produce results. At 2200, the first BBC News bulletin was heard. It was badly worded and must have been very worrying to the families of Leander's ships company. A signal was dispatched asking for a more accurate press release to allay the fears of those at home. All day Wednesday was spent clearing up and drying out the steering motors. And all this time the storm raged on. One Officer was to describe it as the worst he had experienced in 20 years at sea. Bacchante and the Naval tug Rollicker were despatched from Iceland to standby, and the tug Typhoon sailed from Plymouth. Now a new element was to creep into the Leander saga.

The ship was heading for Canada at three knots with her steering motors still out of action. Unless the Leander could be turned by midday on Thursday, there would not be enough fuel to get her home. Weather charts indicated that the storm had not yet run its course and the size of the seas ruled out hand pump steering. The ship had to be turned on her main engines. In the circumstances, this meant there was a danger of the ship capsizing. All that afternoon Lieutenant-Commander Pink waited for a chance to turn. Eventually, at 0400 on Thursday Leander's luck changed. The sea calmed down, the turn for home was completed without mishap, and four hours later one steering motor was back in action. Although the seas were to build up again, Leander was home and dry. The remainder of the passage to Faslane was, indeed, uneventful.'

Chris Pink, as the acting Commanding Officer, has different memories:

> *'We sailed from the areas with a Force 10 forecast but although rough, the sea was bearable. When we got up in the morning, I sent my Mate of the Upper Deck, Ben Vernon, out to assess damage. Most guardrails had gone, as had all the flight deck nets; three liferafts were missing and the port accommodation ladder was swinging in the breeze so to speak. As he came to the bridge to report this, it ripped out of the side. The main roof[106] was hanging all around the funnel and most of the screen ladders had been pulled away from the bulkhead and bent aft. It was obvious at this stage that if we were to continue we would end up with nothing, so I decided to heave to. In fact, I turned into the sea and left eight knots rung on. We were making good somewhere between 4 and 5. The sea continued to build until the waves were approx 70 foot high. It was actually me who suggested to DWEO[107] to spray the steering motors with Rocket. Subsequently, both started but one was arcing so badly, I had it shut down but the other ran like a dream. I actually went to emergency stations in the Dogs[108] before we finally made our turn, as we were seeing odd*

[104] Navalese for bunks.
[105] The Weapons Electrical Branch. So called because, in earlier days, the Branch's Officers wore green distinguishing cloth between their gold rings on their uniform sleeves.
[106] The High Frequency radio aerial, which consisted of a large number of wires between the two masts.
[107] The Deputy Weapon Engineering Officer.
[108] The watches between 1600 & 2000.

The Hull trawler Loch Eribol. (Jón Páll Ásgeirsson)

patches of confused water where I hoped to turn the ship on main engines without broaching.
However just as I was about to do it, I was called to the MCO[109] and Admiral Tony Troup was on the blower; his words were "If I were a young two and a half, right now I would be thinking about turning", to which I responded "Sir, we are at Emergency Stations just looking for an opportunity to turn". His response was "leave it a few more hours", which I agreed to, pointing out that I had to turn by 0300 or I would not have enough fuel to make the Clyde. Just gone midnight, Pete Melson, my OOW, called me and said that the barometer had just fallen off the bottom and the wind had dropped completely. We were right in the middle of a new, very intense depression, but the sea was no longer breaking so the chance of broaching had reduced significantly. As soon as I arrived on the bridge, I went Full Ahead Starboard, Full Astern Port and round she went. A short while later we had one steering motor back and were able to crank up the speed. Bacchante (Captain Tony Dunn) tried to stop me turning but I chose to ignore him. His argument was that we had a rendezvous with the tanker in the morning, further to the west. In the prevailing conditions, there was no way we could fuel and as it turned out the tanker was miles away taking shelter. Having turned, Bacchante came with us and tried to persuade us to go to Rosyth, but Tony Troup intervened and detached her to Rosyth and we continued towards the Clyde. Meanwhile, Mike Thomas, my MEO and the Squadron MEO came to me and said that Fleet Technical Staff would demand a Board of Enquiry, so he, SWEO and SSO formed a Board as Squadron Staff and when Fleet's staff walked onboard and informed me that there must be a Board, I had great pleasure in telling him that it had been done and gave him the report!!'

Next morning the order was given at 0730 to withdraw the patrol initially, to outside 60 miles and at midday, the frigates were withdrawn outside 200 miles and the Royal Air Force reconnaissance flights were suspended. *Bacchante* and the Royal Maritime Auxiliary Service tug *Rollicker* returned to the UK, HM Ships *Falmouth* and *Naiad*, with the RFA tanker *Olwen* remained outside the claimed limit, ready to return should harassment of the trawlers continue. A third frigate was kept at 12 hours notice in Scottish waters, the fourth and fifth stand-by frigates were put at 48 hours notice to sail to

[109] Main Communications Office.

Rosyth. Two civilian defence tugs remained with the fishing fleet, their operational control being transferred to the Ministry of Agriculture, Fisheries and Food (MAFF). It was hoped that these arrangements would provide a climate in which real negotiations could take place and the 44 trawlers on the fishing grounds could fish in peace.

Prime Minister Geir Hallgrímsson accepted an invitation for early talks in London and arrived on 25th January 1976. His negotiating position was very weak in that he believed that any concession would be viewed in Iceland as a failure, likely to lead to his political downfall. His aim was a short-term agreement for a small British catch, 65,000 tons was mentioned, phasing out over a few months. The Foreign Office were now leading on this dispute, rather than the MAFF and over three days of meetings at Chequers, No10 Downing Street and in the Prime Minister's room in the House of Commons, the British side tried to get a long-term agreement for a substantial catch, hoping that the proven ability to catch 100,000 tons per annum under protection would help their case.

Despite the assurance that Dr Luns had been given, harassment continued on the fishing grounds. An Icelandic request that the trawlers be withdrawn during negotiations was turned down and it seemed to be important, domestically, that the Coastguard be seen to be active. In spite of the efforts of the defence tugs, *Tyr* managed to cut *Boston Blenheim's* warps - news of which actually came in whilst the two Prime Ministers were meeting. Geir Hallgrímsson and his followers always suspected Ólafur Jóhannesson, the Minister of Justice and hence head of the Coastguard, of having allowed (organised?) this action in order to scuttle the London talks, either because he feared that his Prime Minister would be too placatory or that Ólafur Jóhannesson hoped to enjoy the spoils of a successful Cod War peace. Despite this provocation, the British did not give up and Harold Wilson personally appealed to the skippers to remain on the grounds, promising compensation for lost fishing time.

HMS Juno keeps an eye on the Hull trawler Kingston Beryl. *(Jón Páll Ásgeirsson)*

Back in Iceland, Geir Hallgrímsson and his cabinet were under increasing pressure to be seen to be taking strong action and eventually decided on 3rd February that the British proposals were unacceptable. The skippers threatened withdrawal unless the frigates returned and on 5th February, with no sign of any movement in the negotiations, and the third warp cutting of the talks period - of *Loch Eribol's* by *Baldur* - the British Government decided that protection had to be resumed.

Protection returns

Operation DEWEY was brought back into being and on the morning of 6th February 1976, HMS *Juno*, commanded by Captain Ted Anson, who was the OTC, HMS *Diomede* and RFA *Olwen* resumed protecting a group of 33 trawlers in the DFA, which was 90 miles long off the east coast of Iceland. Royal Air Force reconnaissance flights restarted and the tugs *Lloydsman*, *Euroman* and *Statesman* were taken back under naval control. HMS *Lowestoft* (Commander Richard Carpendale) arrived from Scottish waters on the 7th to bring the patrol back to full strength.

As had happened before, the Icelandic government had proved to be unable, or perhaps unwilling, to engage in negotiations. The risks of any kind of compromise were just too great for the fragile coalition and, as events were to show a couple of weeks later, the Icelandic government had limited control over its representatives - a problem that extended beyond the Coastguard.

CHAPTER 18

THE THIRD COD WAR FEBRUARY 1976

Up to the withdrawal on 20th January 1976, three or four frigates had been on patrol for eight weeks, supported by a Royal Fleet Auxiliary tanker and daily Royal Air Force reconnaissance flights. Nine trawlers had lost one or both warps, three frigates had been in collisions and one of the tugs had been threatened with gunfire after another collision. The gunboats had been active and, at times very aggressive, but they had failed to co-ordinate their attacks and the fishing had been good. Given further protection, the trawlermen were on target to exceed an annual catch of 100,000 tons.

Once the frigates returned, the first confrontation was not long in coming. On 6th February, the patrolling Fokker Friendship saw the returning forces and, that evening, *Olwen's* Wessex 3 detected *Tyr* closing the DFA. HMS *Juno* marked as *Tyr* crossed the 12-mile limit and, by 1945, as she was approaching a group of trawlers, *Juno* had closed in to half a cable. Five minutes later, *Tyr* attempted to cross *Juno's* bow and, despite avoiding action by the frigate, they just touched.

Fifteen minutes later, with the ships 50 feet apart at 20 knots, *Tyr* tried again. From this range and at this speed, even *Juno's* hard a starboard and half-astern were not enough to avoid a collision and the gunboat struck the frigate's pitching focsle. Her stern then swung in to catch *Juno* under her 4.5-inch turret. *Juno's* avoiding manoeuvres brought her to within half a cable of the trawlers and *Tyr* took advantage of the confusion to attempt several warp-cuttings. She succeeded in cutting one of *Ross Altair's* warps before HMS *Diomede* intervened.

Dave Winning, who was on his first draft as an Electronic Warfare (EW) operator in HMS *Diomede* remembers being allowed to use the ship's jammers:

> *'We also used our EW gear to good effect. At the time the radar jammers we had onboard were quite powerful and their peacetime use*

Tyr makes a very close - later too close - pass down HMS Juno's port side. (Chris Brown)

The ICGV Baldur – a converted, ice-strengthened trawler. She developed the trick of swinging her stern into frigates' sides and caused more damage to the Royal Navy than any other Coastguard vessel.
(Donald Harrison)

was subject to strict limitations. This was due to the fact that if the unit you were jamming was too close, you could severely damage the crystals in the target radar. We managed to put Thor's radar out of action for a few weeks by targeting her navigation radar with our jammers on full power when she was only a couple of hundred yards away, therefore totally burning out the set. They soon got wise to this and we only managed to use this tactic once as after this incident they would turn off all radar's when within a mile.'

Next day, as already noted, HMS *Lowestoft* joined the defending forces and the physically toughest of the gunboats made her first appearance. *Baldur* was a Polish-built stern trawler, hired by the Coastguard in late 1975. She had an ice-strengthened bow, a strong, sharp transom stern and was armed with a 57mm gun forward; her stern was to be her main weapon. On this occasion, her initial attempts at warp cutting were foiled by *Juno*.

The next two months were to see the Coastguard keeping up a high level of operations. Whenever the weather was suitable, there would be two, three and sometimes four gunboats in the DFA on a daily basis, threatening to cut warps and so disrupting the fishing. Close marking became routine as did close protection by the defence tugs. All this close-quarters manoeuvring inevitably led to near misses and collisions and it seemed, to the British frigate captains at least, that the gunboats were more and more likely to go for the frigate if denied access to the trawlers.

The DFA was between 100 and 150 miles long and remained off the east coast, with its ends swinging between Rifstangi in the north and Stokksnes in the south. As before the temporary withdrawal, the previously agreed conservation and small boat areas were observed, but the new conservation areas, declared unilaterally and without consultation by Iceland, were ignored. However, in order to show that Britain did recognise the need for conservation, fishing inside 20 miles from the Icelandic baselines was banned from 10th February. A renewed request for the defence forces to be allowed up to the edge of Iceland's 4-mile territorial waters was again turned down.

Baldur makes her presence felt

On 11th February 1976 the DFA was well to the north when, in calm weather, *Baldur* was detected off Thistilfjord at 1030. She headed for some trawlers and was, at first, fended off by *Euroman* and *Statesman*. *Juno* successfully marked her from 1100 to 2245 with *Lowestoft* joining after 2100. *Ægir* was detected at 2244 and *Juno* headed south to mark her, leaving *Lowestoft* with *Baldur*.

Ægir tried to get in amongst the trawlers but was prevented from doing so by *Juno* and at 0345, still within the DFA, she came to a stop for the rest of the night, marked by HMS *Diomede*. *Baldur* did not give up so easily and, with her small turning circle, at 2301, she eventually managed to out-manoeuvre *Lowestoft* and break free of her marker. She successfully cut one of *Ross Rodney's* warps, before *Lowestoft* re-established the 'mark'.

Unfortunately *Lowestoft* suffered a steering gear failure at 0120, allowing *Baldur* to break free again and this time, she cut one of *William Wilberforce's* warps. *Lowestoft* retired from the scene to make repairs, leaving the defence tugs to deter successfully *Baldur* until she retired towards the coast at 0300.

Ægir, marked by *Diomede*, remained in the DFA all night and throughout the next day. *Lowestoft*, now repaired, took over marking at 1945 on the 12th, when *Diomede* headed off to refuel from *Olwen*. At 2046, still on her way to the tanker, *Diomede* detected *Baldur* returning to the DFA. She closed to mark and ride *Baldur* off from a group of trawlers about 7 miles distant. Having taken station a cable on *Baldur's* port beam, *Diomede* matched her alteration of 30º to starboard to a course of 160º. Captain Bob McQueen's report tells what happened next:

'When Diomede steadied on the new course, the Baldur already at one cable on the beam, edged further in until the two ships were only fifteen yards apart. The ICGV[110] *then turned away bringing his stern within fifteen feet of Diomede's side. He immediately turned in again, steadying thirty degrees in on Diomede's course and drawing slowly ahead to about 60 degrees on Diomede's starboard bow. The range closed rapidly. At half a cable he made a radical turn to port making a collision inevitable. 'Full astern' was immediately ordered and it is estimated that 110 revolutions astern were achieved before the collision occurred.*

Just before the moment of impact Baldur swung his stern onto our starboard bow. Baldur continued to turn away, but then swung in again apparently to have a second attempt. This time however he passed under the bow. Diomede's course had been steady throughout.'

Fortunately there was little damage to either ship. FOSNI, Vice Admiral Troup took, and continued to take, a robust line in support of his frigate Commanding Officers. His covering letter on

ICGV Baldur swings her stern into HMS Diomede... (Jón Páll Ásgeirsson)

[110] Icelandic Coastguard Vessel - an acronym that became common during the Third Cod War.

Contact ...... ICGV Baldur & HMS Diomede
(Jón Páll Ásgeirsson)

Captain McQueen's collision report stated:

> 'HMS *Diomede was handled correctly and firmly both before and after the collision. During close marking phases it is vital that there should be no weakening of resolve on the part of the Commanding Officer in achieving the aim of riding off ICGVs and Captain McQueen acted in accordance with my operation orders,'*

After the collision, *Baldur* joined *Ægir* inside the 12-mile limit and, to the extreme irritation of both the defence forces and the trawlers, a reporter in *Ægir* [111], who had not been there or seen things firsthand, was heard reporting to Iceland on the radio telephone a one-sided pro-Icelandic account of the *Diomede/Baldur* collision. The BBC reporter in *Juno* was quickly given *Diomede's* version, together with some 'uninhibited' advice from the trawler skippers on the patriotism of his organisation. *Diomede* had decided to rig a line of tyres along her ship's side as a form of protection, as Chief ERA[112] Stuart Johnson remembers:

> *'I remember seeing another frigate with a neat row of car tyres hung around her making a sort of continuous fender. Knowing how the Royal Navy frowned on fenders when underway, one may be forgiven for thinking that this gave her the appearance of a garbage-scow. Actually, it looked quite smart because the tyres were all the same size and perfectly in line. She was a Leander - being flush-decked and thus possible to line them all up.'*

During close encounters, *Diomede's* Buffer[113] would muster the off watch at the 'spud' locker on 02 deck, where they would then proceed to open fire on the gunboat. This hail of potatoes would usually, as Dave Winning recalls, succeed in clearing the gunboat's upper deck. This may not have been strictly within the Rules of Engagement.

Memory is always a tricky source of the facts and *Diomede's* Navigating Officer, Chris Miller, has clear recollections that neither did *Diomede* hang tyres over her side[114] nor would her crew ever have been permitted to hurl potatoes at an Icelandic vessel. He says:

> *'We were on strict instructions, particularly from the First Lieutenant, that we were not to provoke Baldur's crew in any way, particu-*

[111] A BBC man according to the Naval Staff History, but there is no other record of a BBC reporter being at sea at this time.

[112] Chief Engine Room Artificer - the senior rating in the ship's Engineering Department.

[113] The Chief Bosun's Mate – the senior seaman onboard. Possibly so called because he was the 'buffer' between the officers and the sailors.

[114] In fact, several photographs taken from Icelandic vessels show *Diomede* complete with a neat row of tyres.

larly by throwing things such as vegetables or by making hand signals. This led to the amusing incident on 30th March (3 days after the multiple collisions) when Bob McQueen became very angry at one point and ran out onto the port bridge wing and gave a very blatant v-sign to the Baldur's captain (who was at the time only a few feet away!), underlining his gesture by inviting the serious looking Icelander to 'F' off. None of us dared look at the First Lieutenant, Lieutenant Commander Hugh Powlett, who was on the bridge at the time and witnessed this scene!'

By 15th February 1976, the weather had changed again and a force 9 gale was blowing when HMS *Scylla* arrived to relieve HMS *Juno*. Captain Arthur Checksfield, in *Scylla*, took over as OTC from Captain Ted Anson. HMS *Bacchante* relieved HMS *Diomede* on the 18th. Once the gale had subsided, *Thor*, *Ægir* and *Tyr* reappeared and spent most of the period 18th-20th in the DFA.

Thor was marked by *Lowestoft* overnight on the 17th/18th, whilst *Scylla* marked *Ægir* from about 0600 and *Bacchante* marked *Tyr* from 0915. At 0800, *Ægir* slipped past *Scylla* and made an unsuccessful run at *Vianova*, followed by a successful one at *William Wilberforce*, although, once again, only cutting one warp. *Tyr* also managed to slip her marker and made an unsuccessful run at *Boston Lightning*. There were a series of near misses over this three-day period, but only one collision.

During the forenoon of 18th February, both *Lowestoft* and her mark *Thor* were resting - lying stationary after a period of close marking. They were about two cables apart and were lying parallel to each other on a heading of about 040º. At 1135 *Thor* got under way, turned towards *Lowestoft* and drove straight into her. *Lowestoft* had started to move slowly ahead, following *Thor* movements on a heading of 040º, and went full astern as soon as *Thor* turned towards. She was stationary by the time *Thor* struck her starboard bow at about 5 knots, before pulling off astern. *Thor* appeared to take no avoiding action; the sea was calm, the wind light and the visibility excellent. There was little damage to either ship.

The nearest trawlers were 6 miles away blocked from *Thor* by *Lowestoft*. This pre-meditated calculated ramming was a new departure. That it provided the final excuse to break off diplomatic relations may not have been a coincidence. The harassment continued and at 0930 on the 19th, *Ægir* slipped past *Scylla*, this time managing to cut both of *Royal Lincs's* warps. The backlash of one of the warps struck a fisherman on deck, fortunately only causing minor bruising.

HMS Lowestoft on Cod War patrol - once again note the Fishery Protection flag on her funnel. Why some RN ships wore the Fishery Protection flag & some retained their squadron funnel numbers is unclear.
(Jón Páll Ásgeirsson)

Diplomatic Relations are Broken Off

Ashore, the Icelandic Foreign Minister, Einar Ágústsson, had sent the following message to all NATO Foreign Ministers on 19th February 1976:

'After the British frigates once again entered the Icelandic fishing grounds the logical consequence would have been the implementation of the Icelandic Government's January announcement and immediately sever diplomatic relations with Britain. But in view of the fact that the Secretary General of NATO, Dr Luns, offered to use his good offices in an attempt to have the warships withdrawn once more, and urged the Icelandic Government to postpone any unilateral action until he had fully looked into the matter, a final decision on the severance of diplomatic relations has been withheld for almost two weeks.'

A move of Icelandic Ambassadors was, coincidentally, under way. Niels Sigurdsson had been transferred from London to Bonn and Sigurdur Bjarnason, from Copenhagen, was going to London. On the 9th of February 1976, when the London post was already vacant and the Ambassador-designate was ready in Reykjavik, the Foreign Minister had announced that the new Ambassador would not be taking up his post 'for the time being' as the government was contemplating cutting off diplomatic relations with Britain. This decision had been under consideration in Icelandic Government circles since before Christmas. Meanwhile, in Moscow, there had been further diplomatic moves. Howard Smith, the newly arrived British Ambassador, had sent the Icelandic Ambassador, Hannes Jónsson, the usual protocol letter concerning the presentation of credentials. The Icelandic Ambassador did not reply to his diplomatic colleagues letter 'in conformity with correct diplomatic behaviour for representatives of two belligerent states posted in a third and neutral country'[115]. Perhaps believing that Iceland and Britain were still NATO allies, Howard Smith requested a courtesy call on his Icelandic opposite number on 16th February. Ambassador Jónsson refused to see him and this diplomatic snub came to the attention of the Reuters bureau in Moscow, who made further enquiries. This caused Dr Jónsson to issue the following statement to the international press agencies based in Moscow:

'In logical consequence of the decision of the Icelandic Government not to send the newly-appointed Icelandic Ambassador to London for the time being, because of the aggression of British frigates, hindering Icelandic Coastguard vessels in performing their duties to enforce the law off the shores off Iceland, the Icelandic Ambassador in Moscow has not replied to the new British Ambassador's Protocol letter of February 9th expressing 'the hope that the friendly relations between our countries may continue to be reflected in the relations, both official and personal, between our two missions', because to talk about the present relations between Iceland and Britain as being 'friendly' is nothing but hypocrisy.
Furthermore, the Icelandic Ambassador in Moscow has today turned down a request by the British Ambassador and Mme[116] Smith for a Protocol visit to the Icelandic Ambassador and Mme Jónsson by having his Russian secretary convey the following message over the telephone to the secretary of the British Ambassador:
"Concerning the request of the new British Ambassador and Mme Smith to make a Protocol visit to the Icelandic Ambassador and Mme Jónsson, the Icelandic Ambassador has asked me to convey to you that as long as the British frigates are in Icelandic waters, hindering by aggressive actions the Icelandic Coastguard vessels in performing their duties to enforce the law off the shores of Iceland, the Icelandic Ambassador will not receive the British Ambassador in Moscow"'.

It is clear from his book that Dr. Hannes Jónsson issued this press statement without consulting his government in Reykjavik, as he notes that this statement 'became a news-bomb in Iceland' and quotes the Foreign Minister as saying that the Icelandic Ambassador in Moscow had 'jumped ahead of us to

[115] To quote Dr Jónsson from his book '*Friends in Conflict*'.
[116] Dr Jónsson is here writing in the era when French was the language of diplomacy - hence Mme as the abbreviation for Madame.

break relations with Britain.' It does look as if it wasn't only the Coastguard who were pursuing their own agenda.

The British Ambassador in Reykjavik, Kenneth East, had been keeping up the appearance of normality as much as possible, although he was clearly a bit of an embarrassment to some of his hosts. The Young Social Democrats actually called upon him and presented him with a one-way air ticket to London, but he declined on the grounds that he would have to give a gift of equivalent value and he had nothing suitable to offer them. When the ticket was then posted to his office, he forwarded it to the leader of the impoverished Social Democrat Party, acknowledging the point but saying that he was sure that the party could apply the funds to more worthwhile party ends.

Eventually on 19th February, Kenneth East got the expected call from the Permanent Secretary at the Foreign Ministry requesting him to leave the country. Unfortunately Icelandic Airlines were on strike at the time and it was several days before flights resumed and the Ambassador was able to depart. Whilst waiting, he retired to stay with friends outside Reykjavik and the whole of the rest of the Embassy staff became, legally, the 'British Interests Section of the Embassy of France', under the nominal control of Jacques Pradelles de Latour Dejean, the French Ambassador.

As soon as diplomatic relations were broken off, because of the 'continued deployment of British warships in Icelandic waters' and 'recent developments on the fishing grounds[117]', the UK Government proposed that NATO observers should be embarked in both frigates and gunboats 'in order to refute allegations of aggression and to demonstrate the purely defensive nature of the British operation'. If the Icelandic Government was not prepared to have observers onboard their ships, they could still be embarked in the frigates. The Icelandic Government rejected this proposal completely on the grounds that it would be an infringement by NATO of the Icelanders' legal right to patrol their own fishing grounds.

Probably not being that keen to get involved in this dispute anyway, the other NATO nations did not pursue this matter any further. Another example of this unwillingness to get involved was the US's rejection of an Icelandic request to hire or buy two small naval ships for the Coastguard.

Once back in London, Kenneth Young found himself an office in the Foreign Office, not without difficulty as the system made no allowance for 'non-resident Ambassadors' who needed a room, a telephone, secretarial services and to be on the distribution of the relevant papers. All those who have worked in any major bureaucracy will appreciate his difficulties. Fortunately Roy Hattersley, the Minister of State in the Foreign Office, was now personally involved in the Icelandic problem and wanted the 'Ambassador's' input, so Kenneth Young was able to stay in the loop.

Back at Sea

Back at sea, the oncoming HMS *Yarmouth* was told to speed up and she arrived a day earlier than planned to relieve *Lowestoft* after her collision. *Yarmouth* had no settling-in period, she refuelled from *Olwen* at 2000 on the 19th February 1976 and then was straight into close marking on *Tyr*. She got the 'let's test the new boy' treatment from *Tyr*, in whose close company she spent most of the next three days. All the frigates were kept very busy close marking. Things were to get much tougher on the fishing grounds - there were to be 17 collisions between 24th February and 27th March.

[117] The *Thor* /*Lowestoft* collision of 18th February 1976.

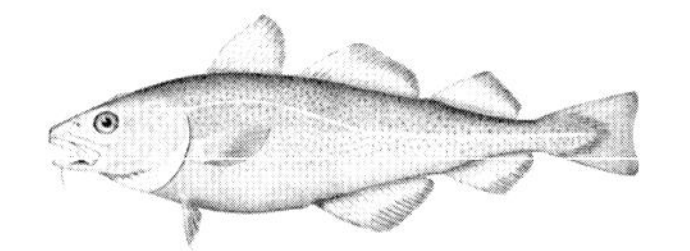

CHAPTER 19

THE THIRD COD WAR
FEBRUARY - MARCH 1976

The severance of diplomatic relations made little difference to activities on the fishing grounds. On 23rd and 24th February 1976 there were again four gunboats out in the DFA. The weather started poor (wind force 6-8 and overcast), but improved to fairly calm on the 24th. The DFA was 100 miles long off Iceland's northeast coast and there were 25 trawlers at work.

Tyr appeared first and was marked, for over 48 hours, by HMS *Scylla* from 0725 on the 23rd. That afternoon, she slipped, at high speed, through a small gap between *Scylla* and *Luneda* and managed to cut both the trawler's warps. Meanwhile, a group of 4 trawlers fishing near the northwestern edge of the DFA reported *Baldur's* appearance at 1000. They hauled their nets until HMS *Bacchante* arrived at midday, when they recommenced fishing. *Baldur* once again proved that she could outmanoeuvre a frigate and got away to cut both of *Arctic Vandal's* warps at 1345. Meanwhile, HMS *Yarmouth* was marking *Òdinn*. Both *Òdinn* and *Baldur* retired inshore overnight, whilst *Tyr* remained, marked by *Scylla*.

It was whilst only one gunboat was on task that *Yarmouth's* Wasp flight had one of those 'difficult' experiences. The helicopters were often used to transfer messages to trawlers, as this was the only way to avoid the gunboats hearing what was planned. Usually, the Wasp would hover over the trawler and then lower the bag to the crewman who would unhook it and take the contents to the trawler's skipper. The Wasp would then winch in the wire and hover alongside until the crewman signalled that he had the bag ready to return. On this occasion, the crewman hooked the winch wire onto the guardrail, a highly dangerous practice and against all the safety rules, and disappeared swiftly into the wheelhouse. Fortunately, it was flat calm and so the pilot decided to risk staying hooked on, although he was ready to use the explosive cutter to sever the winch wire. Equally fortunately, the crewman wasn't gone long and when he returned, the bag contained a bottle of whisky.

Next morning, *Scylla* was still marking *Tyr*, whilst *Bacchante* was covering *Òdinn*, who remained inshore of the 12-mile line, near Langanes. At 1000,

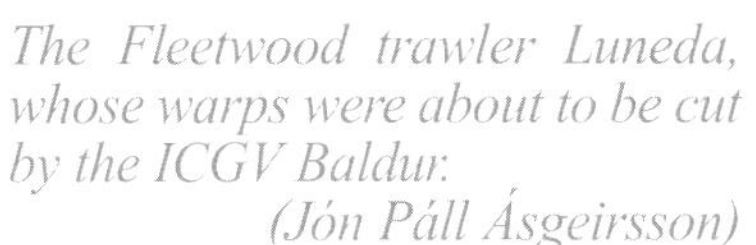

The Fleetwood trawler Luneda, whose warps were about to be cut by the ICGV Baldur.
(Jón Páll Ásgeirsson)

ICGV Thor *(Peter Harrison)*

a group of seven trawlers reported *Thor* approaching and that they were hauling their nets. The on-task Nimrod located *Thor* and *Yarmouth*, 25 miles to the south, wound up to 30 knots to join the threatened trawlers. On arriving in *Thor*'s vicinity, *Yarmouth's* captain, Commander Mike Jones, warned *Thor* that he would tolerate no interference with British trawlers fishing legally in international waters.

Yarmouth took station 100 feet on *Thor's* starboard beam at 1118. Once established on a parallel course to the southwest, *Yarmouth's* captain reported that he 'steered him round to the south east to firmly establish my position and attitude.' The trawlers were to the north and by 1123, both ships were on a course of 140º. *Thor* tried to shake off *Yarmouth* by large variations of speed - much easier to change rapidly in a diesel ship, such as *Thor*, with controllable-pitch propellers than in a steam-turbine frigate, but was unsuccessful.

At 1130, *Thor* turned five degrees in towards *Yarmouth* and the two ships collided, beam to beam. Fifteen minutes later, *Thor* repeated this manoeuvre and, perhaps because *Yarmouth* rang on full astern and *Thor* was still going ahead, the frigate's port bow collided with *Thor*'s starboard side. Damage to *Yarmouth* was minor, but *Thor*'s starboard bridge wing was completely crushed and needed two weeks to repair

That evening, FOSNI decided to reinforce the patrol and signalled:

> *'As a result of the number of Icelandic gunboats now deployed in the DFA and their increasingly aggressive behaviour HMS Andromeda is being sailed as a temporary reinforcement. I hope this will demonstrate our determination to provide adequate protection in accordance with HMG[118] policy.'*

HMS *Andromeda* arrived on station at 1200 on 26th February 1976 to bring the frigate numbers up to four. The 27th was quiet and on the 28th the weather was again fine and reasonably calm. Once again, *Tyr* was the first on station and at 0725, she slipped past *Scylla's* guard and cut *Boston Stirling's* warps. For the second time, the backlash as the weight of the net came off the warp caught one of the fishermen on deck, but he was not seriously injured. *Òdinn* was

[118] Her Majesty's Government.

successfully marked by the newly-arrived *Andromeda* and soon left the DFA.

David Jones, who was the Chief Radio Supervisor in HMS *Scylla*, has several anecdotes of this period:

> *'I do recall that as a Communicator, the lads were in two watches for the entire duration of the patrol i.e. 6 hours on and 6 hours off and knew little of what was going on outside of the world of the Comcen*[119] *... and trying to maintain an HF 'Maritime Rear Link' back to Whitehall Comcen was somewhat trying and a fulltime juggling exercise of frequencies pre Satellites.*
> *On the day we were relieved, I was standing next to one of the young Radio Operators, he and I blinking like moles in the sunlight, looking at the gunboats darting around between us, the relieving frigate and the trawlers when he commented "Cor Chief - so this is what has been going on up here."*

As he notes, life for communicators during the Cod War was very much limited to the written word on paper and voice messages. Often exciting, but within their enclosed world of the Comcen, they felt rather remote from the actual activity outside. He also has a couple of (possibly apocryphal, but equally possibly true) stories that illustrate the sailor's sense of humour.

> *'In the darkening gloom of an Icelandic twilight, with one of the gunboats ducking and diving around the stern of the frigate, a line of five matelots appeared. They were the only beings on the upper deck at this time, in full foul weather clothing, with only their eyes visible through the hoods. Standing in a row alongside the guardrails of the heaving and pitching flight deck, holding up large cards to the gunboat - giving her marks out of 9.*
> *The frigates spent long hours steaming up and down lengthy patrol lines, usually into a heavy sea and, before turning back, the tannoy would announce "The ship is about to turn to starboard and may roll heavily". In severe weather the pipe of "The Upper Deck is out of bounds" would also be made. One of the popular movies at the time was 'The Poseidon Adventure', about a huge liner that turned across an enormous wave and turned over. On one patrol, this movie was being*

HMS Scylla on patrol.
(David Mathias)

[119] Communication Centre.

HMS Yarmouth's bow after she had collided with ICGV Baldur. A whole new bow section was subsequently fitted by Chatham Dockyard. (Reykjavik Museum of Photography)

shown with the projector, on its spindly legs, being held by a couple of sailors as the ship bounced around. As the liner's captain decides to turn across the threatening wave, a quiet voice said, "the ship is about to turn to starboard and may roll heavily". Shortly afterwards, by which time the liner was upside down, the same voice intoned, "The upperdeck is out of bounds".

Baldur got into the southern end of the DFA undetected, but was spotted by the Nimrod at 0930 and marked by *Yarmouth* from 1145, at which time she was heading for a group of 7 trawlers, seven miles to the north. As he had with *Thor*, Commander Mike Jones took a robust position and warned *Baldur* that under no circumstances were trawlers to be harassed while fishing on the high seas. *Yarmouth* headed for a marking station on *Baldur*'s starboard side on a northerly course, keeping between the gunboat and the trawlers. Immediately, *Baldur* demonstrated her tight turning circle and turned nearly a full circle to port under *Yarmouth's* stern and back towards the trawlers. *Yarmouth* followed *Baldur* round and increased speed in order to regain her station on *Baldur*'s starboard side. As she did so, *Baldur* executed another circle to port, settling on a northeasterly course towards the trawlers - now at only 3 miles. To avoid a stern chase with the trawlers so close, Commander Jones turned to starboard at 24 knots, aiming to get up onto the gunboat's port beam and then to ride him off to starboard, away from his warp-cutting course. *Baldur* did not give way and a collision became inevitable[120]. In spite of ringing on full astern, *Yarmouth* struck *Baldur's* port quarter at 1206. Damage to *Baldur* was minor, not so to *Yarmouth*.

[120] By this stage of the conflict, both side's commanding officers were concentrating more on achieving their aim - either getting to, or stopping the other side getting to, the trawlers. The Rule of the Road seems to have been of secondary importance, except in the media exchanges. Commodore Paul Canter, quoted in *The Last Waltz,* says 'We always tried to match them and always have a collision on the port side so that under international law, we would be seen as being "in the right"'. It should be noted, however, that the term 'right of way' does not appear anywhere in the rules. Even the ship entitled to 'stand-on' has a duty to prevent collisions. The Rules were not written to regulate ships manoeuvring aggressively in very close company.

After 20 minutes of further sparring, *Baldur* retired and *Yarmouth* was able to assess the damage. Her bow was split and bent back through about 90º, with some slow flooding. Her safe speed was reduced to about 12 knots and she would need to be dry-docked to repair the damage.

After shoring up the forepeak, it was decided that *Yarmouth*, accompanied by the Royal Maritime Auxiliary Service tug *Rollicker*, would leave the patrol area as soon as it was dark. As was the case with the damaged *Leander*, the weather immediately turned foul and *Yarmouth* and *Rollicker* had to stem the gale at 4 knots, heading towards Greenland. After about 24 hours the weather moderated and the two ships were able to turn home towards Rosyth. Rosyth dockyard was too busy to undertake the necessary repairs and so *Yarmouth* was sent on to Chatham. Here a whole new bow section was constructed and fitted. *Yarmouth* was on her way back to rejoin the Cod War when the dispute was finally settled.

Meanwhile, HMS *Naiad* was immediately sailed to bring the frigate numbers back to four. *Baldur* was back in the DFA within 48 hours. The Coastguard Fokker Friendship had been overhead throughout these manoeuvrings and so Icelandic pictures were soon available to the press.

One downside of this was that families back in the UK knew from Icelandic sources, that '*Yarmouth* had been hit and badly damaged'. The MoD was unwilling or unable to confirm any of the details, so leaving the families fearing the worst for 'several days'[121]. This problem was not solved until well into the Falkland's War - many will remember the MoD spokesman confirming that a Type 42 whose name began with 'C' had been sunk, so leaving both *Coventry's* and *Cardiff's* families desperately worried.

The *Yarmouth*/*Baldur* collision well illustrates the problems faced by Commanding Officers, who had to balance the risk of collision and serious damage against their brief to show sufficient firmness to deter an aggressive gunboat, so that fishing could continue uninterrupted. The gunboats' captains' policy seemed to be to test the resolve and nerve of their opposite numbers, especially the newcomers, by prolonged, dangerous close quarters manoeuvring. Captain Hóskuldur Skarphedinsson in *Baldur* had already shown that he was a determined and aggressive opponent. The difference between 'riding off' and 'ramming' can be a very fine one and may not be apparent until the incident is over. The DEWEY OpOrder gave the following guidance:

> *'In the past prevention of warp-cutting by HM Ships has been remarkably successful but pride in this achievement must not be permitted to cloud judgement as to the best course of action to promote the long term aim (a negotiated settlement) which is prejudiced by*

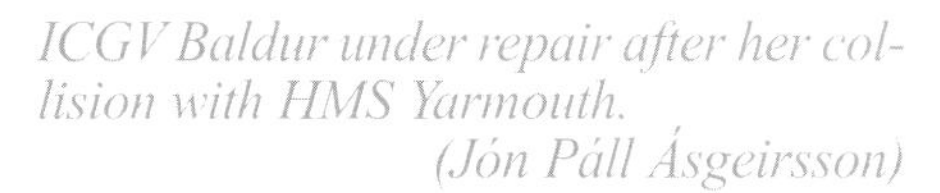

ICGV Baldur under repair after her collision with HMS Yarmouth.
(Jón Páll Ásgeirsson)

[121] See www.swmaritime.org.uk/article.php?articleid=339&atype=a

every violent clash. Thus, whilst encouragement to gunboats and discouragement to trawlers should be avoided whenever reasonably possible, nice judgement is needed at all times as to when some interruption to fishing is inevitable if serious repercussions are to be avoided.'

It would be interesting to be able to compare this with the guidance, if any, that was given to the gunboat captains.

Operations off Iceland, including time spent by ships in dockyard hands for repairs, were beginning to affect the Fleet's programme and both the 1976 group deployment to the Far East and some participation in NATO training exercises had to be abandoned. As the British will have had to notify NATO of any withdrawals from planned exercises, Iceland should have been aware of this reduction in the Fleet's training activity, but there is no direct evidence of this. The fact that the Cod War was reducing the Royal Navy's readiness for 'hot war' would have provided them with useful propaganda.

In late February 1976, the Naval Staff proposed that ships should be brought forward from the Standby Squadron. HMS *Lincoln* had just completed post-refit sea trials and HMS *Jaguar* was about to commence hers, so both were in a good state of maintenance. In normal circumstances, *Lincoln* would have gone straight into preservation and *Jaguar* would have followed once she had completed sea trials. The problem was manpower. The Admiralty Board approved the Naval Staff's proposal in early April and both ships were to be commissioned, with reduced crews, for six months from 1st June 1976.

To prepare them for Icelandic operations, it was decided to strengthen their bows and quarters with external heavy wooden padding, to fill the forepeak with steel drums and to fit bow wire-cutters on the forefoot. *Lincoln* (*see photo on previous page*) and *Jaguar* commissioned just too late for operations off Iceland, but were most valuable in carrying out general fleet tasks at a time when frigate numbers were very tight.

The high level of aggressive activity continued over the next fortnight. The following five extracts from Captain Checkfield's Report of Proceedings as OTC between 15th February and 7th March 1976 are typical:

'Scylla/Tyr: 26th February: Close Marking

At varying speeds Tyr headed northwest across the southwest flank of the main trawler group, the closest trawler passing two miles

Left - HMS Lincoln brought out of reserve for the Third Cod War & fitted with a reinforced bow section. She rejoined the Fleet too late to serve in the Cod War, but filled a valuable gap in the frigate strength whilst other, more modern, frigate were repaired. *(MoD/Crown Copyright)*

Right - HMS Scylla and ICGV Tyr jostle for position...... *(Peter Harrison)*

.....*ICGV Tyr closing HMS Scylla. Note power coming on as she accelerates.*
(Peter Harrison)

to starboard. Scylla marked initially 2 cables on Tyr starboard side. On two occasions Tyr steered into Scylla's path.

Incident One - Tyr closed to 20 feet on Scylla's port bow before turning away. Incident Two - Tyr closed to 10 feet, slowed down to pass down Scylla's port side, and turned away when abreast Flight Deck missing Scylla's port side by 5 feet.

Scylla/Tyr: 26th February: Attempted Warp-Cutting

Tyr approached starboard quarter of trawler Benella streaming cutter with 5 cables to run. Scylla initially between Tyr and Benella. Tyr reduced speed then accelerated crossing ahead of Scylla but out of position to cross Benella's stern. Tyr then commenced a tight anticlockwise loop around Benella, with Scylla manoeuvring to block. Benella's trawl recovered before cutter could engage.

Bacchante/Tyr: 28th February: Attempted Warp-Cutting

Tyr turned to port at high speed towards lone trawler at 4 miles. Bacchante chased at high speed and warned Tyr to clear on VHF. Tyr came in to ten feet on Bacchante's port beam with both ships at 20 knots then slowed and went round Bacchante's stern to her starboard quarter. Royal Vanguard hauled just before Tyr made final close pass.

Andromeda/Tyr: 1st March: Close Marking

Tyr accelerated close up Andromeda's starboard side under full power and turned violently to starboard when her bridge was abeam of Andromeda's bow. Collision averted by Andromeda ordering full astern both engines and full port rudder. Tyr's stern passed two feet clear of Andromeda's bow.
Naiad/Tidepool/Baldur: 5th March: Emergency Breakaway from RAS(L)[122]

At 051100 Naiad and Tidepool carrying out RAS(L) course 340° speed 12. Baldur, close

[122] Replenishment At Sea (Liquid) = refuelling.

marked by Andromeda, sighted at 5 miles bearing 000°. Baldur remained on steady bearing despite international code Uniform flashed at Baldur and speed decreased. At 1120 emergency breakaway executed when Baldur at one mile. Baldur course throughout was 240° speed slow to cross the bow of RAS units at one cable. When emergency breakaway was executed Baldur accelerated to cross Tidepool's bow at 2.3 cables.'

Captain Ted Anson took over again as OTC when HMS *Mermaid*[123] arrived to relieve *Scylla* on 7th March 1976. Captain Anson transferred to his own ship, HMS *Juno*, when she arrived to relieve *Naiad* on the 11th. The other two reliefs in this turnover period were HMS *Diomede* (arrived on the 9th) and HMS *Galatea* (on the 10th). On 10th March, there were three gunboats active and another collision.

Baldur, being marked by *Mermaid*, commanded by Commander Roger Heptinstall, had been making strenuous efforts to reach a trawler, coming within a few feet of the frigate several times. Finally, according to the formal British records, she tried to cut across *Diomede's* bow and misjudged it. The glancing collision caused little damage to either ship.

Chris Miller, who was *Diomede's* Navigating Officer at the time, remembers these events rather differently:

'...we deliberately rammed the Icelandic vessel amidships at about 18 knots. We had as-built drawings of Baldur onboard and had calculated that her hull area, adjacent to her engine room, was her only vulnerable area[124]*. She was an extremely strongly built vessel and, in particular, her stern with its solid A-frame provided her with a useful weapon during collisions - thus the Icelandic Captain's continuous attempt to swing one or other of her quarters into our side, where he knew we were weak.*
When we eventually hit the Baldur on her starboard side (we had started the run in at her from some considerable distance away), to our alarm she rolled over to port some 45 degrees to a point where we thought she might capsize. It was clear from the expression on the faces of her crew that they also thought that this may well happen.

HMS Mermaid, built as the Presidential Yacht for President Nkrumah of Ghana & taken on by the Royal Navy after his overthrow. *(Jón Páll Ásgeirsson)*

[123] *Mermaid* was a one off in the Royal Navy. Originally designed as the Presidential Yacht for President Nkrumah of Ghana, she was never delivered after his departure from office. She was converted for Royal Navy service and spent several years based in Singapore. Mechanically, she was similar to the Cathedral and Big Cat diesel frigates.

[124] In conversation, Chris Miller also remembers examining the plans of *Baldur* with Vice Admiral Troup and Captain McQueen during the pre-deployment briefings and discussing the best point at which to ram her.

ICGV Tyr rams HMS Juno (Paul Canter)

> *However, to my relief, she came back on to an even keel. Needless to say, Diomede sustained considerable damage to her bow.'*

The Royal Navy was now, I believe, intent on playing the game to the Icelander's rules and minor collisions were becoming almost commonplace. Next day, *Tyr*, *Baldur*, *Thor* and *Ægir* were all active, the last succeeding in cutting *Ross Kashmir's* warps.

Now that there were four frigates and two or three defence tugs with only one DFA to cover, the gunboats were finding themselves effectively marked. Inevitably they would manage to break away from their marker from time to time, but fishing was continuing with a very manageable level of disruption. The comparatively light construction of the frigates, certainly when compared to *Baldur*, was now clear to all. In any serious collision, the frigate would come off worse and would have to retire, probably with one of the defence tugs in company, to a UK dockyard for repair. The result was an increased unwillingness by the gunboat captains to give way when being ridden off and so more frigate collisions were inevitable.

Baldur had already taken advantage of her stronger construction on 10th March. On 12th and 13th, *Tyr* and *Thor* followed suit with seven collisions in four separate incidents. From 11th March to 22nd April no warps were cut, but there were 25 collisions.

On 12th and 13th March there were about 35 trawlers enjoying reasonable fishing in the DFA. The weather was overcast, the wind gusty and it was pretty rough. *Tyr* and *Thor* were on task. HMS *Juno* was under the commander of her First Lieutenant, Lieutenant Commander David Fremantle. Captain Ted Anson (the OTC) was due to rejoin from HMS *Falmouth* that evening.

At midday, *Juno* and *Tyr* were heading south towards a group of trawlers about 4 miles away. *Juno* was maintaining station between *Tyr* and the trawlers, giving the usual radio warnings and sound signals. Eventually, at 1210 *Tyr*, making directly for the trawlers, closed the frigate and struck her port side forward with her bow, scraping back down *Juno's* side and causing further damage. Four minutes later, with *Juno* still steady on the same course and still blocking her way to the trawlers, *Tyr* dropped back to a position half a cable on the frigate's port side aft. She then made a sharp alteration to starboard and hit *Juno's* port quarter. 'Harry' (Donald) Harrison was the LMEM[125] on duty in the Tiller Flat during this incident:

> *Being a Killick Stoker, I was in the tiller flat during action stations. My main function was to change over to Mechanical Wheel emergency steering if the need arose, or to hand pump steering as a last resort. I was with a Killick Seaman who would steer the ship. Nothing unusual about this you would think, but the main hatch out of the tiller flat was lashed down and our only exit was through the Greenies mess and up through the Burma Way.*
> *Needless to say, my Seaman friend had his very sharp knife at hand to cut away the lashings if needs must. Also directly above the tiller flat was the petrol stowage and I am sure that on one occasion the Gunboat Tyr rammed us by the Tiller flat which caused a fire in the Petrol stowage and some very brave or foolhardy seaman put out the fire and received some award at a later date for his bravery. But what about me and my oppo in the Tiller flat who were thrown across the tiller flat by the force of the ramming, and were unaware that we could have been toast. The tiller flat we were told had to be lashed down, because on some other ship, it had been left open in roughers and the tiller flat was flooded out.*

Fortunately all was well. Close manoeuvring, in amongst the trawlers by now, continued for the next 20 minutes.

Later in the same afternoon, *Mermaid* had a similar experience with *Thor*. At 1620, *Mermaid* crossed ahead of *Thor* and took up station on her port bow, between the gunboat and a group of trawlers 7 miles away. *Mermaid* then dropped back to *Thor's* port beam and tried to 'ride off *Thor* and turn him to starboard away from the trawlers'[126]. *Thor* declined to be ridden off and steered in towards *Mermaid*. The two touched beam-to-beam and after a further period of close manoeuvring, *Thor* stopped. Then, she

> *'...got underway at 1725, again making for the trawler group. Mermaid accelerated and sounded six short blasts and again attempted to ride her off from the trawlers. Thor did not give way and when the ships were 10 feet apart, went astern on her engines. Mermaid went half astern both engines (18 knots speed set) but Thor turned violently to starboard, the rate of turn possibly increased through interaction, and her starboard bow hit Mermaid just forward of the funnel, damaging the superstructure and the whaler. Both ships gathered sternway, Thor then moved ahead again, accelerating quite quickly and Mermaid followed suit. Thor shaped to pass across Mermaid's bow and it was appreciated that she would swing her stern into Mermaid's bows as she passed ahead. To prevent this and to take the seemingly inevitable collision on the anchor and anchor fleet, Mermaid turned to port and the ships collided, Mermaid's port bow hitting Thor just abaft the bridge.'*

Mermaid sustained minor damage to her whaler, davits and upper deck fittings, some ship's side dents and a 4-inch split in the port bow well above the waterline. *Thor* suffered superficial damage to her superstructure and, after lying stopped for 15 minutes, she returned to Seydisfjord, leaving the trawlers to fish in peace.

That evening, with Captain Anson back in command, at 1845 *Juno* had her third collision with *Tyr*. Again the gunboat was being prevented from getting amongst the trawlers and, after a very close encounter, *Tyr* tried to get across *Juno's* stern. When *Juno* matched her deceleration, the gunboat went full ahead and headed to cross her bow. After a slight lag[127], *Juno* matched *Tyr*'s acceleration and a collision

---

[125] Leading Marine Engineering Mechanic aka Leading (or Killick - from the anchor worn on the arm as a badge of rank) Stoker.

[126] *Mermaid's* Collision Report dated 15 March 1976. The Royal Navy has a form on which to report Collisions and Groundings. This is the 'dreaded' S232. It's not that naval officers are superstitious, but a navigating officer will never steer 232° and will, instead, always set a course of 231½ °. It is also no accident that the numbering of the Royal Navy's Type 23 frigates runs from F230 to F239, missing out F232. HMS *Lancaster*, originally numbered F232, was redesignated as F229 before her launch.

[127] As has been mentioned before, the gunboats have a system of diesel engines combined with controllable-pitch propellers. This allows a quicker initial reaction time than a steam turbine frigate, but once power comes on, the frigate will accelerate more quickly and has a much higher speed.

Even during the hours of darkness there was no letting down your guard. ICGV Tyr about to hit HMS Diomede's flight deck
(David Nealon)

was inevitable as the gunboat crossed the frigate's bow. After this third collision, *Juno's* operational status was unaffected but the buckled plates and damaged fittings would, subsequently, require substantial repairs. *Tyr* remained in the DFA overnight, still marked by one of the frigates.

It was *Diomede's* turn next morning. She had been marking *Tyr* for nearly four hours when, at 0849, after several close passes, all of which she pulled out of in time, *Tyr* came in too close, did not back off and hit the frigate abreast the flight deck with her bows. Damage was not serious.

DIY Diplomacy

It was on February 14th 1976 that the MP for Hull East, John Prescott, decided, against the advice of the FCO, to visit Iceland and look for a solution himself. He met Captain Gudmundur Kjærnested, the British press's 'Mad Axeman' onboard *Tyr* in Reykjavik and, with the TV cameras ever present, was shown around, including damage inflicted by the British. As Captain Kjærnested later said:

'He turned out to be a personable young man

and he had a lot to say for himself, as is the custom of politicians. No one could get in a word sideways, but I didn't mind. I just ate my doughnut.'

Roy Hattersley, the Minister of State at the Foreign Office, says of Prescott's foray into diplomacy:

'John Prescott mounted an independent operation and the Foreign Office kept telling him to come home. He wouldn't come home. He came to see me when he did come home with his own peace plans.'

The Foreign Office ignored Prescott's proposals, which he was later to claim was better for Britain than the final agreement.

Political Considerations

As a result of the incidents on 12th and 13th March 1976, the rules of engagement (RoE) were reviewed. Captain Anson signalled his concern over *Tyr*'s collision with *Juno*:

'His action was either an impossibly badly judged attempt to pass under Juno's stern or a deliberate attempt either in anger or in cold blood to damage the frigate. I think the latter more likely and more sinister. Icelandic Coastguard vessels are considerably stronger than frigates and have yet to suffer serious damage. They appear now to appreciate this and Tyr seemed intent on causing damage perhaps with the hope of sending Juno home. This I believe to be an escalation of the conflict and worthy of political attention.'

FOSNI signalled his support, adding that, after seven collisions in four days damage repair had become a serious factor in the frigate deployment programme. He also recommended that the RoE should be reviewed. After looking at the possibilities of escalation and de-escalation, he recommended that ... 'a firm and controlled demonstration of intent to use gunfire ... in self-defence against deliberate ramming' might achieve the desired aim of cooling the situation and should be seriously considered in Whitehall. The Commander-in-Chief Fleet agreed. The Naval Staff prepared a submission, emphasising the weakness of the frigates' position in the face of deliberate ramming and recommended that to maintain effective naval protection would entail an escalation in the RoE to permit such measures as counter-ramming by defence tugs and the use of gunfire to enforce an exclusion zone. The alternative was to withdraw naval protection.

Whilst all this staffing of the Captain Anson's signal was going on, on 16th March 1976 the British Prime Minister, Harold Wilson, resigned and was replaced by the Foreign Secretary, Jim Callaghan. Tony Crosland, who was the MP for the fishing port of Grimsby, became the new Foreign Secretary. Once the dust of Wilson's resignation had settled, this meant that there was a much greater interest at the top of the political system in resolving the dispute with Iceland.

The next fortnight passed quietly. There were only one or two gunboats out and no collisions or warp-cuttings. There are several possible reasons for this lull - the gunboat operating cycle, the need for repairs to *Tyr* and *Thor*, the awful weather and perhaps a pause for reflection after the spate of collisions. There were also political/presentational reasons for reducing the tension. The third UN Conference on the Law of the Sea (UNCLOS3) reassembled in New York on 16th March and the Icelandic government hoped that, after all the careful preparatory work, there would be swift international agreement on a 200-mile Exclusive Economic Zone (EEZ). In the event, UNCLOS3 proceeded very slowly, but the Icelandic position was boosted when both the United States and Canada declared that they would be declaring a 200-mile EEZ in 1977, whatever the Conference decided. As the British government also wanted a 200-mile EEZ for Common Market fishing policy reasons, time was clearly running out for the UK.

The other main political reason for the lull was that the Norwegian Foreign Minister, Knut Frydenlund, had bravely decided to try to broker a peace between Iceland and Britain and there was international pressure to avoid incidents whilst the Norwegian proposal was considered. Knut Frydenlund, who was to be driven further than his advisers thought prudent over the next few months, was very concerned at the risks to NATO of the continuing Anglo-Icelandic dispute. His suggestion was for an agreement based on the number of trawlers in Icelandic waters rather than on a total catch.

The other NATO nations were, indeed, losing patience with the Anglo-Icelandic dispute. There seemed to be, in private at least, a general acceptance that the British, at the moment, had the law on their side and that the Icelanders were acting obstinately and dangerously, but there was also a groundswell that Britain should be able to sacrifice a few thousand tons of cod for the security of the Western world. It was believed that the government in Iceland might well close the Keflavík base or even withdraw from NATO. The Norwegian initiative seemed to be the only hope of a reasonable settlement.

Catches in March were down, below the level that would produce an annual catch of 100,000 tons. In a normal season, the trawlers would have been working the northern and western grounds, so there was strong pressure for the opening of a second DFA. The Navy was able to show that, against the level of harassment experienced recently, it would not be possible to offer protection in two widely separated DFAs. It was decided to stick with one DFA and to move it to the northwest in early April, when gales and icing would be unlikely.

An Anti-Warp-Cutter-Cutter

There was also a renewed search for a counter to the warp-cutter. If the warp-cutter could be rendered ineffective, then riding off would no longer be necessary and the tension presently inherent in the dispute would be reduced. In November 1975, right at the start of the Third Cod War, the MAFF had asked what defensive devices were available. The towed grapnel trialled in 1973 was not considered effective and had never been used off Iceland.

At a meeting on 17th February 1976, the MoD had undertaken to investigate the provision of the kind of explosive cutters used in minesweeping and on 18th March, HMS *Glasserton* carried out trials with a tug. The results were inconclusive, but encouraging enough for the project to continue. The standard explosive cutter used by the Royal Navy was too heavy for easy handling, but a new Swedish light-weight cutter was entering Royal Naval service. Despite the diplomatic reservations, work was put in hand to modify 200 of the Swedish cutters for use by trawlers, with the aim of having them ready for issuing by mid-May. The industry's reservations about handling explosives were largely overcome and, by the end of March, there was some hope that trawlers could be fitted with self-defence protection against the warp-cutter. A second sea trial using the modified Swedish cutter in the trawler *Norina* and HMS *Cuxton* on 15th May was also inconclusive, but plans went ahead to offer the device to the industry.

The British Government Considers

On 25th March 1976, the new Ministers considered the proposal that the defending forces should either escalate or withdraw. However, the MoD's proposal had to compete with the FCO's one, which was to avoid any further damage to the NATO alliance and to keep things quiet whilst the Norwegian initiative was considered. MAFF was, of course, keen that the industry should have the protection necessary to be able to achieve good catches. In the absence of any incidents in the preceding fortnight, Ministers were unwilling to change the status quo and so no new decisions were made regarding protection.

There were five collisions in the following two days, emphasising the vulnerability of frigates under the current RoE.

CHAPTER 20

THE THIRD COD WAR
MARCH - APRIL 1976

With the Third UN Conference on the Law of the Sea underway in New York, a Norwegian peace initiative under discussion and a new Prime Minister (Jim Callaghan, an ex-Royal Navy man) in No10 Downing Street, there was some hope at the end of March of, what would now be called, talks about talks. There is little doubt that the tide had changed in political terms in Britain. As one FCO official said after the talks in London in late January:

'I became aware that for the first time the Foreign Office had taken a grip on the situation and MAFF were no longer running the show. The damage to the frigates and the wider political implications now loomed larger than the requirements for which the trawler owners were holding out.'

In addition, the new Foreign Secretary, Antony Crosland sat for a Humberside constituency and 'his colleagues felt that anything he endorsed must be the best obtainable.' The Norwegian proposal would have been dismissed six months before as a sell out. It amounted to no more than a limited number of 'trawler days' for six months. Antony Crosland asked his staff if the proposal had the support of MAFF. The question provoked a loaded silence, after which one of the officials present observed that the only real choice was between a solution or the support of MAFF. From then on, the Foreign Office was behind the Norwegian proposal.

However, someone in Iceland decided that now was an appropriate moment to wind up the pressure, perhaps because there was a window for compromise, and *Baldur* was to be the (self?) chosen instrument. She was involved in one collision on the 26th March and four on the 27th.

Baldur gets stuck in...

On the morning of 26th March 1976, after two weeks of undisturbed fishing, *Baldur* entered the DFA off Langanes and approached a group of trawlers. At 0700 HMS *Galatea* took up a defensive waiting station between *Baldur* and the nearest trawler, the *Maretta*, who was still fishing. *Baldur* went on past and turned north towards the other two trawlers, the *Kingston Pearl* and *Westella*, who were just recovering their nets.

Galatea (Captain Willie Gueterbock) took up a marking position 100 feet on *Baldur's* port beam and the two vessels proceeded north, on slowly converging courses. At 0722, now two miles south of *Kingston Pearl* and *Westella*, with both ships at 17 knots, *Baldur* altered 30º to port from a position 40 feet on *Galatea's* starboard bow. *Galatea* stopped engines and went slow astern. A minute later, *Baldur* altered hard to starboard so that her port quarter swung across and cut into the frigate's bow, which was holed. The small hole was repaired in a few hours.

Baldur was out again next day, marked by HMS *Diomede*. In his Collision Report, Captain Bob McQueen reported:

'The Coastguard vessel was heading towards the main trawler fleet. At 6 miles from the trawlers Diomede took station astern of Baldur and at 4 miles from the nearest trawler, called the ICGV on channel 12 and ordered him to stay clear of the trawlers, who were going about their lawful business in international waters. The defence tug Euroman was ordered to place herself between the trawlers and the Baldur. During the subsequent afternoon's events the

Euroman attempted on several occasions to gain a good 'riding off' position, but was frustrated by the Baldur's superior speed. Despite this she was most useful as a back up and provided good support.
From 1356 to 1625 there followed a series of manoeuvres by the ICGV which were extremely dangerous and which resulted in four collisions between the two ships, in the last of which Baldur tore her starboard quarter into Diomede's vulnerable midships section. In all it is estimated that the ICGV attempted on 30[128] *occasions to ram the Diomede and his actions were thwarted on 26 of these. 268 wheel and engine orders were given in these two and a half hours ... though Baldur attempted on several occasions to gain the advantage and pass Diomede to make a run at the trawlers, she was at all times prevented from doing this.'*

Captain McQueen's frustration and anger can well be imagined, but short of hauling off and allowing *Baldur* free rein amongst the trawlers, there was nothing the RoE allowed him to do, except place his ship between *Baldur* and her prey. Captain Hóskuldur Skarphédinsson of *Baldur* was according to the British briefing notes 'very aggressive'[129]. In *The Last Waltz*, Captain Skarphédinsson comments on this collision:

> *'The struggle started in the traditional manner.* HMS *Diomede was defending a group of trawlers. We tried to get inside and use the cutters. The upshot was that she rammed us, quite severely it can be said. The Coastguard vessel was damaged. In the end, she went too far.'*

Captain Bob McQueen's response, in the same TV programme, was:

> *'It seemed to me, on that particular afternoon, that he was determined to damage my ship, 20 attempts at collision, 4 successful.'*

At about 1800, *Juno*, *Galatea* and *Lloydsman* joined *Diomede* and escorted *Baldur* back to the 12-mile

ICGV Baldur crosses HMS Diomede's bow. (Mick Tolhurst)

[128] From Captain McQueen's signalled report - 25 years later, in the TV programme *The Last Waltz,* he quoted only 20 attempts – see below in the main text.
[129] There is some evidence that, by this stage, the relationship between Captain McQueen and Captain Skarphédinsson had become 'personal.'

HMS Diomede's ship's side after the final collision with ICGV Baldur. Fortunately the calm weather lasted just long enough to repair the hole. *(Jón Páll Ásgeirsson)*

line. *Diomede* had suffered extensive damage, including a 12-foot gash along her portside - destroying the wardroom. She was, fortunately, already planned to return to the UK next day.

Electronic Warfare Operator Dave Winning's account illustrates some of the aspects of this very serious collision that the extract from the official report above fails to cover:

> *'We sustained considerable damage during these collisions to both the starboard side and the port side. There was heated debate amongst the ship's company as to which was the most severe, due to the fact that the Beer Store was holed on the starboard side and we were losing precious cases over the side whilst manoeuvring! The damage to the port side actually took out the wardroom.*
>
> *At the time, the Midships First Aid Party were closed up as we were at 'Dioguard Stations' (a modified Action Stations). As the Baldur came 'inboard', one of the stewards actually dived through the serving hatch connecting the pantry to the wardroom, which undoubtedly saved his life!*
>
> *On our return to Chatham - of which he was a native - the local newspapers ran stories of the incident, which contained photographs of him holding a lump of metal left behind by the Baldur.*
>
> *In fact we were very lucky that the damage was on the port side, because had the damage been on the starboard side, then we would have been in serious trouble. This was due to the MCO[130] and Operations Room being located here with all the associated electrical equipment and a lot more people within these compartments.*
>
> *The ship was very badly damaged and the captain ordered our 20mm guns to be uncovered and warned Baldur not to attempt another ramming or he would open fire under the RoE at the time.*
>
> *Quite sensibly the Baldur heeded this warning. Over the next few hours, the ship's company worked like demons to get the damage repaired before the weather changed for the worst, as luckily it was calm at the time. Our main priority was to get the gash down the ship's side repaired; again luck was on our*

[130] Main Communications Office.

Top: A close up of the 12 foot gash in HMS Diomede's port side caused by the collision with ICGV Baldur. *(Jón Páll Ásgeirsson)*

Bottom: The repairs to HMS Diomede's ship's side in the wardroom and the team of engineers who carried out those repairs. *(David Nealon)*

side. Rumour had it that we could not have repaired the gash as effectively as we did had it not been for the fact that the metal plates that we had for damage control purposes had been supplied in metric and not imperial sizes. The gash at its widest was slightly over 3 feet, but slightly under 1 metre, so the plates fitted perfectly to enable them to be welded and shored. We eventually managed to repair all the damage and the Captain addressed the ship's company, informing us that we had been ordered back to the UK for docking down, but he also warned us that we should be prepared to abandon ship if we happened to hit any severe weather.'

David Nealon was the Squadron Gunnery Officer onboard HMS *Diomede*. He was on watch in the Operations Room when the collision happened. He remembers the shock of the collision, followed by all the lights going out. As they came back on, the whole Ops Room team checked all their displays and other equipment and settled back down to business. It was, he says 'complete professionalism' as one would have expected, but reassuring none-the-less when it happens. David also says that not only were the 20mm guns uncovered, but also the ship's main armament, the 4.5-inch twin turret was ready. The hoists (the hydraulic system that feeds the shells and cartridges to the turret) were loaded with HE[131]. He still uses a piece of *Baldur* as a doorstop in his Devon home. It was recovered from the Forward TAS[132] Store, so had come in through the hole just forward of the 'F' on the ship's side.

This collision was the most flagrant example yet of calculated aggression by the Coastguard and again raised the question of escalation or backing down. That evening, FOSNI signalled to the OTC:

'While UK position is reconsidered, to avoid further major damage to frigates you should no longer feel inhibited from ordering ships to switch to marking gunboats using Method Two defined in the DEWEY Operation Order when faced with deliberate attempts to ram.'

David Nealon holding a doorstop made from a piece of ICGV Baldur found inside HMS Diomede after the final collision. (Andrew Welch)

The relevant section of the DEWEY OpOrder says:

'Method Two. The frigate marks from the quarter, broadcasting the gunboat's position and ordering trawlers in the vicinity to haul or get under way.
The frigate must be prepared to describe a close circle around any trawler who has not hauled before the gunboat approaches it.'

FOSNI's instructions were confirmed when, on the First Sea Lord, Admiral Sir Edward Ashmore's per-

131 High Effect, often wrongly thought ('though perhaps more accurately) to mean High Explosive.
132 Torpedo and Anti-Submarine.

sonal instructions, the MoD signalled that the RoE were not to be changed, but that:

'Pending further ministerial consideration of the situation, frigates are if practicable to avoid action damage. If circumstances dictate, this consideration is as a temporary measure to take priority over continuity of fishing.'

This, as was pointed out to Ministers, meant a significant reduction in the effectiveness of naval protection and more interruptions to fishing. As soon as the Coastguard realised that the policy had changed, they would take full advantage of it. Ministers did not dissent from the new policy, which was not communicated to the fishing industry for both domestic political reasons and because, as soon as the industry knew, the Coastguard would too.

In Iceland the Captain of *Baldur* was treated as a hero by the press. *Diomede* was accused of making more than 20 attempts to ram *Baldur* and *Galatea* was accused of manning her guns and of threatening to open fire. It is true that her 40mm guns were uncovered and manned, but no threat was made. Iceland accused the British of a dangerous escalation of the dispute and protested in the United Nations. The British responded by protesting to the Icelandic government and by putting the British case, condemning Icelandic gunboat aggression, in the UN. As so often in that great talking shop, protests in the UN had no influence on the dispute.

Chris Miller, *Diomede's* Navigating Officer, remembers this incident well:

'Galatea did uncover and man all her weapons on the 28th, including her Seacat[133] *and trained them on Baldur (including illuminating the gunboat with her gunnery radar). Although he almost certainly would have been unaware of this latter point, the Icelandic Captain's subsequent accusation was accurate.*

The reason for Galatea's reaction was that communications during these running battles between the bridge of a frigate and her team in the Ops Room were extremely problematical. The Captain was inevitably driving the ship on the bridge and was therefore absent from his (by then) usual action station in the Ops Room. The team down below were completely blind as to what was going on topsides (at extremely close quarters their radars were useless) and they relied on somebody on the bridge giving them a running commentary.

In our case this task was allocated to a Midshipman. It was inevitable that as our fight with the Baldur developed that Saturday afternoon, things on the bridge became more and more 'interesting'. The young Mid inevitably became very excited and his descriptions to the crew in the Ops Room became increasingly colourful; for their part they were well aware of the collisions and the sudden movements of the ship - and in addition their big fear was that Baldur might well suddenly appear through the hull into their darkened space.

However, and this is really the critical point leading to Galatea's actions, it was up to our PWO[134] *to pass on to the other Royal Navy Ships present a blow by blow description of the battle. We therefore had a classic 'send three and fourpence, we're going to a dance*[135]*' situation and by the time the process had been reversed in Galatea (i.e. the message passed from her PWO to her Captain) the latter became convinced that Baldur had every intention of sinking Diomede; thus his order to man and arm his weapon systems.'*

The Watch changes

On 28th March 1976, Captain David Armytage arrived in HMS *Scylla* to take over as OTC, with HM

[133] First-generation manually-guided anti-aircraft missile with a, very much, secondary anti-ship capability.
[134] Principle Warfare Officer – the officer, who watch-keeps in the ship's operations room. He conducts operations on behalf of the Command and, ultimately, has the delegated authority to initiate action if the speed of response (such as an incoming missile attack) requires it.
[135] Just before Waterloo in 1815, Wellington is reputed to have sent a message saying 'Send reinforcements, we're going to advance'. It is said that the message was received as 'Send three and fourpence, we're going to a dance'.

Ships Bacchante and *Tartar* in company. HMS *Salisbury* arrived on 30th to complete the changeover. *Diomede*, *Mermaid* and *Galatea* departed on 28th March, *Juno* following a day later. Chris Miller remembers that, as the group crossed the 200-mile limit, a small Russian squadron passed them, heading to a port visit in Iceland. As he notes, probably not a co-incidence.

One of the new OTC's prime concerns was to formulate a policy to contain *Baldur*. This entailed cautious marking by at least two frigates, whilst avoiding damage to the frigates, warning trawlers to haul early and using the defence tugs as much as possible. In the event, *Baldur* returned to Reykjavik on 31st March, quite probably to allow the press to interview her captain, and did not return until 8th April.

Three days of foul weather allowed the new team to settle down free of interference from the gunboats. By 1st April, the weather had moderated, visibility was good and there was little icing when, at about midday, *Tyr* appeared right at the northern end of the DFA off Langanes. The on-task Nimrod made the initial detection and then HMS *Salisbury* (Commander Hugo White) took up a marking station. There were 31 trawlers, mostly in two groups, eight near the northern corner of the DFA and 16 further south on the Vopna Bank. *Lloydsman* was in close support of the northern group and *Statesman* was with the southern one.

At 1245, *Salisbury* was joined by HMS *Tartar* and for the next eight hours the two frigates, sharing the close marking task, kept *Tyr* from approaching either group. Fishing did continue uninterrupted, but *Tyr* had seven collisions, five with *Salisbury* and two with *Tartar*. The frigates did manage to stop *Tyr* getting past and towards the fishermen, but the consequences, to all three ships, were minor splits, dents, bent guardrails and fittings and buckled plates. However, nothing that affected the operational capability of any of the three British units, but *Tyr* did end up with a cut in her hull below the water line. Years later, Dave Willis, who was one of the Radio Operators on *Tartar's* bridge at the time, wrote the story up (as he admits, with more than a bit of poetic licence….) for the retirement of the helmsman, Marine Alan Haskell, from the Metropolitan Police in November 2004. As Dave Willis gives a rather more dramatic version that the usual reports on collisions, I include his entire tale here, only very lightly edited.

'In 1976 Iceland decided that "foreign" fishing boats were stealing all "their" fish so they declared - with immediate effect - a 200-mile exclusion zone around their island within which "foreign" vessels were not allowed to fish.

Contrary to international law - which requires nations to wait a prescribed amount of time before enforcing such declared limits - Iceland decided to deploy its entire fleet of Gunboats immediately, with orders to drag hooked cables that would summarily detach the trawling gear of British trawlers. What idiot in his right mind would tamper with an Englishman's Fish & Chips....not a good career move by anyone's standards!

In addition to causing severe financial loss to the British fishing trawlers, this simply wasn't cricket and the Admiralty - in its infinite wisdom - deployed several Frigates with orders not to shoot, but simply to get between the "Icelandic Coast Guard Vessels" (for we weren't allowed to call them Gunboats) and the trawlers.

So incensed was the Admiralty that they even deployed HMS Tartar under the Fishery Protection flag - which was a really odd thing to do in the waters surrounding Iceland, since the Tartar was a "warm weather vessel" fresh from the West Indies squadron and sporting open gun turrets. I guess this didn't matter too much, since we weren't allowed to use them anyway.

The entire fleet of ICGV's consisted of 4 vessels named Tyr, Thór, Baldur and Ægir, and their tactic for dealing with the British frigates was to steam alongside the bow and then use their dual-screws to rotate the back-end of their tough little vessels into the quarter inch steel plate of the lightly built frigates bow and punch a hole in it……and then to take a picture from their helicopter hangar which made it look like they had been rammed by the evil British sailors! Damned uncouth what! During these "close marking" situations, of course, the off-watch

ICGV Tyr and HMS Tartar collide on 28th March 1976. Note that Tyr's starboard funnel has already suffered in one of her many previous collisions. (David Mathias)

sailors onboard the frigate had to leave their beds to sit in the Burma Road[136], which - unlike their warm bunks - is above the waterline.

Jolly inconvenient if you ask me.... and quite frustrating given the frequency of our meetings with the ICGV's

And so it was that Tartar, with Marine Alan 'Janner[137]' Haskell at the helm, arrived on station on the morning of April 1st and discovered the ICGV Tyr ... Of course, when I say, "discovered" we were actually greeted with something that might easily have been taken as a threat to our Port side!!

Damn cheek!

It wasn't long before Tyr felt that she'd made her point and set off in a new direction at top speed..... hell-bent for the nearest clutch of trawlers. Claxons wailed the call to "Action Stations"……er….sorry, "Close Marking Stations" and a flurry of activity followed as ever-grumpy sailors sought out their assigned places and closed all watertight doors behind them. Someone reported the utterance "Bring it on baby!!, Time to Rock and Roll !!!" emanating from the wheelhouse and, on closer inspection, the gleeful (perhaps a little maniacal) grin of the helmsman.

Fortunately I was already on watch at my assigned station - the radio circuit on the Bridge - and I was blissfully unaware of whose hands my life actually rested in. Had I known I suspect that my lifejacket might have been a little closer to hand. Still, my location was a pretty good place to watch the skipper jockey for position between the Tyr and the trawlers, which was not an easy thing to do given the physical characteristics of the Tartar. Over the radio as the Tyr approached, we repeated our rehearsed safety warning that we thought might deter them from the tactic we knew they were going to employ:

[136] The main passageway inside the ship from bow to stern. Also often called the 'Main Drag'.
[137] A native of Plymouth.

"Icelandic Coast Guard Vessel Tyr .... this is warship Tartar.....be warned, we are a single-screw vessel with stabilizer fins amidships - 10 feet below the waterline protruding 6 feet from the ship's side" The "single-screw" simply indicates that, once we start to turn we can't readily stop turning, and the presence of submerged blades should have been obvious (but apparently not as it turned out). Had I known I could also have added "Oh yes,....and 'Janner' Haskell is at the wheel" but I'm not sure it would have done any good.

Closer she came..... and closer..... and closer.... And suddenly we were in "extremely close" marking as she proceeded along out Port side for the familiar swing of her stern.

Well we twisted and turned with her for a while and, suddenly, she started the swing manoeuvre.... But....rather than shying away this time I hear the skipper yell, "Full speed ahead, hard a Port and follow her round". Did the skipper really think that 'Janner' Haskell could actually see what was going on....he's in the wheelhouse 3 decks down, half theships length aft and amidships....there ain't no windows amidships!

But it's uncanny. It's as though 'Janner' Haskell can see what's going on....can see that the flightdeck of the Tyr is now level indicating that she has discontinued her turn.... And Haskell still has the wheel hard over....I mean HARD OVER !!!

An involuntary "Oh Crap!! FULL ASTERN, Hard-a-Starboard!!!" from the skipper breaks what had become an uncanny silence. And I'm peeking over the bridge window thinking, rather peacefully, "Hmmm, 15 feet to go, 2,800 tons doing 15 knots with the wheel hard-a-Port and the skipper thinks that a delayed "full astern, hard-a-starboard" is going to do it? No! And with Haskell at the wheel DEFINITELY NOT!!!! So I brace for impact.... Waiting....waiting....ooooooh a slight tug of reverse thrust - someone in the engine room is on their toes!.....waiting ..... a a a a a a a a a n n n n n n n d d d d d Caaaaarrrrrruuuunnnncccchhhh !!!!! It's not really all that bad and it's not the impact that actually scares the pants off me, it's the spontaneous eruption of 240 below-deck sailors cheering in unison that fills the bridge with a cacophony of sound. It's all rather embarrassing and eventually the Bosun's Mate has to pipe "Stand to!" over the ships intercom in an attempt to stifle the outburst before the ICGV's crew can record it and play it back on the 6-o'clock news!

But it's not over.... As we bounce off we're a little mesmerized by our improvement of Tyr's Starboard funnel, but a little concerned by what we later learn is a 4 foot by 2 foot gash in the Port side of our bow.

But momentum is momentum, and the dance goes on: Tartar is bouncing away to Starboard and the skipper yells "Amidships" to centre the rudder (so we don't swing our stern into the Tyr). Tyr meanwhile has gained quite a bit of energy from our temporary union and is presently rolling to Port exposing the hull below her waterline. And...there's a bit of Newton straining for recognition in my head...for every action there is an equal and opposite reaction.... Thinks.....exactly what significance might that have right now? And just as I'm putting the pieces together - and adding the variable of "Haskell at the wheel" I feel Tartar lurch as the Port stabilizer fin punctures Tyr's hull below the waterline. Oh dear....how unfortunate!

Each vessel pauses to evaluate the damage and, while Tartar is to remain on station, the Tyr heads back to Reykjavik for dry-dock repairs. This is no time to pause for, in just a couple more days, we do a similar dance with the Ægir.

For now, however, the bridge is responding to the skippers orders: "Number 1[138]*....get the hell down to the wheelhouse and pat that man on the back.....then get him the hell off the helm of my ship!!!"*

Later that evening, a muffled toast is overheard in the wardroom "Helmsman Haskell....God Bless Him!!!"

Overheard on the bridge much later, as the

[138] Number 1 is the First Lieutenant and Second in Command.

Tartar is coming alongside in an unnamed Scottish port for supplies, "Number 1.....Haskell's not at the wheel is he?!"'

Tartar's captain, now Vice Admiral Sir James Weatherall's only comment on this account is that his memory is that the actual events were rather more cold-blooded!

As Dave Willis remarks above, the Tribal class frigates had been designed for operations in the Persian[139] Gulf and so were very much hot-weather ships. They also had a unique propulsion system - a large single screw, with twin rudders, driven by a combined steam and gas turbine system. This complex system, as would be expected, had advantages and disadvantages. One of the disadvantages was that to get out of the gas turbine boost mode (which provided 'full' speed), the ship had to be stopped so that the clutch could be disengaged. Commander Jim Weatherall (as he then was) was what is known as a 'Dagger N[140]', a specialist navigating officer who had commanded several ships and had taught ship handling to commanding officers.

During his pre-patrol briefings he had been told, privately, by Vice Admiral Troup, FOSNI, to 'get stuck in'[141]. He was not to deliberately damage his ship, but if he was involved in a collision, he would get the Admiral's full support. With these robust instructions, Commander Weatherall made his preparations. *Tartar* had a pair of large retractable protruding stabilisers. These were fixed out and strongly braced with damage control timber across the width of the engine room. The pecker motors[142] were isolated so that the propulsion would respond much more swiftly.

Commander Weatherall's policy was one of 'controlled aggression'. His intention was to get close to any threatening gunboat, preferably on her starboard side, because the big single crew meant that *Tartar* turned better to port, and to ride the gunboat away from her quarry. He did not intend to let any gunboat get past *Tartar* and in this he succeeded. However, his determination to ride off the gunboats led to two collisions with *Tyr* and two with *Ægir*. When asked if he'd deliberately rammed, he said no, but - yes - he had caused collisions. In the circumstances where two commanding officers have totally contradictory aims, one has to give way or there will be a collision. By this stage of the Third Cod War, the Royal Navy was not giving way and nor were the Icelandic Coastguard. The Rule of the Road was only of interest to the Press Officers ashore who were trying to put the best gloss on their own side's activities. The final retrospective comment from Vice Admiral Weatherall was that he hadn't enjoyed hazarding his ship and he had doubted the wisdom of the British Government's position, but orders were orders.

Whilst *Salisbury* and *Tartar* were jousting with *Tyr*, *Òdinn* made a sortie from south of Langanes and was marked by *Scylla*, who, as OTC, subsequently reported:

'I immediately marked her at 2 or 3 cables, and altered course to port in 2 degree steps so that over a 30 minute period Òdinn's ship's head was altered round 20 degrees to port. On two occasions Òdinn closed Scylla's port side but there were no incidents. After a period of some two hours Òdinn was still more than 20 miles from the trawlers ... Òdinn reversed course and returned to Langanes without sighting a trawler. This was probably an examination day for the newcomers Scylla, Tartar and Salisbury.'

It seemed as if the firm posture shown by all three frigates had not given away that an 'Avoid Damage to Frigates' policy was now in place. In *The Last Waltz*, Captain Gudmundur Kjærnested admits (probably about this collision):

[139] As it was then called. With the fall of the Shah of Iran & the increased importance of Arabia, it became RN policy to refer to it as the Arabian Gulf.

[140] At the time, most Seaman Officer specialisations were divided into the short course (known as a 'little n, g, tas, c' etc and shown in the Navy List by the lower case letter), the long course (a capital 'N, G' etc in the Navy List) & the deep specialists, who had the symbol of a dagger alongside their long course designation – hence a 'Dagger N, Dagger G' etc.

[141] Just after the bicentenary year, it is too tempting not to quote Nelson before Trafalgar 'In case signals can neither be seen or perfectly understood, no captain can do very wrong if he places his ship alongside that of the enemy'.

[142] I am indebted to John Hollidge, a serving Marine Engineering Officer, for an explanation of the 'pecker motor', named because of the pecking motion which it executed to engage with a toothed wheel and thereby turn valves etc. On main engine throttles they were mounted in groups of four, two to open two to close the throttles. (*Continued at foot of next page*)
These motors were used to open and control the main engine throttles on all remote and/or auto control steam plants. Prior to remote

'... and then I collided with the bastard. This I did on purpose. I can admit this now. They were quite cunning when colliding with us to appear to be in the right visually. According to navigation law they were considered to be in breach of the rules since they had overtaken us. There it says that a vessel which overtakes another vessel shall give way, but they sailed behind us and overtook us. I suppose it can be argued that the wiser man relents, but there were times that one didn't like to budge. One didn't alter course and speed as prescribed in the navigation law, which of course resulted in a collision. However it is also stated in the navigation law that a collision should be prevented if at all possible. But one cannot be expected to remember everything at the same time.'

Captain Kjærnested, in this honest (post-retirement) admission is only, I believe, reflecting the dilemma that all Commanding Officers, on both sides, faced. They had to balance their governments' aims and objectives, the safety of their ships and people, the reputations of their Services, the Rule of the Road, the media campaign and, no doubt at times, their egos too. This difficult balancing act, though, is exactly why Commanding Officers are carefully selected.

On 3rd April 1976, after a period of attempting, but failing, to interrupt fishing, *Òdinn* had a minor collision with *Scylla*. Captain David Armytage assessed this collision as being caused by the failure of his opposite number to take into account the pressure and suction effects and so being sucked into the frigate's bow area.

As noted earlier, the Icelandic Government had, unsuccessfully, asked the United States to sell or lease them more Coastguard vessels. Enquiries had also been made in Norway, Denmark and Germany and, Ólafur Jóhannesson, once again pursuing his own domestic political agenda, had publicised these enquiries without his Prime Minister's knowledge, let alone approval, including the suggestion that Iceland might look to a loan of small frigates from the Soviet Union. Nothing came of these enquiries in time to affect the dispute, but on 5th April, the Coastguard did commission *Ver*, another hired stern-trawler and *Baldur's* sister ship.

The DFA is moved

The 5th of April 1976 also saw the start of the move of the DFA to the northwest. An extra frigate, tanker and defence tug had been organised to cover the move, which had been planned for the first week in April, the exact date being left to the OTC. HMS *Andromeda*, the fifth frigate joined the patrol on 2nd April. The tanker RFA *Tidereach* joined a day later and, as well as providing a second tanker to cover the move, pumped much of her cargo over to RFA *Olwen*, the patrol tanker. Finally on 4th April, *Euroman* arrived to reinforce *Lloydsman* and *Statesman*.

The skippers were consulted about the move and, initially, on 3rd April only seven voted for the move. By the 5th, fifteen wanted to move, but nineteen voted to stay, of whom ten were nearly at the end of their trip. After consultations with Whitehall, the OTC decided to order the move from pm 5th April. At 1800 *Scylla*, *Tartar*, *Olwen* and *Statesman* led a convoy of 16 trawlers and the two civilian support ships around the north of Iceland, with *Bacchante* and *Euroman* bringing up the rear. The tug RMAS *Roysterer* was sent round south about and *Andromeda*, *Salisbury*, *Tidereach* and *Lloydsman* remained in the eastern DFA with 18 trawlers until that DFA was closed on 9th April. Royal Air Force surveillance flights were provided in both DFAs from 3rd to 7th April.

The Icelandic government had been informed of the intention to shift the DFA to the northwest and *Ægir* shadowed the convoy from a distance. As the numbers decreased in the eastern DFA, the gunboats all moved west. On 9th April, *Andromeda* joined the other frigates in the new DFA and *Salisbury*,

---

control, the "silver wheels" were simply operated by hand of the throttle watchkeepers. Under the pecker motors, the speed of response was predictable but fairly slow, manually (under the control of a good throttle watchkeeper) the response was much faster but it needed careful co-ordination between boiler room and engine room to avoid priming (water carry over with the steam) the boilers or dropping the water level out of the bottom of the gauge glass. Both could result in boiler damage (or shutdown), disastrous in a close quarters situation. The trick was to spin both the ahead and astern throttles at the same time, opening one whilst closing the other. By so doing the steam take off from the boilers was unchanged (the steam was simply diverted from the ahead to the astern turbine, or vice versa, within the main engine), hence avoiding boiler power changes. A skilled team of watchkeepers could out manoeuvre almost any other type of machinery, but it was all down to skill!

ICGV Tyr streaming a warp cutter. *(Peter Harrison)*

Tidereach and *Lloydsman* returned to the UK.

The new DFA, which ran from Straumnes to Bjargtangar, came into force overnight 6th/7th April. Fishing for the 16 trawlers initially in this new DFA was excellent. By 12th April, there were 29 trawlers fishing mainly on the Hali and Kogurgrunn Banks, off Iceland's northwest corner. For the next fortnight, *Ægir*, *Baldur* and *Tyr* appeared infrequently and were comparatively peaceful, with no attempts being made at warp cutting.

Unfortunately, as the numbers built up in the new DFA, the catches decreased markedly and the skippers wanted to move again. An extension to the east, along Iceland's north coast, was ruled out because the British Government, as a conciliatory gesture, decided to recognise a newly declared Icelandic conservation area. An extension to the south could only be a short-term one because the British Government had agreed to the conservation area off Breidifjord, which came into effect on 1st May.

Accordingly, the OTC, supported by FOSNI, recommended an early move back to the east. In fact, the DFA was extended temporarily to the south, but by 16th April there were only 13 trawlers in the area. The remainder had either gone to Greenland or were, against all their instructions, risking fishing in other areas off Iceland without naval protection.

The British Government reviews the dispute

On 13th April 1976, Ministers met again to discuss the dispute and to revisit the same arguments they had faced three weeks before. The MoD's view was that effective protection would become impossible without more robust Rules of Engagement, MAFF wanted the best protection with the minimum disruption to fishing and the FCO wanted firmness, but no incidents on the fishing ground, in order to encourage Icelandic agreement to the now very promising Norwegian initiative. Faced with a recent record of 10 fairly peaceful days in the DFAs, Ministers endorsed the 'Avoid Damage to Frigates' policy, refused to strengthen the RoE and supported efforts to achieve the best settlement available under the Norwegian initiative.

The DFA is moved back

After continued bad weather and poor fishing, Whitehall agreed to the OTC's suggestion that the

DFA should return to the west. The next group of frigates, HM Ships *Galatea*, *Naiad* and *Gurkha*, arrived on 18th April under Captain Willie Gueterbock as OTC. *Scylla*, *Bacchante* and *Tartar* returned to the UK, whilst *Andromeda,* under Captain Tony Pearson, remained on task for another week. With FOSNI's approval, the new OTC closed the western DFA at 1230 on 19th April and led the assembled trawlers and their protecting forces eastwards. *Naiad* remained behind to shadow *Ægir*, who had appeared early that morning. The reopened eastern DFA came into effect at 0600 on 20th April and, initially, ran from Langanes to Dalatangi. By that evening, there were 20 trawlers fishing within it.

No gunboats were seen on 20th or 21st and by the evening of the 21st, trawler numbers had grown to 40. The weather on the 22nd was moderate and there was a lot of fog around, when *Ægir*, *Òdinn* and *Tyr* all made appearances. The trawlers were in two main groups - one to the north off Glettinganes and a southern group off The Whaleback. *Ægir* was the first gunboat out, at midday, when she made a high speed run in thick fog, without her cutter streamed, through the northern group of trawlers and then returned to Seydisfjord. She returned after lunch and was marked by *Andromeda* and *Lloydsman*, who successfully kept her away from any trawlers.

Òdinn was next on scene, being reported initially by the southern group of trawlers and then being sighted by the defence tug *Euroman* at 1245. Both HMS *Gurkha* (Commander Tim Lee) and *Euroman* marked *Òdinn* and just managed to thwart two warp-cutting runs at *C S Forester* and *Irvana*. *Naiad*, meanwhile, had detected *Tyr*, approaching the northern group at 1145. For several hours *Tyr* circled the trawlers from a distance, shadowed by *Naiad*. Then, at 1800, she made a determined run at the trawlers and cut one of *Northern Gift's* warps. Pressing on, disregarding her marker, she then cut both of *Benella's* warps at 1930 and one of *Arctic Vandal's* at 2100. Other trawlers, warned by *Naiad*, hauled their nets and so fishing was disrupted for several hours.

Captain Tony Casdagli of *Naiad* reported that *Tyr* had constantly manoeuvred within feet of him, but that under the RoE in force, he was forced to give way, as he could not prevent the warp cutting without risking collision. He also reported that:

> *'... trawlers are naturally very angry and one stated that if the Navy could not hold off Coastguard vessels they might as well not be there.'*

The skippers in the northern group, who had witnessed three warp-cuttings, the first for over six weeks, and had suffered lengthy interruptions to their fishing were angry and dismayed, and rightly suspicious that the Navy's instructions had changed. In his daily OTC's report that evening, Captain Gueterbock said:

> *'Cut warps and loss of gear are causing bitterness among the trawlers. While no frigates have been damaged there can be no guarantees that the type of manoeuvres indulged in by Tyr, Òdinn and Ægir today will not cause damage to both sides in the future if it continues..... If the Icelandic Coastguard vessels continue as they have today further warp-cutting will result under the present rules of engagement and instructions. As the Icelanders become more aware of the constraints under which the defence forces operate they will be even less easy to frustrate.... Authority for a more robust response from the frigates and tugs is required if our trawlers are to be provided with adequate protection.'*

HMS *Mermaid* relieved *Andromeda* on 23rd April 1976. *Ægir*, *Tyr* and *Òdinn* all appeared in the DFA during the day and there were some interruptions to fishing, but no successful warp-cuttings thanks to the early warnings given by the frigates.

Next day, the same three gunboats succeeded in halting fishing by the main group of 20 trawlers for several hours. Those skippers who did not heed the frigate's warnings lost their warps. *Ægir* cut both of *Maretta's* and one of *C S Forester's*, whilst *Tyr* took both of *Ross Canaveral's*. Then at 1620, *Tyr* collided with *Naiad*, who had been following the gunboat in 'marking method two', whilst warning the trawlers to haul. Surprisingly, at the same time, trawler numbers were up to 55, the highest since the Third Cod War began.

At 2½ miles from the trawler *Irvana*, *Naiad* had pulled ahead and placed herself very close to the trawler's quarter to prevent a warp-cutting run. *Tyr*

The damage to HMS Naiad's bow after her collision with ICGV Tyr. *(MoD/Crown Copyright)*

decided to try to get between the two at high speed, which she succeeded in doing, but only by barging *Naiad* out of the way and striking the nearly stationary frigate's bow with her port quarter. The cutting run was unsuccessful, *Tyr's* superstructure was damaged and *Naiad's* bow was split, both above and below the waterline. After some hours shoring and repairs, *Naiad* was able to continue her patrol.

An Attempted Arrest

The final event on this busy day started at 1800 when *Òdinn* detected the trawler *Crystal Palace* a mile inside the 12-mile limit south of The Whaleback with fishing gear not stowed. The inference of this offence is that she had been fishing inside the 12-mile limit. The skipper initially denied that he had been inside the 12-mile limit, but later admitted that he had been. After the *Lord St Vincent* Hot Pursuit affair on 13th August 1973, the Cabinet had considered the issue and the Navy's orders concerning attempts to arrest a trawler accused of illegal fishing had been rewritten.

They now emphasised that Commanding Officers were obliged to make every effort to avoid interference, including telling the skipper not to risk the lives of his crew, preventing other trawlers from interfering, keeping out of the immediate vicinity and not allowing the skipper onboard one of HM Ships. Nevertheless, Commanding Officers were authorised, in the last resort, to take action in defence of the trawler if he considered that the gunboat was using unnecessary or unreasonable force.

Òdinn and *Crystal Palace* both stopped outside the 12-mile limit, where they were joined by the support ship *Hausa*. The Support Commander visited both vessels to establish the facts and *Ódinn's* Captain made clear his intention to arrest *Crystal Palace* and escort her into port. *Crystal Palace's* skipper consulted his owners who advised him not to submit to arrest unless he was fired upon and, if he was, to act as he thought best for the safety of his crew. It should be remembered that the Coastguard (and the Navy) were capable of listening in to the skipper's conversation with his owner and it would be very surprising if they were not doing so.

The facts were reported to Captain Gueterbock, in *Galatea*, who had closed the scene, but was remaining clear in accordance with the DEWEY OpOrder. He advised all the participants that he recognised *Ódinn's* right of hot pursuit and that the skipper should not take any actions that might endanger the lives of his crew. The skipper consulted with his owners again and received the same advice. He then set off southeast with *Òdinn* and *Hausa* in company and *Galatea* following at a distance.

Òdinn sought permission from headquarters to use gunfire to stop *Crystal Palace* but, as in the *Lord St Vincent* incident, this was refused. The Icelandic authorities were not prepared to take the risk that resistance from the trawler or return gunfire from *Galatea* might cause casualties. The little convoy proceeded southeast all night to the median line between Iceland and the Faeroes, where at 0850, *Òdinn*, *Galatea* and *Hausa* turned back and *Crystal Palace* returned to the UK.

The DFA is changed

The trawler skippers, never shy in making their feelings public, were becoming increasingly vociferous on the trawler radio net, which was constantly monitored by the Coastguard and there were a couple of, fortunately half-hearted, attempts to retaliate against the gunboats. The British Government imposed 20 mile fishing limit was a particular irritation and it became clear that not just the skippers, but also their owners were no longer prepared to be bound by this restriction. The skippers proposed that, as protection was no longer effective, they should no longer be confined to a DFA and should be allowed to fish anywhere outside 12 miles, with the frigates and defence tugs marking the gunboats and warning trawlers to haul as necessary.

The OTC, aware by now that both the skippers and the Coastguard realised that a lower level of protection was all that was now available, agreed in principle and proposed a free fishing area outside 20 miles covering the whole east and southeast coast of Iceland from Langanes to Ingolfshöfdi, an area 250 miles long at the inner edge. FOSNI approved an area 200 miles long, but insisted that it still be called a Defended Fishing Area, so that the Instructions to Skippers would remain in force and naval control could be maintained. This extended DFA was to remain in force right up to the end of the dispute and was very much in line with the 1972 concept, before the Second Cod War, of as much freedom to fish as possible with gunboats being marked by defence forces.

The Final Month

The final month of actual 'hostilities', before talks began on 23rd May 1976, was to see nine warp cuttings, 22 collisions, another arrest attempt, hot pursuit and one firing.

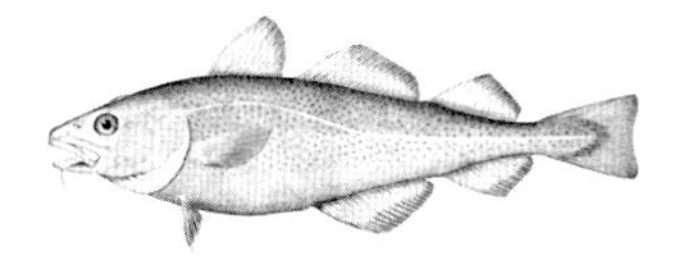

CHAPTER 21

THE THIRD COD WAR
APRIL - MAY 1976

The new 'extended' DFA came into effect on 25th April 1976. *Andromeda* had been relieved by HMS *Mermaid* the day before, so the defending forces now consisted of *Galatea* (Captain Willie Gueterbock as OTC), *Naiad*, *Gurkha* and *Mermaid*, with the tanker *Tidepool* in support. After the busy day on the 24th, the 25th was quiet, although there were four gunboats, *Ægir*, *Baldur*, *Òdinn* and *Tyr* active in the now larger DFA.

Each gunboat was marked by a frigate, but there was no warp cutting and no collisions, despite several near misses. Fishing was badly interrupted, as the trawlers would not risk shooting their nets in the proximity of gunboats. With all four frigates engaged on marking and the gunboats remaining in the DFA overnight, refuelling became a bit of a problem. Captain David Thompson in RFA *Tidepool* had to transit from one frigate to another and await a chance to replenish as gunboat activity permitted.

The gunboats were now remaining on station in the DFA for longer periods, were using jamming and spoofing[143] on the trawler circuits and were, in general, keeping up the pressure on the British fishermen. In the enlarged DFA some skippers were able to fish undisturbed, others spent long hours with their nets hauled.

The defence forces were reinforced by the tug *Statesman* on the morning of 26th April. This brought the defence tug strength back to three, which was just as well as the Nimrod sighted the fifth gunboat, *Thór*, 30 miles to the west of the DFA. She appeared to be operating in the vicinity of a group of Icelandic trawlers, but was close enough to join the other four and give the OTC more problems. The OTC was already concerned about *Naiad's* seaworthiness after her collision, should the weather turn bad, and *Mermaid* had intermittent main engine defects[144]. From what Shaun Jones, one of *Tidepool's* Deck Cadets, also remembers, her steering gear wasn't that good either, as they had a very near shave when it failed during a replenishment.

At 1430, the tug *Euroman* collided with *Ægir* whilst trying to protect the trawler *Irvana* from a series of persistent attempts to cut her warps. The Defence Commander reported:

> *'Euroman came ahead to get between the trawler and Ægir who held her course and speed. When it was apparent that a collision was inevitable Euroman turned hard over and reduced speed. But for this action Euroman would have hit Ægir's most vulnerable part stem on with almost certain damage to the ICGV. As it was, Ægir was struck hard on her port quarter by Euroman's bow. Ægir heeled over alarmingly and visible damage was done to her helicopter deck and other above waterline fitments. Far from deterring Ægir the incident appeared to have the opposite effect and for a further 30 minutes she made a number of attempts - all unsuccessful - to cut warps.'*

This official version does not, however reflect what actually happened. Bob Turner was *Naiad's* Wasp pilot and recounts a less-guarded version:

> *'Whilst the embarked Wasp helicopters were primarily tasked with reconnaissance, or stores and passenger transfer missions they began to develop harassing tactics against the Icelandic gunboats. This arose to some extent through frustration with the Rules of*

[143] In this context, jamming is denying the use of a radio circuit by transmitting a constant signal on it. Spoofing is transmitting false information in the hope of causing confusion.
[144] Although she did have quite a lot of spare mechanical capacity, with 4 diesels on each shaft.

Engagement, under which the ships were constrained in their riding off manoeuvres and by the fact that the ships were sometimes too far away from an incident when the gunboat began to close in to cut the nets.

From mid April onwards, Naiad Flight had started to get very close to the gunboats' bridges as they started their approach to the final circular track around the victim fishing vessel. The aim was simply to disrupt the Icelanders' ship handling and buy sufficient time to enable the fishing vessel to recover her nets before the gunboat could cut them. The Wasp was extremely manoeuvrable and could be positioned very close to the bridge wing of the gunboat. This created a very heavy and disruptive downwash, often enhanced by whipped off wave tops and deafening noise. This cumulative effect made ship handling, bridge communication and the passing of conning orders virtually impossible, and on several occasions caused the gunboats to break off from their cutting manoeuvre. Most importantly, it gave a degree of confidence and comfort to fishing vessel skippers that even though the nearest Royal Naval escort was possibly 30 miles away, there was still some mutual support and limited protection provided by the helicopter.

The Captain of HMS Naiad, Tony Casdagli, was himself a very experienced helicopter Pilot and was aware of the risks. He satisfied himself that the aircrew, myself and Leading Aircrewman "Titus" Oates were driving to the edge of the operational limits of the aircraft, but not beyond. However, on 26th April an opportunity arose which moved the stakes a little higher. We had been tasked on a search mission to find the unlocated Ægir. Some time after take off we received a radio message that Ægir was closing the fishing fleet at speed, and that apart from the ocean going tug Euroman, there was no protection. Euroman was very strong but much slower than any gunboat. Arriving at the scene, we got stuck into our harassment role. We had the Starboard front undercarriage wheel actually nestling within Ægir's bridge wing. The bridge team in Ægir were really unhappy and there was lots of spray, noise and confusion. A heaving line and wheel spanner were produced as a deterrent to the helo, but the attempt to lob them up into the rotor was blasted away by the downwash, much to Titus Oates' amusement.

Meanwhile, looking across the cockpit, I could see that Euroman was approaching from the port side and despite her speed disadvantage, lining up for a possible ramming attempt. I told Titus to keep the Ægir bridge team's attention and from the faces on the bridge wing I could see that he certainly was achieving that. I found out later that he was gesticulating and performing forms of obscenity probably well outside the Geneva Convention. By this stage, Euroman was disappearing from my view below the helicopter, but I could see that she was under heavy helm to port. I called to Titus to give me the "up up" call at the right moment and he did just that. As Wasp 324 disappeared vertically from the scene, with Titus still energetically performing his lewd routine, Euroman passed under us and struck Ægir fair and square on her port side. As we flew past moments later we could see that Ægir had hauled off and that there was some damage to her hull. It was a great feeling, which helped to overcome the frustrations felt by all the Navy, Royal Maritime Auxiliary Service and Fishermen in previous months. We called this tactic the "Rammex". There was plenty of chatter between the fishing fleet on the radio after this incident and Mike Osborne, our MAFF liaison officer was particularly happy. We had to admit that we had been lucky with the relative wind over the Ægir's deck at the time, and the small fuel load then in 324. These factors had given us the scope to fly the Wasp right to its limits and get in really close."

At the same time, in another part of the DFA, *Baldur* was evading a ramming attempt by an irate trawler skipper, who had had more than enough of being harassed. Commander Roger Heptinstall in HMS *Mermaid* managed to restore the peace.

ICGV Ver with HMS Gurkha in the background. Ver was chartered by the Coastguard for the last 2 months of the Third Cod War.

(Jón Páll Ásgeirsson)

Another gunboat joins the fray

The recently commissioned *Ver* made her first appearance on 27th April 1976; the defence forces now had six gunboats to contend with. The OTC reminded his ships that it was now even more important to avoid damage to the frigates. He also signalled FOSNI, asking, once again, for ships and helicopters to be allowed into 4 miles (the limit of Icelandic territorial waters). His reasoning was that this would ease his detection and marking problem now that he was faced with six opponents. He backed up his request with his concerns about the weak EW[145] assets in his force, *Naiad's* damaged bow, *Mermaid's* main engine defects and a defect in the Wessex 3 helicopter, limiting it to daylight flying only.

FOSNI and CinCFleet strongly supported the OTC's request and the MoD agreed to reconsider the proposal, along with several others that were then under discussion. The Commander-in-Chief, Admiral Sir John Treacher, also asked the MoD to examine the possibility of increasing fixed wing (i.e. Royal Air Force Nimrod) air support. To contain six gunboats with four frigates and two defence tugs, it was necessary to employ the Royal Maritime Auxiliary Service tug *Typhoon* (Master Mike Dooley) and the tanker, *Tidepool* (Captain John Moffat) as surveillance assets whenever possible, as well as relying on the trawlers to report all sightings.

Fortunately, just before *Ver* arrived, *Tyr* retired into Seydisfjord to repair the damage suffered in her collision with *Naiad* and she did not reappear until 1st May. The four frigates were marking *Ægir*, *Baldur*, *Òdinn* and *Ver* on the 27th when *Thór* entered the western edge of the DFA and cut one of *Irvana's*[146] warps. Later that evening it was decided that the operational risk of HMS *Naiad* remaining on station with her damaged bow were too high and HMS *Falmouth* was sailed to relieve her.

On 28th April, *Thor* was well to the west, leaving the frigates with one gunboat to watch each again. *Tidepool's* Wessex 3 helicopter was now grounded and so the OTC asked for an extra daily maritime patrol aircraft (MPA) sortie. With CinCFleet's support, this was arranged and the first extra sortie was on task that afternoon.

Òdinn was the first into action, cutting both

[145] Electronic Warfare - in this case, the ability to detect and analyse radar signals, and sometimes radio conversations, from the gunboats.

[146] It is interesting that certain trawlers appear again and again as targets of gunboat action. Either the gunboats had a 'black list' or certain skippers had a knack of being in the wrong place at the wrong time!

Gerontius's warps at 0840. *Galatea* was 80 feet on the trawler's beam at the time, but the gunboat (33 foot beam) came between them at 16 knots for this successful cutting run. The other incident on 28th April was a pair of minor collisions between *Statesman* and *Ver*, the first at 0925. *Ver* was being marked by both *Statesman* and *Gurkha* as she made several determined attempts to cut a trawler's warps. Twice *Statesman* 'fended her off' as *Ver* cut too close across *Statesman's* bow. There was little visible damage to either ship and *Ver* continued attempting to cut warps for another two hours.

All the 21 trawlers still in Icelandic waters were reporting poor catches, even when they were able to fish undisturbed. The total catch was running at about 20% below that needed to achieve the 100,000 tons annual target. The fishermen's frustration and anger was once again unleashed on the gunboats when a trawler tried, unsuccessfully, to ram *Baldur*. The skipper then voiced his concerns forcefully to his owners on the radiotelephone, demanding the restoration of full naval protection. The owners agreed that the situation was unsatisfactory and told the skipper that the concerns were being put to Ministers on the morrow. The trawlers would be informed of the outcome. Like virtually all the skippers' conversations with their owners, this one was monitored by the Coastguard, who, no doubt, took great comfort from the success of their tactics.

Political Considerations

At the end of a bad week with 8 warp cuttings and 4 collisions, plus significant operational defects to cope with, Captain Gueterbock signalled asking for an escalation in the Rules of Engagement.

> *'Now that it is widely recognised that the defence forces are constrained from any defensive action which might cause damage to ICGV, fishing is being interrupted more and more frequently for longer and longer periods.... ICGV warp-cutting runs are pressed home regardless of danger to trawlers and HM Ships who are lying close aboard to protect them, and with scant attention to the defence tugs which were at one time a very considerable deterrent .... Request rule of engagement three four six*[147] *to include authority for defence tugs to ram ICGV when within 2 miles of a British trawler.... Any ICGV approaching within 5 miles (will) be warned by voice radio.... Without providing this ability to contain the ICGV the effectiveness of the defence forces will be practically worthless in a few days, now that all vestiges of the bluff we have been relying on over the last few weeks have been called.'*

It looks very clear that Captain Gueterbock did not think that he and the forces under his command were being fairly supported. This is often a problem when the Services are being asked to hold some kind of line for political reasons, but the politicians can only ignore the legitimate concerns of the front line for so long. Once those in the front line start to believe that the politicians aren't listening, or worse, don't care, the RoE will begin to be bent, as had already happened on the 26th April 1976 when *Euroman* was 'conned' into position to ram *Ægir*.

FOSNI supported the OTC's request for more robust RoE, but CinCFleet, closer to the corridors of power[148], replied 36 hours later:

> *'CTG's difficulties and embarrassment are appreciated but there is no chance at present of approval being given to change to rule of engagement proposed... There is considerable activity in Whitehall examining a number of other ideas which could alter significantly the general situation. Results may appear about mid next week but are in any case most unlikely to include any relaxation to rules of engagement.'*

Faced with the apparent failure of the protection policy and a vociferously complaining fishing industry,

[147] RoE 346 - Riding off the unit which is engaged in harassing is permitted.

[148] I am certain that CinCFleet was, in this instance, being used to pass the MoD's answer back. This may have been because the Naval Staff knew what the answer would be and so didn't even submit the OTC's request or Ministers' Private Offices may have decided not to submit for the same reason or maybe Ministers were made aware, but didn't wish to know, so they could claim subsequently that they weren't consulted. Please excuse the cynicism - it's based on experience.

Ministers met again on 29th April 1976. Whilst endorsing diplomatic efforts to bring the dispute to an orderly end, they were prepared to accept neither ineffective protection nor offensive rules of engagement. The sort of arguments deployed[149] were:

> *'There was no immediate threat of military action by the Soviet Union so that the number of vessels operating off Iceland could be safely increased,[150]'*

> *'The task of protecting trawlers must take precedence over all other activities,'*

and

> *'Valuable resources were being wasted if the Navy could not carry out this priority task.'*

The naval staff were therefore ordered to undertake a rapid, but full examination of all the possibilities and to report back to Ministers within the week. The areas for consideration included altering the rules of engagement, increasing the frigate force on task, using other types of naval vessels, hiring or buying more civilian defence vessels, naval manning of the defence tugs, countermeasures against the warp-cutter and self-protection measures against collision damage.

Back at Sea

On the fishing grounds, the initiative remained firmly with the Coastguard. An incident free 29th April was followed by one collision, one warp-cutting, several near misses and badly disrupted fishing. *Ægir*, *Baldur* and *Òdinn* were all in the DFA and all three were both active and aggressive.

At 1040 *Euroman*, trying to protect the trawler *Kingston Pearl*, passed six feet astern of the gunboat and severed her cutter wire. *Òdinn* immediately turned on her other marker, HMS *Naiad* and appeared to make a deliberate attempt to ram, which missed by only 20 feet. Shortly afterwards HMS *Falmouth* arrived on station and *Naiad* was able to leave for the UK to have her bow section repaired.

Bob Turner, the helicopter pilot onboard *Naiad* recounts that just before starting south, they embarked a returning journalist:

> *'There had been considerable media interest in the action in the Designated Fishing Area, both by Television Crews and Journalists. To participate, they were normally committed to at least ten days away from the UK and so each unit returning home often carried at least one journalist for the transit.*
> *Peregrine Worsthorne of the "Sunday Telegraph" was transferred from RFA Tidepool to HMS Naiad by Wasp Helicopter on 29th April, a trip that he clearly did not enjoy. However, he was soon finely accommodated, as a personal guest of the Captain, and settled in quickly to the routine transit South.*
> *At this stage, the First Lieutenant, Bill Christie thought it would be a good idea to hold a Ship's Variety Concert, commonly known in the Fleet as a "Sods' Opera." This was soon to be renamed "The EuroNaiad Song Contest" and each department onboard was expected to contribute.*
> *The contest was to be compèred by the Captain's Steward, Leading Steward Jimmy Green who was a particularly garrulous and likeable rogue whether afloat or on a run ashore. Jimmy Green had already eyed Peregrine 's fine dark green velvet smoking jacket and persuaded him to loan it for the duration of the Contest.*
> *The Contest commenced after supper in the Junior Ratings' dining hall on the evening of 2nd May. HMS Naiad was by then on track down the Irish Sea in deteriorating weather. Peregrine was seated next to the Captain who had thanked him for lending the smoking jacket to the compère and explained the form for the evening, including how he should vote. Peregrine was amused by the concept, humour and quality of the earlier acts. The ship's company was in a relaxed "up channel night" mode and the tins of beer were flowing freely and perhaps not totally in accordance with the Queen's Regulations. As the show*

[149] I have not seen the primary sources, these three 'reasons' are as quoted in the Naval Staff History.
[150] That is, the Navy's readiness for war with the Warsaw Pact could be reduced.

went on, the weather deteriorated further, as did the quality of the acts. By now, Naiad was rolling heavily, the Captain calmly explained some of the lyrics to Peregrine, the rows of steel chairs slid from side to side in unison and empty beer cans rattled across the deck. Peregrine was becoming increasingly worried by the state of his velvet jacket as Jimmy Green wound up the tempo at the same rate as he was spilling beer. Although "Nil Points" was a common score (and the Supply Department even scored a minus point as supper had included Arctic Roll for pudding yet again) the Stokers were in the lead after an epic performance from some of their more robust Leading Hands. A serious looking Signalman then appeared, barged to the front, and spoke to the Captain. He quickly withdrew from the Dining Hall along with the Operations Officer and a number of key players. Clearly something was afoot.

Shortly afterwards the pipe was made and we were off on a Search and Rescue mission to assist the French trawler fleet caught in storm force winds to the South of Ireland. This happened quickly and effectively and Peregrine was heard to remark how amazed he had been by the Royal Navy's ability to switch from the exacting and arduous task in the fishing grounds, to a humour enriched and relaxed party mode, then immediately and seamlessly switch back again to the serious business of search and rescue in storm conditions. He had also lost track of his smoking jacket, but this was returned later the next day. It had received considerable attention from the Chinese laundry man but was still not looking quite as sharp as when it had first arrived onboard. Peregrine was later to write favourably of his experiences.'

At 1435 *Baldur* cut one of *Boston Kestrel's* warps and then, at 1523, *Òdinn* tried for the third time to cut *Arctic Corsair's* warps. She was marked by HMS *Mermaid* at the time and both *Galatea's* and *Falmouth's* Wasp helicopters were carrying out low level approaches and passes overhead of *Òdinn* (or in most people's language, harassing her). As *Òdinn* cut close across *Arctic Corsair's* bow, Skipper Charlie Pitts took the opportunity to ram *Ódinn's* starboard quarter hard[151]. He would probably have said, not hard enough, as despite what looked like significant damage, *Òdinn* was only in harbour for repairs for two days.

The *Arctic Corsair* was badly damaged in the bows and her forward section rapidly filled with seawater. *Galatea's* damage control teams boarded the trawler and helped with immediate repairs. Meanwhile Skipper Pitts spoke with Boyd Line, his owners, and as *Arctic Corsair* was nearly full of fish anyway, it was decided that she should return home to Hull. HMS *Mermaid* escorted her out of the immediate area just in case one of the other gunboats tried to arrest her and then another returning trawler accompanied her home.

[151] I am indebted to the *Arctic Corsair* website for this account, which is much more believable than the Naval Staff History which, necessarily, only admits 'The ICGV (*Ódinn*) tried to go close across the trawler's bow and was hit hard on the starboard quarter'. The *Arctic Corsair* is still (2006) preserved afloat in Hull.

Left to right: 30th April 1976 - Revenge at last! The Hull trawler Arctic Corsair rams the ICGV Ódinn, whilst Wasp helicopters from HM Ships Galatea & Falmouth observe (MoD/Crown Copyright). Top right: ICGV Ódinn's damaged starboard quarter after being rammed by Arctic Corsair (Jón Páll Ásgeirsson)

Despite his owner's instructions to take care on the homeward journey, Skipper Pitts had proceeded at nearly full speed (possibly to keep his catch as fresh as possible). The consequence of this was that the *Arctic Corsair's* forward watertight bulkhead was badly buckled and the damage was worse than it had been just after the collision. Whilst praising his conduct at the time of the incident (*Òdinn* was clearly in the wrong as far as the International Rules for the Prevention of Collisions at Sea was concerned), Boyd Line were less pleased at his subsequent behaviour. Had the watertight bulkhead failed, she would surely have foundered and he had put his crew in unnecessary danger. Skipper Boyd was dismissed and relieved of his command for a short period. Her catch sold for a good price, making a useful sum for the owners, skipper and crew.

That evening *Euroman* left the patrol for maintenance and a crew change and, fortunately, the *Tidepool's* Wessex helicopter was repaired and fully operational again. Despite the helicopter's return to health, it was agreed to continue two MPA sorties a day until 3rd May, when the requirement would be reassessed. The Government also agreed with the British Trawler Federation's (BTF) oft-repeated request to be allowed to fish inside the, self-imposed, 20-mile limit and trawlers were allowed into 15. Once again, the OTC's request to be allowed to patrol as far as the 4-mile limit of Icelandic territorial waters was refused.

The Icelandic Coastguard realised that they were winning and made great efforts to keep as many gunboats at sea as possible so as to keep the pressure up on the British. The 1st May brought the first gale for a couple of weeks and a pause in gunboat activity. Whilst the gale was blowing, the trawler *Kipling* left for home early because the crew mutinied, presenting an ultimatum to the skipper, refusing to fish unless there was a promise of compensation for loss of earnings.

More Politics

In reality, by this stage the Navy was being used to hold the ring off Iceland, whilst politicians in London worked out how to keep the fishermen quiet whilst they arrived at a solution that the Icelanders would accept and could be sold to the industry.

On 2nd May 1976, at 1500, the skippers held a three-hour discussion on the radio (monitored, of course, by the Coastguard) during which they agreed to send a message to the British Government via the Defence Commander. This message urgently requested the resumption of adequate naval protection and demanded compensation for lost earnings during the period that protection was ineffective. They threatened to leave Icelandic waters by midday 4th May unless a satisfactory answer was forthcoming. The OTC reported:

> *'The frigates' rules of engagement are now so well known that the ships are reduced to a role of reporting the movements of ICGV. The defence tugs still provide some discouragement if the ICGV allow them to get close. The*

trawlers are now hauling when an ICGV is within 7 or 8 miles.'

At this time, based on the rumour that there were three frigates under repair in the dockyards, the UK press was running headlines such as:

'Cod War defeat: Bloody nose for Britain as Royal Navy runs out of frigates to help harassed trawlers.'

with quotes from a 'Reykjavik spokesman.'

'For us there is no longer a Cod War. It finished today with complete British surrender.'

At midday on 3rd May 1976, the MAFF sent an interim reply, stating that Fred Peart, their Minster, would be meeting representatives of the industry (crews, officers and owners) the following evening and that the trawlers should be urged to stay on the fishing grounds. *Baldur*, *Òdinn*, *Tyr* and *Ver* had, just by their presence, virtually brought fishing to a halt and those still fishing were facing severe harassment. At 1440 on 3rd May, with the gale passed, *Òdinn*, having been swiftly repaired, was back at work and cut both *Boston Kestrel's* warps. HMS *Falmouth* had been protecting *Boston Kestrel*, but was obliged to give way to avoid being damaged. Next morning, at 0745, *Tyr* cut both of *Lord St Vincent's* warps, having outmanoeuvred the tug *Statesman* and the trawler *Prince Philip*, who was not fishing but had stationed herself to protect *Lord St Vincent's* warps.

On 4th May, Captain Gueterbock again requested the rules of engagement necessary to allow him to fulfil his tasking:

'If normal fishing is to be restored there is no half way stage. It cannot be reiterated too strongly that the period of bluff is over. From now on bluff of any kind will not work with the ICGV.
Force alone including the use of guns and/or mortars will have to be used to show the ICGV that we mean to protect the trawlers. Defence tugs will need clear authority to ram ICGV in all circumstances. The ICGV are making a maximum effort to finally clear the British from Iceland. At present Baldur, Òdinn and Tyr are weaving in and out of trawlers lying stopped in the main group. If we are to remain off Iceland a major escalation will have to be made and seen to be made by UK.'

Fred Peart, the Minister, sent a personal reply to the skippers' ultimatum which was broadcast as a telegram by Gorleston Coastguard on 4th May 1976

When the trawlermen refused to continue fishing because of the inadequacy of RN protection under the 'Avoid damage to Frigates policy', one of the steps considered was to reinforce the patrol with HMS Blake & her 4 Seaking helicopters. In the event, she was never sent to Iceland.
(David Weller)

and was received by the trawlers (and, no doubt the Icelandic Coastguard) at 2100. By this time there were only 14 trawlers still off Iceland, none of them fishing. The Minister stated that the situation at sea had been explained to him with clarity and force, that he understood the fishermen's anxieties, and that a decision on further protection would be taken within 48 hours.

The trawlermen were unimpressed, particularly with the lack of any mention of compensation, and by 2130 there was only one trawler, the *Carlisle*, still on the fishing grounds. All the others had left for the Faeroes. The owners managed to reverse this exodus and all returned, but did not agree to restart fishing. By the afternoon of the 5th, two trawlers were back in the vicinity of The Whaleback, one of them, the *Boston Lightning*, fishing with a close escort of two tugs and a frigate. By that evening, there were 15 trawlers in the DFA, but only the one fishing. The others stood by their pledge not to resume fishing until they had a favourable reply to their ultimatum. Ministers again discussed the dispute on 6th May 1976. The naval staff's proposals covered reinforcement, escalation, changes in the fishing patterns and passive defence measures. The possible reinforcements included more frigates, more civilian defence vessels and, if the DFA was to be enlarged further, the helicopter-cruiser HMS *Blake*[152] with her four Seaking helicopters to provide better surveillance. It was clearly pointed out, however, that no amount of reinforcement would be any use if ships were still not authorised to use the force (already) available.

RoE changes proposed for Ministerial consideration included the use of gunfire when threatened with ramming, counter-ramming by frigates or (naval manned) tugs, retaliatory warp-cutting of Icelandic trawlers by British vessels, improving surveillance by allowing the protection forces in to the 4-mile limit of Icelandic territorial waters and, most simply, reverting to the RoE in force before the '*Avoid Damage to Frigates*' policy had been imposed. The risks in this last and most obvious course were two fold, casualties and serious damage to the frigates from collisions with the more heavily constructed gunboats.

Other measures proposed by the naval staff included the fitting of protective padding to *HM Ships Jaguar* and *Lincoln*, for both defence and for counter-ramming, the fitting of bow wire-cutters to both ships and the offer of self-defence explosive cutters to the trawlers.

Ministers also had to consider the diplomatic factors. There were signs that the Icelandic Prime Minister, Geir Hallgrímsson, might be edging towards gaining enough support within his coalition for at least a short-term agreement. Knut Frydenlund, the Norwegian Foreign Minister, had proposed a six-month agreement based on an average of between 22 and 25 British trawlers fishing within the 50-mile limit. The next NATO ministerial meeting was being held in Oslo on 20th and 21st May and the subject of 'British naval activities in Icelandic waters' was on the agenda. There were also the usual Icelandic rumblings about the Keflavík airbase and even withdrawing from NATO to consider. Britain's NATO allies were getting very tired of the dispute and were putting pressure on her to settle. Unfortunately, at around this time, Dr Luns bolstered Iceland's hand by describing Keflavík as 'the most important piece of real estate in NATO.'

The latest session of the Third UN Conference on the Law of the Sea was due to close on 7th May without agreement on Exclusive Economic Zones EEZs. It was believed that the USA, Canada and Norway were going to declare their own 200-mile EEZs shortly, whatever the result of the UNCLOS3 session, and France, Denmark and Ireland were believed to be thinking of taking the same action. Britain wanted to declare her own 200-mile EEZ by the end of 1976 and a 200-mile European Economic Community EEZ was being discussed.

NATO's Oslo meeting was seen as a good opportunity to bring the Third Cod War to an end through bilateral talks with the Icelandic Foreign Minister. However, until that time the Government was determined that fishing and the necessary protection should be seen to continue. If the trawlers left the fishing grounds, the Icelanders would have won and would have no need to settle.

From all these conflicting considerations, Ministers decided to order reinforcements of two frigates and one civilian defence vessels, with the DFA to remain

[152] The possible deployment of HMS *Blake* was reported in the UK press on 12th May 1976, possibly as an indication to Iceland of Britain's intent not to be defeated at sea.

unchanged. It was also decided to drop the '*Avoid Damage to Frigates*' when riding off gunboats policy immediately, without awaiting the arrival of the reinforcements. The proposals to fit *Jaguar* and *Lincoln* with protective sheathing and bow cutters was approved, as was that of providing the fishing industry with explosive cutters. This latter suggestion was quickly rejected by the industry as impractical in the vast majority of British trawlers, which were still of the older side trawl type. The Royal Air Force and the Royal Navy decided to continue with only one Nimrod MPA sortie per day (down from two since 3rd May), with a second sortie available in case of operational need.

These decisions were signalled to the OTC on the afternoon of 6th May 1976 together with orders that 'warnings are to be passed … to make it abundantly clear to ICGVs that frigates are not circumscribed by high authority in riding off.' Simultaneously, the Minister of Agriculture, Fisheries and Food sent another personal message (again via Gorleston Coastguard, with the consequence that the Icelandic Coastguard could listen in) to the trawlermen informing them that reinforcements were coming and stating that:

> *'No decision has yet been taken about compensation but I am confident that the protection which the Navy will now be able to give will allow a return to worthwhile fishing off Iceland as before.'*

The Defence Commander read this message out on the trawler radio net at 1730 and by 1900 about half of the trawlers had resumed fishing. The remainder delayed, hoping for some word on compensation. The gunboats, who believed that they had won the war, were now disillusioned. *Baldur*, *Tyr*, *Òdinn* and *Ver* were all in or near the DFA and immediately launched a vigorous offensive.

CHAPTER 22

THE THIRD COD WAR
MAY - JUN 1976

On the evening of 6th May 1976, as the message sank in that the '*Avoid Damage to Frigates*' policy had been reversed, reinforcements were en route and British trawlers had recommended fishing in the disputed waters, the Royal Navy must have been expecting a fairly sharp reaction from the Icelandic Coastguard. It was not long in coming.

There were four gunboats, *Baldur*, *Òdinn*, *Tyr* and *Ver* in or near the DFA, in which 15 trawlers, in a fairly tight group, had resumed fishing. All of the gunboats were being marked and the two defence tugs were in close escort on the trawlers.

Nine Collisions in under Three Hours

HMS *Gurkha* marked *Òdinn* from about 1830 and at 2030 the gunboat started to move northeast towards the trawlers. At 2125, as the distance closed, *Gurkha* took up a close marking position on *Ódinn's* starboard side, between her and the nearest trawler, now about 5 miles away. As the two ships moved round to the northwest of the trawler group, *Òdinn* made a series of moves towards *Gurkha* to see if she would give way, closing to within a few feet and turning hard away to swing her stern close to the frigate's side. *Gurkha* maintained her marking position, only manoeuvring at the last moment to avoid collision. *Òdinn* reversed her course at 2151, followed round by *Gurkha*. Ten minutes later, *Òdinn* closed once again and this time struck *Gurkha* amidships with her quarter. There was no significant damage to either ship.

Meanwhile, *Baldur* had appeared from within the 12-mile limit at 1945 and was marked by *Mermaid*. Over the next hour and a quarter, *Baldur* made seven attempts to ride off *Mermaid* and to get to the trawlers. At the eighth attempt, at 2105, *Baldur* again swung her stern hard into *Mermaid's* side. This time her quarter struck the frigate amidships, causing a 5-foot horizontal gash, 8-inches wide in the conversion machinery space.[153] By this time *Galatea* and *Statesman* were nearby and *Baldur* retired to within the 12-mile line, watched over by both frigates. The hole in *Mermaid's* side was above the waterline, but as the sea was moderate to rough, enough water was coming in for there to be a significant risk of losing power to the ship's compasses, radars and weapons. Taff Jones was onboard *Mermaid* for both her Cod War patrols. He was in his bunk when *Baldur's* quarter came through *Mermaid's* side:

> *'A patrol started mainly from Rosyth and lasted about three weeks give or take a day or two. We did not know really what to expect at first apart from the weather, which a few of us knew would not be very kind to us. For those of us that had been up to that part of the world, we feared the worst and we would not be disappointed! I think in all the patrols that we did we could count on one hand the calm days we experienced. I had been in the Navy around ten years and I thought I had seen rough seas!! A good example was one day I was on the bridge looking out when I over heard the Captain telling the OOW that we would be lucky to survive the next wave that came our way!! Mind you some of them were 60 feet high at times!*
>
> *Once up north the days were quite long and boring except when we came in contact with one of the Icelandic gunboats. The rules of*

[153] The role of the Conversion Machinery Space is to convert the standard 440V 60Hz 3 Phase supplies from the ship's main generators to the various voltages and frequencies required by many of the ship's electronic systems. Everything from compass repeats to radars, weapon systems to telephones.

ICGV Baldur swings her stern in to hole HMS Mermaid on 6th May 1976 (Jón Páll Ásgeirsson)

engagement changed daily, but I don't think any of us really took much notice of them most of the time. As some of the photos showed collisions were the order of the day. They would be between gunboats and Royal Navy ships or gunboats and UK trawlers. Some of these collisions were dangerous at times. One example was one night lying in my bunk when a pipe was made by the OOW "standby collision port side". Within ten seconds a bow of a gunboat came through the mess bulkhead!! Luckily my bunk was on the other side of the mess, and the bunks that came in contact were empty (lads on watch). We went to lifeboat stations with a view to abandon ship. Luckily we managed to shore up the hole and kept on going. I think we went back to Rosyth shortly afterwards.

We did manage to have some fun, mostly during the nights when the gunboats went back alongside. Bingo was played in the dining hall or a film was shown. On the Mermaid there was an ice cream machine so ice cream was served between reels! The usual cards were played in the messdeck and of course the famous uckers[154]! So it wasn't all gloom and doom. Morale was always high. But then what do we expect from the best Navy in the world! On a few occasions there was a chance to make a phone call home if the SCO[155] was in a good mood! The idea was who could spot who first, and where they were coming from. The radar was used by both sides, but my job on board was as an EW rating who had a bit of kit that could pick up their radar well before they could detect us. Needless to say I was in the Captain's 'good books' on more than one occasion. He did actually send a case of beer down the mess once!!

Guess what was on the menu nearly every day?

Do you want to phone a friend? No. Was it cod and chips? Correct! Good job most of us liked fish and chips. I think the fish cost the Captain a few bottles of his best malt! The poor seaboat crew worked hard to keep us in fish, backwards and forwards to the trawlers each time we passed one of them. I think the Captain saw them all right with a few cases of beer.

At the end of one of the patrols we were going

[154] A naval variant of the game of Ludo.

[155] Ship's Communications Officer - not called just the CO, because that is, of course, the Commanding Officer.

back home to Pompey. Sailing down the North Sea the Captain made a pipe and asked us if we wanted to go straight back or did we fancy a run ashore in Grimsby. Guess where we voted for? What a run ashore Grimsby is after a cod war patrol! I don't think we spent a penny on beer, taxis, food or anything else! Thinking back it was quite an experience, but at times frightening! All for fish some would say.
Well guess where most of the trawlers that sell their fish up here in Hull come from? Correct again! Iceland!!!!!!!!!!'

At 2000 *Falmouth* had taken over marking *Tyr* from *Galatea* and was 100 yards on the gunboat's port quarter. *Tyr* had already managed to cut one of *Carlisle's* warps, which turned out to be the last warp cutting of the dispute. At 2010, *Tyr* suddenly slowed down and as *Falmouth* came up onto her port beam, turned hard towards and rammed the frigate amidships, causing some minor damage. As she hit *Falmouth's* flight deck fairleads, *Tyr* came off slightly worse, with a hole in her bow 10 feet above the waterline.

The nearest trawler was now only two miles away and *Falmouth* had to manoeuvre violently to avoid being rammed again. At 2200, whilst lying stopped 5 cables clear of the also stationary *Tyr*, *Ver* approached *Falmouth* from the northwest. Commander Gerald Plumer, the Commanding Officer of *Falmouth*, realised that *Ver* was heading straight for him and had to ring on full ahead to avoid being quite deliberately rammed on his starboard quarter. At 2215, *Tyr* got under way again and headed towards the trawlers, whilst *Galatea* took over marking *Ver*.

By now it was quite clear to the OTC, Captain Willie Gueterbock, that the gunboats were determined to regain the upper hand, if necessary by ramming and damaging the frigates. *Mermaid* had a dangerous split in her side, both *Gurkha* and *Falmouth* had been rammed once and *Falmouth* had narrowly escaped a second ramming from *Ver*. The short period of darkness was about to begin and gale force winds were forecast.

Faced with these circumstances, Captain Gueterbock came to the conclusion that he would need more robust Rules of Engagement (RoE), if he was to be able to hold the gunboats off without incur-

ICGV Baldur pulls away from HMS Mermaid after colliding. 6th May 1976 *(Jón Páll Ásgeirsson)*

ring further damage to his ships and, possibly, casualties. At 2250 *Baldur* reappeared from inside the 12-mile limit and was marked again by *Mermaid*. Her Commanding Officer, Commander Roger Heptinstall, signalled the OTC suggesting that permission to use force should be sought. The OTC agreed and, at 2302, he signalled:

> *'Request approval for all frigates to open fire in self-defence with guns and mortars*[156]*. Mermaid and Falmouth both damaged. Mermaid taking water. ICGV still attempting to ram.'*

FOSNI immediately asked for amplification, which Captain Gueterbock supplied at 0020, by which time *Falmouth* had been in two further collisions. Within an hour, the MoD had refused any change to the RoE. Meanwhile, the gunboats were continuing to keep up the pressure. *Baldur* approached several trawlers, none of whom were fishing, and returned to The Whaleback area at 0020. *Mermaid* had marked her throughout, whilst the damage control teams onboard worked to repair the split in her hull.

Gurkha succeeded in keeping *Òdinn* away from any trawlers, but suffered three more bumps in the process. *Galatea* was marking *Ver* and *Falmouth* covered *Tyr*. The final incident of this very dangerous period was to see both *Falmouth* and her attacker, *Tyr*, badly damaged and forced to retire from the fishing grounds.

At 2245 *Tyr* was doing 20 knots with her cutter streamed and was a mile short of a trawler, whom she believed to be fishing. *Falmouth* was at 28 knots and was taking up a marking position 100 feet on *Tyr's* port quarter. Commander Plumer's collision report indicated the difficulties and dangers he faced that evening:

> *'Considering it too dangerous to attempt to overtake in the limited sea room available, I sounded one short blast hoping the Tyr would appreciate the danger she was in and ease away to starboard.*
>
> *No action was taken by Tyr. A full minute later when I had moved up slightly to 40° on her quarter at 100 feet and the trawler was only 6 cables away being closed at 20 knots by an Icelandic Coastguard Vessel with her cutting gear streamed, I had no option left to prevent Tyr cutting the warp apart from turning to starboard. I sounded a further single blast and turned to starboard hitting Tyr on her port side forty feet from her stern. I immediately gave the order for full astern. If Tyr had turned away to starboard at the same time then collision might have been averted. The effect of the collision was awful; Tyr heeled over 70° to starboard as she rapidly pivoted round my stem until the two ships were lying stem to stern, our port sides grinding past at 3-4 knots.*
>
> *While I appreciated that my bow must be damaged, I was concerned at the possibility of damage to the hull of Tyr and whether any lives had been lost. Tyr pulled away quickly astern and I searched the sea for any men who might have been thrown overboard - there appeared to be none.*
>
> *Very shortly after this collision, on the orders of CTG 600.1 (the OTC, Captain Gueterbock in Galatea) I broadcast to all Icelandic Coastguard Vessels on VHF that any further harassment of British trawlers could result in severe damage. The reply from an unknown station was not clear but appeared abusive.*
>
> *Approximately ten minutes later, at 2300, Falmouth was again close marking Tyr from her port quarter. Tyr, with his cutter still streamed, was heading at 20 knots for another trawler believed to be fishing some 14 cables ahead. Falmouth again closed to mark from 100 feet on the port quarter and on reaching 5 cables from the trawler, I again sounded one short blast clearly indicating my intention of turning to starboard. If anything Tyr altered slightly to port towards the trawler whose range was closing rapidly. Again I could see no option than to turn to starboard if I was to prevent Tyr passing close astern of the trawler and cutting the warp. After sounding a second and third single short blast, separated by about ten seconds, I turned to starboard and as Tyr did*

[156] A pattern of 550lb anti-submarine mortar bombs fired to burst at shallow depth close ahead of a gunboat would certainly have produced a big enough shock wave to disable the gunboat, if not actually to sink her.

not turn away the two ships collided in almost similar circumstances to the first occasion. Tyr again heeled sharply to starboard and swung around to port moving slowly down my port side as the two ships stopped or went astern. On this second occasion, I was even more concerned that serious damage had been done to Tyr and that there was the possibility of men having been thrown overboard. I asked Tyr on VHF whether she required assistance to which she replied, "I want no help from you". As soon as she was clear Tyr made off at 14 knots in a NW direction towards the 12-mile limit. As there were no trawlers in that direction I stayed in the vicinity of the collision to see if there were any men in the water and to inspect my own damage. I then proceeded to follow 3 miles astern of Tyr as she entered the 12-mile limit. At this stage all Icelandic Coastguard Vessels broke off their action and retired to the north-west. I believe that the course I took was the only one consistent with achieving full protection of the trawlers under attack. Any other course of action would have resulted in warps being cut or of my being placed in a position of extreme disadvantage.'

Tyr returned to The Whaleback at 14 knots, badly shaken up with her port quarter stove in, her port shaft bent, propeller blades damaged, as well as the hole in her bow from the first collision two and a half hours before. By 0200 all four gunboats were grouped together within the 12-mile limit. Shortly afterwards, *Tyr* retired to the shelter of Reydarfjord and two days later returned to Reykjavik for a hero's welcome.

Falmouth had flooding in her lower forward compartments and her bow was crumpled and wrapped round to port between the waterline and six feet above. She was fortunately due to be relieved that morning anyway and so, after temporary repairs and shoring, she returned to the UK. *Lowestoft* joined the defending forces, for her third patrol, late in the forenoon. *Mermaid* had made her ship's side watertight again but as a precaution, she was also ordered to return to the UK, accompanied by the Royal Maritime Auxiliary Service tug *Typhoon*.

7th May - A Quiet Day: Only One Collision

Captain Gueterbock prepared for a resumption of the Coastguard's offensive on 7th May 1976. The Nimrod sortie was brought forward to 0500 to check the fjords and all approaches to the DFA for gunboat

ICGV Baldur crewmembers survey the latest damage. (Jón Páll Ásgeirsson)

activity. In the event, *Baldur* retired inshore and no additional Coastguard resources were deployed. *Ver* and *Òdinn* made sorties into the DFA at about 1400. *Ver* was marked by *Galatea* and subsequently *Lowestoft*. On being warned not to interfere with the fishing, she retired to the 12-mile limit without attempting any warp cutting runs.

Òdinn was, however, more persistent. For two hours *Gurkha* maintained a marking position between *Òdinn* and the trawlers, *Òdinn* holding station at about 150 feet from the frigate. After passing two trawlers with their nets down, at 1647, *Òdinn* decided to make a determined run at the *Ross Ramilles*. *Gurkha* was not prepared to give way and, in fact, by this stage, was not able to do so without colliding with *Ross Ramilles* herself. In spite of warnings, *Òdinn* altered towards *Gurkha* and a collision became inevitable. There was little damage, the trawler's warps were protected and, when *Galatea* joined *Gurkha*, *Òdinn* retired towards the 12-mile limit at 1730.

Having had to send two damaged frigates home that day, Captain Willie Gueterbock concluded that *Òdinn* had deliberately tried to disable *Gurkha* so the use of force might be necessary if further frigates were not to be rendered non-operational by ramming. He also assessed that warning shots would not only be effective, but also that the risk of casualties would be lower than with the sort of dangerous collisions that had taken place between *Falmouth* and *Tyr* the night before. He therefore, as soon as he heard of this latest collision, once again signalled asking for approval to use force if necessary, saying:

> *'Request authority to use gunfire and mortar fire at ICGV Òdinn who has just rammed Gurkha and tried to force Gurkha onto trawler Ross Ramilles.*
> *Òdinn had been warned by Gurkha. Galatea joining Gurkha with dispatch.'*

Self-Defence?

MoD turned this request down within two hours, but FOSNI did remind the OTC of his inherent right of self-defence in extreme circumstances. Despite this swift negative response, the OTC's request had raised two significant questions in Whitehall. The defence forces were, and remained throughout until the end, under Rules of Engagement Option Charlie, which instructed the OTC to attempt to deter and frustrate harassment allowing force to certain specified levels, not including gunfire. The DEWEY OpOrd also contained Option Delta allowing the use of gunfire.

Option Delta included the rules for the use of direct gunfire as the culmination in a series of escalatory options - warning, training of weapons, blank shots, shots across the bow etc. A change from Option Charlie to Option Delta required ministerial approval, which at this stage (two weeks before the NATO Ministerial Summit in Oslo) was extremely unlikely to be given.

However, quite separately, there was the question of opening fire in self-defence, as FOSNI had reminded the OTC. Under the Royal Navy's standing instructions in the classified '*Guide to International Maritime Law*', a Commanding Officer had the inherent right, irrespective of the rules of engagement in force, to open fire in self-defence to ensure the safety of his own ship, ships under his protection and all their crews, when under armed attack. There had to be 'an instant and overwhelming necessity for self-defence, leaving no choice and no moment for deliberation'.

The Guide assumed that the adversary had opened fire, but the question had now been raised as to whether an attempt to sink by ramming might justify opening fire in self-defence. It took the MoD two weeks to answer this, admittedly complex politico-legal, question and on 19th May 1976 a letter was issued laying down the very narrow circumstances in which a Commanding Officer, faced with an adversary intent on ramming, could open fire.

The CinCFleet once again raised the question of passive defence measures against ramming. The MoD agreed and ships were invited to offer their own proposals for extra shoring or fendering, nothing that might be portrayed as offensive would be permitted. A proposal for dockyards to fit extra fendering would have cost £75,000 per ship and taken 5 weeks to fit. In the end, the dispute ended before any proposals could be followed up.

Meanwhile in Iceland

After *Falmouth's* robust treatment of *Tyr*, the balance of power in the DFA seemed to have swung back to the British. Certainly the Coastguard were surprised

HMS Falmouth's bow after her 6th May collision with ICGV Tyr
(David Mathias)

at the response generated by their attacks and now recognised that they could not force British trawlers out of their claimed 200-mile limit. There were going to have to be some kind of negotiations.

The British Embassy was still closed, but the usual staff, with the exception of the Ambassador, were still at their posts, albeit as the British Interests Section of the French Embassy. One of the remaining team was told shortly after the events described above that there had been no Coastguard headquarters plan or government instructions for the combined attacks on 6th May 1976. The incidents had been solely initiated by the immediate and angry reactions of the Coastguard captains in the area at the time when they heard the telegram indicating that the British were not leaving and were, in fact, reinforcing their defence forces.

Control over the Icelandic gunboat captains was becoming ever weaker as their press-inflated reputations and chauvinism-fuelled popularity increased. The Prime Minister had, in fact, complained to the Norwegian Ambassador that some of the Coastguard captains wanted to be 'national heroes' and did not obey instructions to refrain from action at sensitive moments in the dispute. Predictably the Icelandic press accused the frigates of dangerous attempts to ram and sink their gunboats in accordance with British Government policy.

One unusual factor in the events of 6th May was the presence of an Icelandic journalist, Mr Óli Tynes, onboard *Falmouth*. He had asked to view events from a British ship and his application had been accepted on the basis that an open press policy outweighed the risk of hostile reporting and that the opportunity to prove that British warships did not ram Icelandic gunboats was too good to miss.

He had been in HMS *Gurkha* (Commander Tim Lee) for three weeks and had witnessed the British embarrassment of the '*Avoid Damage to Frigates*' period, when the gunboats had the upper hand and the trawlers left the fishing grounds. He was then keen to return to Iceland, but no Icelandic ship would accept him directly from the British, so he was transferred to *Falmouth*, as she was the next frigate returning to the UK.

Consequently, he was onboard and a first-hand witness to the three collisions between *Tyr* and *Falmouth*. His subsequent report made it clear that he had witnessed deliberate ramming by a British frigate. However, having spent time at sea with the Icelandic Coastguard as well, his view was that both sides should equally share the blame for collisions. Otherwise, his reports showed sympathy and understanding for those involved in fishery protection, which was in marked contrast to the virulent anti-*Falmouth* line taken in his newspaper. When Mr Tynes was landed in the UK, his message to the British press was polite and muted.

In *The Last Waltz*, Óli Tynes recounts the *Falmouth/ Tyr* collisions as he remembered the view from *Falmouth's* bridge:

> *'The noise was horrendous and the Tyr began to capsize. The port propeller came out of the water and whisked the sea. ... I heard somebody shout, "My God, she's going over". ... (Just before the second collision) I heard someone downstairs cry, "My God, what kind of man is this Captain Kjærnested?" On board the frigate, all hell broke loose of course. ... I was quite horrified like many others onboard because we thought that she would capsize. But when she sailed at full speed again towards the next trawler, the tiny Icelandic heart almost burst with pride.'*

By this stage, the British press, although favourable to the Navy, in contrast to the earlier accusations of failing to protect 'our fishermen' during the '*Avoid Damage to Frigates*' phase, was beginning to question the wisdom of the Government's whole policy towards the dispute. Questions were being raised about whether the Navy was being asked to fight without weapons and what the whole future of the distant-water fishing industry should be, once there was an EEC common fishery policy in a world of 200-mile EEZs.

Reinforcements arrive, a Brief Lull and then Gunfire

After the bruising activity of the 6th and 7th May 1976, there were several days of much reduced activity. Captain Willie Gueterbock was relieved as OTC by Captain John Tait on 11th May, by when there were five newly-arrived frigates on patrol - HM Ships *Leander*, *Tartar*, *Lowestoft*, *Salisbury* and *Eastbourne*, backed up by two defence tugs - *Statesman* and *Euroman*, one tanker - *Tidepool* and the Royal Maritime Auxiliary Service tug *Roysterer*. A sixth frigate, the single-screw HMS *Dundas*, another tanker, RFA *Blue Rover*, and an additional civilian defence vessel, the chartered stern trawler *Southella* were also on their way to add to the defences. Twenty trawlers were on the grounds and fishing had improved.

When not engaged in combating gunboats, the usual task of the Fishery Protection Staff continued. Ian Daniels, a Leading Seaman in *Leander* at the time, remembers one particular inspection trip:

> *'Most of the time we were on Defence Watches, 6 hours on watch and 6 off. We never knew if we were getting up for breakfast, lunch or dinner. It was our job to take the fishery protection men over to the fishing boats so they could measure the net size and inspect the catch.*
> *On one occasion I was part of the boarding party at about 2 am and it was really wet and cold. The Gemini dinghy was lowered over the side in quite a big swell so it was not easy to slip the boat. We managed that and came alongside to pickup the Fishery men. It took several attempts because of the swell and the fishery men were hanging on the Jacob's ladder for some time. The worst part was trying to get them both onto the fishing boat. The swell was so big that we kept losing sight of the fishing boat. As we got closer we could see the swell going from the fishing boats hull right up to the gunnels. We made several attempts again to get alongside. We had to catch it just as the water was at the gunnels so the men could jump off and then bear off and wait for them to call us along side again to pick them up.*
> *On this occasion whilst we were waiting we were called alongside given a few baskets of fish, which they tipped into our Gemini. It was frozen of course and very heavy. We went back alongside when requested and picked up the fishery protection men.*
> *We got back to the Leander and the 2 chaps went up the Jacob's ladder and we went under the davits to be lifted clear of the water. We managed to hook up in the swell and started being lifted. There was an almighty crack and we hung on the safety ropes for life. The fish had been so heavy that the strengthening boards in the bottom of the boat had snapped. Although it was dangerous we laughed for hours.'*

The brief lull was shattered by a call from the Hull trawler *Primella* 400 miles to the west of the DFA, reporting that *Ægir* had fired at her and was attempting to board. Fishing outside the DFA had become more common since the disillusionment that set in with the standard of naval protection offered during the '*Avoid Damage to Frigates*' period and many trawlers, en route to Greenland, would try their hand at a bit of fishing off western Iceland if the coast looked to be clear.

On 11th May 1976 the Coastguard realised that there were six British trawlers fishing about 40 miles off Straumnes and *Ægir* was dispatched on 12th to clear them out. She was in the area by 0800 and ordered the trawlers to haul their nets. According to the captain of *Ægir*, all did so and scattered, except for *Primella* who attempted to start fishing again, an accusation that the skipper of *Primella* denied. At about 1000, *Ægir* sent her armed boarding party over to attempt to arrest *Primella*, at which her skipper escaped south at 14 knots.

Ægir gave chase and over the next two hours repeatedly ordered *Primella* to stop and submit to arrest. During this chase *Ægir* fired four warning rounds, three blanks and a live shot missing the trawler's stern. On receipt of *Primella's* first radio call at 1100[157], the OTC had dispatched the on-task Nimrod, HMS *Lowestoft* and RFA *Blue Rover*[158]. The Nimrod was over the incident at about 1230, having been briefed that, if *Ægir* continued to threaten, her captain should be warned that British units were authorised to return fire[159]. Captain Tait, the OTC, had rightly calculated that *Ægir's* Captain would not be certain if, or with what, the Nimrod was armed and that there was nothing to lose and everything to gain by this gambit.

When the Nimrod arrived, *Ægir* had just fired her eighth round and was threatening to fire an aimed round into the hull of the *Primella*. Accordingly, the Nimrod's Captain passed the authorised warning. There were communications difficulties and so the Nimrod's warning had to be relayed by another trawler, which was done three times. The effect of this warning was that *Ægir*, despite continuing to threaten the trawler for a time (each threat being answered with the Nimrod's 'self-defence' warning), dropped astern of *Primella* and, finally, at 2100 turned away to the north. Additional Nimrods were launched throughout the day and escorted *Primella* until *Lowestoft* met her off Reykjanes at 0030 and escorted her back to the DFA.

It later became clear[160] that *Ægir's* Captain had not sought permission to open fire (which he would probably not have received) and decided not to call the Nimrod's bluff[161], with the possible risk to life if the Nimrod was not bluffing. Hans G Andersen, the Foreign Ministry's chief Law of the Sea Adviser from 1946 to after the Third Cod War, was of the opinion that *Ægir's* captain had either acted on his own initiative (burnishing his image as a 'national hero') or, as on previous occasions, had been ordered to be aggressive by Ólafur Jóhannesson, the Minister of Justice/Head of the Coastguard, just when a negotiated settlement seemed to be in sight.

The press reaction to this incident was inevitable and predictably over the top. Formal protests were made at government-to-government level. The British protested about the use of gunfire against a trawler fishing legally on the high seas. Iceland responded that *Ægir* was merely carrying out normal policing duties and that the threat to open fire by a 'Nimrod Spy Plane' was a dangerous escalation. Overall, the reputation of the defending forces, both as opponents and protectors, was enhanced and the owners took steps to tighten up trawler discipline.

Back in the DFA, the lull continued and by 15th May 1976 there were more than 30 trawlers fishing. The weather was mostly calm, with increasingly frequent thick fog. *Ægir*, *Thór* and *Ver* were all around, but entered the DFA only rarely and then singly. Each visit could therefore be met by two frigates and, often, a defence tug. HMS *Dundas* joined the patrol

[157] Three hours after this incident started. I assume that the skippers did not wish to admit that they were fishing in Icelandic waters, outside the DFA, against the owners' Instructions to Skippers. Had the OTC known what was going on at 0800, the Nimrod could have been there by about 0900.

[158] After a full speed passage of 400 miles, *Lowestoft* would need refuelling to remain at the high fuel state that was required.

[159] This warning was required by ROE 101 before opening fire in self-defence.

[160] It is a reasonable assumption that the British were listening to the gunboats' communications with their HQ and had a number of Icelandic interpreters available to translate. Additionally, in a small capital city like Reykjavik, the diplomatic community will be very incestuous and everyone will have been interested in the progress of the dispute. Keeping details of incidents secret will have been nigh on impossible.

[161] As far as I can tell, at the time, Nimrods were not fitted with any weapons that could have been used against *Ægir* in these circumstances.

on the evening of 14th May, bringing the frigate strength up to six. She was the first Type 14 single-screw frigate to have been deployed on Cod War duties since 1961, it having been decided that these ships were too frail to risk collision with gunboats. The fact that Type 14s were now being deployed was mainly a reflection of the shortage of more capable frigate hulls.

Stuart Johnson was the Chief ERA[162] of *Dundas* and recalls her transition from Training Ship back to the Front Line:

> *'We had come out of refit, completed our trials etc and returned to Portsmouth ready for Easter seasonal leave. There was a chance of a long weekend beforehand, however I was sent for and told "Iceland on Saturday".*
> *Having just finished work-up at Portland, I suppose we were reasonably trained up already for most things, but we were then warned about a bit more, namely 50 foot waves and ice - so shovels, picks and grease in large quantities were embarked. Apart from that, there was little time to get ready; certainly nothing could be done about the final stages of my wife's pregnancy!*
> *On the notice board in the main passageway, there were official photographs of all the uniformed skippers of the Icelandic gunboats that we were going to meet. Someone said that it looked like a rogues' gallery of U-boat commanders - anything to cheer us up!*
> *Unusually for a small ship like Dundas, Surgeon Lieutenant (Doctor) joined the ship just before we sailed - very reassuring!*
> *Thirty years ago, we had several very successful classes of anti-submarine frigate, of which Dundas was one of the smallest. I'm sure that the greatest admirer of our Navy would have to admit that none of these thin-skinned 1000-ton ships were really suitable for barging other vessels out of the way, 'though of course we had the speed and endurance to remain at sea for quite a while.*
> *As I understood things, we were not allowed to wilfully ram another ship; several of ours had been damaged by the opposition. The First Sea Lord, Admiral Sir John Treacher, had told us that the previous week he said to the Prime Minister, Harold Wilson, "Someone is going to get killed."*
> *When we arrived in Rosyth, on the way to Iceland, a friend of mine came across from his own ship Mermaid (damaged), looked down on to our ship and said to be "Be careful, they'll cut you in half".*
> *Actually, things turned out alright. A Type 14 had one very large single propeller, which when spun from full ahead to full astern tended to throw the stern to one side. This enabled us to avoid any actual contact with the gunboats when they got in amongst our fishing fleet and we managed to turn the Icelandics away from our vessels. This required a certain amount of agility "down below", especially in the boiler room by keeping the steam pressure and water levels steady during this quite violent manoeuvring, which was unusual for a peacetime navy.*
> *Actually it was quite exciting and the Captain (Lieutenant-Commander Mark Bush) sent for me after one particularly close encounter with the dreaded Baldur to say how successful this had been "Couldn't have done it without you fellows down below". Later that evening I received a signal - my third daughter had arrived.*
> *There was a fisherman from one of the trawlers who had to return to Grimsby for compassionate reasons (See 'Colin' the next anecdote), so we transferred him by boat and they filled our boat with fresh fish. Our galley was knee deep in cod; I was surprised how big they are. It was a number of years since the fishermen had seen a Type 14 and they were amazed how fast we could go. Dundas was an agile old lady.*
> *Instead of Action Stations, we had Gunboat Stations, which meant exactly the same thing really. Our fisherman passenger was quite astounded at what happened then - meals left unfinished and the Mess cleared in seconds!'*

Bryan 'Tiny' Height, who served in HMS *Palliser* in the First and Second Cod Wars, was now back again

[162] Chief Engine Room Artificer.

in *Dundas*, which must be something of a record. He remembers them all cheering one of the tugs on as she rode off a gunboat. His final thoughts on the Cod Wars are:

> *'The last two cod wars that I did cannot match the one we did in the early sixties. I remember HMS Agincourt alongside in Reykjavik, who would argue with her? Even HMS Decoy in 1958 and the other big destroyers who took part.*
> *Every time I go into the local fish and chips, people do not have a clue what risks were taken for their weekly treat. On the Dundas we brought back a trawlerman, Colin I think his name was from Hull. He lived in the PO's Mess and had recently lost a brother on a trawler that went down, also another brother before that. We certainly looked after him. I have been to Fleetwood and Hull, and now you see all the empty docks clear of trawlers.'*

The DFA is shifted to the Northwest and then back again

There had been discussion for some days about moving the DFA to the northwest again. The OTC had made it clear that there could not be two DFAs and so waited for the majority of the skippers to vote on a move. In the Liaison Skipper's daily round up at 1700 on 15th May 1976, by 17 votes to 15, the skippers agreed to the move and Captain Tait ordered an immediate shift to a new DFA, 100 miles long, between The Horn and Dyrafjord on Iceland's northwest corner.

At 1800 *Tartar*, *Eastbourne* and *Blue Rover* led the straggling convoy of 20 trawlers north-about in patchy fog, with *Dundas* and *Tidepool* in amongst the trawlers and *Lowestoft*, *Roysterer*, *Statesman* and *Euroman* bringing up the rear. *Ægir*, *Baldur* and *Thór* were around, but did not interfere. The Eastern DFA was closed, but *Leander* and *Salisbury* remained for another 12 hours, both to mark *Thór*, who was at sea, and to cover the last ten trawlers who were either topping up before heading home or delayed in moving to the new DFA.

By midday on 17th May, there were 27 trawlers in the new DFA, but as on the previous occasion in April, the grass was not 'greener on the other side of the road' and there were calls for a return to the east even before the stragglers had their nets in the water. That evening, the DFA was shifted back to the east after the skippers' round up.

On 18th May, *Southella* joined the patrol. Her arrival meant that three of the four civilian defence vessels - *Euroman*, *Lloydsman*, *Statesman* and now *Southella* - would always be on patrol. When they returned from the west the trawlers initially spread out all over the DFA, but fortunately for the defending forces, they soon coalesced into two groups, 100 miles apart. The foggy weather persisted, making gunboat location difficult and *Lowestoft* had to return home with technical defects.

A Draft Agreement is Reached so there are Five more Collisions.

Ægir, *Baldur* and *Thór* all entered the DFA on 18th and 19th May 1976, but only *Ægir* made a serious effort at harassment. On the evening of the 19th, the new British Foreign Secretary Antony Crosland went to Oslo for the NATO Ministerial meeting. That evening and over the next two days, he had discrete talks with his Icelandic opposite number, Einar Ágústsson, and finally, on the afternoon of 21st May, with the Icelandic Prime Minister, Geir Hallgrímsson.

Thanks to all the careful preparation by Knut Frydenlund, the Norwegian Foreign Minister[163], there was almost full agreement on the terms of the agreement. A daily average of 24 British trawlers would be permitted to fish between 20 and 200 miles for six months. The Icelanders had a few reservations over some of the details, particularly those concerning the EEC and asked for a little time to finalise these and to consult with their coalition partners. It was, however, agreed that both sides would move as quickly as possible so that an agreement could be announced and the defence forces could be withdrawn within a few days.

Some of the problems faced by the Icelandic Government are illustrated by an editorial in the inde-

[163] There remain strong feelings in Iceland that the Norwegian mediation efforts throughout all three Cod Wars were primarily driven by self-interest and, mainly, by the desire to keep Iceland in NATO so that there would be no pressure on Norway to host the facilities that the airbase at Keflavík provided.

pendent newspaper "*Dagbladid*" on 21st May in which it was stated that Einar Ágústsson should not have attended the NATO meeting. But should have stayed at home to protest against the:

> *'murder attempts of the British against the officers and men of the Coastguard vessel Tyr and other British acts of aggression.'*

The *Dagbladid* editorial concluded with:

> *'We ought to tell the NATO leaders clearly that if they do not yield to our demands in this matter of our vital interests, we will, following the recall of our ambassador (to NATO) and the closing of the base (Keflavík), withdraw from the alliance and send American forces home.*
> *If we lose the fishery limits war, there will be little to defend here.'*

Whilst the politicians were in discussion in Oslo, there were two more collisions, followed by three more on the day the Icelandic delegation returned home with the draft agreement. Once again the British Government had to wonder if the Icelandic Prime and Foreign Ministers were negotiating in good faith or just had no control over their government's servants. As one Foreign Office official noted:

> *'Matters were not made easier by the feeling of everyone who had been involved that Icelandic behaviour had been intolerable from first to last and it was a thankless task for the Ambassador (then resident in London) to attempt to explain why they acted as they did. It remains a conundrum whether there was a mastermind at work, perhaps Ólafur Jóhannesson[164], deliberately planning their campaign, or whether they simply out-muddled us.'*

HMS Salisbury & ICGV Aegir 'jousting' on 20th May 1976. They collided, with minor damage to each, twice that day.
(David Mathias)

[164] Ólafur Jóhannesson was Minister of Justice at the time, hence head of the Coastguard (the Coastguard comes under the Ministry of Justice). He was also Chairman of the Progressive Party, then in coalition with the bigger Independence Party, of which Prime Minister Geir Hallgrímsson was Chairman.

HMS Eastbourne - the Engineer's Training Ship - note the absence of a turret on her fo'c'sle
(Jón Páll Ásgeirsson)

That said, the Royal Navy had had enough and the response to attempted warp cutting in these final days was very robust.

The Final Act at Sea

On 20th May 1976, *Ægir* came out in the morning, between 0200 and 0630, and was successfully marked by *Salisbury* and *Dundas*. She reappeared in the afternoon and approached the group of trawlers south of The Whaleback at 1630. *Salisbury* (Commander Hugo White) warned *Ægir* to keep clear and took up a marking position 200 feet on her starboard beam. From there, *Salisbury* steered 5° in on *Ægir's* course so as to 'ease' her away from the nearest trawler. *Ægir* declined to be ridden off and, when the two ships were about 40 feet apart, altered sharply away to port, swinging her stern into *Salisbury's* side.

After this encounter, the two ships paralleled up and, about half a minute later, *Ægir* altered towards and struck *Salisbury* with her bow. *Salisbury* altered away at the last moment and avoided serious damage. HMS *Eastbourne* had been stationed a mile away on *Salisbury's* disengaged bow, ready to move in should *Ægir* have slipped past her marker. No warps were cut on this occasion, but once again a gunboat had shown that she was fully prepared to go for a frigate

ICGV Baldur collides with HMS Eastbounre on 20th May 1976. Both ships suffered significant damage in this incident. Note the warp cutter at Baldurs' stern.
(Robert Marshall)

if denied a trawler.

News of the likely settlement seems to have spurred the gunboat captains to a final flurry of aggression on the 22nd May. The weather was calm, with widespread fog. There were 41 British trawlers in the DFA, mainly in two groups south and southeast of The Whaleback. The OTC, mindful of the need to avoid incidents at this delicate stage of negotiations, advised the trawlers to haul early if a gunboat appeared, but his restraint was to be in vain.

Ægir was first into the DFA at 0715 when she appeared south of The Whaleback, heading south, marked by *Tartar*, still under Commander Jim Weatherall's command. At 0903, *Ægir* streamed her cutter and made towards the *Prince Philip*, fishing 2½ miles away. *Tartar* moved into a position 2 cables on *Ægir's* port beam and warned her not to interfere with any British trawlers. By steering a slightly converging course, *Tartar* succeeded in forcing *Ægir* away from her target.

Once past *Prince Philip*, *Ægir* stopped and *Tartar* followed suit. They lay stopped for 45 minutes until the tug *Euroman* came up from the east, when *Ægir* got underway again and headed towards another trawler, about 5 miles distant. *Tartar* followed and took station half a cable on *Ægir's* starboard beam this time, again steering a converging course.

This time *Ægir* did not give way but at 1033, when the range was down to 10-15 feet, turned hard to port and swung her stern into *Tartar*. *Tartar* matched the turn, so minimising any damage, and forced *Ægir* round 90° to port before breaking off. Neither ship was much damaged and when the civilian defence vessel *Southella* joined *Tartar*, *Ægir* retired to the northwest, into the 12-mile line.

Baldur appeared at about 1130 and was marked by *Eastbourne*, with *Dundas* in company. Visibility was about half a mile as the three ships headed south towards the trawlers. In spite of warnings not to harass British trawlers fishing legally on the high seas, *Baldur* persisted and by 1220 was within 2 or 3 miles of several trawlers. The trawlers had been advised to haul by the OTC, but by sending *Dundas* ahead to check out the situation, it was clear that some had decided to ignore this advice.

As *Baldur* now had several potential targets, the frigates stationed themselves at two cables on each quarter, ready to intervene once *Baldur's* intentions became clear. Eventually, at 1234, the *Lord Jericho*, still hauling her nets, became visible in the fog fine on the port bow at 7 cables and *Baldur* immediately altered course towards to cut her warps. Lieutenant Commander Mark Kemmis Betty, the Commanding Officer of *Eastbourne* marking from *Baldur's* port quarter, was determined not to let her do this and so, whilst again warning the gunboat, he came up to full

The damage to HMS Eastbourne after her collision with ICGV Baldur.
(Robert Marshall)

The ICGV Ægir runs the gauntlet with HMS Tartar marking her to port.
(Bryan Height)

speed to get between *Baldur* and *Lord Jericho*.

Neither Commanding Officer was prepared to give way and about a minute later *Eastbourne*, now doing 25 knots, hit *Baldur*, doing about 18, port side amidships. *Baldur* altered to starboard just before the collision and *Eastbourne* followed suit, thus narrowing the angle of impact, but the damage was still significant. *Eastbourne's* bow sheared *Baldur's* forward trawler gantry away from the deck on the port side. *Eastbourne* herself received two gashes in her starboard bow and had some secondary buckling and splitting.

Baldur made a final but unsuccessful attempt to cut the *Lord Jericho's* warps and then retired across the 12-mile line. She was back in the DFA three days later with her whole forward gantry removed. *Eastbourne* was the Engineering Apprentices Training Ship and so had 52 eager MEA[165] apprentices plus their training staff onboard. All the apprentices had recently completed their NBCD[166] course at HMS *Phoenix*, so the challenge of patching and shoring *Eastbourne's* bow section was met with relish. She remained on patrol fully operational.

The day's activities were not over yet. HMS *Leander* (OTC) and *Ver* were in company from about 1430. *Ver* made several aggressive, but unsuccessful, warp cutting runs, getting within feet of *Leander* and once coming so close that her cutter wire caught on the frigate's bow. At 1513, *Ver* stopped for 20 minutes and then approached the trawlers once more.

After further very close quarters high-speed manoeuvres in her attempt to get at the trawler *Jacinta*, *Ver* and *Leander* collided. Only a last minute order of full astern by *Leander* reduced the violence of the impact. It has been estimated that *Leander* was doing 24 knots and *Ver* about 18 when they hit. *Leander's* port bow struck *Ver's* starboard bridge wing at an angle of about 40°. *Ver's* bridge wing was destroyed and her superstructure holed and badly distorted down to main deck level. She returned to Reykjavik for repairs (funded as usual by Lloyds of London) and took no further part in the dispute.

Leander's bow was badly distorted and holed, with flooding in the forepeak. After shoring the forward bulkheads, she was seaworthy enough to remain on patrol as the command ship, with a maximum safe speed of 10 knots.

Despite this mutual aggression, there were still occasional incidents of mutual co-operation. On 22nd May, the British trawler *Vianova* and the Icelandic *Bjartur* accidentally entangled their nets.

[165] Marine Engineering Artificer aka Tiffy
[166] Nuclear, Biological and Chemical defence and Damage control

HMS Exmouth, the Royal Navy's gas turbine trials ship, was deployed on Icelandic patrol for the last week of the last Cod War. By this stage, the shortage of frigate hulls was severe.
(Jón Páll Ásgeirsson)

The more-powerful *Bjartur* gradually towed *Vianova* over the 12-mile line as Commander Jim Weatherall in *Tartar* watched nearby. The Defence Commander in *Southella* was able to arrange a truce with the captain of *Ægir*, who sent three of his men over to help disentangle the two trawlers' nets.

Talks start in Oslo

One outcome of the Foreign Ministers' talks in the margins of the NATO meeting had been an agreement that the two Fishery Ministers should meet and this meeting took place in the Icelandic Embassy in Oslo on 23rd May 1976. The rash of collisions did not derail the peace process, if anything it strengthened it. The British view was that the Royal Navy's robust defence of the trawlers had made it clear that British fishermen would be protected until a settlement was reached. The Fishery Ministers' meeting agreed to aim for a final agreement within a week.

There was a reduction in gunboat activity immediately after the 22nd. *Tyr* and *Ver* were in Reykjavik having collision damage repaired and *Òdinn* was just finishing a maintenance period. She was expected back on patrol on 27th May. *Ægir*, *Baldur* and *Thór* were at sea, policing Icelandic fishermen as well as making the occasional foray into the DFA, where there were plenty of defending assets to contain them.

On 23rd May, HMS *Exmouth,* commanded by Lieutenant-Commander John Davies, arrived to replace *Lowestoft*. *Exmouth* was a Type 14 frigate that had been extensively modified to act as the Royal Navy's gas turbine propulsion trials ship. She had one Olympus and two Proteus gas turbines driving a single controllable-pitch screw and so could both accelerate and decelerate very quickly. *Baldur* was the first gunboat to meet *Exmouth* and it was clear that her acceleration and manoeuvrability caused some surprise. *Exmouth* was a mixed blessing to the OTC. She required more frequent refuelling and suffered a number of breakdowns.

Ægir slipped unseen into the DFA on 24th May and made an unopposed warp cutting run on *Jacinta* (the trawler that *Leander* had been damaged protecting). Luckily for *Jacinta*, the cutter wire parted. The 25th saw the departure of the tanker *Tidepool* (Captain David Thompson), after 32 days on station. This was the longest period that any Royal Navy or Royal Fleet Auxiliary ship had spent off Iceland since *Wave Ruler* (Captain Bob McKenzie) had spent 36 days on station in September/October 1958. The other lengthy patrol was of 39 days by *Olwen* (Captain Jim Coull) covering the period of the peace talks in January/February 1976, when defence forces were withdrawn to wait outside 200 miles.

The final turnover, in fact, happened next day, 26th, when Captain Bob McQueen in HMS *Diomede* relieved Captain John Tait in HMS *Leander* as OTC and HMS *Achilles* relieved HMS *Eastbourne*. RFA *Olwen* was the new tanker. Both *Leander* and *Eastbourne* returned to the UK for major repairs. *Eastbourne* had been the first ship on patrol in the First Cod War in September 1958. She missed being the last one on patrol in the Third by 5 days.

The Final Collision

The final collision was on 26th May 1976 and it was perhaps fitting that *Ægir*, driven by the 'Mad Axeman', the British press's favourite 'bogeyman' should be involved. Commander Jim Weatherall, of HMS *Tartar*, reported the day's events in his Collision Report:

> *'HMS Tartar and HMS Diomede loose marked Ægir stopped 15 miles NE of the main UK trawler group throughout the night of 25/26 May. At 0240 Ægir started making ground towards the nearest of the trawlers to the southwest. HMS Dundas and HMS Tartar closed to mark at ½ a cable at 0445, the Dundas to starboard and the Tartar to port. At 0520 Lloydsman was controlled to approach from ahead. This caused Ægir to break from his approach and cut across the bows of HMS Tartar, circling to port before making off to the northwest. It was decided to steer Ægir away from British trawlers fishing nearby and then to the 12-mile limit, where Lloydsman would be detached to return to her trawler group. Shortly after the nearest trawler had reached his closest point of approach ½ mile to port, Ægir was very close to starboard and drawing slightly ahead of HMS Tartar. What may have been an attempt to swing his stern resulted in a swing to port across HMS Tartar's bow considered to be caused by interactions. The Tartar went full astern in order to avoid this collision, but Ægir's stern came into light contact with the Tartar's starboard bow. Under firm escort of two frigates and one defence tug, Ægir then proceeded inside the*

HMS Tartar vs ICGV Aegir on the final day of actual hostilities - 26th May 1976 (David Mathias)

12-mile limit without causing further problems.'

This account makes it clear that by this stage, the Royal Navy had the initiative within the DFA. An occasional warp cutting was still attempted, right up to the end and the British forces had to maintain their full defensive posture.

The Final Agreement

The draft agreement was discussed both in Iceland and within the EEC and on 28th May 1976 it was decided that Foreign Ministers should meet in Oslo on 31st to clear up the final details and to sign the agreement. The 28th May agreement also stipulated that the defending forces would be withdrawn outside 200 miles and that the Coastguard would not cut any warps, provided trawlers hauled when ordered to do so.

The Icelandic Fisheries Minister remembers Antony Crosland saying to him:

'I shouldn't be surprised if my constituents finish me off for having done this. But for you the situation is quite different. You will return home as victors.'

Operations DEWEY and HELIOTROPE were suspended from 2100 on 30th May. The frigates, tankers and Royal Maritime Auxiliary Service tug withdrew, Royal Air Force Nimrod surveillance flights stopped and the civilian defence vessels reverted to MAFF control and were also withdrawn. HM Ships *Diomede* (OTC), *Achilles*, *Tartar*, *Exmouth*, *Naiad* (having relieved *Dundas* on 27th May) and *Torquay* (having relieved *Salisbury* on 30th), together with RFAs *Olwen* and *Blue Rover*, RMAS *Rollicker*, the defence tugs *Lloydsman* and *Euroman* plus the civilian defence vessel *Southella* remained just outside 200 miles until the evening of 1st June. *Statesman*, having been en route, was immediately sent back to Dundee. Two weeks later, she was back at her normal job, acting as lead tug for the *Brent Spar* tow.

On the afternoon of 1st June 1976, Antony Crosland the British Foreign Secretary and Einar Ágústsson, the Icelandic Foreign Minister signed the agreement ending the Third Cod War. At 1830 the MoD signalled:

'1. UK and Icelandic mediators have reached agreement settling dispute over fisheries off Iceland.
2. Operation DEWEY is cancelled.
3. HM Ships, RFAs, embarked aircraft and RMAS tugs allocated to DEWEY may be withdrawn and tasked as required.'

The Cod Wars were over. Kenneth East returned to Iceland as British Ambassador a day or so later. However, there was still much to do, not least in explaining to the fishing community what this agreement meant and in trying to help those who would now lose their livelihood.

Nothing Gained

Jim Dalrymple of the "*Sunday Independent*" was onboard HMS *Naiad* for that last patrol. His poignant report (published on 13th June 1976) well illustrates how the Royal Navy felt:

'The nasty little war ended with four silent ships stopped on an icy and painted ocean, moodily glowering at each other like boxers between rounds. We were nine miles off the southeast coast of Iceland and the vessel in the centre of the little cameo was the squat, powerful gunboat Ægir, her helicopter flight-deck buckled and her hull ripped and scraped along its length from a dozen skirmishes.
Around her, in perfect triangulation, stood the Royal Navy frigates Naiad and Diomede - and the huge ocean-going tug Statesman. Away to the south-west the lads from Hull and Fleetwood lay in a bunch, steam rising from their winches, dirty and businesslike, pulling in the cod as if there was to be no tomorrow. And we all knew that there would be no tomorrow for most of them.
It was silent, beautiful and menacing - the wolf, the shepherds and the flock frozen in a pure liquid bowl of the sea and sky where you can see forever. The air was immaculate. Nothing shameful can live. The shame was about to end, finished finally around a table in Oslo by the ham-handed politicians who had started it all in the first place.
The airwaves between our small flotilla, the

giant Ministry of Defence barn in Whitehall and the peace-talking politicos in Oslo were alive with signals.

At last one came. The one everybody wanted to hear.

Without ceremony the shepherds - the frigates and the big tugs - turned away from the wolves and made 15 knots to the edge of Iceland's 200-mile limit. The floating factories of Hull pulled in their nets.

The war the Navy hated was over.

Captain Tony Casdagli, 44-year-old skipper of HMS Naiad, veteran of four patrols to The Ice - as the Navy calls the Cod War - stood a few feet away from me on the bridge and smiled: "At least you saw a gunboat. Looked pretty peaceful didn't he?"

There was no bitterness in his voice. Throughout the eight nights and days I spent in his ship he made no remark that could have been remotely critical of his Whitehall masters. Just as he barely raised his voice when his frigate ... had played dodgems with armour-hulled gunboats on the most ferocious winter seas in the world.

For the last six months he, and senior officers like him, were reduced to the status of American footballers running interference - and making sure nobody got killed in the process. Down below, the 250 men who lived in the Naiad and who had worn their nerves and their bodies to a frazzle were not so reticent.

The ship's Wasp helicopter pilot, Lieutenant Bob Turner, is also the ship's joker and born mimic.

He rolled grandly on the wardroom carpet when the ceasefire news came through, groaning like an elderly admiral with gout: "Gad Sir, the burning shame of it", he roared. "D'ye know what day this is dammit? It's the day the Battle of Jutland ended. Jutland, by God. What are we reduced to? What have we come to?"

And he sobbed mightily. But there was an edge to his performance. It WAS the day Jutland ended - and not so long ago at that.

The First Lieutenant, Lieutenant-Commander Bill Christie took 25 years to come through the ranks and he is proud of the Navy and its role. He doesn't make with the jokes. He told me before we set off for the ice: "Both my wife and my father have made it plain to me that they don't like what we are doing up there."

"I suppose it is a feeling that is shared by a big majority of people in the country and in many ways you can't blame them. When we came up in January we learned a kind of warfare that is totally alien to us, using these very sophisticated ships in a role that was bizarre, to say the least.

But we learned how and we learned quickly and we passed our knowledge to others that followed.

Nothing, absolutely nothing has been gained. We can only hope that the so-called Cod War will not leave lasting bitterness between ourselves and the Icelanders. They are fine seamen who, over the years, have saved the lives of many of our fishermen. I hope they will consider that we had a job to do, like them, and now it is over."

That said, though, nobody onboard Naiad would deny that the greatest moment of the entire waste of time came on April 24 when the 'little lady' finally gave them what for.

Naiad, her huge turbines going full astern, put a hole in the side of Tyr after a high speed, nerve-rattling run for the trawlers. Technically Tyr rammed Naiad. Like the man who thumped the other fellow's fist with his nose.

"It was a good moment for the ship that" said Bill Christie. "It made a hell of a mess of our bows and it was highly dangerous, but the ship's morale shot up because we are after all, an aggressive service and we felt that we had shown our worth."

The collision, and dozens of other incidents involving near things, were hairy enough on Naiad's bridge. On the engine-room plates it had been like something written by Dante. Frank McDonald, the quiet-spoken Marine Engineering Officer said: "For some of the younger lads down below it was, frankly terrifying. The First Lieutenant - old Golden Larynx himself - gave the men a full running

commentary of what was happening[167].
But they knew that at any second the bows of a gunboat could come battering through the ship's plates, above and beside them, and through the boilers beside their heads."
This kind of strain went on all the time, even when the seas were running before a force nine gale, in temperatures where exposure to water even for a few seconds would stop the blood of a man and kill him as surely as a bullet through the brain.
And the trawlermen being protected? Were they grateful? Not really.
As one petty officer put it: "Those guys would have had us using missiles on a gunboat. When we missed the gunboat and it made a warp cutting run we were effing cissies. When we stopped they wondered why we didn't sink it. They're wild you know. They drink like ship's engines most of the time and I saw one trawler skipper whose warps had just been cut standing on his bridge throwing knives and forks at a gunboat.
He was cursing and raving and trying to chase it, telling it not to be an effing coward and turn round and fight. There's no agreement on earth that'll stop those lads fishing inside the 200-mile limit. As the kind of money those skippers make, around £30,000[168] *a year, they'll be running the gunboat blockade until they're either boarded or sunk. The Cod War is over for us, but not for them."*
For us it was over. Under the midnight sun we watched our shepherds - the frigate task group - break off and stream down from the Arctic for, hopefully the last time. We were led by the jaunty little Tartar[169]*, immortalised on radio by Tony Blackburn as being a saucy thing after she made a monkey out of the angry Ódinn.*
In Naiad's wardroom we had cod and chips, fresh from the belly of a friendly trawler, and talk about ship's 'buzzes' - the rumours that flash up in a minute and last for days. "Amazing things buzzes", said Frank McDonald. "I once started one in the engine room, paused in the heads on the way to the bridge, and was given an expanded version of the same buzz by a watchkeeper up there. My own rumour had beaten me by seconds." The buzz was that we were off to the Clyde for rest and recreation. It was right. The captain confirmed it. Another rumour was that the flotilla's padre had exorcised the gunboat Baldur - a particularly tenacious and brutal type - but that was unconfirmed.
We munched our fish and chip suppers and cracked jokes about gunboat skippers, trawler skippers and hairy moments during the Cod War.
Nobody talked about politicians. Then it wouldn't have been a joke any more.'

Dave Winning of HMS *Diomede* thought that:

'A lot of people in naval circles scoff when you mention the Cod Wars as they were not a true war. I believe that of all the conflicts the Royal Navy has been involved in during the last 3 decades, only during the Cod Wars and the Falklands have the Royal Navy's ships sustained severe enough damage to test our damage control procedures to the limits. Having spoken to many people who were involved in the Cod Wars we all agree on two things:
We all get quite annoyed when people who were not there pass snide comments about how it was only a glorified fish patrol and, secondly, of all the campaign medals we hold it is a shame that one was never issued for our service off the Icelandic Coast.'

One cannot but agree with these sentiments. On the latter point, the politicians could hardly have been asked to issue a medal for something that had been such an unmitigated political disaster but when a bar

[167] In almost every ship, the First Lieutenant would have given a running commentary on the action so that all those down below knew what was going on & were better able to prepare in case …
[168] By some measurements, equal to £250,000 in 2006.
[169] There is no record of a run in between *Tartar* & *Ódinn*. Jim Dalrymple or Tony Blackburn may well have meant to say *Gurkha* - who had several very close encounters with *Ódinn*.

to the General Service Medal for 'Gulf' was issued to the ships that 'escorted[170]' British tankers into and out of the Arabian Gulf during the Iran-Iraq War, you do have to wonder about the criteria for issuing medals.

[170] At the time the term 'escorting' was not allowed to be used, the Armilla patrol ships used to 'accompany' the tankers. The 'Gulf' bar to the GSM was actually issued, so legend has it, because a poorly-briefed Minister (or perhaps he just hadn't listened) told a sailors' messdeck that they would get a medal. As one contributor also observed - no medal was awarded for the Battle of Copenhagen either. Nelson was not happy.

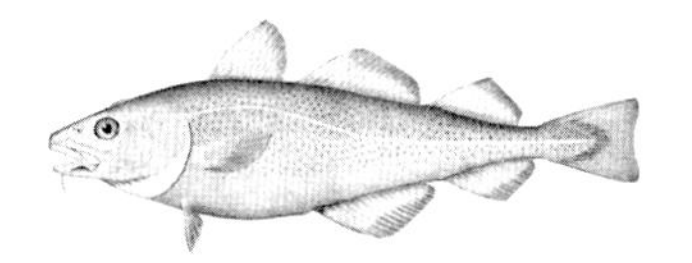

CHAPTER 23

AFTERMATH AND ASSESSMENT

The immediate political problem in Britain on 1st June 1976 was to explain the terms of the settlement to the fishing industry. The Oslo Agreement allowed a daily average of 24 British trawlers to fish between 20 and 200 miles off Iceland's coasts for a further six months. There were more conservation areas, including extra prohibited areas. It was calculated that the agreement would provide a catch of about 30,000 tons over the six-month period.

The British fishing industry was shocked when they realised the extent of the 'sell-out' that had been negotiated. Whilst most people in the industry had realised that the writing was on the wall for British distant-water fishing[171], the scale and suddenness of the change caught almost everyone involved by surprise. The grudging realisation that realism and commonsense had prevailed did not help much on Humberside, especially as the EEC's Common Fishery Policy (CFP), which had been negotiated on the eve of Britain's entry to the EEC, favoured the continental nations at the expense of the British.

Unless the CFP could be re-negotiated, the declaration of an EEC 200-mile Exclusive Economic Zone, whilst excluding non-EEC nations, would have the effect of opening up all British waters between 12 and 200 miles to the fishing vessels of all the other EEC nations. Antony Crosland, the Foreign Secretary, made the following statement in Parliament on 7th June 1976:

> *'Since my predecessor, now Prime Minister (Jim Callaghan), last made a statement to the House on this dispute on 4th February, much has changed.*
>
> *The Law of the Sea Conference has met again and, while no final agreement was reached, the trend towards 200-mile limits is now clearly irreversible. Thirteen countries have already declared such limits. Canada, the United States, Norway and other countries have publicly announced their intention to extend to 200 miles, and Britain is inviting the EEC to do the same at an early date. It was against this background, of an inexorable world-wide move towards 200 mile limits, a move from which Britain and the EEC cannot long remain exempt, that the Government had to decide whether once more to seek an agreement with Iceland - an agreement that would inevitably be on the lines of the one that I concluded last week.*
>
> *What were the alternatives? There was in fact only one. That was to continue to pursue the Cod War, with the certainty of dangerous escalation, with international and especially NATO opinion moving sharply against us, at a mounting cost in terms of naval protection, with our moral position steadily eroding as nation after nation accepted the principle of 200 miles, until, after only a few months, Britain and the EEC ourselves accepted 200 miles. At that moment, any claim on waters off Iceland would disappear; meanwhile, we should have lost goodwill on a massive scale, and our bargaining position with the Community over the common fisheries policy would have been seriously complicated.*
>
> *No informed observer has argued for this option, and that includes many of those*

[171] It was not only the problems with Iceland that impinged upon the industry's future. The OPEC oil price rises fed directly through into the fishing industry. The fuel bill for the whole of the UK fishing industry was £8million in 1972; by 1976 it was over £33 million. The 45 oil-burning steam trawlers had been the first to go in 1974/5. From the beginning of 1974 to the end of 1975, the British distant-water fleet decreased by 27% and the middle-water fleet by 16%.

trawler owners and others who have been so vociferous in their public condemnation of this agreement .....

I should like to express my thanks to Mr Knut Frydenlund, the Norwegian Foreign Minister, for his invaluable help in making possible the contacts which led to this agreement, and also to the NATO Secretary General for his efforts in the same direction.

This agreement has been as passionately denounced in Reykjavik[172] *as it has on Humberside. I regard it as a concession only to common sense. There is no point in yearning for the unattainable. We must now concentrate on the future. This is the first step in a long process of adaption which the British fishing industry, like other fishing industries, will have to face in the new world of 200 mile limits. The next steps will be an urgent study by the Government of what help can be given towards the restructuring of the industry, the revision of the common fisheries policy, and a decision by the EEC on its own 200-mile limit.*

..... I am certain that with help from the Government and the EEC, while relying on its own resilience and initiative, the British fishing industry will emerge from these changes a different but still a vital and prosperous industry.'

In answer to a question on starting negotiations with Iceland in order to achieve a new agreement before the six months ran out, the Foreign Secretary said:

'Another Cod war at the end of six months is the last thing that I should have thought anyone would want, on either side of the House. As regards starting the negotiations quickly, the negotiations will be undertaken by the EEC, as the agreement makes plain, and we have made it clear to the EEC that there is a great need for hurry in this matter to avoid an awkward gap at the end of the six month period.'

In retrospect, there was no real chance of any extension beyond the initial six months. As a result of the Oslo Agreement, Iceland had been granted the EEC tariff concessions that had been denied for so long and the EEC had little else to offer Iceland, certainly there was no interest in reciprocal fishing rights within the EEC's 200 mile limit. Added to this problem was the fact that the Community was still arguing internally about access to each others waters (the CFP again), and that two EEC nations (West Germany and Belgium) already had quota agreements in Icelandic waters. What were the EEC to offer in exchange for these agreements?

The West German agreement with Iceland expired on 28th November 1977 and was not renewed. After that date, only a few Belgians, Norwegian and Faeroese fisherman had the right to fish in Icelandic waters under small-scale quota arrangements.

Out at Sea

On the fishing grounds, the new regime had to be explained to the unhappy trawlermen, who whilst now spared harassment and warp cutting, had to move further out to sea, from 12 to 20 miles, and were faced with additional closed areas. With the advice and support of the civilian support ships, serious incidents were avoided.

The Royal Air Force restarted their regular 'Cold War' surface and sub-surface surveillance flights from 2nd June 1976, initially keeping well clear of all fishing vessels and gunboats, but once the ban on the Royal Air Force using Keflavík was lifted on 24th June, normal patrol patterns were re-established. The Royal Navy reintroduced distant-water fishery patrols, although all activity in Icelandic waters was left to the civilian support ships. Frigates patrolled to Norwegian waters in October and November 1976, the latter, by *HMS Berwick*, being the Royal Navy's last ever distant-water fishery patrols and the ending of a 500-year-old task.

The last British trawler left Icelandic waters on 1st December 1976. On 1st January 1977, the EEC 200 mile Exclusive Economic Zone (EEZ) came into effect. The USA, Canada, Russia and Norway, amongst other nations, declared 200 mile EEZs at

[172] There were left wing protests in Iceland that even 30,000 tons over 6 months was too much, but the vast majority were content to have settled the dispute.

about the same time. The EEC did manage to negotiate an annual quota with Norway, but as this had to be shared by all the Community's fishing nations, the British share was a fraction of what Britain had traditionally caught in these areas.

The Russians closed their EEZ to foreigners and, without the Icelandic fishing grounds as an alternative and a stop-off on the way to and fro, it was no longer economic for British trawlers to fish off Greenland. By mid-1977 all of the traditional British distant-water fishing grounds were covered by 200 mile EEZs. The pattern of British fishing changed rapidly with, necessarily, much more emphasis on Community waters. Distant-water trawlers were laid up and paid off in huge numbers from 1977 and within a year or so, the British distant-water fishing fleet had all but disappeared.

Some trawlers were converted to oil rig support vessels, two were sold to Greenpeace, *St Giles* and *Westella*, some went to work off New Zealand, South Africa, Australia, Norway, Nigeria and Iran and five were requisitioned as minesweepers during the Falklands War - the *Junella*, *Cordella*, *Northella*, *Farnella* and *Pict*. This wholesale scrapping or sale of trawlers obviously affected both the fishermen and the, much larger[173], numbers who worked in the support sectors of the industry - everything from fish processing and distribution, through victualling and ship repairs. The impact on employment and general economic activity in Hull, Grimsby and Fleetwood was disastrous. Whole communities were destroyed. Aberdeen, the other major distant-water fishing port was shielded from the worst by the North Sea oil boom.

Many, if not most, of the trawler skippers, mates, engineers and radio officers were able to find employment somewhere in the world, but for the deck hands, with few if any qualifications, life was much harsher. Having signed on and off for each trip, they were classed as temporary 'casual' workers and so not entitled to redundancy payments. Some ex-gratia payments were made between 1993 and 1995, but the main battle to right this patent injustice lasted until 28th July 2000, when the Compensation Scheme for former Icelandic Water Trawlermen was announced. The Government finally recognised:

> *'... that former Icelandic water trawlermen suffered an injustice. Many lost their jobs as a result of the settlement of the 'Cod Wars' and received little or no help.'*

The compensation scheme provided £1000 per year served at sea, with a maximum of £20,000. In the 20+ years that the campaign for compensation lasted many of those who would have been eligible died. An additional scheme, covering those who had been unreasonably excluded from the two previous ones, was announced in October 2001. The trawler owners received £23 million in compensation soon after the Third Cod War ended, with about £175 million more later (much of it EEC funds) for scrapping their trawlers.

Conservation

Sadly, people seem to find it very difficult to be objective about conservation and, whilst it may be better to overcorrect a bit than to leave things until too late, unless there is some degree of consensus, any conservation restrictions will be ignored by some, if not most, of those they aim to control. The fate of the cod fisheries on the Grand Banks and the herring off northern Iceland show us that even the most bountiful fish stocks are vulnerable to overfishing, but the trouble is that pressure groups and nations have brought the science of conservation into grave disrepute by using so-called facts for their own political purposes.

There is no doubt that Icelandic cod stocks would not have survived had they been subject to unregulated fishing using the most modern methods, but there is no such certainty about the figures presented as justification for declaring the 50-mile limit in 1971 or the 'Black Report' that the British were 'bounced' with in October 1975. The British fishing industry has moved on, if that is the right expression, from disputing the scientific basis of Icelandic conservation measures to the discredited EU quota system, which is a prime example of what happens to conservation measures[174], when they are widely perceived to be more the result of political manoeuvring than

[173] Estimated at 8 people 'behind' each fisherman. It was also estimated that 33% of Hull's total income was derived from the trawlers.

[174] The Times of 30th April 2005 reported that 'Up to 50 per cent of all fish caught in Britain are landed illegally'.

agreed scientific facts. Iceland, who led in the introduction of fishing conservation areas and used their 'facts' politically, must share some of the blame for the lack of respect that fishermen have for quotas and conservation generally.

The Royal Navy's Lessons Learnt

The Royal Navy's Aim[175] and the Government 'perceived' Aim

The Navy's aim, though expressed differently between 1958 and 1976, was constant - to protect trawlers from interference and to provide an environment in which fishing could continue uninterrupted. This aim was, on the whole, achieved although less successfully after the advent of the warp-cutter and barely during the period of '*Avoid Damage to Frigates*' in April and May 1976.

Her Majesty's Government never really established an 'aim'. The concept is problematical for politicians and anathema to diplomats, who like to have the freedom to bend to the political wind until the last possible moment. From the naval perspective, it seemed that HMG's long-term aim was to ensure that fishing continued for as long as possible under the latest legal international rules and agreements and to negotiate advantageous arrangements for the future.

There was always the implicit acknowledgement that the rules were changing, but a refusal to recognise any changes until they were internationally legally agreed. This strict adherence to the legal process did not find favour with the Icelandic government or people. Commodore Anderson's briefing at No 10 Downing Street in 1958 'Stand no nonsense .... do your best to avoid any incidents', perhaps unfairly, illustrates the politicians' view that a holding operation was all that was needed.

If this perception of HMG's aim is correct, it was certainly never achieved. All of the three Cod War settlements required the British Government to accept Icelandic positions that had been unacceptable when that particular conflict had started and, in every case, the final settlement was worse for the British fishing industry that the final offer made by Iceland before naval intervention. The British fishing industry had a powerful voice and its survival was considered (rightly) to be at risk, foreign interference with British ships on what were legally the High Seas was not acceptable and Britain did try, at every opportunity, to negotiate with Iceland before sending the Royal Navy in.

There is no evidence that any negotiating strategy or acceptance of any of the Icelandic offers would have made any difference to the final outcome.

Military Advice to Her Majesty's Government

The Navy, rightly, had no say in the decision to intervene or not - that was a political decision. However, it is vital that political decision makers understand the practical implications of any intervention and this is where military advice is essential.

In 1958, it was assumed that the defensive task would be of short duration and even once it became clear that this was not to be so, there was agreement between the politicians and the Services as to how to fulfil it.

In 1972/3, the Navy was keen to avoid another open-ended defensive commitment[176] and tried hard to persuade Ministers that a short, sharp offensive, using overwhelming force, would be more effective. This was not politically acceptable. From then onwards until the end in 1976, the MoD continued to advise Ministers about the difficulty of providing protection without using weapons, the vulnerability of the thin-skinned frigates to ramming by the gunboats, the effect on the Navy's other commitments and the dangers to NATO.

Whilst acknowledging these factors, Ministers decided, again and again, that the protection of British fishing vessels on the high seas had a higher priority. Given that political ruling, the navy continued to do as well as it could in the circumstances. The one period when naval protection failed was during the '*Avoid Damage to Frigates*' period (27th March to 6th May 1976) and, interestingly, it was FOSNI, Vice Admiral Troup, who initiated this policy and Ministers who merely rubber-stamped it. Arguably, the robust reaction of the ships on task when the policy was reversed reflected, at least partly, the seagoing Navy's embarrassment at their failure to protect the trawlers.

[175] Service teaching is that there can only ever be one 'Aim' in an operation, with supporting 'Objectives', every one of which must be checked to see that it does, indeed, support the 'Aim'.

[176] 'Mission Creep' in today's jargon.

The Use of Force

Once committed to an operation, the Services need to know how much force they are going to be permitted to use to achieve their aim. By the Second Cod War the Rules of Engagement (RoE) system was well understood and provided the means by which careful graduations in force could be matched to changing circumstances. There were still a few areas of doubt - for example the question over the 3 or 4-mile limit of Icelandic territorial waters in 1972 and the matter of 'hot pursuit' in the case of the *Lord St Vincent* in 1973, but on the whole Commanding Officers commented on the clarity of their instructions.

In 1958 however, Commanding Officers were just issued with 12 paragraphs[177] on 'the use of force'. These made it clear that gunfire was available and could be used in support of the 'utmost endeavours to prevent the arrest of British fishing vessels on the high seas, and to secure the release of any such vessel which had been arrested.' There were graduated circumstances for using blank warning shots, live warning shots and direct fire, with the final caveat that 'the object of such fire would be to destroy the Icelandic vessel's gun. No attempt should be made to sink the Icelandic vessel.'

Fortunately these comparatively generous rules were not needed as, certainly after the Northern Foam incident, the clear and robust determination of the destroyer and frigate commanding officers to defend the trawlers was sufficient to deter the gunboats from attempting arrest in the Royal Navy's presence.

The advent of the warp-cutter completely changed the balance of power between the Royal Navy and the Icelandic Coastguard. To prevent warp-cutting meant getting into increasingly hazardous close quarters situations, situations in which the frigates were more vulnerable to serious damage than the gunboats. These close quarters 'jousts' also provided the gunboat captains with a valuable national - and self - publicity platform. The correlation of embarked press and TV crews and collisions in the Second and Third Cod wars was much too close for there to be any doubt about the cause and effect.

The Royal Navy had no effective defence against deliberate ramming other than gunfire, or as it can be argued happened two or three times, more ramming. To avoid getting into this situation, the heavily-built tugs could be brought into play, but their speed disadvantage meant that good, early intelligence of the gunboats movements was needed. A degree of bluff and, sometimes unjustified, confidence on voice circuits would sometimes do the trick and keep a gunboat from making that final effort to get past her marker to the trawler target, but when that bluff was called, as during late April and early May 1976, the Navy was powerless and fishing came to a stop.

The British Government's dilemma was always how much force could be authorised whilst remaining totally within international law and whilst causing the least international disquiet or causing a rift in NATO. For the Navy this dilemma crystallised into how much protection could be given without rendering the frigate giving that protection non-operational as the result of a collision.

It is not surprising that gunfire was never authorised, or even seriously considered by Whitehall during the Second or Third Cod Wars. The norms of international behaviour had changed since 1961. The Palmerstonian response of 'Send a Gunboat' was no longer acceptable to the rest of the international community. It is also not a surprise that the authority to 'ride off' was, in effect, withdrawn for a period. Had it not been, however, the final three weeks might not have been so violent.

The Effect on Operational Effectiveness

Despite the concerns about training and operational effectiveness expressed from time to time, all three Cod Wars provided the Navy with useful experience, some inevitably, being re-learnt. In February 1959 the First Sea Lord, Admiral Lord Louis Mountbatten, wrote:

> *'For small ships to have to keep on station in the open sea in the face of full Arctic gales has been an experience in seamanship and countering hardships which has given their ships' companies a quality of training previously only obtained under conditions of war.'*

[177] Today's Rules of Engagement fill a substantial book.

Commodore Anderson, the Commodore Fishery Protection Squadron at the start of the First Cod War, replied to the concern that the Iceland patrol was 'paralysing fleet training' with:

> *'In my opinion, shared by many Captains(D), operations off Iceland have been and are providing valuable training for our Commanding Officers and ships' companies in keeping their ships going for long periods; RAS in all weathers; exacting seamanship; and team spirit within ships. In addition these operations are taking place in waters in which we may well operate in time of war. Apart from this, many and varied defects in the design of our new ships and their equipment have come to light.'*

And Admiral Troup, in his final report as Flag Officer Scotland and Northern Ireland (FOSNI) at the end of the Third Cod War, wrote:

> *'A whole mass of lessons were relearned the hard way by operations in Arctic conditions, particularly RAS.'*

Weather was, of course a, if not the, ruling factor, not just in where it was safe to fish once the shelter of the Icelandic fjords was denied, but also in the safety of men and ships whilst conducting their operational tasks. The Coastguard, of course could, and usually did, stay in harbour or sheltered in the lee of land when the weather was particularly foul. The frequency and sudden onset of violent storms and the dangers of icing were ever-present concerns.

All aspects of seamanship were regularly tested to the limits, in particular boatwork and replenishment in marginal conditions. The Navy also relearnt many of the basics of operating regularly in severe weather, such as the fundamental importance of securing for sea, weather deck safety, arctic clothing and keeping ships with their complex weapon and sensor systems fully operations in icing conditions. Ship handling at close quarters was also rigorously tested. Admiral Lucey, FOSNI during the Second Cod War, reported:

> *'The final point must be my admiration of the expertise, endurance and ship handling of the Commanding Officers. The often expressed doubt as to the capabilities of present day frigate captains has been shown, off Iceland, to be unfounded.'*

One of the major pluses for the Navy was that they had a clearly defined, worthwhile task to do and this, as always, was good for morale. To quote Admiral

The sort of conditions faced during winter off Iceland – 2 views onboard RFA Tidepool in October 1973. (Alan Patterson)

Lucey again:

> *'The most heartening aspect of this operation has been the morale of the ships' companies involved.*
> *However unpleasant the conditions, they seemed to relish a difficult but real job to be done.'*

And Admiral Troup again:

> *'It was most noticeable how the morale of ships' companies improved during the period when they were given a difficult, unpleasant but specific task to undertake. More than one ship which I visited was transformed from the mediocre to the very good during three weeks of Iceland patrol.'*

Perhaps the most serious long-term effect on naval effectiveness was the loss of the distant-water fishing fleet, which had gallantly and stalwartly provided the men and the vessels for minesweeping and patrol duties during two world wars. This reserve of fine seagoing men no longer exists.

Logistics

Logistics are usually the unsung, unglamorous side of any sustained operation. Whilst fuel was fundamental to the ships' ability to stay on task, there was also a mass of operational stores, spares and mail to be delivered. In the First Cod War, all these items went north in trawlers or relief escorts. The first Nimrod mail drop took place in June 1973 and thereafter mail and high priority stores items were air-dropped, with the heavier items going to the patrol area in relieving frigates, tankers and tugs.

Aviation

The Wasp helicopter first flew 18 months after the First Cod War ended and so by the time the Second started, they were becoming a regular feature of naval operations. They contributed significantly to the surveillance effort, as well as acting as a transport for mail, stores, personnel and, of course, underslung nets full of cod. From September 1973, the 'O' and 'Tide' class fleet tankers carried a Wessex 3 helicopter and sometimes an additional Wasp.

Operating these aircraft was often severely weather-limited and peacetime safety rules were maintained throughout. Both aircraft were single-engined and so had to operate close enough to a suitable flight deck fitted ship to provide a good chance of crew survivability in the event of a ditching. This meant that the Wasp was not permitted to operate outside 20 miles from a flightdeck-fitted frigate or tanker and the Wessex 3 had to keep within 30 miles of the tanker.

Many useful lessons were learnt about helicopter operations at the limits in Arctic conditions - hanger doors needed strengthening, hangers needed heating, ice was a problem[178] and additional lashing points were required, just to mention a few.

One of the Royal Navy's major difficulties was knowing where the gunboats were, especially as the government consistently refused to allow the defence forces full use of the high seas - having made the 'goodwill' gesture of keeping warships and defence tugs outside 12 miles rather than the 4 of Icelandic territorial waters, this restriction seems to have become an inviolate point of principle, despite regular requests from the OTC, FOSNI and the CinCFleet for it to be lifted.

Fortunately helicopter borne radar in the Wessex 3 and the sensors in the Royal Air Force's Nimrods (less so in the Britannias and the Hastings) allowed contacts to be plotted within the 12 mile zone, but identification was impossible until the contact was visible - which with many foggy days and the long winter nights often meant that a ship or aircraft had to get very close in order to achieve a positive ID. The Nimrods, with their ability to cover vast areas, were fundamental to the Navy's ability to maintain the picture of who was where. The cost to the Nimrod force was definitely a temporary decrease in their anti-submarine effectiveness, however as Admiral Lucey reported:

> *'Without air surveillance the task of marking the Icelandic gunboats would have been very*

[178] Perhaps a BGO (Blinding Glimpse of the Obvious), but the problem was much bigger than had been anticipated. The Royal Navy does Arctic trials on all its warships and equipment, but a carefully planned (and inevitably costly) trial can never produce the kind of experiences that a lengthy period of operating in the same environment will.

difficult, and negative intelligence was almost as valuable as positive identification. Furthermore, I am sure trawler discipline would have been more lax without the threat of being seen and reported from the air.'

Communications

Communications are fundamental to the success of any naval operation, but become of even greater importance when there is close political control. HF conditions are notoriously poor off Iceland, but the Navy, both seagoing and shore-based, managed to work through and around them and the traffic continued to flow both ways.

Frigates were fitted with additional VHF sets so that they could talk to the trawlers and UHF sets were fitted to the defence tugs so that they could talk discretely to the frigates. Attempts at using coded positional information on the trawler net foundered as it caused more confusion to friends than enemies.

Meteorology

During the First Cod War, the Navy provided the essential local weather forecasts for the fishing fleet. By the Second Cod War, the civilian support ships had taken over this function. Extra meteorological officers were provided at sea, frequent forecasts were provided from ashore and, in due course, frigates were provided with Mufax machines for the receipt of synoptic charts. All these combined to produce a reasonable forecast service in an area very prone to sudden and violent changes in the weather.

Intelligence

The OTC's success was heavily dependant upon his knowledge of where the gunboats were. Once at sea, he could use all his forces to detect and track them, but these resources could be deployed much more efficiently if he knew when they entered and left port.

In 1958, the British Embassy was very good at keeping the OTC informed about all gunboat movements in Reykjavík. Necessarily, movements in other ports were only reported on a rare opportunity basis and the presumption was that, if not in Reykjavik, they were at sea.

During the Second Cod War, the Embassy did not provide any intelligence until some time after the dispute started. The delay was less during the Third Cod War. The paucity of intelligence mattered little in the first dispute because the problem was mainly to prevent arrest. With the advent of the warp-cutter, much bigger Defended Fishing Areas (DFAs) and the ban on entering the 12-mile limit, the paucity of shore intelligence was more keenly felt.

The major intelligence failure was the lack of warning of the warp-cutter. This device was discretely trialled in 1958, but was not deployed because it was considered to be too aggressive and retaliation against Icelandic trawlers and the smaller gunboats was feared. Additionally, only *Thór*, and possibly the older *Ægir*, were powerful enough to tow it. The existence of this device was reasonably well known in Icelandic fishing circles, where secrecy is hardly a habit, so it is unfortunate that the cutting of *Peter Scott's* warps by *Ægir* on 5th September 1972 was a surprise. It is quite possible that those who knew about it thought that it wasn't worth reporting, because it was such a simple device and its existence appeared to be well known.

As has been recounted earlier, the search for a simple user-friendly defence was never successful.

The Press

The 'Silent Service' did not welcome the press in the sixties or seventies. They were 'not to be trusted and would twist the words of simple sailormen'. Whilst there was, and is, much truth in this view, even back in the 1970s, Iceland was fighting a media campaign as well as the one on the fishing grounds. For basic geographical reasons, Iceland was always going to have the advantage. Incidents could be generated at times that suited the Icelandic cause (or at least one part of the governing coalition in Iceland) and embarked newsmen could get their copy, photos and film ashore very soon after the incident.

In 1958, reporters were offered passage in warships and destroyers, but after a few days, interest waned and there was little press interest in the dispute. By 1973, television had joined the media scrum and newspapers, radio and television were offered places in trawlers, tugs, tankers and Royal Air Force Nimrods. Places in frigates were not offered because it was considered that Commanding Officers, and especially the OTC, already had quite enough to contend with.[179] Trips in ships were not that popular because of their duration. Some reporters however, including some British ones, did take short trips out with the gunboats.

One, Larry Harris of the BBC, spent two trips in *Tyr* during the Third Cod War, where he experienced some hostility because of the BBC's lack of 'partiality' towards the Icelandic position. Captain Gudmundur Kjærnested claimed, in "*The Last Waltz*" that he had been advised by a 'foreign correspondent' to 'attack the British at 1800 so as to disrupt their evening meal'. Larry Harris denies being the originator of this advice, but did say to me 'It's too good a story to muck up with the facts'.

In spite of the efforts at sea and ashore, the Icelandic viewpoint sometimes featured in the British media, much to the annoyance of the Navy, their families and the fishing industry and in 1975 there was a determination to improve the British press coverage. The press, including once an Icelandic reporter, were embarked in frigates, Commanding Officers gave interviews, naval 'spokesmen' were made available to the TV, facsimile picture transmission equipment (actually a modified weather map transmitter) was fitted and on two occasions in 1976, film of a collision was flown back to the UK in a Seaking helicopter, using a Rover class tanker as a midway fuelling stop.

The assessment of all this public relations effort was disappointing. It had no effect in Iceland, where everything said by Icelandic sources was unhesitatingly believed to be the truth. Internationally, Britain's friends were embarrassed by the dispute and her enemies rejoiced in her discomfort. Reporting from the fishing grounds made no difference to their views and domestically, the public were, if not as uncritically as in Iceland, on the side of the Royal Navy and the trawlermen anyway.

The Cost

Icelandic Prime Minister Jónasson said to the British Ambassador, Sir Andrew Gilchrist, on the evening of 31st August 1958:

> *'You will make cheap cod as expensive as salmon[180]'.*

Much was made of the cost of the three Cod Wars and calculating 'additional' costs is not straightforward. One of the few statistics in the records is the fact that in April 1959, the additional cost of fuel for HM ships on Icelandic patrol was £50,000 per month. In reply to a parliamentary question in June 1976, the Under Secretary of State for Defence for the Royal Navy stated:

> *'With the exception of repair costs, the costs incurred by the Royal Navy and Royal Air Force protection forces were broadly those that would have been incurred wherever the vessels and aircraft had been deployed.'*

Like all answers to parliamentary questions, this one is very carefully crafted and fails to say that the number of ships and aircraft deployed was significantly in excess of those that would have been deployed in normal circumstances. The repair costs for the 15 frigates damaged in the Third Cod War was just under £1 million, it was much less in the Second Cod War. In fact, because of the cancellation of the 1976 Task Group Deployment, there was a saving of about £270,000 in travel and associated allowances. So overall, in terms of the defence budget, the cost of the three Cod Wars was not significant.

The Ministry of Agriculture, Fisheries and Food, however, had to foot the bills for chartering the defence tugs, which in 1976 came to about £100,000 per tug per month.

The Icelandic Coastguard

The Royal Navy always had a healthy respect for the professionalism and seamanship of the Icelandic Coastguard. They made interesting opponents. The two main areas that the Royal Navy never really understood were the lack of control that Coastguard HQ, or anyway the Icelandic Government, seemed to have over the

[179] But see the first line of this section …

[180] He was right. Checking a supermarket whilst writing this book, I found fresh cod at £8.23/kg and fresh salmon at £6.47/kg. It is not easy to establish equivalents for 1958. The Office for National Statistics has no data for salmon prices in 1958, showing what a luxury it was before farmed salmon appeared on the markets. The Sainsbury Archive shows that no fish was sold in their shops until the 1960s, when they started selling frozen fish. Sainsbury's sales of fresh fish started in 1980. Tinned salmon was available at between three shillings & sixpence (17.5p) and five shillings & sixpence (27.5p), depending on brand, in 1954. The consumer magazine *Which*? records cod fillets at 2 shillings (10p) a pound in 1957.

The former ICGV Thor at Reykjavik in May 2003, Having previously served as a floating restaurant she was seen here, painted gold, awaiting a new lease of life as a floating disco.
(Steve Bush)

actions of individual gunboat captains and the lack of co-ordination in the use of the gunboats.

Interestingly, in "*The Last Waltz*", Captain Sigurdur Arnasson, who commanded in all three cod wars says of Pétur Sigurdsson, who became the Director of the Coastguard in 1952 (and remained in that post until 1981):

> *'Whatever the season, whatever the time of day, Sigurdsson could always be reached. He was at his desk literally 24 hours a day all the time.'*

To quote Captain Gudmundur Kjærnested on his Director from the same documentary:

> *'But when one got older and more domineering, our policies might diverge on occasions. But he was the boss and at sea we are used to obeying.'*

Now 46 years old, the ICGV Òdinn is seen here undergoing maintenance in May 2003 at Reykjavik.
(Steve Bush)

There were several occasions when there were enough gunboats at sea in the right place for them to have mounted a joint attack that would have overwhelmed the available defence forces, but this never happened, for which the RN remained grateful, if puzzled. Even on the 6th May 1976 when four gunboats reacted angrily to the resumption of protected fishing, they all acted as individuals.

As well as being daring and expert seamen, by the Second Cod War they had excellent well-found ships, as Admiral Troup commented in 1976:

> *'I believe that there are many lessons to be learned from the design of the Icelandic Coastguard Vessels which we might incorporate in a future design of our own. Their robustness, speed, manoeuvrability and sea keeping qualities are quite remarkable - after six months of endless collisions they still managed to field four out of six at sea which says a lot for their design.'*

The Trawlers

Relations between trawlers and the Navy were never going to be easy. Life in a trawler off Iceland was hard, unpleasant and often dangerous. The compensation was very good money after a successful trip, but because trawlermen were paid by results, they did not like being told where to fish and really didn't want the other trawlers to know where they were either.

They looked upon naval protection as a right but did not acknowledge any linked responsibility to follow the Navy's advice or their owners' instructions. They were generous with their fish when the Navy was in favour and withdrew any cooperation when they felt let down. Despite all these problems, relations were pretty good and much of this was due to the Liaison Skippers, retired, experienced trawler skippers, embarked in most frigates. As well as their 'management' role, there are several reports of Liaison Skippers teaching sailors how to gut cod. I remember a large delivery of Cod to *Charybdis's* flight deck by the Wasp helicopter. The galley staff looked at all this just-dead fish & called for help. A 'production' line was established around our liaison skipper, Eric Thudercliff, who sat on a wooden stool in the middle of the flight deck and proceeded to gut the whole lot, whilst eager hands handed whole fish to him, took the gutted ones away and washed both fish and deck clean.

The British Trawler Federation (BTF) were keen to help the Navy protect their trawlers, but there was often a suspicion that individual owners were not too unhappy if a skipper broke the rules, embodied in the BTF's Instructions to Skippers, provided they brought a good catch home. If the skipper and crew made good money out of a successful trip, the owners made more.

Had the trawlers been under firmer naval control and subject to sanctions if they broke the rules, several of the more difficult incidents, which often involved trawlers fishing on their own could have been avoided. Similarly, one possible reason why no effective counter to the warp cutter was ever deployed was that the fishermen were not prepared to use anything that might interfere with their fishing. As the Naval Staff History tactfully says:

> *'A measure of naval control of trawlers in return for protection might have been a helpful feature.'*

Was the Result Inevitable?

I believe that the short answer to this is yes. Could the British have produced a managed decline in their distant-water fishing industry? Just possibly, but only just.

The end of the Second World War and the consequent end of the colonial era, produced two interlinked movements in world politics - a rejection by the emerging nations of the old 'colonial' basis for such international law as there was and a desire for wider national control over coastal waters. Amongst 'emerging nations' I would include Iceland - keen to prove herself a 'nation', but without the domestic political maturity to behave like one on the international scene and certainly without any established traditions of loyalty and obedience towards the will of the elected government.

Britain was undoubtedly, at the beginning of this period, still stuck in the 'Great Power' colonial mindset and continually failed to take the developing threat to her fishing interests seriously enough. However, as one of the centres, if not the centre, of

International Maritime Law, Britain was deeply committed to acting within that law and had very good national reasons for upholding the law as it stood. Had Britain taken a leading part in the evolution of what became the UN Convention on the Law of the Sea, rather than having resisted all the changes, the consequences, certainly for the fishing industry, might have been spread over a longer period.

The Fifth Report from the Expenditure Committee on the British Fishing Industry, published by the House of Commons on 13th April 1978, acknowledges this:

> *'Paragraph 265. .... The widespread establishment of fishery zones extending to a maximum of 200 miles both by member states of the EEC and by a number of non-member states has, it is claimed, crystallised into a new rule of customary international law ...*
>
> *Paragraph 266. It emerges from the narrative in Appendix 1 that during the protracted Law of the Sea Conference the Foreign and Commonwealth Office were so obsessed with maintaining right of passage and freedom of the high seas that they were slow to recognise the political force of the move towards exclusive 200-mile fishery zones, which was initiated by Peru, Chile and Ecuador in 1952 and which was later adopted as desirable policy, although not immediately implemented, by many other countries. Had (Her Majesty's Government) appreciated in time the advantages to the UK of adopting a strategy of exclusive fishery zones, instead of continuing to resist it until 1974 and even 1975, they might have stood out more firmly in 1970-2 against the undesirable 'common access' features of the Common Fisheries Policy. Had they done so, the EEC negotiations might have had a different outcome.'*

As it was, Iceland not so much realised which way the wind was blowing, as 'whistled up' that wind. She was pushing at a relentlessly opening door that Britain was vainly trying to keep closed. If your opponent is a nation state that refuses to be bound by international law, even if they have earlier agreed to abide by it, as Iceland had in 1973, there is little you can do except use sufficient force to compel acquiescence. In the circumstances of the Cod (and Cold) Wars, Britain was, probably rightly, not prepared to use sufficient force, especially against a NATO ally and hence, the result was inevitable.

To quote an anonymous Foreign Office source:

> *'I have often wondered what might have happened if Mrs Thatcher had been Prime Minister (during the Third Cod War). Would she have seen the livelihood of the fishermen of Humberside, like that of the Falkland Islanders, as warranting a blank cheque in lives, resources and diplomatic fallout? Would she have ordered her Admirals to take ever-stronger action against the Icelandic Coastguard until they desisted from harassment?*
> *Would she then have met from Washington the stern check, which Eisenhower administered to his old comrade Eden at the time of Suez? This is the stuff that nightmares are made of; but who in 1976 would have dreamed that we would one day go to war in the South Atlantic?'*

And Sir Gerald Fitzmaurice, The Foreign Office's Legal Adviser, in 1958 at the beginning of this process and also in the era when 'Mandarins' both could, and were permitted to, quote the Classics:

> *'The lesson of the Sibylline Books is to accept the possible when it is still timely.'*

CHAPTER 24

A TAILPIECE

On 19th September 1979, HMS *Bacchante*, as part of NATO's Standing Naval Force Atlantic (SNFL), visited Reykjavik. SNFL consisted of 6 frigates at the time and not all could berth alongside in Reykjavik, but it was decided that *HMS Bacchante*, as the first Royal Navy ship to visit Iceland since the end of the Third Cod War, should be alongside.

I was the Operations Officer onboard and that evening was lucky enough to be one of the *Bacchante* officers invited to dinner by Kenneth East, the Ambassador who had been expelled in 1976. Also invited to the dinner were a number of Coastguard Officers. Peace was made over several hours and many toasts were drunk. Unsurprisingly, I don't remember very much about this evening, but for the fact that my captain, Commander John Brigstocke, and a beard-hater, ordered me to shave off my beard. This was not a legal order, but I obeyed, on condition that I could start growing again next morning. A bar-chit was duly signed recording this agreement and I shaved off. Despite the Master-at-Arms's objections, as the regulations say that there must be a two-week gap between ceasing shaving and shaving again and vice versa, I was permitted to start growing again immediately. I still have the same beard - it even survived the Falkland's War. My wife has never known me without my beard and, having seen this photograph, doesn't wish to.

A beard-less and chilly Lieutenant Andrew Welch at Colours onboard HMS Bacchante in Reykjavik on 20th September 1979, peace having been made with the gunboat captains over a lengthy dinner in the British Embassy the night before. (Andrew Welch)

And a Poem
By Ken Knox

"The Fox and the Hound"[181]

The gunboat Thór patrolled the ground,
A certain trawler just had to be found.
He'd searched and searched, his one intent,
To find the skipper, he had his scent.

The trawler he hunted, to live and to die for,
Was new and named after a famous author,
Its skipper was also known by name,
A legend based on his knowledge and fame.
For years this skipper trawled Iceland's grounds,
Catching the prime fish, the flat and the round.
Cod-fish, haddock, plaice and sole,
The more the better, his only goal.

This notorious skipper had given him hell,
A damned elusive pimpernel.
The search had gone on long enough,
He'd set a trap and he'd make it rough.

The limit line was like a fence,
To go inside by law an offence.
Three miles, six miles, twelve miles, more,
For trawler skippers like closing a door.
To open that door and go inside,
Enticement too much, "let's open it wide".

The Thór was the hound and he'd choose a box,
He'd lure this skipper, this clever old fox.
The place he chose was a well-known ground,
And many ships trawled all around.
He knew his prey was among this group,
So he made his plans to make his swoop.

His ten man Gemini[182] *he'd leave in place,*
Six men and first officer would lie in wait.
Fifty horse power and thirty knots,
Far too fast for our clever old fox.

---

[181] This poem is 'loosely' based on the 'exploits' of Skipper Dickie Taylor, who was notorious, as far as the Icelandic Coastguard were concerned, and who admitted to fishing inside the limits in the TV programme '*The Last Waltz*'. Skipper Ken Knox also sent me the following anecdote in January 2006 – 'Today I had lunch with two Icelandic businessmen, both of whom had been skippers. The subject of Dicky Taylor was brought up by one of them. He mentions a story that has been told in Iceland. "At a school in Iceland a class of 10 year olds where asked who knew of Brigitte Bardot. Three girls put their hands up. Then asked who knew of Dick Taylor. Everyone in class put their hands up." Ken finished with – "I'm sure there are many such stories around like this".'

[182] The inflatable rubber dinghy.

"While you lie in wait in the fjord so calm,
I'll steam away to a set false alarm.
Out of sight from their radars I'll wait.
Before the dawn we'll seek his fate.
As soon as you see him, on your radio call,
Here we'll snare him, our own net will fall".

The call for assistance far down the south side,
Had left them alone, the doors open wide.
The fox among others saw the gunboat leave,
Disappearing off radar, new plans to conceive.

Two hours later and the coast looking clear,
The fox went inside with no sign of fear.
With minimal lights the fiord dark and calm,
He'd pay out his nets for the codfish and prime.

The officer saw the loom of the lights,
"Call the Thór on the radio, we have him in sight".
In the quiet the fox heard the Gemini start,
"Get them nets back on board we must depart".

On the surface it floated, fishing line wrapped in weed,
Fouled the Gemini's screw, abruptly stopping its speed.
Then an act of nature with Iceland's freak weather,
Brought a wind down the fjord, all acted together.

The Gemini disabled and to the officer's grief,
He and his men would soon be on reef.
He called the Thór and to his dismay,
Fifteen miles distance, too far away.

The experienced fox, a seaman of old,
Surmised the danger, it left him cold.
"Engines full, from this fjord we'll flee,
Instead he put Gemini safely under his lee.

He took them onboard with their craft made secure,
No dangers now do you have to endure.
Have a rum and some food, there's plenty more,
I'll soon have you back to your mother ship Thór.

At thirteen knots for fifteen minutes,
He met with the Thór right on the limits.
They tied up close, both fox and the hound,
"You'll need these men that I've just found".

Two captains looked across the gap,
One with gold braid the other flat cap,
The fox with eyes so brown and intent,
The Icelanders blue, no sign of contempt.

"Look on your chart skipper, you'll see a red line,
One side's yours the other side's mine.
This special time I'll overlook,
You're a seaman special, not for my log-book.

Thirty years later and both retired,
Two old seamen sat weary and tired.
With whisky in hand, their second round,
They toasted themselves,
The FOX and the HOUND.

APPENDIX ONE

CHRONOLOGY OF THE FIRST COD WAR (1 SEP 58 TO 11 MAR 61)

listing HM Ships and Royal Fleet Auxiliaries employed on operations off Iceland and incidents involving the Icelandic Coast Guard (ICG).

1958

24 May	The Icelandic Minister of Fisheries, Lúdvík Jósepsson, announced his government's decision to extend their fishing limits to 12 miles.
30 Jun	The Icelandic Minister of Fisheries signed the regulation bringing the 12-mile fishing limit into force.
1 Sep	The Icelandic 12-mile limit came into effect. British trawlers continued to fish inside the new limit.
1-5 Sep	HMS *Hound* on patrol.
1-12 Sep	HMS *Eastbourne* (OTC) on patrol.
1-19 Sep	HM Ships *Russell* and *Palliser* on patrol.
2-11 Sep	RFA *Black Ranger* on station.
2 Sep	*Thor* and *Maria Júlia* attempted to arrest *Northern Foam* (GY490)[183]. Counterboarding by HMS *Eastbourne*. *Thor's* boarding party were taken to HMS *Eastbourne* (see 13 Sep). A crowd protested outside the British Embassy in Reykjavik.
2 Sep	*Òdinn* attempted to arrest *Churchill* (GY585).
2 Sep	*Maria Júlia* attempted to arrest *Lifeguard* (GY395).
3 Sep	*Albert* attempted to arrest *Burfell* (GY346). Resulted in a minor collision.
4 Sep	A large public meeting was held in Leakjartorg Square in Reykjavik to protest at the British actions.
5-27 Sep	HMS *Lagos* on patrol.
5 Sep	*Thór* and *Maria Júlia* attempted to arrest *Lancella* (H290) and *St Nectan* (H411)[184]
6 Sep	*Òdinn* attempted to arrest *Aston Villa* (GY42).
7 Sep	*Ægir* attempted to arrest *Craddock* (GY11).
7 Sep	*Maria Júlia* and *Hermodur* attempted to arrest *Stella Canopus* (H244) and *Brontes* (H236).
8 Sep	*Òdinn* attempted to arrest *Warwick Deeping* (H151).
9 Sep	*Òdinn* attempted to arrest *King Sol* (GY338).
10 Sep	*Òdinn* attempted to arrest *Loch Fleet* (FD43).
12 Sep	*Maria Júlia* attempted to arrest *Coldstreamer* (GY10) and *Bayella* (H72).

[183] H = Hull registered, GY = Grimsby registered, A = Aberdeen registered & LO = London registered. Port of Registry was not always the same as Home Port – for example, all the LO registered trawlers worked out of somewhere other than London. That said, GY trawlers are usually Grimsby based etc etc.

[184] The Naval Staff History lists this incident as involving the *St Meltane*, however there is no trawler of that name on record, although there was a *St Meltan*. However, *St Meltan* was not in commission at this time, so I have assumed that the *St Nectan*, as the most similar name, was the vessel concerned.

13 Sep	HMS *Eastbourne* dropped the members of *Thor's* boarding party off in Faxa Bay.
13-29 Sep	RFA *Wave Baron* on station.
13-30 Sep	HMS *Hogue* (OTC) on patrol.
15 Sep	*Thor* attempted to arrest *Red Lancer* (LO442).
18 Sep	*Ægir* attempted to arrest *Valafell* (GY383). *Valafell* accused of attempting to ram *Ægir*.
19 Sep	*Ægir* attempted to arrest *Welland* (GY300).
20 Sep - 2 Oct	HMS *Diana* on patrol.
20 Sep - 3 Oct	HMS *Decoy* on patrol.
21 Sep	*Ægir* attempted to arrest *Lincoln City* (GY464).
25 Sep	*Òdinn* and *Maria Júlia* attempted to arrest *Paynter* (GY480). The boarding took place whilst HMS *Diana* was landing a sick man in Iceland. The boarding party withdrew as soon as HMS *Diana* reappeared.
28 Sep	*Albert* attempted to arrest *Northern Gem* (GY204) and *Northern Foam* (GY490).
29 Sep	*Ægir* attempted to arrest *Afridi*. Warning shots were fired.
30 Sep - 6 Nov	RFA *Wave Ruler* on station.
1-10 Oct	HMS *Ulster* (OTC) on patrol.
1-22 Oct	HMS *Russell* on patrol.
2 Oct	*Thor* and *Saebjörg* attempted to arrest *St Just* (LO434).
3-23 Oct	HMS *Hardy* on patrol. OTC from 11-13 Oct.
4-25 Oct	HMS *Palliser* on patrol.
4 Oct	*Ægir* attempted to arrest *Banquo* (FD99). Resulted in a minor collision.
6 Oct	*Maria Júlia* attempted to arrest *Kingston Emerald* (H49). Warning shots were fired.
11 Oct	*Òdinn* attempted to arrest *Neath Castle* (GY52). Warning shots were fired.
13-30 Oct	HMS *Blackwood* (OTC) on patrol.
14 Oct	*Thor* attempted to arrest *Cape Campbell* (H383). Warning shots were fired.
23 Oct - 8 Nov	HMS *Hogue* on patrol.
24 Oct - 15 Nov	HMS *Zest* (OTC) on patrol.
26 Oct - 11 Nov	HMS *Lagos* on patrol.
31 Oct - 11 Nov	HMS *Dundas* on patrol.
7-18 Nov	RFA *Wave Victor* on station.
12-19 Nov	HMS *Orwell* on patrol.
12-30 Nov	HMS *Russell* on patrol.
12 Nov	*Thor* attempted to arrest *Hackness* (FD120). Warning shots were fired. HMS *Russell* intervened.
12 Nov	An unidentified ICG vessel attempted to arrest *Spurs* (GY515).
16 Nov - 2 Dec	HMS *Duncan* (OTC) on patrol.
20-27 Nov	HMS *Grafton* on patrol.
20-27 Nov	RFA *Wave Baron* on station.
20 Nov - 16 Dec	HMS *Llandaff* on patrol. (OTC from 3 Dec)
20-27 Nov	RFA *Wave Baron* on station.
2-12 Dec	HMS *Diamond* on patrol.
5-18 Dec	HMS *Paladin* on patrol.
13-18 Dec	HMS *Palliser* on patrol. OTC 17-19 Dec.
19 Dec - 5 Jan	HMS *Solebay* (OTC) on patrol.
19 Dec - 5 Jan	RFA *Wave Victor* on station.
19 Dec - 6 Jan	HM Ships *Lagos* and *Hogue* on patrol.

1959

6-19 Jan	RFA *Wave Chief* on station.
6-23 Jan	HM Ships *Duncan* (OTC) and *Russell* on patrol.
7-20 Jan	HMS *Palliser* on patrol.
9-11 Jan	RFA *Tidereach* on station.
13 Jan	*Thor* attempted to arrest *Reneva* (FD7).
20 Jan - 6 Feb	RFA *Wave Baron* on station.
24 Jan - 11 Feb	HM Ships *Agincourt* (OTC) and *Corunna* on patrol.
1 Feb	*Thor* attempted to arrest *Valafell* (GY383). The boarding was not achieved, but *Valafell* was ordered into Iceland by her owners for trial as both *Thor* and HMS *Agincourt* considered that she had been fishing inside the 4-mile limit. *Valafell's* fishing gear and catch were confiscated and the owners were fined IKr 74.000 (£1,700). Many in Iceland considered this fine to be unduly lenient.
7-19 Feb	RFA *Wave Ruler* on station.
12 Feb - 1 Mar	HM Ships *Duncan* (OTC), *Russell* and *Palliser* on patrol.
20 Feb - 17 Mar	RFA *Wave Chief* on station.
2-9 Mar	HMS *Vigo* on patrol.
2-17 Mar	HM Ships *Zest* (OTC) and *Eastbourne* on patrol.
9-17 Mar	HMS *Whitby* on patrol.
9-29 Mar	RFA *Wave Baron* on station.
17 Mar - 3 Apr	HMS *Palliser* on patrol.
18 Mar - 5 Apr	HM Ships *Duncan* (OTC) and *Russell* on patrol.
25 Mar	*Thor* attempted to arrest *Carella* (FD319), who was alleged to be within the 4-mile limit. HMS *Palliser* refused to admit or discuss *Thor's* claims.
26 Mar - 13 Apr	RFA *Wave Chief* on station.
28 Mar	*Albert* attempted to arrest *Swanella* (H141).
6-24 Apr	HM Ships *Scarborough* (OTC), *Tenby* and *Grenville* on patrol.
14-24 Apr	HMS *Salisbury* on patrol.
14-29 Apr	RFA *Wave Ruler* on station.
14 Apr	*Òdinn* and *Ægir* attempted to arrest *Swanella*, allegedly within the 4-mile limit. HMS *Scarborough* refused to admit or discuss the ICG's claims.
23 Apr	*Ægir* attempted to arrest *Lord Montgomery* (FD13). The boarding was not achieved, but *Lord Montgomery's* owners ordered her into Iceland for trial as both *Ægir* and HMS *Tenby* considered that she had been fishing within the 4-mile limit.
25 Apr - 9 May	HMS *Contest* on patrol.
25 Apr - 10 May	HMS *Cavendish* (OTC) on patrol.
25 Apr - 10 May	RFA *Wave Baron* on station.
25 Apr - 11 May	HMS *Exmouth* on patrol.
29 Apr	*Albert* attempted to arrest *Ashanti* (GY16).
30 Apr	*Thor* attempted to arrest *Arctic Viking* (H452). Warning shots were fired.
2 May	*Thor* attempted to arrest *Kelly* (GY6).
9 May	*Thor* attempted to arrest *Avon River* (A660).
10-28 May	HMS *Carysfort* on patrol.
11-28 May	HMS *Agincourt* (OTC) on patrol.
11-31 May	RFA *Wave Baron* on station.

12-28 May	HMS *Chaplet* on patrol.
12-18 May	HMS *Malcolm* on patrol.
16 May	*Òdinn* attempted to arrest *Samuel Hewitt* (LO117).
17 May	*Òdinn* attempted to arrest *Junella* (H399).
19 May - 1 Jun	HMS *Broadsword* on patrol.
19 May	*Thor* attempted to arrest *Lord Rowallan* (H9).
19 May	*Òdinn* attempted to arrest *Burfell* (GY346).
22 May	Minor collision between HMS *Chaplet* and *Òdinn*.
29 May - 16 Jun	HM Ships *Duncan* (OTC) and *Russell* on patrol.
31 May	*Maria Júlia* attempted to arrest *Lord Lloyd* (FD52). Warning shots were fired.
1-8 Jun	HMS *Malcolm* on patrol.
1-23 Jun	RFA *Wave Ruler* on station.
3-16 Jun	HMS *Apollo* on patrol.
17 Jun - 4 Jul	HM Ships *Trafalgar* (OTC), *Jutland* and *Dunkirk* on patrol.
23 Jun	*Thor* attempted to arrest *Cape Palliser* (H354).
24 Jun - 11 Jul	RFA *Wave Baron* on station.
29 Jun	*Thor* attempted to arrest *Wyre Mariner* (FD34).
1 Jul	*Maria Júlia* attempted to arrest *Lancer* (GY65). Warning shots were fired.
5-11 Jul	HMS *Vigo* on patrol.
5-23 Jul	HM Ships *Duncan* (OTC) and *Russell* on patrol.
7 Jul	*Òdinn* attempted to arrest *Robert Hewitt* (LO65). Warning shots were fired.
7 Jul	*Ægir* attempted to arrest *Northern Dawn* (GY289). Warning shots were fired.
8 Jul	*Ægir* attempted to arrest *Conan Doyle* (H251). Warning shots were fired.
12-18 Jul	HMS *Malcolm* on patrol.
12 Jul - 4 Aug	RFA *Wave Chief* on station.
18 Jul	*Thor* attempted to arrest *Coventry City* (GY422). Warning shots were fired.
19 Jul - 5 Aug	HMS *Broadsword* on patrol.
21 Jul	*Thor* attempted to arrest *Statham* (GY25). Warning shots were fired.
23 Jul - 11 Aug	HMS *Carysfort* on patrol.
24-29 Jul	HMS *Cavendish* (OTC) on patrol.
29 Jul – 10 Aug	HMS *Palliser* on patrol.
5-23 Aug	RFA *Wave Ruler* on station.
6-25 Aug	HMS *Malcolm* on patrol.
11-24 Aug	HM Ships *Duncan* (OTC) and *Exmouth* on patrol.
14 Aug	An ICG Catalina aircraft fired flares over *Leeds United* (GY261) ordering her to stop and await arrest by an ICG gunboat.
24 Aug - 13 Sep	RFA *Wave Victor* on station.
25 Aug - 9 Sep	HMS *Trafalgar* (OTC) on patrol.
25 Aug - 10 Sep	HMS *Jutland* on patrol.
26 Aug - 10 Sep	HMS *Dunkirk* on patrol.
31 Aug	*Thor* attempted to arrest *Cape Campbell* (H383) and *Man O'War* (H181).
10-29 Sep	HM Ships *Venus* (OTC) and *Urchin* on patrol.
11-29 Sep	HMS *Carron* on patrol.
14 Sep - 4 Oct	RFA *Wave Chief* on station.
24 Sep	*Albert* attempted to arrest *Viviana* (GY233).
26 Sep	*Ægir* attempted to arrest *St Alcuin* (H125).
27 Sep	*Thor* attempted to arrest *Red Knight* (LO445).
30 Sep - 16 Oct	HM Ships *Chaplet* (OTC) and *Malcolm* on patrol.
30 Sep - 18 Oct	HMS *Palliser* on patrol.

2 Oct	*Thor* attempted to arrest *Stoke City* (GY114).
5-18 Oct	RFA *Wave Ruler* on station.
13 Oct	*Ægir* attempted to arrest *Northern Sky* (GY427).
17 Oct - 6 Nov	HM Ships *Trafalgar* (OTC) and *Dunkirk* on patrol.
19 Oct - 31 Oct	RFA *Wave Sovereign* on station.
19 Oct - 6 Nov	HMS *Jutland* on patrol.
26 Oct	*Ægir* attempted to arrest *Northern Chief* (GY128), who was accused of damaging Icelandic fishing lines.
28 Oct	*Maria Júlia* attempted to arrest *Gavina* (FD167).
29 Oct	*Albert* attempted to arrest *Lord Lloyd* (FD52), threatening to open fire in the process.
1-25 Nov	RFA *Wave Baron* on station.
5 Nov	*Maria Júlia* attempted to arrest *Stella Dorado* (H307).
7-27 Nov	HM Ships *Saintes* (OTC) and *Camperdown* on patrol.
7-29 Nov	HMS *Armada* on patrol.
26 Nov - 21 Dec	RFA *Wave Sovereign* on station.
28 Nov - 16 Dec	HMS *Palliser* on patrol.
28 Nov - 17 Dec	HMS *Russell* (OTC) on patrol.
1 Dec	*Ægir* attempted to arrest *Samuel Hewitt* (LO117) and *Wyre Gleaner* (FD23). Warning shots were fired.
4 Dec	*Thor* attempted to arrest *Lord Essendon* (H312).
16 Dec - 6 Jan	HMS *Undine* on patrol.
18 Dec - 5 Jan	HMS *Duncan* (OTC) on patrol.
20 Dec - 8 Jan	HMS *Troubridge* on patrol.
22 Dec - 6 Jan	RFA *Wave Baron* on station.

1960

6-23 Jan	HMS *Ulysses* (OTC) on patrol.
7-21 Jan	RFA *Wave Chief* on station.
7-24 Jan	HMS *Torquay* on patrol.
22 Jan - 8 Feb	RFA *Wave Ruler* on station.
24 Jan - 11 Feb	HMS *Barrosa* on patrol.
25 Jan - 11 Feb	HM Ships *Armada* (OTC) and *Malcolm* on patrol.
9-22 Feb	RFA *Wave Baron* on station.
12 Feb - 1 Mar	HM Ships *Apollo* (OTC) and *Palliser* on patrol.
21 Feb	*Albert* attempted to arrest *James Barrie* (H15). Warning shots were fired. HMS *Palliser* intervened.
23 Feb - 14 Mar	RFA *Wave Chief* on station.
29 Feb	*Thor* attempted to arrest *Camilla* (H193). Warning shots were fired.
1 Mar	*Albert* attempted to arrest *Bengali* (GY61). Warning shots were fired.
2-14 Mar	HM Ships *Paladin* (OTC) and *Undine* on patrol.
3 Mar	British trawlers were accused of trawling across the nets of Icelandic vessels from Olafsvik, causing considerable damage to their nets.
15 Mar - 27 Apr	British Trawlers withdrew from the fishing grounds in order to facilitate the International Conference of the Oceans in Geneva. The Royal Navy's patrol was gapped.
26 Mar	The Geneva conference broke up without any agreement.
28 Apr - 18 May	HMS *Delight* (OTC) on patrol.
28 Apr - 19 May	HMS *Palliser* on patrol.
28 Apr - 22 May	RFA *Wave Ruler* on station.

29 Apr - 11 May	HMS *Barrosa* on patrol.
30 Apr	The Icelandic Government issued a general pardon for all British trawlers who had been accused of fishing illegally from 1 Sep 58 to 29 Apr 60.
1-19 May	HMS *Battleaxe* on patrol.
19 May - 8 Jun	HMS *Dainty* (OTC) on patrol.
20 May - 4 Jun	HMS *Russell* on patrol.
20 May - 8 Jun	HMS *Malcolm* on patrol.
22 May - 12 Jun	RFA *Wave Prince* on station.
9-16 Jun	HMS *Apollo* (OTC) on patrol.
9-21 Jun	HMS *Crossbow* on patrol. OTC 17-21 Jun.
13 Jun - 4 Jul	RFA *Wave Ruler* on station.
11-29 Jul	HMS *Undine* on patrol.
17-21 Jun	HMS *Pellew* on patrol.
21 Jun - 10 Jul	HMS *Duncan* (OTC) on patrol.
22 Jun - 10 Jul	HMS *Palliser* on patrol.
22 Jun	*Albert* attempted to arrest *Thuringia* (GY321). Warning shots were fired.
23 Jun	ICG Catalina aircraft fired flares over *Grimsby Town* (GY246) and ordered her to stop and await arrest by IGC gunboat.
23 Jun	*Thor* attempted to arrest *Northern Sceptre* (GY297).
28 Jun	*Thor* attempted to arrest *Northern Queen* (GY124). The boarding party withdrew peacefully when HMS *Duncan* launched a boat with her counterboarding party.
30 Jun	*Thor* attempted to arrest *Lifeguard* (GY395). Warning shots were fired.
4 Jul	*Òdinn* attempted to arrest *Kingston Jade* (H149).
5-24 Jul	RFA *Wave Prince* on station.
10 Jul	*Òdinn* attempted to arrest *Grimsby Town* (GY246). Warning shots were fired, followed by solid shot hitting *Grimsby Town's* superstructure.
11-29 Jul	HMS *Defender* (OTC) on patrol.
14 Jul	*Albert* attempted to arrest *Hull City* (GY282). Warning shots were fired.
14 Jul	An unidentified ICG gunboat chased *Coldstreamer* (GY10). An ICG Catalina aircraft also fired flares over *Coldstreamer* and ordered her to stop.
16 Jul	*Maria Júlia* attempted to arrest *Wyre Gleaner* (FD23). Warning shots were fired.
25 Jul - 13 Aug	RFA *Wave Ruler* on station.
30 Jul - 11 Aug	HM Ships *Russell* (OTC) and *Palliser* on patrol.
12-29 Aug	HM Ships *Daring* (OTC) and *Crossbow* on patrol.
15 Aug - 7 Sep	RFA *Wave Prince* on station.
30 Aug - 12 Sep	HM Ships *Delight* (OTC) and *Battleaxe* on patrol.
7-16 Sep	No RFA on station
13-16 Sep	HMS *Saintes* (OTC) on patrol.
13 Sep - 2 Oct	HMS *Vigilant* on patrol.
14 Sep	*Wyre Mariner* (FD34) arrested in an Icelandic port after towing in another damaged trawler. *Wyre Mariner's* skipper was tried for a previous fishing offence.
16-29 Sep	RFA *Wave Laird* on station.
16 Sep - 6 Oct	HMS *Malcolm* (OTC) on patrol.
27 Sep - 24 Oct	RFA *Wave Ruler* on station.
3-23 Oct	HMS *Paladin* on patrol.
7-20 Oct	HMS *Defender* (OTC) on patrol.
21 Oct - 3 Nov	HMS *Daring* (OTC) on patrol.
24 Oct - 10 Nov	HMS *Dainty* (OTC) on patrol.
25 Oct - 18 Nov	RFA *Wave Chief* on station.

4-10 Nov	HMS *Zest* on patrol.
11-29 Nov	HM Ships *Duncan* (OTC) and *Malcolm* on patrol.
13 Nov	An unidentified ICG gunboat fired warning shots at *William Wilberforce* (H200) whilst attempting to arrest her.
19-27 Nov	RFA *Wave Prince* on station.
28 Nov - 15 Dec	RFA *Wave Ruler* on station.
30 Nov - 18 Dec	HMS *Palliser* on patrol.
30 Nov - 19 Dec	HMS *Russell* (OTC) on patrol.
16 Dec - 9 Jan	RFA *Wave Prince* on station.
20 Dec - 9 Jan	HMS *Troubridge* (OTC) on patrol.
20 Dec - 7 Jan	HMS *Whitby* on patrol.

1961

6 Jan	An ICG Catalina aircraft ordered *Red Knight* (LO445) to stop and await arrest by an ICG gunboat.
8-19 Jan	HMS *Blackpool* on patrol.
9-16 Jan	HMS *Undaunted* (OTC) on patrol.
10-16 Jan	RFA *Wave Baron* on station.
17-28 Jan	HMS *Torquay* (OTC) on patrol.
20 Jan - 8 Feb	HMS *Loch Alvie* on patrol. OTC from 29 Jan.
23 Jan - 5 Feb	RFA *Wave Chief* on station.
29 Jan - 16 Feb	HMS *Palliser* on patrol. OTC from 9 Feb.
6 Feb - 1 Mar	RFA *Wave Prince* on station.
17 Feb - 11 Mar	HMS *Malcolm* (OTC) on patrol.
26 Feb - 2 Mar	HMS *Keppel* (OTC) on patrol.
2-10 Mar	RFA *Wave Master* on station.
3-11 Mar	HMS *Rhyl* (OTC) on patrol.
11 Mar	The British Government accepted the Icelandic 12 mile limit. The Icelandic Government agreed that British trawlers could fish up to the 6-mile limit for a further three years.

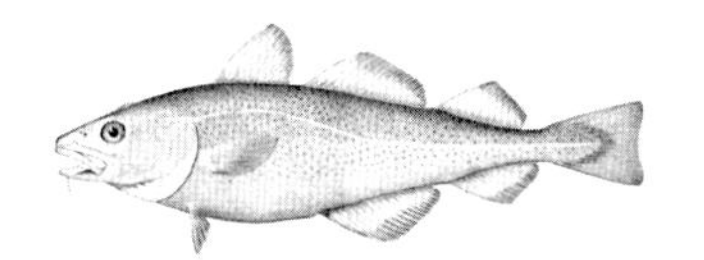

APPENDIX TWO

CHRONOLOGY OF THE SECOND COD WAR (1 SEP 72 TO 13 NOV 73),

listing HM Ships, Royal Fleet Auxiliaries and Civilian Defence Vessels (Tugs) employed on operations off Iceland and incidents involving the Icelandic Coast Guard.

Phase One - Before Naval Intervention 1 Sep 72 to 19 May 73

1972

15 Feb	The Icelandic Parliament passed a bill extending the national fishing limits to 50 miles.
17 Aug	The International Tribunal in The Hague pronounced that Iceland did not have sovereignty over the areas between 12 and 50 miles. The Icelandic Government protested and decided to ignore this decree.
1 Sep	The 50-mile fishing limit came into effect. The West German Government sent three tugs (*Frithjof*, *Meerkatze* and *Poseidon*) into the disputed area to prevent the arrest of West German trawlers. Despite many requests, the British Government decided not to send the Royal Navy into the disputed area.
5 Sep	*Ægir* cut *Peter Scott's* (H103) warps. This was the first use of the ICG's 'secret weapon'. In all, the UK claims that 82 trawlers had their gear cut during the Second Cod War; Iceland claims only 69.
10 Sep - 1 Oct	HMS *Aurora* on patrol.
12 Sep	*Ægir* cut *Lucinda's* (H403) and *Wyre Victory's* (FD181) warps.
19 Sep	HMS *Aurora* rescued survivors from Icelandic fishing vessel *Jón Eiríksson*. *Jón Eiríksson* subsequently sank whilst under tow to the Faeroes.
22 Sep	*Òdinn* cut *Kennedy's* (FD139) and *Wyre Captain's* (FD228) warps.
1-11 Oct	HMS *Palliser* on patrol.
11-23 Oct	HMS *Achilles* on patrol.
17 Oct	*Ægir* cut *Wyre Corsair's* (FD27) warps.
17 Oct	Shooting incident - *Òdinn* /*Wyre Vanguard* (FD36).
18 Oct	*Ægir* cut *Aldershot's* (GY612) warps. Iceland claimed that *Aldershot* rammed *Ægir*.
19 Oct - 14 Nov	HMS *Phoebe* on patrol.
27-30 Oct	HMS *Berwick* on patrol.
29 Oct	Shooting incident - *Òdinn* /*Real Madrid* (GY674).
30 Oct - 4 Nov	HMS *Falmouth* on patrol.
14-29 Nov	HMS *Juno* on patrol.
23 Nov	*Òdinn* cut *Vianova's* (GY590) warps.
29 Nov - 14 Dec	HMS *Jaguar* on patrol.
14-18 Dec	HMS *Apollo* on patrol.
18 Dec - 5 Jan	HMS *Rhyl* on patrol.

27 Dec	*Òdinn* cut *Benella's* (H132)warps. Iceland claimed that *Benella* rammed *Òdinn.*

1973

5-16 Jan	HMS *Lowestoft* on patrol.
7 Jan	*Òdinn* cut *Westella's* (H194) warps.
7 Jan	*Ægir* cut *Boston Blenheim's* (FD137) warps.
12 Jan	*Òdinn* cut *Ross Renown's* (GY666) and *Ross Kandahar's* (GY213) warps.
16-22 Jan	HMS *Yarmouth* on patrol.
16 Jan	*Tyr* cut *Vanessa's* (GY257) warps.
17 Jan	*Tyr* cut *Luneda's* (FD134) warps.
22 Jan - 19 May	CDV *Statesman* on station.
22 Jan - 13 Feb	HMS *Berwick* on patrol.
23 Jan	*Tyr* cut *Ross Altair's* (H379) warps.
23 Jan	Westmann Islands volcanic eruption. IGCVs withdrawn for relief operations until 5th March
12 Feb - 2 Mar	HMS *Caprice* on patrol.
15 Feb - 19 May	CDV *Englishman* on station.
2-24 Mar	HMS *Gurkha* on patrol.
5 Mar	*Ægir* cut *Ross Resolution's* (GY527) and *Port Vale's* (GY484) warps.
5 Mar	*Òdinn* cut *William Wilberforce's* (GY140) warps.
6 Mar	*Òdinn* cut *Real Madrid's* (GY674) warps.
6 Mar	*Ægir* cut *Ross Kelvin's* (GY60), *Brucella's* (H291) and *Vanessa's* (GY257) warps.
7 Mar	*Ægir* cut *Spurs's* (GY697) warps.
7 Mar	*Thor* cut *Grimsby Town's* (GY246) warps.
8 Mar	*Ægir* cut *Real Madrid's* (GY674) warps.
10 Mar	*Ægir* cut *Newby Wyke's* (H111) warps.
11 Mar	*Ægir* cut *Ross Canaveral's* (H267) warps.
13 Mar	*Thor* cut *Irvana's* (FD141) warps.
14 Mar	*Thor* cut *Boston Explorer's* (FD15), *Northern Sceptre's* (GY297), *Boston Blenheim's* (FD137) and *Benvolio's* (H22) warps.
15-17 Mar	Joint SAR operation for Icelandic Trawler *Sjoestjarnan*. *Ægir* assisted by HMS *Caprice,* RFA *Wave Chief*, CDVs *Ranger Briseis*, *Statesman* and *Englishman*, Royal Air Force Nimrod and some trawlers. No survivors found.
17 Mar	*Òdinn* cut *Robert Hewitt's* (LO65) warps.
18 Mar	Shooting incident - *Òdinn* /CDV *Statesman.*
24 Mar - 11 Apr	HMS *Rothesay* on patrol.
25 Mar	*Ægir* cut *Wyre Defence's* (FD37) warps.
25 Mar	Shooting incident *Ægir* /*Brucella* (H291).
26 Mar	Shooting incident *Ægir* /*St Leger* (H178) and *Ægir* cut *St Leger's* warps.
2 Apr	*Ægir* cut *Kingston Emerald's* (H49) and *Ross Resolution's* (GY527) warps.
2 Apr	Shooting incident - *Ægir* /CDV *Englishman.*
3 Apr	*Tyr* cut *St Leger's* (H178) warps.
7 Apr	*Òdinn* cut *St Dominic's* (H116) warps.
11 Apr-3 May	HMS *Arethusa* on patrol.
11 Apr	*Òdinn* cut *Wyre Victory's* (FD181) warps.
12 Apr	*Thor* cut *Belgaum's* (GY218) and *Primella's* (H98) warps.
12 Apr	Shooting incident - *Thor*/CDV *Englishman*. On the same day there were shooting incidents involving *Thor* and 2 separate groups of Trawlers and the *Irvana* (FD141).

12 Apr	*Òdinn* cut *Joseph Conrad's* (H161) warps.
16 Apr	*Òdinn* cut *Boston Kestrel's* (FD256) warps.
17 Apr	Shooting incident - *Thor*/*Primella* (H98).
18 Apr	Unknown ICGV cut *Aldershot's* (GY612) warps.
22 Apr	*Ægir* cut *Volesus's* (GY188) warps.
23 Apr	Shooting incidents - *Árvakur*/*Brucella* (H291)/*Portia* (H24)/German trawlers.
23 Apr	*Thor* cut *SSAFA's* (FD155) warps.
23 Apr	Shooting incidents - *Thor*/a group of trawlers/*St. Leger* (H178)/*Macbeth* (H201). Iceland claimed that *St. Leger* rammed *Thor*.
25 Apr	Unknown ICGV cut *Lord Jellicoe's* (GY709) warps.
3-19 May	HMS *Cleopatra* on patrol.
4 May	*Tyr* cut *Wyre Victory's* (FD181) warps.
7-19 May	CDV *Irishman* on station.
12 May	Shooting incidents *Thor*/CDV *Englishman*/CDV *Irishman*.
14 May	Shooting incidents *Tyr* /a group of trawlers/*Macbeth* (H201).
16-19 May	HMS *Plymouth* on patrol.
18 May	British trawlers skippers refused to fish within the disputed area any longer, unless Royal Navy protection was provided.

Phase Two - Inside 50 Miles
19 May to 3 Oct 73

1973

19 May - 19 Jul	CDV *Irishman* on station.
19 May - 27 Sep	CDV *Englishman* on station.
19 May - 3 Oct	CDV *Statesman* on station.
19-22 May	RFA *Wave Chief* on station.
19-29 May	HMS *Plymouth* (OTC) on patrol. The British decision to send frigates into the 50-mile limit surprised the Icelandic Government as negotiations were, at the time, in progress between the two governments. Consequently, the Icelandic Government withdrew from negotiations and banned British military flights from landing in Iceland.
19 May - 1 Jun	HMS *Cleopatra* on patrol.
20-22 May	HMS *Lincoln* on patrol.
22 May - 2 Jun	RFA *Blue Rover* on station.
22 May - 5 Jun	HMS *Jupiter* on patrol.
26 May	*Ægir* ordered *Everton* (GY58) to stop and fired on her when she refused. *Everton* was sinking, but she was salvaged by CDV *Statesman* and HMS *Jupiter*.
29 May - 20 Jun	HMS *Scylla* (OTC) on patrol.
1-14 Jun	RFA *Wave Chief* on station.
1-17 Jun	HMS *Jaguar* on patrol.
1 Jun	*Árvakur* cut *Gavina's* (A871) warps.
1 Jun	*Árvakur* collided with CDV *Irishman* thrice and with *Vivaria* (GY648) once. Incident observed by HMS *Scylla*.
5-21 Jun	HMS *Ashanti* on patrol.
7 Jun	Collision between *Ægir* and HMS *Scylla*.
10 Jun - 3 Oct	CDV *Lloydsman* on station.
12-20 Jun	RFA *Orangeleaf* on station.

16 Jun - 6 Jul	HMS *Leopard* on patrol.
18-24 Jun	RFA *Wave Chief* on station.
20-25 Jun	RFA *Green Rover* on station.
20 Jun - 15 Jul	HMS *Charybdis* (OTC) on patrol.
21 Jun - 8 Jul	HMS *Falmouth* on patrol.
21 Jun	Collision between *Òdinn* and CDV *Lloydsman*.
24 Jun - 10 Jul	RFA *Olwen* on station.
27 Jun	*Thor* cut *Arctic Vandal's* (H344) warps.
29 Jun - 4 Jul	RFA *Green Rover* on station.
2 Jul	*Ægir* fired blank warning shots in the vicinity of HMS *Leopard* during an incident with German trawlers.
2 Jul	Possible attempt by *Thor* to board *St Leger* (H178) frustrated by HMS *Charybdis*.
6-27 Jul	HMS *Lincoln* on patrol.
8-11 Jul	RFA *Green Rover* on station.
8-16 Jul	HMS *Gurkha* on patrol.
10-15 Jul	RFA *Wave Chief* on station.
11 Jul	*Ægir* cut *Boston Explorer's* (FD15) warps.
13 Jul	*Ægir* cut *Wyre Vanguard's* (FD36) and *Ian Fleming's* (H396) warps.
14-27 Jul	RFA *Olwen* on station.
14-31 Jul	HMS *Arethusa* (OTC) on patrol.
16-31 Jul	HMS *Berwick* on patrol.
16 Jul	*Ægir* cut *Boston Blenheim's* (FD137) warps.
17 Jul	Collision between *Ægir* and HMS *Lincoln*.
19 Jul	Collision between *Òdinn* and HMS *Arethusa*.
24 Jul - 3 Oct	CDV *Welshman* on station.
26 Jul - 12 Aug	HMS *Argonaut* on patrol.
27 Jul	Discussions in Geneva indicated increasing support for a 200 mile Exclusive Economic Zone (EEZ).
27-30 Jul	RFA *Green Rover* on station.
30 Jul - 10 Aug	RFA *Olwen* on station.
30 Jul - 14 Aug	HMS *Sirius* on patrol.
31 Jul - 24 Aug	HMS *Andromeda* on patrol.
2 Aug	Collision between *Albert* and CDV *Lloydsman*.
4-9 Aug	RFA *Green Rover* on station.
10 Aug	Collision between *Òdinn* and HMS *Andromeda*.
11-14 Aug	RFA *Wave Chief* on station.
11 Aug - 1 Sep	HMS *Plymouth* on patrol.
13 Aug - 10 Sep	HMS *Lynx* on patrol.
13 Aug	*Ægir* fired warning shots at *Lord St Vincent* (H261) whilst in Hot Pursuit. Incident witnessed by HMS *Sirius*.
14-19 Aug	RFA *Green Rover* on station.
19-25 Aug	RFA *Olna* on station.
23 Aug	*Ægir* and *Thor* fired warning shots at *Zonia* (FD236). Boarding frustrated by HMS *Andromeda*.
24 Aug - 21 Sep	HMS *Apollo* (OTC) on patrol.
26 Aug - 2 Sep	RFA *Green Rover* on station.
27 Aug	*Ægir* cuts *Ella Hewitt's* (LO94) and *Wyre Corsair's* (FD27) warps.
29 Aug	Collision between *Ægir* and HMS *Apollo*. This collision resulted in the only recorded death during all three Cod Wars when one of *Ægir*'s electricians, repairing damage to her

	hull with a welding torch, was electrocuted and died.
31 Aug - 16 Sep	HMS *Jaguar* on patrol.
1-6 Sep	RFA *Olna* (Wasp embarked) on station.
6-14 Sep	RFA *Green Rover* on station.
7 Sep	*Òdinn* cut *Kingston Sapphire's* (H95) warps
8 Sep	*Thor* cut *Northern Isles's* (GY149) warps
10-22 Sep	RFA *Olna* (Wasp + Wessex 3 embarked) on station.
10-28 Sep	HMS *Whitby* on patrol.
10 Sep	Collision between *Thor* and HMS *Jaguar*.
11 Sep	The Icelandic Government threatened to break off diplomatic relations with the UK unless British forces withdrew from the 50 mile limit. NATO mediated and a formal break was averted.
14 Sep	*Thor* cut *St Giles's* (H220) warps.
14 Sep	*Òdinn* cut *Boston Concord's* (GY730) warps.
16-24 Sep	HMS *Lincoln* on patrol.
19-22 Sep	RFA *Green Rover* on station.
20 Sep	*Ægir* cut *Ross Aquila's* (H114) warps.
21 Sep - 3 Oct	HMS *Charybdis* (OTC) on patrol.
22 Sep - 3 Oct	RFA *Olmeda* (Wessex 3 embarked) on station.
22 Sep	Two collisions between *Ægir* and HMS *Lincoln*. A TV crew, embarked in an ICG aircraft, filmed one of these collisions and this gave the Icelandic propaganda campaign a clear win.
24 Sep - 3 Oct	HMS *Ariadne* on patrol.
24 Sep	*Òdinn* fired warning shots at CDV *Englishman* and CDV *Welshman* sheltering inside the 12 mile limit.
26 Sep - 1 Oct	RFA *Blue Rover* on station.
27 Sep	Collision between *Thor* and HMS *Whitby*.
28 Sep - 3 Oct	HMS *Leopard* on patrol.
30 Sep	*Thor* cut *Arctic Warrior's* (H176) warps.

Phase Three - Outside 50 Miles
3 Oct to 13 Nov 73

1973

3 Oct - 13 Nov	CDV *Statesman* on station.
3 Oct - 13 Nov	CDV *Lloydsman* on station.
3 Oct - 13 Nov	CDV *Welshman* on station.
3-10 Oct	RFA *Olmeda* (Wessex 3 embarked) on station.
3-13 Oct	HMS *Ariadne* on patrol.
3-17 Oct	HMS *Charybdis* (OTC) on patrol.
3-20 Oct	HMS *Leopard* on patrol.
11-13 Oct	RFA *Blue Rover* on station.
12-31 Oct	HMS *Jaguar* on patrol.
14-27 Oct	RFA *Olmeda* (Wasp + Wessex 3 embarked) on station.
15-18 Oct	RFA *Grey Rover* on station.
15 Oct - 5 Nov	HMS *Apollo* (OTC) on patrol.
20-24 Oct	HMS *Whitby* on patrol.

24 Oct - 13 Nov	HMS *Ariadne* on patrol.
28-31 Oct	RFA *Grey Rover* on station.
28 Oct - 6 Nov	HMS *Yarmouth* on patrol.
4-13 Nov	RFA *Grey Rover* on station.
5-13 Nov	HMS *Phoebe* (OTC) on patrol.
7-9 Nov	HMS *Charybdis* on patrol.
9-13 Nov	HMS *Danae* on patrol.
13 Nov	Agreement was reached between the British and Icelandic Governments that larger trawlers would be banned from the 50-mile limit, whilst smaller ones would have strictly limited fishing quotas.

Note: The Tugs were on station throughout except for periodic returns (approx. monthly) to a northern UK port for crew change and maintenance.

APPENDIX THREE

CHRONOLOGY OF THE THIRD COD WAR (15 NOV 75 TO 1 JUN 76)

listing HM Ships, Royal Fleet Auxiliaries, Royal Maritime Auxiliary Service Vessels and Civilian Defence Vessels employed on operations off Iceland and incidents involving the Icelandic Coast Guard.

1975

15 July	The Icelandic Minister of Fisheries, Matthias Björnsson, issued a regulation extending the national fishing limits to 200 miles from 15 Oct 75. The British, West German and other EEC countries protested.
13 Nov	The agreement, reached after the Second Cod War, allowing some British trawlers to fish within the Icelandic 50 mile limit expired.
15 Nov	*Thor* cut *Primella's* (H98) warps.
15 Nov	*Tyr* cut *Boston Marauder's* (FD168) warps.
17 Nov	Dialogue between the British and Icelandic Governments ceased.
18 Nov	*Tyr* cut *St Giles's* (H220) warps.
19 Nov	*Tyr* cut *Benella's* (H132) warps.
19 Nov - 1 Jun	CDV *Lloydsman* on station.
19 Nov - 14 Dec	CDV *Star Aquarius* on station.
19 Nov - 16 Dec	CDV *Star Polaris* on station.
19 Nov - 16 Dec	CDV *Star Sirius* on station.
21 Nov	*Tyr* cut *Real Madrid's* (GY674) warps.
22 Nov	*Tyr* cut *Ross Sirius's* (H277) warps.
25 Nov	The Icelandic and West German Governments reached agreement over limited quotas within the 200-mile limits.
25-30 Nov	HMS *Leopard* on patrol.
25 Nov	*Ægir* cut *William Wilberforce's* (GY140) warps; coinciding with HMS *Leopard's* arrival on station.
29 Nov - 13 Dec	RFA *Tidepool* (Wessex embarked) on station.
29 Nov - 16 Dec	HMS *Falmouth* (OTC) on patrol.
29 Nov - 18 Dec	HMS *Brighton* on patrol.
1 Dec	*Árvakur* cut *Port Vale's* (GY484) warps. *Port Vale* was fishing well outside the declared Defended Fishing Area (DFA).
2 Dec - 1 Jun	CDV *Euroman* on station.
3 Dec	*Ægir* cut *Boston Comanche's* (GY144) warps.
5 Dec	*Thor* cut *Ramilles's* (GY53) warps.
6 Dec	*Thor* cut *Northern Reward's* (GY694) warps. Collision between *Thor* and CDV *Euroman*.
6 Dec	*Ægir* cut *Kingston Jacinth's* (H198) warps.
9-12 Dec	HMS *Galatea* on patrol.
9 Dec	*Thor* cut *St Giles's* (H220) warps.

11 Dec	*Thor* fired warning shots at CDV *Star Aquarius* and CDV *Lloydsman* sheltering inside the 12-mile limit. Collisions between *Thor* and both CDV *Star Aquarius* and CDV *Lloydsman* (twice)
13 Dec - 5 Jan	RFA *Olwen* (Wessex embarked) on station.
13-19 Dec	HMS *Leander* (OTC) on patrol.
18 Dec - 8 Jan	HMS *Lowestoft* on patrol.
18 Dec	*Òdinn* cut *Crystal Palace's* (GY683) warps.
19 Dec - 8 Jan	HMS *Andromeda* (OTC) on patrol.
28 Dec - 6 Jan	HMS *Gurkha* on patrol.
28 Dec	Collision between *Thor* and HMS *Andromeda*.

1976

3-14 Jan	RMAS *Roysterer* on station.
3 Jan	*Ægir* cut *Prince Philip's* (GY138) and *Ross Resolution's* (GY527) warps.
4 Jan - 17 May	CDV *Statesman* on station.
5-15 Jan	RFA *Tidepool* (Wessex embarked) on station.
7-27 Jan	HMS *Naiad* on patrol.
7 Jan	Collision between *Thor* and HMS *Andromeda*.
9-14 Jan	HMS *Bacchante* on patrol.
9-19 Jan	HMS *Leander* (OTC) on patrol.
9 Jan	Collision between *Thor* and HMS *Leander*.
10-30 Jan	HMS *Falmouth* on patrol. OTC from 19 Jan.
15-21 Jan	RMAS *Rollicker* on station.
15 Jan - 23 Feb	RFA *Olwen* (Wessex embarked) on station.
19-20 Jan	HMS *Bacchante* on patrol.
19 Jan	Collision between trawler *Lord Jellicoe* (GY709) and *Thor*
26 Jan	*Tyr* cut *Boston Blenheim's* (FD137) warps.
27 Jan - 15 Feb	HMS *Juno* (OTC) on patrol.
30 Jan - 18 Feb	HMS *Diomede* on patrol.
2 Feb	*Tyr* cut *Ross Khartoum's* (GY120) warps.
5 Feb	*Baldur* cut *Loch Eribol's* (H323) warps.
6 Feb	*Tyr* cut *Ross Altair's* (H279) warps.
6 Feb	Two collisions between *Thor* and HMS *Juno*.
7-19 Feb	HMS *Lowestoft* on patrol.
10-24 Feb	RMAS *Roysterer* on station.
11 Feb	*Baldur* cut *Ross Rodney's* (GY34) warps.
12 Feb	*Baldur* cut *William Wilberforce's* (GY140) warps.
12 Feb	Collision between *Baldur* and HMS *Diomede*.
15 Feb - 7 Mar	HMS *Scylla* (OTC) on patrol.
17 Feb - 8 Mar	HMS *Bacchante* on patrol.
18 Feb	*Ægir* cut *William Wilberforce's* (GY140) warps.
18 Feb	Collision between *Thor* and HMS *Lowestoft*.
19 Feb	Iceland broke off diplomatic relations with the UK. NATO attempted to mediate.
19 Feb	*Ægir* cut *Royal Lincs's* (GY18) warps.
20-29 Feb	HMS *Yarmouth* on patrol.
20 Feb	*Thor* cut *Ross Leonis's* (H322) warps.
23 Feb - 23 Mar	RFA *Tidepool* (Wessex embarked) on station.
23 Feb	*Baldur* cut *Arctic Vandal's* (H344) warps.

23 Feb	*Tyr* cut *Luneda's* (FD134) warps.
24 Feb	Two collisions (Iceland claims 3) between *Thor* and HMS *Yarmouth*.
24 Feb	Collision between *Tyr* and HMS *Scylla*
25 Feb - 11 Mar	R*MAS Rollicker* on station.
26 Feb - 7 Mar	HMS *Andromeda* on patrol.
28 Feb	*Tyr* cut *Boston Stirling's* (FD247) warps.
28 Feb	Collision between *Baldur* and HMS *Yarmouth*. *Yarmouth* returned to the UK with severe bow damage.
1-11 Mar	HMS *Naiad* on patrol.
7-28 Mar	HMS *Mermaid* (OTC) on patrol.
9-28 Mar	HMS *Diomede* on patrol.
10 Mar	Collision between *Baldur* and HMS *Diomede*.
10-28 Mar	HMS *Galatea* on patrol.
11-29 Mar	HMS *Juno* (OTC) on patrol.
11 Mar	*Ægir* cut *Ross Kashmir's* (GY122) warps.
12-27 Mar	RMAS *Typhoon* on station.
12 Mar	Three collisions between *Tyr* and HMS *Juno*.
12 Mar	Three collisions between *Thor* and HMS *Mermaid*.
13 Mar	Collision between *Tyr* and HMS *Diomede*.
16 Mar	Harold Wilson resigns as Prime Minister. Jim Callaghan takes over and Antony Crosland (MP for Grimsby) becomes Foreign Secretary
24 Mar - 22 Apr	RFA *Olwen* (Wessex embarked) on station.
26 Mar	Collision between *Baldur* and HMS *Galatea*.
27 Mar	Four collisions between *Baldur* and HMS *Diomede*. *Diomede* was seriously damaged in these collisions. The '*Avoid Damage to Frigates*' policy was promulgated that evening.
28 Mar - 11 Apr	RMAS *Roysterer* on station.
28 Mar - 18 Apr	HM Ships *Scylla* (OTC), *Bacchante* and *Tartar* on patrol.
30 Mar - 9 Apr	HMS *Salisbury* on patrol.
1 Apr	Five collisions between *Tyr* and HMS *Salisbury*. Two collisions between *Tyr* and HMS *Tartar*.
3-24 Apr	HMS *Andromeda* on patrol.
3 Apr	Collision between *Òdinn* and HMS *Scylla*.
5 Apr	New DFA established off the northwest coast.
6-10 Apr	RFA *Tidereach* on station.
9 Apr	Eastern DFA closed.
12-26 Apr	RMAS *Rollicker* on station.
18-29 Apr	HMS *Naiad* on patrol.
18 Apr - 11 May	HM Ships *Galatea* (OTC) and *Gurkha* on patrol.
19 Apr	Western DFA closed
20 Apr	Eastern DFA re-opened
22 Apr	*Tyr* cut one of *Northern Gift's* (GY704) warps, both of *Benella's* (H132) and one of *Arctic Vandal's* (H344).
23 Apr - 8 May	HMS *Mermaid* on patrol.
23 Apr - 25 May	RFA *Tidepool* (Wessex embarked) on station.
24 Apr	*Ægir* cut both *Maretta's* (FD245) and one *of C S Forester's* (H86) warps.
24 Apr	*Tyr* cut *Ross Canaveral's* (H267) warps.
24 Apr	*Òdinn*, in Hot Pursuit, attempted to arrest *Crystal Palace* (GY683), who returned to the UK.
24 Apr	Collision between *Tyr* and HMS *Naiad*.

26 Apr	Collision between *Ægir* and CDV *Euroman*.
27 Apr - 8 May	RMAS *Typhoon* on station.
27 Apr	*Thor* cut one of *Irvana's* (FD141) warps.
28 Apr	*Òdinn* cut *Gerontius's* (H350) warps.
28 Apr	Two collisions (Iceland only claims 1) between *Ver* and CDV *Statesman*.
30 Apr - 7 May	HMS *Falmouth* on patrol.
30 Apr	*Baldur* cut *Boston Kestrel's* (FD256) warps.
30 Apr	Two collisions between *Òdinn* and trawler *Arctic Corsair* (H320).
3 May	*Òdinn* cut one of *Boston Kestrel's* (FD256) warps.
4 May	*Tyr* cut *Lord St Vincent's* (H261) warps.
6 May	Collision between *Baldur* and HMS *Mermaid*. *Mermaid* returned early to the UK with potentially serious damage. The first serious incident after the resumption of the 'riding off' policy.
6 May	Four collisions (Iceland only claims 3) between *Òdinn* and HMS *Gurkha*.
6 May	*Tyr* cut one of *Carlisle's* (GY681) warps. The last warp cutting.
6 May	Three collisions between *Tyr* and HMS *Falmouth*. Both retired with serious damage.
7 May	Collision between *Òdinn* and HMS *Gurkha*.
8-20 May	HMS *Lowestoft* on patrol.
8-26 May	HMS *Leander* on patrol. OTC from 11 May.
10-24 May	RMAS *Roysterer* on station.
10 May - 1 Jun	HMS *Tartar* on patrol.
11-26 May	HMS *Eastbourne* on patrol.
11-30 May	HMS *Salisbury* on patrol.
12 May	*Ægir* attempted to board and arrest *Primella* (H98). Warning shots were fired. Hot Pursuit was frustrated by a Nimrod's warnings.
13 May - 1 Jun	RFA *Blue Rover* on station.
14-27 May	HMS *Dundas* on patrol.
19 May - 1 Jun	CDV *Southella* on station.
20 May	Two collisions (Iceland only claims 1) between *Ægir* and HMS *Salisbury*.
20-21 May	Anglo-Icelandic Ministerial Meetings during the NATO Summit in Oslo.
22 May	Collision between *Ægir* and HMS *Tartar*.
22 May	Collision between *Baldur* and HMS *Eastbourne*.
22 May	Collision between *Ver* and HMS *Leander*. Both retired with serious damage.
23 May	UK and Icelandic Fishery Ministers met in Oslo.
23 May - 1 Jun	HMS *Exmouth* on patrol.
25 May - 1 Jun	RMAS *Rollicker* on station.
26 May - 1 Jun	HM Ships *Diomede* (OTC) and *Achilles* on patrol.
26 May - 1 Jun	RFA *Olwen* (Wessex embarked) on station.
26 May	Collision between *Ægir* and HMS *Tartar*.
27 May - 1 Jun	HMS *Naiad* on patrol.
30 May - 1 Jun	HMS *Torquay* on patrol.
30 May	Operations DEWEY and HELIOTROPE suspended.
31 May	Foreign Ministers met in Oslo to sign the Agreement
1 Jun	The Cod Wars were over. UK and Iceland agreed quotas for British trawlers within the 200-mile limit for the following 6 months.

Note: The Civilian Defence Vessels were on station throughout except for periodic returns (approx. monthly) to a northern UK port for crew change and maintenance.

19 Sep 79 HM Ambassador in Reykjavík, Kenneth East, hosted dinner for the officers of HMS *Bacchante* and the Icelandic Coastguard.

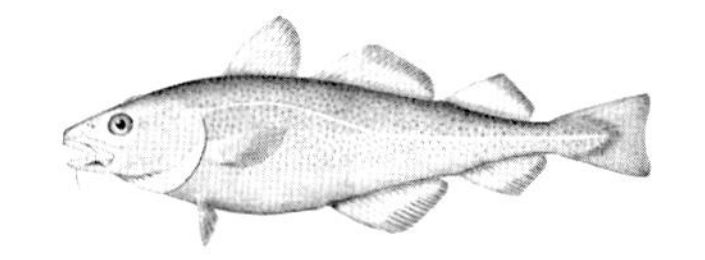

APPENDIX FOUR

ICELANDIC COASTGUARD VESSELS

First Cod War 1958-61

Note: The Commanding Officers were appointed in Command, but not necessarily onboard for every trip.

Ægir	Displacement	507 tons
Captain	LOA[185]	183 ft
Thórarinn	Speed	14 knots
Björnsson	Complement	22
	Armament	1 - 3pdr
	Built	1929 - Rebuilt 1953

Albert	Displacement	200 tons
Captain	LOA	120 ft
Jón	Speed	13 knots
Jónsson	Complement	15
	Armament	1 - 47mm
	Built	1957

Hermodur	Displacement	208 tons
Captain	LOA	119 ft
Gudni	Speed	12 knots
Thorlacius	Complement	13
	Armament	1 - 47mm
	Built	1947

Note: Rated as a Lighthouse Tender, but occasionally employed on Fishery Protection duties. She foundered and was lost with all hands on 18 Feb 1959. A relief Captain was onboard at the time.

Manatindur	Displacement	100 tons
	LOA	80 ft
	Speed	11 knots
	Complement	11
	Armament	Nil

Note: A converted Motor Fishing Vessel used, temporarily, on Coastguard duty 1959-60. She replaced *Hermodur* as a Lighthouse Tender.

---

[185] Length Overall

Maria Júlia	Displacement	138 tons
Captain	LOA	99 ft
Lárus	Speed	12 knots
Thorsteinsson	Complement	12
	Armament	1 - 3pdr
	Built	1950

Òdinn	Displacement	100 tons
	LOA	80 ft
	Speed	11 knots
	Complement	11
	Armament	1 - 3pdr
	Built	1938 - Rebuilt 1954

Note: Renamed *Gautur* in Feb 1960 when the new *Òdinn* was commissioned.

Òdinn	Displacement	1000 tons
Captain	LOA	210 ft
Pétur	Speed	20 knots
Jónsson	Complement	22
	Armament	1 - 57mm
	Built	1960

Suborn	Displacement	100 tons
Captain	LOA	80 ft
Sigurdur	Speed	11 knots
Arnasson	Complement	11
	Armament	1 - 3pdr
	Built	1937

Thorn	Displacement	920 tons
Captain	LOA	206 ft
Eiríkur	Speed	18 Knots
Kristófersson	Complement	22
	Armament	1 - 57mm
	Built	1951

Second Cod War 1972-3

Note: The Commanding Officers were appointed in Command, but not necessarily onboard for every trip.

Ægir	Displacement	1150 tons
Captain	LOA	213 ft
Gudmundur	Speed	20 knots
Kjærnested	Complement	22
	Armament	1 - 57mm fwd
		1 - 47mm aft
		Small helicopter deck
	Built	1968

Note: Captain Sigtryggsson was in command during the incident with *HMS Apollo* on 29 August 1973, after which a mate, Halldór Hallfredsson, was electrocuted whilst welding on the upper deck.

Albert	Displacement	200 tons
Captain	LOA	120 ft
Bjarni O	Speed	13 knots
Helgason	Complement	15
	Armament	1 - 47mm
	Built	1957

Árvakur	Displacement	380 tons
Captain	LOA	142 ft
Helgi	Speed	12 knots
Hallvardsson	Complement	15
	Armament	Nil
	Built	1962

Note: Captain Hóskuldur Skarphedinsson was in command on 1 June 1973 during the incident with the tug *Irishman*.

Òdinn	Displacement	1000 tons
Captain	LOA	210 ft
Sigurdur	Speed	20 knots
Arnasson	Complement	22
	Armament	1 - 57mm fwd
		1 - 47mm aft
		Small helicopter deck
	Built	1960

Thor	Displacement	920 tons
Captain	LOA	206 ft
Captain	Speed	18 Knots
Throstur	Complement	22
Sigtryggsson	Armament	1 - 57mm fwd
aka 'Spörri' -		1 - 47mm aft
the Sparrow		Small helicopter deck
	Built	1951

Tyr	Displacement	630 tons
	LOA	169 ft
	Speed	14 knots
	Complement	15
	Armament	1 - 3pdr

Note: Ex-whaler *Hvalur 9*, hired by Coastguard Sep 1972 to May 1973.

Third Cod War 1975-6

Ægir	Displacement	1150 tons
Captain	LOA	213 ft
Throstur	Speed	20 knots
Sigtryggsson	Complement	22
	Armament	1 - 57mm fwd
		1 - 47mm aft
		Small helicopter deck
	Built	1968

Albert	Displacement	200 tons
	LOA	120 ft
	Speed	13 knots
	Complement	15
	Armament	1 - 47mm
	Built	1957

Árvakur	Displacement	380 tons
	LOA	142 ft
	Speed	12 knots
	Complement	15
	Armament	Nil
	Built	1962

Baldur	Displacement	740 tons
Captain	LOA	200 ft
Hóskuldur	Speed	18 knots
Skarphedinsson	Complement	20
	Armament	1 - 47mm

Note: Stern trawler hired by Coastguard 1975

Òdinn	Displacement	1000 tons
Captain	LOA	210 ft
Sigurdur	Speed	20 knots
Arnasson	Complement	22
	Armament	1 - 57mm fwd
		1 - 47mm aft
		Small helicopter deck
	Built	1960

Thor	Displacement	920 tons
Captain	LOA	206 ft
Helgi	Speed	18 Knots
Hallvardsson	Complement	22
	Armament	1 - 57mm fwd
		1 - 47mm aft
		Small helicopter deck
	Built	1951

Tyr	Displacement	1150 tons
Captain	LOA	213 ft
Gudmundur	Speed	20 knots
Kjærnested	Complement	22
	Armament	1 - 57mm fwd
		1 - 47mm aft
		Small helicopter deck
	Built	1975

Ver	Displacement	740 tons
	LOA	200 ft
	Speed	18 knots
	Complement	20
	Armament	Nil

Note: Sister ship to *Baldur* hired by Coastguard 5th Apr 1976.

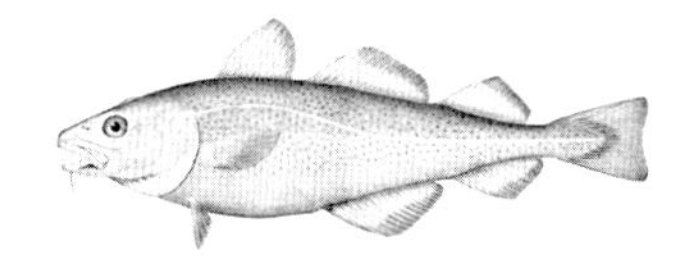

APPENDIX FIVE

ROYAL NAVY PATROL DATES

First Cod War: 1 Sep 58 - 11 Mar 61

Ship	Dates	Commanding Officer
HMS *Agincourt* Battle Class Destroyer	29 Jan - 11 Feb 59 11-28 May 59	Capt E N Sinclair DSC (Capt D4) OTC[186] OTC
HMS *Apollo* Fast Minelayer	3-16 Jun 59 12 Feb - 1 Mar 60 6-16 Jun 60	Capt M G R Lumby DSO DSC Capt L D Empson (OTC) OTC
HMS *Armada* Battle Class Destroyer	7-25 Nov 59 25 Jan - 11 Feb 60	Cdr M W B Kerr DSC OTC
HMS *Barrosa* Battle Class Destroyer	24 Jan - 11 Feb 59 29 Apr - 11 May 59	Cdr R F Plugge DSC
HMS *Battleaxe* Weapon Class Destroyer	1-19 May 60 30 Aug - 12 Sep 60	Cdr J E Maidwell
HMS *Blackpool* Type 12 Frigate	8-19 Jan 61	Cdr M L Stacey
HMS *Blackwood* Type 14 Frigate	13-30 Oct 58 13-24 Oct 58	Lt Cdr D G Kay DSC Capt B J Anderson (CFPS) embarked as OTC
HMS *Broadsword* Weapon Class Destroyer	19 May - 1 Jun 59 19 Jul - 5 Aug 59	Cdr D R Williams MBE
HMS *Camperdown* Battle Class Destroyer	7-27 Nov 59	Cdr P R Wood DSC and Bar
HMS *Carron* Ca Class Destroyer	11-29 Sep 59	Lt Cdr P J Shaw
HMS *Carysfort* Ca Class Destroyer	10-28 May 59 23 Jul - 11 Aug 59	Cdr M M Dunlop DSC OTC 30 Jul-11 Aug

[186] I have included the names of Commanding Officers in the next two Annexes because, despite the modern fashion for omitting CO's names, many people remember their time in a ship by who was in command, rather than by any exact dates.

HMS *Cavendish*	25 Apr - 10 May 59	Capt P U Bayly DSC and 2 Bars (Capt D6)
Ca Class Destroyer		OTC
	24-29 Jul 59	OTC
HMS *Chaplet*	12-28 May 59	Capt R White OBE (Capt D Plymouth)
Ch Class Destroyer		OTC
	30 Sep - 16 Oct 59	
HMS *Crossbow*	9-20 Jun 60	Cdr D Hay. OTC from 17 Jun.
Weapon Class Destroyer	12-29 Aug 60	
HMS *Contest*	25 Apr - 9 May 59	Cdr R H Reynolds DSC AFC
Co Class Destroyer		
HMS *Corunna*	24 Jan - 11 Feb 59	Cdr C Gordon DSC
Battle Class Destroyer		
HMS *Dainty*	19 May - 8 Jun 60	Capt J G Wells DSC (OTC)
Daring Class Destroyer	24 Oct - 10 Nov 60	OTC from 3 Nov.
HMS *Daring*	12-29 Aug 60	Capt C P Mills CBE DSC (Capt D2) OTC
Daring Class Destroyer	21 Oct - 3 Nov 60	OTC
HMS *Decoy*	20 Sep - 3 Oct 58	Capt F P Baker DSC
Daring Class Destroyer		
HMS *Defender*	11-29 Jul 60	Capt G H Carew-Hunt (OTC)
Daring Class Destroyer	7-20 Oct 60	OTC
HMS *Delight*	28 Apr - 18 May 60	Capt P C G Dickens DSO MBE DSC (OTC)
Daring Class Destroyer	30 Aug - 12 Sep 60	OTC
HMS *Diamond*	2-12 Dec 58	Capt J A C Henley DSC
Daring Class Destroyer		
HMS *Diana*	20 Sep - 2 Oct 58	Capt P W W Graham DSC
Daring Class Destroyer		
HMS *Duncan*	16 Nov - 2 Dec 58	Cdre B J Anderson (CFPS) (OTC)
Type 14 Frigate	6-23 Jan 59	OTC
	12 Feb - 1 Mar 59	OTC
	18 Mar - 5 Apr 59	OTC
	29 May - 16 Jun 59	OTC
	5-23 Jul 59	OTC
	11-24 Aug 59	Capt H H Bracken (CFPS) (OTC)
	18 Dec 59 - 5 Jan 60	OTC
	21 Jun - 10 Jul 60	OTC
	11-29 Nov 60	OTC

HMS *Dundas* Type 14 Frigate	31 Oct - 11 Nov 58	Lt Cdr J de Beaufort-Suchlick
HMS *Dunkirk* Battle Class Destroyer	17 Jun - 4 Jul 59 26 Aug - 10 Sep 59 17 Oct - 6 Nov 59	Cdr J Nash DSC
HMS *Eastbourne* Type 12 Frigate	1-12 Sep 58 1-14 Sep 58 2-17 May 59	Lt Cdr R C Mayne Cdre B J Anderson (CFPS) embarked as OTC
HMS *Exmouth* Type 14 Frigate	25 Apr - 11 May 59 11-24 Aug 59	Lt Cdr M R Wilson
HMS *Grafton* Type 14 Frigate	20-27 Nov 58	Lt Cdr J R S Gerard-Pearse
HMS *Grenville* Type 15 Frigate	6-24 Apr 59	Cdr C W Eason
HMS *Hardy* Type 14 Frigate	3-23 Oct 58 11-13 Oct 58	Lt Cdr F E B Brown Cdre B J Anderson (CFPS) embarked as OTC
HMS *Hogue* Battle Class Destroyer	13-30 Sep 58 14 Sep - 1 Oct 58 23 Oct - 8 Nov 58 19 Dec - 6 Jan 59	Cdr V A D Turner DSC Cdre B J Anderson (CFPS) embarked as OTC Cdr J R Pardoe
HMS *Hound* Algerine Class Minesweeper	1-5 Sep 58	Cdr A B B Clark
HMS *Jutland* Battle Class Destroyer	17 Jun - 4 Jul 59 25 Aug - 10 Sep 59 19 Oct - 6 Nov 59	Cdr T W Stocker
HMS *Keppel* Type 14 Frigate	26 Feb - 2 Mar 61	Cdr I G W Robertson DSC (OTC)
HMS *Lagos* Battle Class Destroyer	5-27 Sep 58 26 Oct - 11 Nov 58 19 Dec 58 - 6 Jan 59	Cdr D Jermain DSC & Bar Cdr R P Dannreuther
HMS *Llandaff* Salisbury Class Frigate	28 Nov - 16 Dec 58 3-17 Dec 58	Cdr I F O Alford Cdre B J Anderson (CFPS) embarked as OTC
HMS *Loch Alvie* Loch Class Frigate	20 Jan - 8 Feb 61	Cdr J H Nethersole (OTC)

HMS *Malcolm*	24 Mar - 13 Apr 59	Cdr B H Notley
Type 14 Frigate	12-18 May 59	
	1-8 Jun 59	
	12-18 Jul 59	
	6-25 Aug 59	
	30 Sep - 16 Oct 59	
	25 Jan - 11 Feb 60	
	20 May - 8 Jun 60	
	16 Sep - 6 Oct 60	OTC
	11-29 Nov 60	
	17 Feb - 11 Mar 61	Cdr M A Tibby (OTC)
HMS *Orwell*	12-19 Nov 58	Capt P M Compston
Type 16 Frigate		
HMS *Paladin*	5-18 Dec 58	Cdr K Lee-White MBE
P Class Frigate	2-14 Mar 60	Cdr P D Davey (OTC)
3-23 Oct 60		
HMS *Palliser*	1-19 Sep 58	Lt Cdr G E Hammond
Type 14 Frigate	4-25 Oct 58	
	13-18 Dec 58	
	17-19 Dec 58	Cdre B J Anderson (CFPS) embarked as OTC
	7-20 Jan 59	
	12 Feb - 1 Mar 59	
	17 Mar - 3 Apr 59	
	29 Jul - 10 Aug 59	
	30 Sep - 10 Oct 59	Lt Cdr The Hon J T Fremantle
	28 Nov - 16 Dec 59	
	12 Feb - 1 Mar 60	
	28 Apr - 19 May 60	
	22 Jun - 10 Jul 60	
	30 Jul - 11 Aug 60	
	30 Nov - 18 Dec 60	
	29 Jan - 16 Feb 61	OTC from 9 Feb
HMS *Pellew*	17-21 Jun 60	Lt Cdr P D Jenks
Type 14 Frigate		
HMS *Rhyl*	3-11 Mar 61	Cdr G J Dodd (OTC)
Type 12 Frigate		
HMS *Russell*	1-19 Sep 58	Lt Cdr P F R Corson
Type 14 Frigate	1-22 Oct 58	
	12-30 Nov 58	
	6-23 Jan 59	
	12 Feb - 1 Mar 59	
	18 Mar - 5 Apr 59	
	29 May - 16 Jun 59	

	5-22 Jul 59	
	28 Nov - 17 Dec 59	Lt Cdr J D'O C Lewis Cdr B H Notley (CO HMS Malcolm) embarked as OTC
	20 May - 4 Jun 60	
	30 Jul - 11 Aug 60	OTC
	30 Nov - 19 Dec 60	OTC
HMS *Saintes* Battle Class Destroyer	7-27 Nov 59 13-16 Sep 60	Capt O H M St J Steiner (Capt D3) (OTC) Cdr M J Porter (OTC)
HMS *Salisbury* Salisbury Class Frigate	14-24 Apr 59	Cdr A G Watson
HMS *Scarborough* Type 12 Frigate	6-24 Apr 59	Capt E M Usherwood DSC (Capt F5) (OTC)
HMS *Solebay* Battle Class Destroyer	19 Dec 58 - 5 Jan 59	Capt H J Lee DSC and 2 Bars (Capt D1) (OTC)
HMS *Tenby* Type 12 Frigate	6-24 Apr 59	Cdr W R D Gerard-Pearse MVO
HMS *Torquay* Type 12 Frigate	7-24 Jan 60 17-28 Jan 61	Cdr B H G M Bayham OTC
HMS *Trafalgar* Battle Class Destroyer	17 Jun - 4 Jul 59	Capt C D Madden MVO DSC and Bar (Capt D7) (OTC)
	25 Aug - 9 Sep 59	OTC
	17 Oct - 6 Nov 59	OTC
HMS *Troubridge* Type 15 Frigate	20 Dec 60 - 8 Jan 61	Cdr A H Young (OTC)
HMS *Ulster* Type 15 Frigate	1-10 Oct 58 1-11 Oct 58	Lt Cdr C Rusby Cdre B J Anderson (CFPS) embarked as OTC
HMS *Ulysses* Type 15 Frigate	6-23 Jan 60	Cdr C J Cunningham DSC (OTC)
HMS *Undaunted* Type 15 Frigate	9-16 Jan 61	Capt D H Mason (OTC)
HMS *Undine* Type 15 Frigate	16 Dec 59 - 6 Jan 60 2-14 Mar 60	Cdr L R R Foster
	11-29 Jul 60	Cdr A S Morton
HMS *Urchin* Type 15 Frigate	10-29 Sep 59	Cdr D J Bent DSC

HMS *Venus* Type 15 Frigate	10-29 Sep 59	Capt P N Howes DSC (Capt F DTS) (OTC)
HMS *Vigilant* Type 15 Frigate	13 Sep - 2 Oct 60	Lt Cdr J D B McCarthy
HMS *Vigo* Battle Class Destroyer	2-9 Mar 59 5-11 Jul 59	Capt M P Pollock MVO DSC
HMS *Whitby* Type 12 Frigate	9-17 Mar 59	Lt Cdr C R A O'Brien
HMS *Zest* Type 15 Frigate	24 Oct - 15 Nov 58	Capt A P W Northey DSC and 2 Bars (Capt TS3) (OTC)
	2-17 Mar 59	OTC
	4-10 Nov 60	Cdr M G Fowke

Second Cod War: 1 Sep 72 - 13 Nov 73

HMS *Achilles* Leander Class Frigate	11-23 Oct 72	Cdr H G de Courcy-Ireland
HMS *Andromeda* Leander Class Frigate	31 Jul - 24 Aug 73	Capt A F R Weir (Capt F6) (OTC)
HMS *Apollo* Leander Class Frigate	14-18 Dec 72	Capt R L Garnons-Williams
	24 Aug - 21 Sep 73	Capt R G A Fitch (OTC)
	15 Oct - 5 Nov 73	OTC
HMS *Arethusa* Leander Class Frigate	11 Apr - 3 May 73	Capt A L L Skinner (Capt F8)
	14-31 Jul 73	OTC
HMS *Argonaut* Leander Class Frigate	26 Jul - 12 Aug 73	Cdr C W C Swinley
HMS *Ariadne* Leander Class Frigate	24 Sep - 13 Oct 73 24 Oct - 13 Nov 73	Cdr P A Pinkster
HMS *Ashanti* Tribal Class Frigate	5-21 Jun 73	Cdr R N Blair
HMS *Aurora* Leander Class Frigate	10 Sep - 1 Oct 72	Cdr G F Liardet

HMS *Berwick* Type 12 Frigate	27-30 Oct 72 22 Jan - 13 Feb 73 16-31 Jul 73	Cdr J B D Read Cdr P G V Dingemans
HMS *Caprice* Ca Class Destroyer	12 Feb - 2 Mar 73	Lt Cdr J C E Lloyd
HMS *Charybdis* Leander Class Frigate	20 Jun - 15 Jul 73 21 Sep - 17 Oct 73 7-9 Nov 73	Capt G C Lloyd (Capt F1) (OTC) OTC
HMS *Cleopatra* Leander Class Frigate	3 May - 1 Jun 73	Cdr A R Wavish
HMS *Danae* Leander Class Frigate	9-13 Nov 73	Capt M L'E Tudor-Craig
HMS *Falmouth* Type 12 Frigate	30 Oct - 4 Nov 72 21 Jun - 8 Jul 73	Cdr G F Walwyn
HMS *Gurkha* Tribal Class Frigate	2-24 Mar 73 8-16 Jul 73	Capt D T McKeown Capt V M Howard
HMS *Jaguar* Leopard Class Frigate	29 Nov - 13 Dec 72 1-17 Jun 73 31 Aug - 16 Sep 73 12 Oct - 31 Oct 73	Cdr G W G Hunt Cdr C J Caughey
HMS *Juno* Leander Class Frigate	14-29 Nov 72	Capt A J Whetstone
HMS *Jupiter* Leander Class Frigate	22 May - 5 Jun 73	Cdr J C K Slater
HMS *Leopard* Leopard Class Frigate	16 Jun - 6 Jul 73 28 Sep - 20 Oct 73	Cdr M J Harvey
HMS *Lincoln* Salisbury Class Frigate	20-22 May 73 6-27 Jul 73 16-24 Sep 73	Cdr J D H B Howard
HMS *Lowestoft* Type 12 Frigate	5-16 Jan 73	Cdr M C Powys Maurice
HMS *Lynx* Leopard Class frigate	13 Aug - 10 Sep 73	Cdr C H Layman

HMS *Palliser* Type 14 Frigate	1-11 Oct 72	Lt Cdr G M Tullis
HMS *Phoebe* Leander Class Frigate	19 Oct - 14 Nov 72 5-13 Nov 73	Cdr R A S Irving Capt J A B Thomas (OTC)
HMS *Plymouth* Type 12 Frigate	16-29 May 73	Cdr M J F Rawlinson (OTC)
HMS *Rhyl* Type 12 Frigate	18 Dec 72 - 5 Jan 73	Cdr D A Wallis
HMS *Rothesay* Type 12 Frigate	24 Mar - 11 Apr 73	Cdr T M B Seymour
HMS *Scylla* Leander Class Frigate	29 May - 20 Jun 73	Capt O P Sutton (Capt F7) (OTC)
HMS *Sirius* Leander Class Frigate	30 Jul - 14 Aug 73	Cdr P H Coward
HMS *Whitby* Type 12 Frigate	10-28 Sep 73 20–24 Oct 73	Cdr W J Flindell Capt W J Flindell
HMS *Yarmouth* Type 12 Frigate	16-22 Jan 73 31 Oct - 7 Nov 73	Cdr I W Powe

Third Cod War: 25 Nov 75 - 1 Jun 76

HMS *Achilles* Leander Class Frigate	26 May - 1 Jun 76	Cdr J F S Trinder
HMS *Andromeda* Leander Class Frigate	19 Dec 75 - 8 Jan 76 26 Feb - 7 Mar 76 3-24 Apr 76	Capt R W F Gerken (Capt F6) (OTC) Capt A M G Pearson (Capt F6)
HMS *Bacchante* Leander Class Frigate	9-14 Jan 76 19-20 Jan 76 17 Feb - 8 Mar 76 28 Mar - 18 Apr 76	Capt A J Dunn
HMS *Brighton* Type 12 Frigate	29 Nov - 18 Dec 75	Cdr N I C Kettlewell

Ship	Dates	Commanding Officer
HMS *Diomede*	30 Jan - 18 Feb 76	Capt R McQueen
Leander Class Frigate	9-28 Mar 76	
	26 May - 1 Jun 76	OTC
HMS *Dundas*	14-27 May 76	Lt Cdr M E W Bush
Type 14 Frigate		
HMS *Eastbourne*	11-26 May 76	Lt Cdr M W Kemmis Betty
Type 12 Frigate		
HMS *Exmouth*	23 May - 1 Jun 76	Lt Cdr J Davies
Type 14 Frigate		
HMS *Falmouth*	29 Nov - 16 Dec 75	Cdr G A Plumer
Type 12 Frigate	29 Nov - 12 Dec 75	Capt J M Tait (Capt F3) embarked as OTC
	10-30 Jan 76	
	19-27 Jan 76	Capt J M Tait (Capt F3) embarked as OTC
	30 Apr - 7 May 76	
HMS *Galatea*	9-12 Dec 75	Capt W S Gueterbock (Capt F1)
Leander Class Frigate	10-28 Mar 76	
	18 Apr - 11 May 76	OTC
HMS *Gurkha*	28 Dec 75 - 6 Jan 76	Cdr T R Lee
Tribal Class Frigate	18 Apr - 11 May 76	
HMS *Juno*	27 Jan - 15 Feb 76	Capt E R Anson (Capt F4) (OTC)
Leander Class Frigate	11-29 Mar 76	OTC
HMS *Leander*	13-19 Dec 75	Capt J M Tait (Capt F3) (OTC)
Leander Class Frigate	9-19 Jan 76	OTC
	8-26 May 76	OTC 11-26 May
HMS *Leopard*	25-30 Nov 75	Cdr R H Whyte-Melville-Jackson
Leopard Class Frigate		
HMS *Lowestoft*	18 Dec 75 - 8 Jan 76	Cdr R M Carpendale
Type 12 Frigate	7-19 Feb 76	
	8-20 May 76	
HMS *Mermaid*	7-28 Mar 76	Cdr R H C Heptinstall
Yarrow Type Frigate	7-11 Mar	Capt E R Anson (Capt F4) embarked as OTC
	24 Apr - 8 May 76	
HMS *Naiad*	7-27 Jan 76	Capt A Casdagli
Leander Class Frigate	1-11 Mar 76	
	18-29 Apr 76	
	27 May - 1 Jun 76	

HMS *Salisbury* Salisbury Class Frigate	30 Mar - 9 Apr 76 11-30 May 76	Cdr H M White
HMS *Scylla* Leander Class Frigate	15 Feb - 7 Mar 76 28 Mar - 18 Apr 76	Capt A Checksfield (Capt F7) (OTC) Capt D G Armytage (Capt F7) (OTC)
HMS *Tartar* Tribal Class Frigate	28 Mar - 18 Apr 76 10 May - 1 Jun 76	Cdr J L Weatherall
HMS *Torquay* Type 12 Frigate	30 May - 1 Jun 76	Lt Cdr K W Darby
HMS *Yarmouth* Type 12 Frigate	20-29 Feb 76	Cdr M J Jones

APPENDIX SIX

ROYAL FLEET AUXILIARY, ROYAL MARITIME AUXILIARY SERVICE AND DEFENCE TUG PATROL DATES

First Cod War: 1 Sep 59 - 11 Mar 61

RFA *Black Ranger*	2-11 Sep 58	Capt B V Dobbie
RFA *Tidereach*	9-11 Jan 59	Capt D S Norrington
RFA *Wave Baron*	13-29 Sep 58	Capt G B A Livesay
	20-27 Nov 58	
	20 Jan - 6 Feb 59	
	9-24 Mar 59	Capt T E Hill
	25 Apr - 10 May 59	
	24 Jun - 11 Jul 59	
	1-25 Nov 59	Capt G O W Evans
	22 Dec 59 - 6 Jan 60	
	9-22 Feb 60	Capt R V Warren DSC
	10-22 Jan 61	Capt B V Dobbie
RFA *Wave Chief*	27 Nov - 17 Dec 58	Capt F S Samson
	6-19 Jan 59	
	20 Feb - 7 Mar 59	
	26 Mar - 13 Apr 59	Capt R H Venning
	11-31 May 59	
	12 Jul - 4 Aug 59	Capt P Colfer
	14 Sep - 4 Oct	
	7-21 Jan 60	
	23 Feb - 14 Mar 60	
	25 Oct - 18 Nov	Capt A M Macquire
	23 Jan - 5 Feb 61	
RFA *Wave Laird*	16-29 Sep 60	Capt R K McKenzie
RFA *Wave Master*	2-10 Mar 61	Capt A Waters
RFA *Wave Prince*	22 May - 12 Jun 60	Capt I B Roberts
	5-24 Jul 60	
	15 Aug - 7 Sep 60	
	19-27 Nov 60	
	16 Dec 60 - 9 Jan 61	
	6 Feb - 1 Mar 61	Capt R H Venning

RFA *Wave Ruler*	30 Feb - 6 Nov 58	Capt R K McKenzie
	7-19 Feb 59	Capt F G Evans
	14-24 Apr	Capt D G Cox
	1-23 Jun 59	
	5-23 Aug 59	Capt R V Warren DSC
	5-18 Oct 59	
	22 Jan - 8 Feb 60	Capt W H G Hine
	28 Apr - 22 May 60	
	13 Jun - 4 Jul 60	
	25 Jul - 14 Aug 60	Capt J Coull
	27 Sep - 24 Oct 60	
	28 Nov - 15 Dec 60	
RFA *Wave Sovereign*	19-31 Oct 59	Capt F S Samson
	26 Nov - 21 Dec 59	
RFA *Wave Victor*	7-18 Nov 58	Capt H O L'Estrange DSC
	19 Dec 58 - 5 Jan 59	
	24 Aug - 13 Sep 59	

Second Cod War: 1 Sep 72 - 13 Nov 73

RFA *Blue Rover*	22 May - 2 Jun 73	Capt D P Kindersley
	26 Sep - 1 Oct 73	
	11-13 Oct 73	
RFA *Green Rover*	20-25 Jun 73	Capt S L Read
	29 Jun - 4 Jul 73	
	8-11 Jul 73	
	27-30 Jul 73	
	4-9 Aug 73	
	14-19 Aug 73	
	26 Aug - 2 Sep 73	
	6-14 Sep 73	
	19-22 Sep 73	
RFA *Grey Rover*	15-18 Oct 73	Capt D J Boyden
	28-31 Oct 73	
	4-13 Nov 73	
RFA *Olmeda*	22 Sep - 10 Oct 73	Capt C D G Barker
	14-27 Oct 73	
RFA *Olna*	19-25 Aug 73	Capt J Gulesserian
	1-6 Sep 73	
	10-22 Sep 73	

RFA *Olwen*	24 Jun - 10 Jul 73	Capt R M Thorn
	14-27 Jul 73	Capt G P A MacDougal
	30 Jul - 10 Aug 73	
RFA *Orangeleaf*	12-20 Jun 73	Capt A E T Hunter
RFA *Tidepool*	28 Oct - 6 Nov 73	Capt J C Moffat
RFA *Tidereach*	6-10 Apr 76	Capt R A Cooper
RMAS *Typhoon*	12-27 Mar 76	Master M J Dooley
	27 Apr - 8 May 76	
RFA *Wave Chief*	19-22 May 73	Capt C W P Sumner
	1-14 Jun 73	
	18-24 Jun 73	Capt H J C Wheatley
	10-15 Jul 73	
	21-24 Jul 73	
	11-14 Aug 73	Capt H Nelberg

Defence Tugs on Station Dates

Englishman	15 Feb - 27 Sep 73
Irishman	7 May - 19 Jul 73
Lloydsman	10 Jun - 13 Nov 73
Statesman	22 Jan - 13 Nov 73
Welshman	24 Jul - 13 Nov 73

Note: These vessels were on station throughout the periods listed except for their returns to a northern UK port approximately monthly for crew changes, re-storing and maintenance.

Third Cod War: 25 Nov 75 - 1 Jun 76

RFA *Blue Rover*	13 May - 1 Jun 76	Capt A L Paterson
RFA *Olwen*	13 Dec 75 - 5 Jan 76	Capt J G M Coull
	15 Jan - 23 Feb 76	
	24 Mar - 22 Apr 76	Capt D G M Averill
	26 May - 1 Jun 76	

RMAS *Rollicker*	15-21 Jan 76	Master R F Dunkley
	25 Feb - 11 Mar 76	
	12-26 Apr 76	
	25 May - 1 Jun 76	Master P Parfoot
RMAS *Roysterer*	3-14 Jan 76	Master D Hazell
	10-24 Feb 76	Master R N Tuckett
	28 Mar - 11 Apr 76	Master D Hazall
	10-24 May 76	Master R N Tuckett
RFA *Tidepool*	29 Nov - 13 Dec 75	Capt D R Thompson
	5-15 Jan 76	
	23 Feb - 23 Mar 76	
	23 Apr - 25 May 76	
RFA *Tidereach*	6-10 Apr 76	Capt R A Cooper
RMAS *Typhoon*	12-27 Mar 76	Master M J Dooley
	27 Apr - 8 May 76	

Defence Tugs on Station Dates

Lloydsman	19 Nov - 1 Jun 76
Southella	19 May - 1 Jun 76
Star Aquarious	19 Nov - 14 Dec 75
Star Polaris	19 Nov - 16 Dec 75
Star Sirius	19 Nov - 16 Dec 75
Statesman	4 Jan - 17 May 76

Note: These vessels were on station throughout the periods listed except for their returns to a northern UK port approximately monthly for crew changes, re-storing and maintenance.

APPENDIX SEVEN

CAST LIST

Agústsson, Einar	Icelandic Foreign Minister 1971 and 1975-6
Andersen, Hans G	Chief Law of the Sea Adviser to the Icelandic Foreign Ministry 1946-post 76.
Ásgeirsson, Ásgeir	President of Iceland 1952-68
Arnasson, Captain Sigurdur	Captain of *Saebjorg* in 1CW and *Ódinn* in 2CW and 3CW. Also Captain of *Ódinn* during the *Notts County* rescue.
Beckett, Sir Eric	Foreign Office Legal Adviser 1949
Benediktsson, Bjarni	Icelandic Prime Minister 1963-70
Bevin, Ernest	British Foreign Secretary 1945-51
Bjarnason, Matthías	Icelandic Fisheries Minister 1974-8
Björnsson, Captain Thórarinn	Captain of *Ægir* in 1CW
Boothby, Evelyn	British Ambassador Reykjavik 1962-5
Callaghan, James	British Foreign Secretary 1974-6 British Prime Minister 1976-9
Churchill, Winston	British Prime Minister 1951-5
Crosland, Antony	British Foreign Secretary 1976-7
East, Kenneth	British Ambassador Reykjavik 1975-81
Eden, Anthony	British Foreign Secretary 1951-5 British Prime Minister 1955-7
Eldjárn, Kristján	President of Iceland 1952-68
Frydenlund, Knut	Norwegian Foreign Minister who brokered the Third Cod War settlement.
Gilchrist, Andrew	British Ambassador, Reykjavik 1956-9 Author of "*Cod Wars and How to lose them*"
Greenway, John	British Ambassador, Reykjavik 1950-3
Hafstein, Jóhann	Icelandic Prime Minister 1970-1
Halford-Macleod, Aubrey	British Ambassador Reykjavik 1965-70
Hallgrímsson, Geir	Icelandic Prime Minister 1974-8
Hallvardsson, Captain Helgi	Captain of *Árvakur* in 2CW and *Thór* in 3CW
Hattersley, Roy	British Minister of State for Foreign Affairs 1974-6
Heath, Edward	British Prime Minister 1970-4
Helgason, Captain Bjarni O.	Captain of *Albert* in 2CW
Home, 13th Earl of; later Sir Alec Douglas-Home	British Foreign Secretary 1960-3 and 1970-4 British Prime Minister 1963-4
Jay, Douglas	British Fisheries Minister 1949
Jóhannesson, Gudni Thorlacius	Author of *Troubled Waters. Cod War, Fishing Disputes and Britain's Fight for the Freedom of the High Seas, 1948-1964* and general mentor to the author on things Icelandic.
Jóhannesson, Ólafur	Icelandic Prime Minister 1971-4 and 1978-9 Minister of Justice and hence Head of the Coastguard during the

	Third Cod War.
Jónasson, Hermann	Icelandic Prime Minister 1934-42
Jónsson, Emil	Icelandic Prime Minister 1958-9
Jónsson, Hannes	Author of *Friends in Conflict.* Secretary for Press and Information in the Prime Minister's Office 1972-3 Ambassador in Moscow 1974-80
Jónsson, Captain Jón	Captain of *Albert* in 1CW
Jónsson, Captain Pétur	Captain of second *Ódinn* in 1CW
Jósepsson, Lúdvík	Icelandic Fisheries Minister 1972
Kristófersson, Captain Eiríkur	Captain of *Thór* in 1CW
Kjænested, Captain Gudmundur	Captain of *Ægir* in 2CW and *Tyr* in 3CW
Kurlansky, Mark	Author of "*Cod*"
Lloyd, Selwyn	British Foreign Secretary 1955-60
Luns, Dr Joseph	Secretary-General of NATO 1971-84
Macmillan, Harold	British Foreign Secretary 1955 British Prime Minister 1957-63
McKenzie, John	British Ambassador Reykjavik 1970-5
Mitchell, Austin	MP for Grimsby 1977
Peart, Fred	Minister of Agriculture, Fisheries & Food 1974-6
Sigtryggsson, Captain Throstur	Captain of *Thór* in 2CW and *Ægir* in 3CW. Known as Spörri, the Sparrow.
Sigurdsson, Pétur	Director of the Icelandic Coastguard from 1962-81
Skarphédinsson, Captain Hóskuldur	Captain of *Baldur* in 3CW
Stewart, Andrew	British Ambassador Reykjavik 1959-62
Thorlacius, Captain Gudni	Captain of *Hermodur* in 1CW
Thors, Ólafur	Icelandic Prime Minister 1942, 1944-7, 1953-6 and 1959-63 Icelandic Fisheries Minister 1952
Thorsteinsson, Captain Lárus	Captain of *Maria Júlia* in 1CW
Wilson, Harold	British Prime Minister 1974-6

APPENDIX EIGHT

ACRONYMS AND ABBREVIATIONS

BTF	British Trawler Federation
CFP	Common Fisheries Policy
CFPS	Captain, Fishery Protection Squadron or during the First Cod War, Commodore, Fishery Protection Squadron
CinCFleet	Commander-in-Chief, Fleet
CO	Commanding Officer
CTG	Commander Task Group. *Note*: During the First Cod War, the warships off Iceland were designated Task Group 334.0 and hence the CTG's full title was CTG 334.0.
DFA	Designated Fishing Area
ECM	Electronic Counter Measures
EEC	European Economic Community aka the Common Market. Now the EC - European Community
EEZ	Exclusive Economic Zone
EFTA	European Free Trade Association
ESM	Electronic Support Measures
ETA	Estimated Time of Arrival
EW	Electronic Warfare
FFO	Furnace Fuel Oil
FO	Foreign Office (now the FCO - Foreign and Commonwealth Office)
FOSNI	Flag Officer Scotland and Northern Ireland
FOTI	Fleet Operational and Tactical Instructions
FPS	Fishery Protection Squadron
HMG	Her Majesty's Government
ICG	Icelandic Coastguard
ICGV	Icelandic Coastguard Vessel
loa	length overall
LSBA	Leading Sick Bay Attendant
MAFF	(British) Ministry of Agriculture, Fisheries & Food
MFV	Motor Fishing Vessel
MHQ	Maritime Headquarters. Naval protection operations were controlled from FOSNI's HQ - MHQ Pitreavie, Dunfirmline, Fife.
MoD	Ministry of Defence
MPA	Maritime Patrol Aircraft
No1	The First Lieutenant and Second-in-Command. Also known as XO - the Executive Officer
OpOrd(er)	Operation Order
OTC	Officer in Tactical Command. In effect, the local commander.
RAS	Replenishment at Sea
RFA	Royal Fleet Auxiliary

RMAS	Royal Maritime Auxiliary Service
RoE	Rules of Engagement
RoP	Report of Proceedings
SAR	Search and Rescue
Sitrep	Situation Report
TG	Task Group (see CTG above)
Tiffy	Artificer
UNCLOS	United Nations Conference on the Law of the Sea or United Nations Convention on the Law of the Sea
UTC	United Towing Company
VHF	Literally Very High Frequency, but usually used as the title for the International ship-to-ship/bridge-to-bridge voice circuit

BIBLIOGRAPHY

Arctic Pilot Volume II published by the Hydrographer of the Navy 1996.

Cod by Mark Kurlansky published by Vintage 1999. The Glenfiddich 1999 Food and Drink Awards Winner. Good on background history, 'though the latter part gets bogged down in Canadian detail.

Cod Wars and how to lose them by Sir Andrew Gilchrist. Published by Q Press Ltd 1978. The British Ambassador's personal views from Reykjavik during the First Cod War.

Doom in the Deep by Óttar Sveinsson. Published by Stöng 2003. The story of the loss of the *Ross Cleveland* and the *Notts County.*

Fishermen: The Rise and Fall of Deep Water Trawling by Austin Mitchell and Anne Tait. Published by Hutton Press 1997

Fishing Industry Handbook for Britain & Ireland edited by Peter Brady. Published by Fishing Communications Ltd., Fleetwood

Friends in Conflict: The Anglo-Icelandic Cod Wars and the Law of the Sea by Hannes Jónsson. Published by C Hurst and Co 1982. A very Icelandic viewpoint and I am most grateful to Dr Jónsson for his permission to quote extensively from this book.

Hull's Fishing Heritage by Alec Gill. Published by Wharncliffe Books 2003.
The North Ships by Steven Piper. Published by David and Charles 1974. Life in a Hull trawler in the 60s. Not much on the Cod War, but good on what life in a deep-sea trawler and fishing off Iceland was like at the time.

Sympathy and Self-Interest: Norway and the Anglo-Icelandic Cod Wars by Gudni Thorlacius Jóhannesson 2005. Explains the widely held Icelandic view that Norway's interventions in the Cod Wars were only motovated by self-interest.

Trawler by Redmond O'Hanlon. Published by Penguin 2004. Life in a distant-water trawler at the start of the 21st Century. There are many similarities with the accounts of forty years before.

Trawling: The Rise and Fall of the British Trawl Fishery by Robb Robinson. Published by the University of Exeter Press 1996. A well researched history of the British trawling industry. I am grateful to Robb Robinson for permission to quote from his book.

Trawling with the Lid Off by John Nicklin. Published by Aurora Publishing1996

Other Sources

The Worldwide Web will throw up thousands of pages if you search for Cod War. Just a few are listed below:

Bosun's Watch www.fleetwood-trawlers.connectfree.co.uk
Fishing Industry Handbook www.fishcom.co.uk
Fleetwood's Heritage www.marine-heritage.info.
Grimsby Sidewinder Trawlers http://embark.to/sidewinder
Hull Trawlers http://hulltrawler.net/
SW Maritime History Society www.swmaritime.org.uk

Trawler *Arctic Corsair* www.arcticcorsair.f9.co.uk/corsair/main.html
HMS *Bacchante* www.hmsbacchante.co.uk
HMS *Leander* www.leanders.plus.com/batch1/leander.htm
Civilian Support Vessel *Miranda* http://home.freeuk.net/nigelhadley/codwar.htm
HMS *Rothesay* www.btinternet.com/~warship/Postwar/Frigates/rothesay.htm
HMS *Sirius* www.hmssirius.info/Mick_Pinchen_cod_war_spuds.htm
HMS *Tartar* www.btinternet.com/~warship/Feature/cod/
HMS *Yarmouth* www.hms-yarmouth.com/cod_war.htm

A song about the Cod Wars www.blythpower.co.uk/lyrics/Caesar/viking.htm
& Why to ram the starboard side http://homepage.eircom.net/~admiralty/Colregs%20History.htm